פֶּשַׁע = debt עֲוֹן iniquity

iniquity or transgression
wicked - look up for
consistency
translation

Look @ פֶּשַׁע vs רָעַע

David Skelton

4QInstruction

Studies on the Texts of the Desert of Judah

Edited by

George J. Brooke

Associate Editors

Eibert J.C. Tigchelaar
Jonathan Ben-Dov
Alison Schofield

VOLUME 123

The titles published in this series are listed at *brill.com/stdj*

4QInstruction

Divisions and Hierarchies

By

Benjamin Wold

BRILL

LEIDEN | BOSTON

The Library of Congress Cataloging-in-Publication Data is available online at http://catalog.loc.gov

Typeface for the Latin, Greek, and Cyrillic scripts: "Brill". See and download: brill.com/brill-typeface.

ISSN 0169-9962
ISBN 978-90-04-36144-7 (hardback)
ISBN 978-90-04-36424-0 (e-book)

PRINTED BY DRUKKERIJ WILCO B.V. - AMERSFOORT, THE NETHERLANDS

Dedicated to my loving wife:
Wenhua Shi

and to the apple of my eye,
our beautiful daughter:
Shira Wold

∴

Contents

Acknowledgments

This project was completed through the contributions and support of many others. I would like to thank George Brooke as the series editor of Studies on the Texts of the Desert of Judah for accepting this manuscript for publication and for offering invaluable input on the project over the course of several years. Comments from anonymous peer reviewers were very much appreciated and enhanced the final version of this manuscript. I am grateful for the institutional support that I received from Trinity College Dublin and my colleagues, especially Linda Hogan, David Shepherd, and Daniele Pevarello. Research funding from the National Endowment for the Humanities at the Albright Institute of Archaeological Research, Jerusalem made the successful completion of this monograph possible. My appreciation also goes to the Alexander von Humboldt Foundation, which funded research periods that contributed to this project. Staff at the Israel Antiquities Authority, particularly Pnina Shor, made fragments of 4QInstruction available for consultation which has strengthened this work. Feedback received on sections of this book from Loren Stuckenbruck, Carol Newsom, Eileen Schuller, Émile Puech, Tyson Putthoff, and Matthew Goff has been invaluable, so too their moral support and encouragement. Graduate students at Trinity College Dublin, many of whom now have "Ph.D." proudly after their names, made writing and research a joy; thank you to Michael Morris, Sarah Shier, Geoffrey Wharton, Helen Moran-Cashell, Danny Daley, and Lynn Mills for our many conversations. I am grateful to the library staff at the École biblique, Jerusalem and Israel National Library. Sincere thanks also go to Joey Silver for enriching my family's research environment in the last year of this project.

This book is dedicated to my wife, Dr. Wenhua Shi, and our daughter, Shira Wold. The sacrifices that Wenhua has made for us both deserve the deepest recognition. Wenhua's loving support and constant encouragement mean the world to me. Shira is the joy of our lives and much of this book was written with our little "poem," our "song," in my mind. Dr. Chee Pang Choong and Choon Huah have been a constant support to me, Wenhua, and Shira—thank you. To my family: my mother, my father, Rease, Teckla, and Jasara I am grateful to you for your unwavering love.

Preface

Students of nearly any piece of literature would normally read a text before turning to secondary literature to better understand it. Unfortunately, 1Q/4QInstruction (hereafter "4QInstruction") cannot so easily be read on account of its fragmentary nature and so our conversations are really about a less than half-readable composition. There are different ways to read and assess literature, whether wholly intact or not. As I begin this project my intention is not to offer a new critical edition of 4QInstruction, nor an exhaustive commentary, but rather to attempt to assess this document while avoiding the well-worn topic of the "eschatologizing" of wisdom. This study is comprised of three main chapters each of which explores hierarchies, divisions, as well as exclusionary and inclusionary practices. These chapters take as their focus the categories of and relationships between: (1) speaker and audience; (2) spirit and flesh; and (3) mysteries and Mosaic Torah.[1]

The balance between presenting a readable and succinct study, on the one hand, and offering extensive commentary on reconstructions of often times ambiguous (and often composite) manuscripts, on the other hand, will undoubtedly be viewed more and less positively by different readers. Transcriptions and translations of pertinent passages of 4QInstruction in this study are my own, in consultation with: (1) several of the original manuscripts at the Israel Antiquities Authority, Israel National Museum in 2013 with financial support from the National Endowment for the Humanities; (2) the Leon Levy Dead Sea Scrolls Digital Library and the many re-imaged fragments available to the public at deadseascrolls.org.il; and (3) critical editions. Line-by-line textual notations are simply beyond the scope of this study and I refer my readers to resources available that will hopefully assuage any concerns not addressed here. I have in mind publications by John Strugnell, Daniel Harrington, and Torleif Elgvin in DJD 34 who extensively and exhaustively offer a presentation of fragments; Eibert Tigchelaar, Jean-Sébastian Rey, and Matthew Goff who offer substantive critical editions of most, but by no means all, fragments of 4QInstruction; and Elisha Qimron whose recent and valuable critical edition of 4QInstruction informs this study. I refer my readers to each of these authors,

---

1 The Hebrew term *tôrāh* is used in a variety of ways in biblical and post-biblical tradition. In this study Torah refers to the Mosaic Torah and specifically to the Hebrew term תורה consisting of the five books of Moses.

and the many other contributors to the study of 4QInstruction, and frequently note my indebtedness to them.

I have heard colleagues comment that 4QInstruction is an unusually difficult text to read—I agree. The decision before us is to dare to venture out and say something about it, or to allow the limited nature of this material to cripple us from speaking. My hope is that the reconstructions, translations, and interpretations in the pages that follow are made persuasively on the basis of careful, thoroughgoing analysis of the material. However, a single lacuna or lost column could, naturally, change the entire conversation. I imagine there are few in the world who, like me, dream that one day a complete manuscript of 4QInstruction will be found; until then my curiosity about this intriguing composition leads me to seek meaning among its many fragments.

Introduction

How one understands 4QInstruction's purpose and function is dependent on the assessment of what will be referred to in the following study as hierarchies and divisions. The meaning of these terms are unpacked in the chapters to follow; however, generally, "divisions" refer to a series of distinctions that 4QInstruction draws that are integral to its presentation of learning and "hierarchies" include cosmology, in terms of the structure of the world order, and also the ordering of the social world. One of the most notable lines of questioning about divisions has been expressed in other studies as "wisdom" and "apocalypticism," often with questions about particular speech genres and the social location of their origin.[1] However, such means of categorizing and organizing is not the direction of this study, but rather questions about hierarchy within the speaker's community, perceptions of divisions among humankind, what "wisdom" is, and who has access to it. The relationship of the speaker to their audience, social relations within the community, and even the roles of different members of the family (fathers, mothers, husbands, wives, sons, daughters) are referred to in 4QInstruction.[2] Moreover, within this composition revealed wisdom determines who is within the community and who is outside of it.

Carol Newsom has formulated the various types of questions one could ask about the discourse of the Qumran community.[3] One of her central concerns is why speech in the community was important, how it was regulated, and what it accomplished in terms of the social life of the community. Several of Newsom's questions are applicable here, in particular: how do we discuss what 4QInstruction may have accomplished for its community? How this question is addressed differs from Newsom's study in so far as it is generally agreed that 4QInstruction is not derivative or reflective of the Yaḥad or the wider sectarian movement of which they were part. However, as this study unfolds one way to discern the function of 4QInstruction is to set it alongside the discourse

---

1 E.g., the SBL section on "wisdom" and "apocalyptic"; cf. *Conflicted Boundaries in Wisdom and Apocalypticism*, ed. Benjamin G. Wright III & Lawrence M. Wills, SBL.SS 35 (Atlanta GA: Scholars Press, 2005). Similar formulations are more subtly found in the pairing of "worldly/heavenly" and "wisdom/eschatology."

2 In this study, the speaker is referred to in the masculine singular because his identification as a man is discernible in teachings about women.

3 Carol A. Newsom, *The Self as Symbolic Space: Constructing Identity and Community at Qumran*, STDJ 52 (Leiden: Brill, 2004).

© KONINKLIJKE BRILL NV, LEIDEN, 2018 | DOI: 10.1163/9789004364240_002

of other communities, even those which came to value this composition even though they did not produce it.

Social-scientific theories and social-psychological approaches to "identity" that have been so successfully brought to bear on the Yaḥad, and the wider sectarian community of which they were part, certainly intersect with questions about divisions and hierarchies.[4] The very manner in which distinctiveness and exclusivity is forged derives from competing assertions of authority. However, tensions observed between the Yaḥad (i.e., the assertion that a group has a distinct identity that needs to be constantly attended to) and a larger community may not be at play in the same way or to the same degree in 4QInstruction; indeed, such rhetorical purposes should not be unquestionably applied to this non-sectarian document with an uncertain provenance. With the notion of both "sectarian" and related writings in mind, we may ask why notions of "inside" and "outside," degrees of authoritativeness, and dichotomies develop in different ways in different texts. While commonalities and differences between 4QInstruction and the Yaḥad are topics of discussion throughout, it is only in the conclusion of this study that trajectories can be analyzed and theories postulated as to how and why social movements and theological shifts may have occurred.

Hindy Najman discusses the authorship of biblical texts and the authority they claim for themselves.[5] She points to questions of authorship as central to the study of ancient literature, and the misperception that if we could just discover who wrote a given work, we would understand it historically. Authorial inscription and the authority of ancient documents may be connected, but a great deal can be missed if we do not try to understand why so much of ancient literature seeks to express its own textual production in the ways that it does.[6] Unlike the traditions that Najman addresses, the author of 4QInstruction does not explicitly ascribe his work to named privileged individuals (e.g., Moses or Enoch) so that we are dealing with a "pseudonymous" text. Instead, the speaker in 4QInstruction is an anonymous sage; he has a voice, and questions remain to be asked about the basis for his claimed authority, how the addressees related

Why anonymity? Malleability!

---

4 Newsom, *The Self as Symbolic Space*; Jutta Jokiranta, *Social Identity and Sectarianism in the Qumran Movement*, STDJ 105 (Leiden: Brill, 2013); Maxine Grossman, "Cultivating Identity: Textual Virtuosity and 'Insider' Status," in *Defining Identities: We, You, and the Other in the Dead Sea Scrolls (Proceedings of the Fifth Meeting of the IOQS in Groningen)*, ed. F. García Martínez & M. Popović; STDJ 70 (Leiden: Brill, 2007), 1–3.

5 Hindy Najman, *Seconding Sinai: The Development of Mosaic Discourse in Second Temple Judaism*, JSJSup 77 (Leiden: Brill, 2003), 1.

6 Najman, *Seconding Sinai*, 3–4.

to him, where they themselves fit within the hierarchy of the community (and what those hierarchies are), and what the relationships within such a community may have been.

How may 4QInstruction have expressed meaning in different social locations, not only to its "original" community, but also among early communities that received and copied the text (e.g., the Yaḥad)? When the speaker of 4QInstruction addresses his audience, credibility relates to an appeal to revelation as well as to his being a practitioner of wisdom (i.e., the speaker's own religious experience). Moreover, 4QInstruction as a "speech act"[7] is responding to other discourses and, unlike many of them, he emphasizes revealed wisdom that is called רז נהיה ("mystery of existence").[8] This "mystery of existence" denotes something significant about where authority comes from and who has

---

7   Speech Act Theory was first developed by John L. Austin, *How to Do Things with Words* (New York, NY: Oxford University Press, 1965), which was further refined by John R. Searle, "A Taxonom of Illocutionary Acts," in *Expression and Meaning: Studies in the Theory of Speech Acts* (Cambridge: Cambridge University Press, 1979), 1–29. Speech Act Theory has been developed within Qumran studies, for instance to better understand the function of liturgy by Russell C.D. Arnold, *The Social Role of Liturgy in the Religion of the Qumran Community*, STDJ 60 (Leiden: Brill, 2006).

8   David J.A. Clines (ed.), *Dictionary of Classical Hebrew*, Vol. II ב–ו (Sheffield: Sheffield Academic Press, 1995), 540 היה *Niphal* ptc. as noun meaning: "the present, (present) event, (present) existence, i.e., that which exists, those that exist." The majority of occurrences of נהיה in 4QInstruction are in the construct רז נהיה, where נהיה could be taken as an adjective or *nomen regens* (cf. DJD 34:181). The *Niphal* of היה appears eight times in the Hebrew scriptures (Deut 4:32; 1 Kgs 1:27, 12:24; Joel 2:2; Mic 2:4; Zech 8:10; Neh 6:8; 2 Chr 11:4) and context clearly indicates that it has a past meaning. רז נהיה is found or reconstructed *circa* twenty-five times in 4QInstruction (1Q26 1 1, 4; 4Q415 6 4; 4Q415 24 1; 4Q416 2 i 5; 4Q416 2 iii 9, 14, 18, 21; 4Q416 17 3; 4Q417 1 i 6, 8, 18, 21; 4Q417 1 ii 3; 4Q418 77 2; 123 ii 4; 172 1; 179 3; 184 2; 190 2–3; 201 1; 4Q418c 8; 4Q423 3 2; 4Q423 5 2; 4Q423 7 7). Apart from 4QInstruction it is found in 1QS XI 3–4 and 1Q27 (Mysteries) 1 i 3–4 (par. 4Q300 3 3–4). While there are instances when the future sense of נהיה is relatively clear (esp. 4Q418 69 ii 7; 1QS III 15), the expression רז נהיה indicates temporal meaning that spans the entire plan of God from creation to the end-time, see esp. 4Q417 1 i 3–5; 4Q418 123 ii 3–4 (cf. temporal succession and creation in 1QS XI 11, 1QM XVII 5, 4Q180 1 i 2; 4Q402 4 12; 1QHᵃ XIX 17). Florentino García Martínez & Eibert J.C. Tigchelaar prefer "mystery of existence" in the DSSSE, Jean-Sébastien Rey, *4QInstruction: sagesse et eschatologie*, STDJ 81 (Leiden: Brill, 2009), 287 "mystère de l'existence"; Eibert J.C. Tigchelaar, "4QInstruction," in *Early Jewish Literature: An Anthology*, 2 vols., ed. Archie Wright, Brad Embry & Ronald Herms (Grand Rapids, MI: Eerdmans, 2018), 2:43–56: "The central concept is the *raz nihyeh*, the mystery of existence, which refers to God's overall plan of the world, from creation to judgment, including the place and tasks of all creatures within this plan." Cf. Daniel J. Harrington, "The *Rāz Nihyeh* in a Qumran Wisdom Text (1Q26, 4Q415–418, 423)," *RevQ* 17 (1996): 549–553.

access to it. By studying this ideological sign, and what the text presumes about how recipients relate to it, glimpses are provided into a larger discursive context of ancient Jewish thought. This mystery, regardless of how one translates it, cannot be learned solely by contemplating human experience and pragmatism arising from it. If, as some suggest, the רז נהיה connotes the future, so that it translates as "the mystery to be," then such revelation serves to teach about consequences in the hereafter.[9] This understanding of the mystery is usually connected to a particular deterministic view of the document and division of humanity into two groups; thus, the future is assured and the addressees are to live their lives from the perspective of the eternal. The consequence of living in light of the future is not that the *mēvîn* (the "understanding one") neglects life in the present, but rather that he has wisdom that allows him to live properly in this world.[10] The three chapters of this study deal with the "mystery of existence" in different ways, by asking about: (1) the sage's relationship to it and what that means for his students; (2) how the division of "spirit" and "flesh" shapes views on humankind and who is privileged with access to the mystery; and (3) the relationship of the mystery to Torah and whether one is derived from or subordinate to the other.

4QInstruction may be characterized as teaching about how to live in this world in light of another world. In order to live rightly one must seek revealed wisdom. However, what this revealed wisdom actually is and how it is to be acquired is not clear. What is known is that at nearly every level relationships to teachers, creditors, and members of the community are associated with the mystery. Moreover, this revelation together with "Hagu" (i.e., engraved ordinances) is supposed to enable the *mēvîn* to distinguish between good and evil, although the consequences for not pursuing and acquiring it are not unambiguously grounded in this present world; future judgment for the wicked and

---

9   An exclusive future translation as "the mystery that is to be" is temporally singular to the detriment of the term's fuller signification; cf. translation in future tense by Matthew J. Goff, *4QInstruction*, WLAW 2 (Atlanta, GA: SBL, 2013), 14; DJD 34:157 (נהיה is "probably a future participle, as in Mishnaic Hebrew"); Armin Lange, *Weisheit und Prädestination: Weisheitliche Urordnung und Prädestination in den Textfunden von Qumran*, STDJ 18 (Leiden: Brill, 1995), 57–61; Torleif Elgvin, "The Mystery to Come: Early Essene Theology of Revelation," in *Qumran between the Old and New Testaments*, ed. F.H. Cryer & T.L. Thompson, JSOTSup 290; CIS 6 (Sheffield: Sheffield, 1998), 131–139; cf. DJD 1:103 Józef T. Milik translates the term in 1QMysteries (1Q27) 1 i 3–4 as "le mystère future."

10   John J. Collins, "The Eschatologizing of Wisdom in the Dead Sea Scrolls," in *Sapiential Perspectives: Wisdom Literature in Light of the Dead Sea Scrolls*, ed. John J. Collins, Gregory E. Sterling & Ruth A. Clemens, STDJ 51 (Leiden: Brill, 2004), 49–65 at 60.

reward for the righteous are envisaged. The assessment of divisions and hierarchies below influences perspectives on the composition's eschatology, especially when deterministic and dualistic frameworks suggested by other interpreters are challenged.

4QInstruction was likely composed in the mid-second century BCE, although manuscripts (4Q415–418, 423; 1Q26) date to the late first century BCE
and early first century CE.[11] One reason for suspecting that none of these scrolls
is the original autograph are indications of scribal copying.[12] A date to the
second century is further derived from: (1) viewpoints on the development of
wisdom, and (2) locating terms and ideas in the document on an evolutionary trajectory that falls before so-called "sectarian" writings as a number of
studies have shown. There is, however, no "smoking gun" that would compel
one to agree with this particular date even though the majority opinion falls
to a provenance from the mid-second century. The dating of 4QInstruction is
significant. If it is written earlier, then this complicates the manner in which
particular compositions are grouped together as sharing common ideologies
and theologies as well as how they are associated with identifiable groups
and movements.[13] Because of thematic and terminological correspondences
between 4QInstruction and the Thanksgiving Hymns the hymns seem to provide a *terminus ad quem*.

The author of 4QInstruction appears to have been a pious Jew who composed this roughly thirty-column scroll in the Hebrew language.[14] When compared with other surviving scrolls from the caves around Khirbet Qumran this

---

11   Based upon paleographical analysis.

12   John Strugnell, Daniel J. Harrington and Torleif Elgvin, *Qumran Cave 4 XXIV. Sapiential
      Texts, Part 2: 4QInstruction (Mûsār lĕ Mēvîn): 4Q415ff. with a Re-edition of 1Q26*, DJD 34
      (Oxford: Clarendon Press, 1999), 1 "[e]ach of these [manuscripts of 4QInstruction] was
      once a copy of the same sapiential work." Furthermore, there were different redactions of
      the composition.

13   Dating influences the context of theoretical reconstructions of lacunae and translations;
      e.g., is 4QInstruction contemporary with and similar to the wisdom of Ben Sira? Is this
      composition part of the same intellectual trajectory as the Treatise on the Two Spirits and
      should the latter shape the interpretation of anthropology in the former? How is 4QIn-
      struction to be situated in relationship to Enochic tradition?

14   Annette Steudel and B. Lucassen, "Aspekte einer vorläufigen materiellen Rekonstruktion
      von 4Q416–4Q418," unpublished handout at *Forschungsseminar: Die Wiesheitstexte aus
      Qumran, Tübingen, 22–24 Mai; 20–21 Juni 1998* argue that 4Q418 was at least 30 columns;
      Torleif Elgvin, "The Reconstruction of Sapiential Work A (*)," *RevQ* 16 (1995): 559–580 sug-
      gests that 4Q418 was 23 columns; DJD 34:19 prefer the reconstruction of 4Q418 suggested
      by Steudel and Lucassen.

is one of the longest. 4QInstruction is also known by its Hebrew title *Mûsār lᵉ Mēvîn*, although מוסר למבין is not an expression found in the composition. The noun *mûsār* (מוסר), which is infrequently part of the document's discourse, relates to good conduct and morality, and is often translated as "instruction," "discipline," "training," "exhortation," or "warning."[15] The addressee, the *mēvîn*, is regularly instructed to seek, grasp, gaze upon, and understand the mystery of existence. Although it has become common practice to refer to this document as 4QInstruction, it is technically inaccurate because fragments of a manuscript were discovered in Cave 1 as well as Cave 4.[16] Labels external to the document, whether "4QInstruction" or "*Mûsār lᵉ Mēvîn*," may take on a life of their own and give rise to misleading presumptions about the composition.[17]

What was the purpose of 4QInstruction and how did the author intend it to be used? Though some evidence suggests that 4QInstruction was composed primarily for an elite group of sages in training and that textual production and literacy are indicative of wealth, is it possible that parts of this composition were meant to be read aloud among a socio-religiously mixed company? The rare second person feminine address in 4Q415 2 ii could, for example, be interpreted in different ways: the author may be using *oratio obliqua* to instruct the male *mēvîn* how to teach women (e.g., "You, O *mēvîn*, instruct women in this manner, 'you O woman' ...") or, as seems less likely, if an *oratio recta* it may be directed to women, in this case perhaps within a mixed gathering of men and women. There are strong indications that 4QInstruction is "misogynistic," something found for example in specific terminology for women (e.g., "womb") and teachings about the subjugation of women to men (e.g., 4Q416 2 iii–iv).

---

15   Only three times excluding overlaps and only twice with any discernable context: 4Q416 2 iii 13 (בכול מוסר הבא שכמכה) and 4Q418 169 + 170 3 (מוסר ובאהבת חסד).

16   Devorah Dimant notices that caves contained at least one copy of every composition represented by multiple copies in Cave 4 in "The Qumran Manuscripts: Contents and Significance," in *A Time to Prepare the Way in the Wilderness. Papers on the Qumran Scrolls by Fellows of the Institute for Advanced Studies of the Hebrew University, Jerusalem, 1989–1990*, ed. Devorah Dimant & Lawrence H. Schiffman, STDJ 16 (Leiden: Brill, 1995), 30.

17   1Q/4QInstruction is at times referred to simply as "Instruction," which I do not use here for two reasons: (1) "4QInstruction" has already come to dominate the scholarly discourse, and (2) in order to ensure that this research is found and cited the vagueness of the title "Instruction," when used in an online search, does not turn up clear results (i.e., in online search engines the term "Qumran document 'Instruction'" does not immediately lead you to publications on this composition) whereas "4QInstruction" is sufficiently narrow a term to turn up relevant literature.

Therefore, it is difficult to see how 4Q415 2 ii forms part of a direct speech and, consequently, how this composition would have been intended to instruct anyone other than men.

In the largest single fragment of 4QInstruction (4Q416 2 i–iv), which preserves significant parts of three columns, the *mēvîn* is repeatedly reminded that he is "poor." Poverty and elitism would, seemingly, be irreconcilable. Perhaps much of this language is addressing an original audience that lived at subsistence level, although why they needed reminding of it has been the subject of debate, as will be discussed below. Even if explanations can be found for why someone who lives in abject poverty needs prompting to recall this harsh reality, one cannot help but wonder whether the speaker-sage is contextualizing his message about—to borrow Douglas Adam's language—life, the universe, and everything within the economic hardships of a singular and monolithic audience.[18] Economic language reflects the status of individuals, influences their relationship to others both in and outside of their community, and is an integral aspect of understanding hierarchies and divisions.

If the author's audience was straightforwardly being instructed about material poverty, and there is some agreement that at least on occasion poverty is used metaphorically, then questions arise as to how the Yaḥad, who was not the original audience, adopted it and related to the insistence of a text with the refrain "you are poor."[19] Financial advice directed to others does not necessarily translate to another group's circumstances at another time, especially one that shares all things in common at least a generation later and uses "poor" self-referentially, as a nomenclature for their society. Moreover, attention may be given to scenarios available to explain how 4QInstruction interested the Yaḥad, and perhaps the wider community of which they were part, when it consistently communicates concern for marriage and female members of the family, a commonality shared with the Damascus Document. Economic and marital

---

18   In 4QInstruction the answer is, of course, the רז נהיה and not 42! See Douglas Adams, *The Hitchhiker's Guide to the Galaxy* (New York: Random House/Del Rey, 1979).

19   John Kampen, "Wisdom in Deuterocanonical and Cognate Literature," in *Canonicity, Setting, Wisdom in Deuterocanonicals: Papers of the Jubilee Meeting of the International Conference on the Deuterocanonical Books*, ed. Géza G. Xeravits, Józse Zsengellér & Xavér Szabó (Berlin: de Gruyter, 2014), 89–120, at 112 "Neither temple nor Torah receive significant attention in the composition … It is this change of focus that permitted it to be such an important document for sectarian self-expression and presumably study." However, at 113 Kampen comments that "[w]hat the sectarian authors found in the composition probably far exceeds the intent of the authors, the uncovering of which is itself an ambiguous endeavor."

status are embedded in 4QInstruction and yet these social groupings of the text were received by others, some of whom at least seem to have experienced different social conditions.

To whom the author first wrote and those who transmitted and used this composition should be differentiated. Scribes produced at least eight copies of the composition roughly a hundred years or more after it was first composed, and this suggests its importance during a relatively long time-span.[20] In theory, more copies may have been produced but it is unlikely that we will ever know whether this is the case. That at least eight copies were made indicates importance and that it was read, or read aloud and listened to, by many within a community. Unfortunately, after reconstructing the manuscripts of 4QInstruction only about 30% of the original document survives. What is known about the author and his audience must be inferred based upon these reconstructions and, as noted above, the majority view is that the author is not a member of the Yaḥad or, to use the language of others, it is a "non-sectarian" composition.[21] Nonetheless, the Yaḥad movement was evidently interested in this scroll and its message about the mystery of existence.

In Chapter 1, I argue that 4QInstruction begins with first-person speech; the speaker is a *maśkîl* who teaches students how to live wisely and attain the status of a sage themselves. This specific pedagogic function as a *maśkîl*-text would have found a place within different didactic settings and, the evidence suggests, over an extended period of time. Why 4QInstruction is not preserved outside of Caves 1 and 4 is not known. In Chapter 3, the authority of Torah is discussed and, if the conclusions reached there are convincing, then we may speculate that 4QInstruction lost its appeal when the place of Torah solidified in later Jewish communities. However, how 4QInstruction was valued, and its place within ancient Jewish thought, should not be determined based solely upon inferences that the only extant copies are from Qumran. Moreover, there is no indication that 4QInstruction was forgotten or deliberately "abandoned." Knowledge of the scrolls' existence or whereabouts seems to have simply died away after the inhabitants of Qumran were killed or enslaved by the Romans

---

20 4Q415–418 are in middle Herodian hands (1–25 CE) and 4Q423 and 1Q26 in early Herodian hands (50–25 BCE).

21 Borrowing categories from Devorah Dimant, "The Library of Qumran: Its Content and Character," in *The Dead Sea Scrolls Fifty Years after Their Discovery: Proceedings of the Jerusalem Congress, July 20–25, 1997*, ed. Lawrence H. Schiffman, Emanuel Tov & James C. VanderKam (Jerusalem: IES, 2000), 170–176. Some scholars prefer to describe 4QInstruction as "pre-sectarian" which more firmly locates it in an evolutionary trajectory.

in the Great Revolt.[22] Indeed, one explanation comes from Josephus who tells about Essenes being tortured and killed by the Romans during the Great Revolt (*War* 2.152–153). The numismatic evidence from Qumran indicates that in the year 68 CE, in the midst of the war, the community living at Qumran fled before the advancing Roman army.[23] One assumption is that they hastily hid their scrolls in the surrounding caves before their settlement was destroyed.[24] Perhaps some of them found refuge at Masada, a theory supported by the discovery of the liturgical work Songs of the Sabbath Sacrifice atop the mesa; the only other place this text is known is from multiple copies found at Qumran (4Q400–407; 11Q17).[25] Speculating on where precisely the Qumranites fled is less important than the fact that no one returned to collect these precious manuscripts. Given the value of these scrolls, the best theory is that they did not retrieve them because they could not; they did not so much lose their value to a community as much as they and their owners were lost (i.e., killed or enslaved).

A great many of the Dead Sea Scrolls had and continued a life beyond Khirbet Qumran. Many of the other "non-sectarian" texts such as Jubilees, Ben Sira or Tobit, to name only a few, were clearly read and appreciated longer and more broadly than for a brief time alongside the shore of the Dead Sea. Well-known is that the Damascus Document, a composition considered to be formative for the Yaḥad, was discovered in a cache of manuscripts in the Cairo Geniza in the late 1800s.[26] The Damascus Document attracts our attention because it reflects

---

22 John J. Collins, *Beyond the Qumran Community: The Sectarian Movement of the Dead Sea Scrolls* (Grand Rapids: Eerdmans, 2009), 209–214 writes that "Qumran is not the last Alamo!."

23 See the treatment of the numismatic evidence by Jodi Magness, *The Archaeology of Qumran and the Dead Sea Scrolls* (Grand Rapids, MI: Eerdmans, 2002), 47–70.

24 Daniel Stökel ben Ezra, "Old Caves and Young Caves—A Statistical Reevaluation of a Qumran Consensus," *DSD* 14/3 (2007): 313–333, at 316 presents a scenario in which scrolls were deposited in Cave 1 at a much earlier period.

25 The original provenance of Songs of the Sabbath Sacrifice is unknown, it is thought to be non-sectarian, and yet most copies date to the late first century BCE or early first century CE, the oldest to roughly the mid-first century BCE. See Carol Newsom, *Songs of the Sabbath Sacrifice: A Critical Edition*, HSS 27 (Atlanta, GA: Scholars Press, 1985), 1. The presence of a copy at Masada could indicate an even wider circulation rather than the explanation provided here.

26 Just as questions are asked about how medieval readers gained access to the Damascus Document, one could also ask whether they had access to other texts. The early Karaite movement could theoretically have absorbed other texts known from Qumran. See Maxine L. Grossman, *Reading for History in the Damascus Document: A Methodological Study*, STDJ 45 (Leiden: Brill, 2002), 213.

a social group more diverse than other Yaḥad literature and was used, most likely, by the Karaite community. 4QInstruction was probably written before the emergence of the Yaḥad, was read and copied by the Yaḥad, and conceivably could also have existed outside of Cave 1 and Cave 4 for centuries after the inhabitants of Qumran left.[27] The Damascus Document illustrates that plausible theories, such as suppression, could be considered which offer evaluations of 4QInstruction that during an earlier period of time it was less "marginal."[28] As divisions, hierarchies, and notions of inclusivity/exclusivity in the composition are considered here, it may be seen that its own self-presentation and viewpoints were at odds, or came to be at odds, with literature and movements that later dominated. Indeed, as we will see in Chapter 3, how mysteries and Torah relate to one another may alone have been sufficient reason that 4QInstruction eventually lost its appeal.

The difference in date of composition and transmission indicate that 4QInstruction had significance to audiences in more than one generation. Although "sectarian" as a category is highly problematic, one may surmise that if a document is labeled non-sectarian this implies that it represents a swath of Jewish thought and practice less narrowly defined.[29] Pre-sectarian suggests that a

---

27   Indeed, the discovery of Hebrew, Aramaic, and Greek scrolls found at Qumran are part of a wider occurrence of scrolls being hidden in the Judean wilderness in antiquity. There are two ancient witnesses to this phenomenon. Firstly, the Nestorian patriarch Timotheus I of Seleucia wrote a letter in Syriac from Baghdad around 800 CE in which he describes the discovery of Hebrew manuscripts found "near Jericho." He writes that "trustworthy" converts from Judaism told him that "the dog of a hunting Arab ... entered a cave and did not come out. His master followed him, found a dwelling within the rocks in which were many books, went to Jerusalem and informed the Jews. They came in throngs and found books of the Old Testament and others in Hebrew script ..." The converts also reported to Timotheus I that they discovered "200 hundred psalms of David" and "other biblical manuscripts". Because of the proximity of Jericho to Qumran (c. 20 km) there has been some speculation whether this report actually reflects discoveries at Qumran. Secondly, in the mid-third century CE Origen, as he prepared the Hexapla, comments that he is using "Hebrew and Greek books" that were found "in a jar near Jericho." *The Cambridge History of Judaism*, ed. William Horbury, William D. Davies & John Sturdy (Cambridge: CUP, 1999) 3:840–841.

28   Jubilees and the Book of the Watchers may only be preserved fully in Ethiopic, but part of the Greek and Latin translations of the Hebrew survive. Jubilees and the Book of the Watchers were suppressed.

29   Jutta Jokiranta, "Learning from Sectarian Responses: Windows on Qumran Sects and Emerging Christian Sects," in *Echoes from the Caves: Qumran and the New Testament*, ed. Florentino García Martínez, STDJ 85 (Leiden: Brill, 2009), 177–210.

work is representative of a way of thinking that is on a trajectory toward "sectarianism" and is the fertile soil that gives it sprout. If one is inclined to describe
4QInstruction as non-sectarian, rather than pre-sectarian, as some have, its circulation could conceivably have been broad. It falls into the same division of
scrolls as Jubilees or the Book of Watchers. However, whereas these examples
went on to have a longer and more vibrant life, 4QInstruction disappeared. Perhaps this is indicative of its importance, or lack thereof, in the Second Temple
era. Maybe it is just a fluke that it vanished and arguments from silence should
be avoided.

Sapiential instruction establishes boundaries and hierarchies, typically it
is seen to teach that there are those who measure up to wisdom's standards
by birth, gender, propriety, or achievement and those who do not. "Conventional wisdom," a somewhat misleading but at times useful category, consists
of what is observable in the world around us and its practical character is
taken for granted; a sage can teach how to live in relationship to it and this
can be applied across peoples and cultures. Such wisdom is rooted in the consequences of the here and now, if one acts in such and such a way it will result
in this or that. The divisions and categories used in sapiential teachings shape
a community's world, it orders and forms members' self-perceptions and social
identities. However, 4QInstruction presents its wisdom within a cosmological
framework from the outset (4Q416 1) and how one is to live in the world is
derived from the mystery of existence. Within the discourse of this composition the one's addressed relate to otherworldly beings (i.e., angelic beings)
as well as to one another. The presentation of this worldview as fully integrated with sapiential discourse suggests that hierarchies and divisions within
communities and between communities are in transition. The perspective of
4QInstruction's speaker, details about organization of community and family,
perceptions of humanity, and the question of whether or not the wisdom it
conveys is exclusive are all foundational to understanding this composition and
locating it among other writings in the era.

CHAPTER 1

Maśkîl and *Mēvîn*

Whereas Enoch and John at Patmos boldly proclaim what they have seen and
heard, in 4QInstruction the speaker does not claim to have ascended into the
heavens nor does he relate visionary experiences as one finds in formal apoca-
lypses.[1] The author is never instructed to write what has been revealed to him,
and yet how God imparts wisdom in 4QInstruction is associated with the religious experiences of the author and the pupils whom he addresses.[2] When
constructing his discourse, the author of 4QInstruction does not use a speaker
like in Qohelet, where first-person address appeals to the stature of its purport-
ed author. 4QInstruction does not cultivate self-referential speech as found in
the Thanksgiving Hymns nor does it use the first-person pseudepigraphal idiom.[3] Is there, however, first-person speech and if so what is the author trying
to achieve? First-person forms do indeed occur in 4QInstruction and these are
significant for assessing how this composition is framed. Central to this chapter are passages that use first-person speech, particularly three fragments from
4Q418 (221 + 222, 238) that may be interpreted as a sage (i.e., *maśkîl*) speaking in
the first-person to his pupils, the understanding ones (i.e., *mᵉvinîm*).[4] In addition to these three fragments are a small handful of passages where משכיל occurs, a term that has typically been translated as a participle rather than noun.

1　"I, Enoch, alone saw the visions, the extremities of all things. And no one among humans has
　　seen as I saw" (1 En. 19:3); "Then I turned to see the voice that was speaking to me, and on
　　turning I saw seven golden lampstands" (Rev 1:12).

2　Matthew J. Goff, *The Worldly and Heavenly Wisdom of 4QInstruction*, STDJ 50 (Leiden: Brill,
　　2003), 38–39, 69–73, 94 is non-committal about how God reveals knowledge, and suggests
　　that it took place vis-à-vis a visionary experience; Shane A. Berg, *Religious Epistemologies in
　　the Dead Sea Scrolls: The Heritage and Transformation of the Wisdom Tradition* (Ph.D. disser-
　　tation, Yale 2008), 47 concludes that the "sage shows virtually no interest in the logistics of
　　attending to the רז נהיה, but instead asserts what can be gained" by diligently pursuing it.

3　Cf. Newsom, *Self as Symbolic Space*, 204–229. where she discusses "I" and "you" in the *Thanks-
　　giving Hymns*.

4　The view that first-person speech is used by a *maśkîl* in the opening column of 4QInstruc-
　　tion was first put forward by Eibert J.C. Tigchelaar, *To Increase Learning for the Understanding
　　Ones: Reading and Reconstructing the Fragmentary Early Jewish Sapiential Text 4QInstruction*,
　　STDJ 44 (Leiden: Brill, 2001), 245 helpfully observes that "[s]cholarly analysis of [4Q]Instruc-
　　tion is based on fragments and on fragmentary texts, and the addition of one or two relatively
　　small fragments to another fragment, column or section, may force one to alter one's views."

© KONINKLIJKE BRILL NV, LEIDEN, 2018 | DOI: 10.1163/9789004364240_003

In this chapter, we begin with an identification and examination of first-person speech throughout 4QInstruction, first in 4Q418 55 and 4Q418 69 ii (§1.1.) followed by 4Q418 221+222 and 238 (§1.2.). After locating several in-stances of first-person speech belonging to a sage, each occurrence of משכיל is studied in order to determine whether it is ever used in reference to a *maśkîl*. One previously unrecognized reference to a teacher-sage in 4Q416 2 ii is espe-cially important because it elucidates one of the most contested fragments in the composition, namely 4Q418 81+81a where the activities of an exalted sage are described. In making the case that a *maśkîl* figure is central to our understanding of 4QInstruction, it is necessary to draw upon other Qumran discoveries that are likewise interested in a sage. Attention to *maśkilîm* in these other compositions both support the identification of a sage in 4QInstruction as well as offer models for how other sages were conceived. The picture that emerges from this analysis is that the speaker of 4QInstruction is a *maśkîl* who teaches *mᵉvinîm* in the ways of a sage. The pedagogical outlook taken in 4QIn-struction is inclusive and indicates that the teacher desires for his students to obtain to and live out wisdom to the same degree as him.

1   First-Person Speech

4QInstruction is written primarily as a work addressed to a single individual in second-person speech; the address is directed at one who is told to understand (ואתה מבין), understands (מבין), and at times is simply called "you" (אתה). There are also instances of indirect third-person masculine forms, for instance to describe God's activity ordering the cosmos (4Q416 1). As noted in the introduc-tion, at another point is an unusual indirect address in the second-person fem-inine (4Q415 2 ii). As would be expected, possessive pronouns occur in second and third-person masculine and singular forms. While these forms of speech have been noted and are the subject of commentary, comparatively little has been said about first-person speech and first-person possessive pronouns. This includes a number ambiguous occurrences that could be read either as first or third-person. In order to analyze the speaker's identity and his relationship with the addressee these relatively infrequent first-person forms serve as our point of departure.

Loren Stuckenbruck differentiates first-person speech in documents that mention a *maśkîl* with first-person speech found elsewhere in Qumran dis-coveries,[5] and observes that in documents that refer to a *maśkîl* (e.g., Rule of

---

5   Loren T. Stuckenbruck, "Pseudepigraphy and First Person Discourse in the Dead Sea Docu-

the Community, ShirShabb; Songs of the Sage) first-person address should not be confused with authorial self-ascription.[6] Indeed, if first-person speech is attributed to a *maśkîl* in 4QInstruction, then care is taken in this study not to confuse "speaker" with "author." Before turning to fragments and passages where references to a *maśkîl* may be found (4Q418 frgs. 222 + 221, 238), two other fragments where first-person speech occurs are considered (4Q418 frgs. 55; 69 ii). Except for these occurrences of the first-person there are only two other occasions in 4QInstruction that have this form; however, insufficient context is preserved to decipher how they were used, these are: 4Q418 54 3 "we will have rest" (נרגיעה); and 4Q418 78 2 "we will pursue" (נרדפֿ[ו).

1.1   First-Person Speech in 4Q418 55 and 4Q418 69 ii (+60)

4Q418 55 and 4Q418 69 ii have been extensively commented on for their common use of: (1) the second-person plural form; (2) the first-person plural form; (3) rhetorical questions; and (4) shared vocabulary.[7] These similarities led the editors of DJD 34 to theorize that these are "twin set-pieces" composed sep-

---

ments: From the Aramaic Texts to the Writings of the Yaḥad," in *The Dead Sea Scrolls and Contemporary Culture*, ed. Adolfo D. Roitman, Lawrence H. Schiffman & Shani Tzoref, STDJ 93 (Leiden: Brill, 2011), 295–328, at 324 comments: "The 'I' in the *Yaḥad* and related writings reflects a textual immanence of the real authors, however anonymous to us they continue to be. The first-person writer presents himself *as a present voice about the present*." It has been suggested that the "I" of the protagonist in hymns transmitted in the Thanksgiving Hymns may be identified with each member of the community and later, within a different context, identified with the Teacher of Righteousness, see esp. Michael O. Wise, "מי כמוני באלים: A Study of 4Q491ᶜ, 4Q471ᵇ, 4Q427 7 and 1QHᵃ 25:35–26:10," DSD 7/2 (2000): 173–219, at 218, "The Canticle's assertions were literally true of the Teacher in a way they could not be for anyone else. But on another level, each individual believer could make them true for himself or herself by partaking in the charisma of the Teacher. That happened partially through recitation. In a sense, the group became what the charismatic founder had been." Cf. Annette Steudel, "The Eternal Reign of the People of God—Collective Expectations in Qumran Texts (4Q246 and 1QM)," RevQ 17 (1996): 507–525, at 525; Florentino García Martínez, "Old Texts and Modern Mirages: The 'I' of Two Qumran Hymns," in *Qumranica Minora I: Qumran Origins and Apocalypticism*, ed. Eibert J.C. Tigchelaar, STDJ 63 (Leiden: Brill, 2007), 105–128.

6   On the use of the term in the Qumran literature see Hans Kosmala, "Maskil," *JANESCU* 5 (1973): 235–241; Carol Newsom, "The Sage in the Literature of Qumran: The Functions of the Maskil," in *The Sage in Israel and the Ancient Near East*, ed. John G. Gammie & Leo G. Perdue (Winona Lake, IN: Eisenbrauns, 1990), 373–382.

7   See esp. Tigchelaar, *To Increase Learning*, 208–224 who systematically presents these different forms before adjudicating their relationship to the rest of 4QInstruction.

arately and later integrated into the composition.[8] Eibert Tigchelaar offers a detailed study of this proposal and in conclusion is non-committal that "shared features should be attributed to slight editorial reworkings of a *Vorlage*," and that they "have some features in common with the rest of [4Q]*Instruction* ... which may indicate that they have the same provenance as the rest of [4Q]*Instruction*."[9] Matthew Goff comments that "points in common between fragments 55 and 69 ii are indeed striking, but they do not necessarily provide enough evidence to understand them as having been added later to the work," and that the language and themes "are fully compatible with the rest of the composition."[10] The working assumption here is that fragments 55 and 69 ii do not preserve sections composed separately and that the burden of proof lies with anyone who contends that they were. Moreover, by situating these different forms of speech within the context of a sage speaking to a spectrum of pupils a resolution is provided as to how these fragmentary passages relate to the other remaining sections of 4QInstruction.

4Q418 55 3–7 are characterized by "we" (l. 3 נכרה, נרגיע; l. 4 בלבבנו, בכול דרכנו) and "they" (l. 5 בחרו, שחרו) language. The first-person plural "we" does not appear to refer just to the instructor and *mēvîn*, in a more limited sense, but rather the "we" encompasses the members of a group.[11] Unlike 4Q418 55, in frag. 69 ii first-person speech is preceded by rhetorical questions (תאמרו איכה "how can you say ..." and האמור יאמרו "do they really say ..."), which explicitly introduce indirect speech. Important for the focus here, Tigchelaar comments that it is likely that in "frag. 55 the 1st person speeches were also [i.e., like frag. 69 ii] presented as speech of a group, and that the introduction has been lost."[12] Goff also views 4Q418 55 3–4 as indirect speech, "the author probably conveys what the ideal student-addressee *should* say. A similar rhetorical approach is found in 4Q418 69 ii 11–12."[13] Tigchelaar's and Goff's proposal that first-person speech in 4Q418 55 3–4 mirrors the indirect and rhetorical use in 4Q418 69 ii is questionable; it is dependent upon a perceived relationship of these two fragments, theoretical reconstruction, and assumptions about how first-person speech occurs in 4QInstruction more generally. Moreover, while sense can be made of 4Q418 55 3 within a rhetorical question (i.e., "[*how will you say,*] 'we

---

8   Torleif Elgvin, *An Analysis of 4QInstruction* (Ph.D. dissertation, Hebrew University 1998), 107–111, 248–255, 274–278; DJD 34:13–14, 265–273.

9   Tigchelaar, *To Increase Learning*, 224.

10   Goff, *4QInstruction*, 213.

11   DJD 34:13–14.

12   Tigchelaar, *To Increase Learning*, 218.

13   Goff, *4QInstruction*, 211.

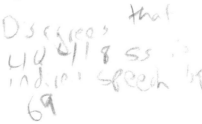

have dug its way with toil'"), line 4 appears to be a hortatory subjunctive and it is unclear how it could be introduced as indirect speech. The reconstruction here follows Elisha Qimron; the speaker laments shortcomings inherent to human beings and calls for vigilance.[14] As such, the speaker of 4Q418 55 is concerned with both his and his community's struggle faithfully to pursue understanding, which is a laborious and fraught task.

The translations of 4Q418 55 and 69 ii below are presented in tables with the right column indicating the form of speech. While Tigchelaar systematically presents and comments on rhetorical correspondences and common forms found in these two fragments, attention here is given to the subject of address and whether speech is direct or indirect. In 4Q418 55 no instances of indirect speech are found.

4Q418 55, Transcription and Translation:[15]

[ ] ○[וּנֹפֹשֹׁוֹ]	1
[ ] vac [ ]	2
[ ] נרגיע vac בעמל נכרה דרכיה [למה]	3
vacat [נא לנפשנו]ושקד יהיֿה בלבבנו [בכול קצים]וֿבטוח בכול דרכינו	4
[והם מאסו עצ]תֿ דעה ולא שחרו בֹּנֹ[ה וברצון אל ל]אֿ בחרו vac הלוא אל [ה]דֿעות	5
[הוא הוא פ]על אמת להכִֿין כול] חפציהם ודעת ב]ֿינה הוא פלג לנוחלי אמת	6
[מה כול פעולתו הלוא]שֹׁקד בא[מת ומה כול מ]ֹעֹשֹׂ[הו]הלוא שלום והשקט	7
[ואתם מבינים הלוא יד]עֹתם אם לא שמעתמה כיא מלאכי קודשׁ[ל]וֹ[ן] בשמים	8
[ ] ויבחרו ב]אֿמת וירדפו אחר כול שורשי בינה וישקדו על	9
[כול עצת דעה כי הם לפי]דֿעתם ֿכבדו איש מרעהו ולפי שכלו ירבה הדרֹֿ	10
[ ]הֿאנוש הם כי יעצל ובן אדם כי יֿדֿמֹה הלוא [○] [ ]○[	11
[○ֹד והם אֿחזֹת עולם ינחלו הלוא ראיתם	12
bottom margin	

---

14   Elisha Qimron, מגילות מדבר יהודה. החיבורים העבריים /*The Dead Sea Scrolls: The Hebrew Writings*, 3 vols. (Jerusalem: Yad Ben-Zvi Press, 2010–2014), 2:150 [Hebrew] only offers a short statement that these are questions from the recipients (שאלות בפי הנמענים) and does not comment on whether this is direct or indirect speech or the relationship of the speaker to this first-person speech. DJD 34:267 the editors ask, "[i]s this 'we' group composed merely of the instructor and his pupil the maven, or made up of a more numerous group, the members of a wider movement of sages?"

15   DJD 34:267; Tigchelaar, *To Increase Learning*, 89; theoretical reconstructions modified from those of Qimron, *Dead Sea Scrolls*, 2:150; cf. Goff, *4QInstruction*, 211; Jean-Sébastien Rey, *4QInstruction: sagesse et eschatologie*, STDJ 81 (Leiden: Brill, 2009), 304–305.

3 [... why] do we pursue its (i.e., truth's) ways with toil?

vac

[let us] have rest 4 [for our souls ...],

and vigilance will be in our hearts [at all times],

and assurance in all our ways

vac

ll. 3–4 "we" speaker and righteous community (direct speech)

5 [For they rejected the counsel of] knowledge,

And they did not diligently pursue understand[ing,

[n]or did they choose [God's good pleasure].

vac

l. 5a "they" are wicked ones

Is not God (a God) of knowledge?

6 [Who made] truth to regulate all [their desires]

[and knowledge of un]derstanding He apportioned to the
    inheritors of truth.

ll. 5b–6 third-person direct speech

7 [What is all its results? Is it not] vigilence in tr[uth?]

[And what are all its d]ee[ds?] Is it not peace and quiet?

l. 7 third-person rhetorical questions (direct speech)

8 [And you understanding ones,

have] you not known, have you not heard,

that the holy angels[ ] unto[him] in heaven [...]

l. 8a "you" (pl.) are righteous community

9 [... and they choose]truth,

and they seek after all the roots of understanding,

and they are vigilant in 10 [all counsel of knowledge.]

ll. 8b–10a "they" are angels, (direct speech)

[According to] their knowledge they will honor a man
    more than his neighbor,

and according to his understanding his glory will be
    increased.

l. 10b "they" righteous community

l. 10c "he" generic member of community

11 [...] are they (i.e., the holy angels) like humankind, for
    he is sluggish,

and a son of man, for he comes to an end,

are not 12 [...]d

and they will inherit an eternal possession,

have you not seen ...

In line 3 the speaker refers literally to "digging" (כרה) out either the ways of "truth" (אמת in ll. 6, 9) or perhaps, less likely, the antecedent of the feminine pronoun is "understanding" (בינה in ll. 6, 9). "Digging" is a verb that occurs in 4QInstruction only here and in Qumran discoveries is infrequent. 4QBeatitudes (4Q525 5 12) uses כרה as an activity pursuing wisdom: "the shrewd will dig out its (i.e., wisdom's) ways" (ערומים יכרו דרכיה). 4Q424 3 6 (4QSapiential Text) warns not to send an undiscerning man "to dig out thoughts" (אל תשלח לכרות מחשבות).[16] In CD VI 1–10 the ones who dig a "well" (= Torah) are the righteous remnant, literally the "returners of Israel" (שבי ישראל), who reside in Damascus during an age of wickedness (CD VI 5).[17] When the speaker in 4Q418 55 includes himself with his addressees, he contrasts them with others who have rejected the counsel of knowledge and not sought after understanding (l. 5). The "us" and "them" in these lines distinguish a faithful community digging laboriously for truth, which in 4Q417 1 i shapes the cosmos and the mystery of existence, from wayward ones who have failed in this task. Throughout this fragment and elsewhere in 4QInstruction the inside group lives with a tension, namely that the pursuit of both knowledge and mysteries is a perpetual undertaking with risk of failure (cf. Ch. 2).

4Q418 55 8–12 continue "they" language, but the speaker changes from "we" to the second-person plural address "you." Angelic beings are the "they" and the addressees are the "you" in a comparison between angels and humans. The "angels of holiness" (מלאכי קודש) are explicit in line 8 and are the likely subject of the verbs in lines 9–10a; as such they: (1) choose truth, (2) seek understanding, and (3) are vigilant in the counsel of knowledge. The characterization of angelic being as pursuers of wisdom is also found in 4Q418 69 ii. Here, in line 11, humans are described as fatigable and mortal whereas, in contrast, angels are not. The speaker's inclusionary address in lines 3–4, despite second-person speech in lines 8–12, avoids presenting himself as superior: he too is "sluggish" and will one day perish.

In this fragment contrasts are drawn and groups and individuals are distinguished from one another on the basis of the degree to which understanding has been acquired. On the extreme end of the spectrum are those who have simply rejected (using the perfect שחרו to indicate completed action) the pursuit of wisdom, which results in an "us" and "them" scenario. Gradations within the community itself are expressed as individuals who are distinguished from one another based upon the extent to which they have obtained knowledge (l. 10). Goff comments that "[t]here is not enough evidence of factionalism or sectarian tensions in 4QInstruction to suggest that the 'they' group of 4Q418 55 4 represents a community that splintered off from the group to which 4QIn-

---

16   Gershon Brin, "Wisdom Issues in Qumran: The Types and Status of the Figures in 4Q424 and the Phrases of Rationale in the Document," *DSD* 4/3 (1997): 297–311, at 300 translates לכרות מחשבות as "to differentiate thoughts."

17   These lines are preserved in 4Q266 3 ii 11; 4Q267 2 9.

struction is addressed."[18] However, his conclusion is rooted in a specific deterministic and dualistic understanding of the composition which is derived from
an interpretation of 4Q417 1 i 13–18 as depicting the creation of two different
groups of humanity, one that ontologically has it within their remit to pursue
wisdom and the other not. This passage, the so-called Vision of Hagu pericope,
comes into focus in Chapter 2 where this particular dualistic and deterministic
framework is challenged. As such, the "us" and "them" in 4Q418 55 need not be
seen as reflecting "factionalism," but rather a depiction of humanity as a whole
being tasked with distinguishing good and evil and divisions occurring based
upon un/faithful pursuit of wisdom. The reason that this is not "factionalism" is
that the "us" and "them" are not expressing a split among the "elect" who were
bestowed special revelation; instead, the "us" and "them" are those among all
humanity who have acted wisely or foolishly.

4Q418 69 ii 1–15 preserve parts of four passages, only two of which are fully
extant. The conjunction "and now" (ועתה) and address "and you" (ואתה), along
with a consistent use of *vacats*, demarcate these pericopae. The two passages
preserved are found in lines 4a–9 and 10–15a.

4Q418 69 ii+60 lines 3–15 (comp. 4Q417 5 [single underline], 4Q418 60 [double
underline]), Transcription and Translation:[19]

‏דתם הלוא באמת יתהלכו‏ ‏[‏ ‏]○○○[‏ ‏]○[‏	‏]‏ 3
‏כו]ל[‏ ‏[מימי]הם ובדעה כול גליהם‏ ‏vacat‏ ‏ועתה אוילי לב מה טוב ללוא‏	4
‏[נ]וצ[ר]‏ ‏[ומה]‏ ‏השקט ללוא היה ומה משפט ללוא נוסד ומה יאנחו מתים על‏	5
‏מ]נוחת ○ם‏	
‏אתם]‏ ‏מהב]ל נוצרתם ולשחת עולם תשובתכם כי תקיץ‏ ‏[○○‏	‏חטאבמ]ה[‏ 6
‏מחשביה]‏ ‏י]צרחו על ריבכם וכול נהיה עולם דורשי אמת יעורו למשפטכ]ם ואז[‏	7

---

18   Goff, *4QInstruction*, 215 concludes that "[i]t is more likely that the 'they' group and their
refusal to seek knowledge represents an attitude that the student-addressees should not
adopt." If the dualistic interpretation of humanity is incorrect, the "they" group does not
represent an undesirable "attitude," but rather wayward humanity who has forsaken wisdom; the addressees are being warned that they should not succumb to laziness and join
the foolish.

19   DJD 34:281; Tigchelaar, *To Increase Learning*, 209–210 who joins 4Q418 60, containing perhaps the first letters of lines 4 and 5 and is underlined above, to frag. 69 ii; Émile Puech, "Les
fragments eschatologiques de 4QInstruction (4Q416 i et 4Q418 69 ii, 81–81a, 127)," *RevQ* 22
(2005): 89–119; Rey, *4QInstruction*, 243–244; Goff, *4QInstruction*, 223–224; Qimron, *Dead
Sea Scrolls*, 2:151.

8 ישמדו כול אוילי לב ובני עולה לוא ימצאו עוד] וכ]ול מחזיקי רשעה יבש]ו כיא[

9 במשפטכם יריעו מוסדי }ה{רקיע וירעמו כול צ]בא מ]ל]אכים וכו]ל אהבי]ל צדק יגילו[

10 vacat   ואתם בחירי אמת ורודפי [צדקה ו]מ֯ש֯ת֯]רי בינה ו]שוקד֯]ים[

11 על כול דע֯ה איכה תאמרו יגענו בבינה ושקדנו לרדוף דעת ב֯]כול עת [בכול מ֯]קום[

12 ולא עי֯ף בכול }נ{שני עולם הלוא באמת ישעשע לעד ודעה [תמיד]תשרתנו זב֯]ני [

13 שמים אשר חיים עולם נחלתם האמור יאמרו יגענו בפעלות אמת ויעפ]נו[

14 בכול קצי֯ם הלוא באו֯ר עולם יתה֯ל]כו ואתם תנחלו כ]ב֯ו֯ד ורוב הדר אתם] כיא[

15 ברקיעי]ן קדוש ו]ב֯סוד אילים כול [נחלתכם   vacat]   ואתה בן [מבין[

bottom margin

3 [   ]○[ ]○○*dtm*,   ll. 3–4a "they" are righteous
will they not walk in truth?   ones

4 In all their [waters] and in knowledge all their waves?

vacat

And now foolish of heart what is good to one not 5   ll. 4b–5 "they" are wicked
    created?   ones, rhetorical ques-
[And what] is quietness to one who is not?   tion/direct speech

And what is judgment to one not born?

And how will the dead groan over their d[eath] (lit.
    sleep/resting?)

6 [In futili]ty you were created and to the eternal pit you ll. 6–7 "you" (pl.) are wicked
    will return;   in direct speech

for you will awaken [   ][y]our sin [   ]

7 its dark places[ ]will cry out against your disputes,

and all who will live forever,

seekers of truth will awaken for [your] judgment,

for] 8 all the foolish of heart and the sons iniquity will be l. 8 "they" are wicked in
    destroyed,   direct speech

they will not be found any longer,

[and a]ll those who hold fast to evil will with[er,

and then] 9 in your judgment {the} foundations of {the} l. 9a "you" is God
    firmament will shout out,

and all the [angelic] h[osts] will thunder,   l. 9b angels are "they"

[al]l lovers of[righteousness will be revealed]   l. 9c "they" are righteous
                                                           ones
10 *vacat*

And you are choosers of truth and seekers of[righteous- ll. 10–11a "you" (pl.) are righ-
    ness],   teous in direct speech

and] on[es] who diligently seek [insight and] watch over l. 11b "we" righteous com-
11 all knowledge,   munity, indirect speech

how will you say, "we have toiled in insight and taken

 care to pursue knowledge at [all times] and in every

 p[lace]."

12 But He does not tire in all the years of eternity.

Does He not take delight in truth forever?

And does not knowledge[continually]serve Him?

And the son[s] 13 of heaven who inherit eternal life, will

 they really say,

"we have toiled in labors of truth, and [we] are tired 14 at

 all times."

Will [they] not walk in eternal light,

[and will you not inherit g]lory and great splendor with

 them?

15 In the [holy] firmament [and]in the council of the

 angels is all [of your inheritance]

vacat

And you, son of [an understanding one]

   bottom margin

ll. 11c–12a third-person statement

ll. 12b–13a third-person rhetorical questions

ll. 13b–14a "we" are angelic beings, indirect speech

l. 14b "they" are angels

ll. 14c–15 "you" (pl.) are righteous ones

The first passage found in lines 4b–9 fluctuates between third-person and second-person forms. The speaker begins by describing the "foolish of heart" (ll. 4b–5) in the third-person, using a series of four rhetorical questions, in the first three "good," "quiet," and "judgment" are as nothing to one who has not been created, is not, and has not been born.[20] The fourth, following Qimron's reconstruction, uses the euphemism "rest" or "sleep" for death (cf. Isa 57:2).[21]

---

20 Cf. 4Q418 81 + 81a 6 where, in contrast, and in direct speech, God says to the exalted and righteous addressee: "I will give my good things to you." Note that Rev 17:8, 10 mock the beast "because it was and is not and is to come," which is a parody of Christ who is, who was, and who is to come.

21 Qimron, *Dead Sea Scrolls*, 2:151 on the meaning of מנוחה comments: המתים אינם נאנחים בקבריהם; he suggests alternative reconstructions (מיתתם, משפטם, משכבם). מנוח and its synonym מנוחה are unusually frequent in 4QInstruction occurring at least five times (4Q415 13 5; 4Q417 2 i 22; 4Q418 7b 5; 4Q418 8 9; 4Q418 188 3; perhaps 4Q418 237 1). The editors, Goff, Rey, and Puech all reconstruct כ[ול יומ]ם ("about their [days]"); Menahem Kister, "Divorce, Reproof, and Other Sayings in the Synoptic Gospels: Jesus Traditions in the Context of 'Qumranic' and Other Texts," in *Text, Thought, and Practice in Qumran and Early Christianity: Proceedings of the Ninth International Symposium of the Orion Center for the Study of the Dead Sea Scrolls and Associated Literature, Jointly Sponsored by the Hebrew University Center for the Study of Christianity*, ed. Ruth A. Clements & Daniel R. Schwartz, STDJ 84 (Leiden: Brill, 2009), 195–229, at 198–199 על מ[ות]ם ("over their own

Of significance here is that the speaker switches to direct second-person plural address in the following lines (ll. 6–7). This is the only place in 4QInstruction where someone other than a positively conceived understanding one is addressed, although on occasion the addressees are "simple ones." The "you" (pl.) here are warned of judgment and future destruction; those who seek truth may anticipate a day of reckoning when the wicked will return to the eternal pit. Who these foolish of heart are is one question, why the speaker uses direct second-person address is another. If these foolish ones are "a rival sapiential school," as Goff suggests, the author could have used a third-person form, which would continue with the "us" and "them" constructs found elsewhere in these fragments.[22] Goff deduces that those in this rival school follow Qohelet's bleak assessment of the human condition (i.e., "vanity of vanities") and are at fault for complaining about their days. When "you" is used in lines 6–7 it is not in a conditional, but a statement about the creation of the wicked and their impending judgment.[23]

That second-person plural forms are literally directed to the foolish, *in a competing school*, is not plausible. There are, seemingly, only two options, either the second-person address is directed to: (1) those outside of the community, or (2) those within the community. In regard to the first point, there is no evidence that 4QInstruction is written to address opponents directly. Regarding the second point, if there is no ontological distinction between groups of humanity (cf. Ch. 2 §2.1.), direct address to the foolish could include those within the community who are being chastised and warned about the dangers of their foolish ways. These are not the ones that 4QInstruction refers to as "fleshly spirit," but rather those on the verge of being errant and are in danger of corrupting their spirit (cf. Ch. 2 §2.2.).[24] Noteworthy is that the Book of Watchers

---

de[ath]"); Tigchelaar, *To Increase Learning*, 211 does not reconstruct but comments that one may consider משכבם (cf. Sir 47:20 (B) אנחה על משכבך); Elgvin, *Analysis*, 115–116 משפטם.

22   Goff, *4QInstruction*, 230.

23   DJD 34:284 confirm that this passage "discusses how 'you', the foolish minded, are bound for the Pit (line 6) and describes the final judgement in which they, and all the cosmos with them, shall be destroyed (line 8)." However, that the unusual address to the foolish is *sui generis* in the document is not discussed.

24   4Q418 126 ii (+122 ii) 6 refers to turning away vengeance from workers of iniquity (להשיב נקם לפעלי און) and elsewhere the addressee turns away wrath from members of the community (4Q418 81 + 81a; 4Q417 2 i). There is concern within 4QInstruction that the speaker's own community may come under judgment and is, therefore, demonstrably concerned directly with unrighteousness ones (cf. Ch. 2 §2.4.).

(1 En. 5:4–10) also contains second-person, direct speech to the wicked, who are described as lacking endurance. The wayward are warned that "the years of your life shall perish and multiply in eternal execration" (1 En. 5:5). In this chapter of the Book of Watchers, the righteous are contrasted with the wicked, using third person address when describing the faithful. Moreover, similar to 4QInstruction (4Q416 1), wickedness is described as a failure on the part of humanity to observe the created order and seasons (1 En. 5:1–2).

Emphasis and repetition on the theme of "not being created" in line 5 stands in sharp contrast to a statement about their creation in line 6: "you were created" (אתם נוצרתם). A direct statement about being created but ridiculing them as though they "are not" is a way to excoriate those acting foolishly within the community. If you treat your own creation with such contempt by abandoning the pursuit of wisdom, then you are as one never created. The "you" in these lines is directed at the speaker's own community, warning them that following in the ways of foolishness will result in judgment and negating the gift of their own creation.[25] These four rhetorical questions are a playful mocking of folly and inanity: one who has not been created cannot enjoy good things, and the dead cannot complain about their "resting" (= death).

Line 8 alternates back to a third-person ("they") description of the "foolish of heart" who are now modified with the "sons of iniquity." The foolish and iniquitous ones are warned of judgment and described as those who continue in their evil ways. Finally, the speaker turns to God's judgment, using the second-person possessive pronoun "your judgment," before anticipating in the third-person how angels ("they") will rejoice and how lovers of righteousness ("they") will be revealed.

Found in the second passage (ll. 10–15a) are first, second, and third-person forms. Unlike the previous pericope, this section begins with a second-person plural address to those who choose truth and seek righteousness. This is the only extant instance of בחיר (one who "chooses" or one who is "chosen") used to describe the addressees in 4QInstruction; noticeably infrequent are terms derived from the root בחר, which by contrast occur frequently in the Thanksgiving Hymns where the psalmist is God's chosen (cf. Ch. 2 §1.2.). The ones addressed here in 4Q418 69 ii 10 are called by nomenclatures that express wakeful and persistent pursuit of understanding, they are: "pursuing" (רודפים), "diligently seeking" (משחרים), and "watching over" (שוקדים) knowledge. So too, they

---

25   This is a creation that is not exclusive to them. Not only does this serve as a warning, but also draws attention to the creation of those who will be judged for not following the created order. These lines root justification of judgment in the creation of humanity.

are "ones who choose truth" (בחירי אמת) rather than "chosen one's of truth" as found frequently in English translations.[26]

Despite the positive description as seekers of knowledge, the speaker draws attention to the imperfect nature of their endeavors by way of a rhetorical question which introduces indirect speech and contains a first-person plural form. Neither instances of indirect speech in this pericope, in which first-person plural speech occurs (ll. 11, 13), are within a rhetorical question, but rather are found in statements set up to answer a rhetorical question posed in preceding direct speech. Lines 11c–12a transition to third-person forms, setting up a contrast between righteous humanity with both God and angelic beings (i.e., "sons of heaven"). God is perfect, he does not weary at any time. God delights in truth. A rhetorical question in lines 12b–13a expresses that knowledge continually serves God. The untiring nature of angelic beings is emphasized in lines 13–14 when the speaker sets up a hypothetical setting, asking if angelic beings would really make such and such a statement. The speaker then asks rhetorical questions about the future of both "them" (l. 14b), who are the angels, and "you" (ll. 14c–15), who are the righteous addressees.

Lines 14–15 portray those who choose truth as sharing glory and splendor with the angelic being (אתם "with them"). The righteous community joins the sons of heaven in the firmament and participates in their council. "Council of angels" and "council of the sons of heaven" are synonymously parallel in 1QH[a] xxv 26 (= Self-Glorification Hymn). In 4QInstruction, "firmament" (רקיע) is only found in 4Q418 69 ii lines 9 and 15. In line 9 the "foundations of the firmament" (מ{וס}דֵי ה{ה}רקיע) may inform the reading of the "[holy] firmament" in line 15, which could be read as a parallel expression to the "council of angels" in the same line.[27] While these lines promise shared future glory together with the angels, this does not necessarily exclude participation with them in the present. How the speaker and addressees relate to angels, especially if present participation is depicted, is an important aspect of the religious experiences of the community (see § 4.1. below).

Among the shared characteristics of 4Q418 55 and 69 ii are the use of first and second-person plural forms. However, these forms are not used identically in these two fragments as may be observed in the following three points. First, 4Q418 55 addresses "you" who are the "understanding ones," whereas atypically in 4Q418 69 ii "you" are the "foolish of heart." Second, the "we" forms in 4Q418

---

26   The active sense of בחירי אמת is preferred here because it is in parallel with "seekers of righteousness"; see comments in DJD 34:288 (cf. 1QH[a] 11 13; 4QTNaph 1 ii 2).

27   סוד ("council") occurs on several occasions in 4QInstruction in the expressions סוד אנשים and סוד אמת see 4Q415 6 1, 6; 4Q418a 12 2; 4Q417 1 i 8, 20; comp. with 4Q418 43–45 i 6, 15.

[handwritten note: Perps read rhetorical? of 1 into the other]

69 ii are found in indirect speech, which are statements that answer an immediately preceding rhetorical question posed in direct speech. When "we" occurs
in 4Q418 55 3, it is found in a sentence that itself forms a question. Third, 4Q418
55 4 is not a statement in response to a rhetorical question either, but rather
appears to be hortatory; line 4 is not a statement in response to an immediately
preceding question or a question itself. Indeed, lines 3–4 are two consecutive
sentences each with first-person plural forms, and in 4Q418 69 ii first-person
plural forms do not occur consecutively because both function within a length-
ier rhetorical construct, which distinguish between angelic beings and humanity. Therefore, a straightforward conclusion that 4Q418 55 3–4 are using indirect
speech in the same way as 4Q418 69 ii is not plausible. Evident from tables
and discussion above are that these two fragments are using a variety of forms
that are not witnessed elsewhere in 4QInstruction and these different forms—
whether first, second, or third-person—do not mirror one another. 4Q418 55
3–4 preserve first-person plural address in which the speaker includes himself
with his students. This provides an important context for the assessment of
first-person forms in three small fragments of 4QInstruction (4Q418 222 + 221,
238 below) as well as several other instances where references to a sage are
found.

In summary, 4Q418 55 and 4Q418 69 ii have been considered problematic
because they use a variety of addresses, including second-person plural and
first-person plural forms, that have been perceived as incongruous with the
rest of 4QInstruction. The assessment here considers the possibility that the
speaker includes himself with the addressees. In 4Q418 55 the speaker is concerned with those who have rejected knowledge ("they") and are outside the
community, which leads him to encourage and exhort them not to weary in
their own pursuit of understanding. 4Q418 69 ii also contrasts the righteous and
wicked ("they") and uses direct speech ("you") to warn the "foolish of heart." The
speaker is addressing an audience composed of a range of students, some are
verging on abandoning the pursuit of wisdom, likely by succumbing to laziness,
and are chastised, warned, and even mocked. Other students, ones that are
more diligent and faithful, are nonetheless imperfect and are encouraged not
to make excuses. These two fragmentary columns do not depict elect "chosen
ones of truth" (4Q418 69 ii 10), but rather one's who *choose* truth. By understanding the widely spread standing of various students, some advanced and others
much less so, and direct addresses to them and indirect teaching about them,
the misperception that these two fragments are inconsistent with the rest of
4QInstruction is corrected.

[handwritten note: ⸮Maskil w/ people]

1.2 Speech of a Maśkîl in 4Q418 222 + 221, 238

4Q418 222 + 221 and 238 may preserve the incipit of 4QInstruction. In the scribal hand of 4Q418, as is the case of other manuscripts of 4QInstruction, the letters *waw* and *yod* are indistinguishable. Despite this ambiguity Harrington and Strugnell shy away from rendering these pronominal suffixes in the first-person.[28] In regard to these ambiguous pronouns in 4Q418 222 + 221, Tigchelaar suggests the possibility that first-person speech occurs in these fragments; moreover, a third fragment (frg. 238 where the word משכיל occurs) may be located in close proximity to these two others. He tentatively locates these three fragments in the first column of the document, in which case the speaker of 4QInstruction may be a *maśkîl* instructing understanding ones.[29]

4Q416 1 is the first column of 4QInstruction, which is evident from the wide right-hand margin. In addition to Tigchelaar, other scholars have speculated that from the outset of the document a seer is referred to who increases learning for the understanding ones. Several factors converge when assessing the possibility that a sage is present: (1) a reconstruction and translation of 4Q416 1 14–15; (2) rendering ambiguous pronouns in 4Q418 222 + 221; (3) the possible location of 4Q418 222 + 221, 238 at the beginning of 4Q416 1;[30] and (4) similarities with other compositions where the speaker is a *maśkîl*. In regard to the

---

28　DJD 34:436–438, 437 "Palaeographic considerations do not especially favour either *yod* or *waw*." The right stroke, or "head," of the *yod* in 4Q418 is often times fuller than that of a *waw*; if this is correct then a *yod* is favored here. Cf. Frank M. Cross, "The Development of the Jewish Scripts," in *The Bible and the Ancient Near East: Essays in Honor of W.F. Albright*, ed. G. Ernest Wright (New York, NY: Doubleday, 1960), 133–202.

29　Tigchelaar, *To Increase Learning*, 245; cf. Eibert J.C. Tigchelaar, "Wisdom and Counter-Wisdom in 4QInstruction, Mysteries and 1 Enoch," in *The Early Enoch Literature*, ed. Gabriele Boccaccini & John J. Collins, JSJS 121 (Leiden: Brill, 2007), 177–194 where he speculates that it is Wisdom who speaks in 4QInstruction and concludes that Enoch's role in 1 Enoch 92:1 is similar to that of Wisdom in 4QInstruction (cf. 1 En. 42:1–2).

30　The editors indicate a "top margin" of 4Q416 1 (DJD 34:81); however, there is no top margin visible in the fragment, therefore one or more lines likely preceded 4Q416 1 1. Cf. Qimron, *Dead Sea Scrolls*, 2:147 who comments on the top of 4Q416 1: חסרה שורה (או יותר). 4Q416 overlaps with 4Q418 2a, 209, 218, 208, 2c (= 213), 212, 217, 224; it is possible that 4Q418 222 + 221 could be located in the line(s) preceding 4Q416 1 1. However, Eibert J.C. Tigchelaar, "Toward a Reconstruction of the Beginning of 4QInstruction (4Q416 Fragment 1 and Parallels)," in *The Wisdom Texts from Qumran and the Development of Sapiential Thought*, ed. Charlotte Hempel, Armin Lange & Hermann Lichtenberger (Leuven: Peeters, 2002), 99–126, at 123 writes: "since the fragment does not overlap with 4Q416 1, and does not provide any plausible textual joins, this identification is no more than a possibility."

final point, frags. 222 + 221 and 238 share similarities with the Songs of the Sage (4Q444, 510–511), where the author clearly calls himself *maśkîl* and refers to himself in the first-person (4Q510 4 "and I, the Instructor," ואני משכיל), and the Thanksgiving Hymns (1QHª XX 14–16—אני משכיל).[31]

There are several possible readings of 4Q416 1 15; Harrington and Strugnell give four options, and one of the most probable requires that a (non-extant) subject of the verb at the beginning of the line 15 be supplied.[32] What verb this is, either from the root כון ("establish," "prepare," "ordain") or בין ("understand"), and how it relates to the following words (צדיק or צדק; conjunction -ו or not), is not agreed upon in critical editions of this column.[33] 4Q418 2 overlaps with the beginning of 4Q416 1 15 and each preserve a different reading of these words; additionally, just how different these readings are is debatable because the crucial letters of להכ֯י֯ן in 4Q416 1 15 may or may not be the same as in 4Q418 2 (להבין). 4Q418 2 reads להבין צדיק ובין ("to cause the righteous to understand and between ...") and 4Q416 1 15 may read להב֯י֯ן צדק בין ("so that the righteousness may distinguish between ..."). Émile Puech offers a theoretical reconstruction of 4Q416 1 14–15 with a reference to a *maśkîl* without associating it with frags. 222 + 221 and 238.

---

31   Stuckenbruck, "Pseudepigraphy and First Person Discourse," 300; the address למשכיל is
      equally as frequent a way of referring to a *maśkîl* (e.g., CD XII 21; 1QS III 13; IX 12, 21; 1QHª
      VII 21). Eileen M. Schuller & Carol A. Newsom, *The Hodayot (Thanksgiving Psalms): A Study
      Edition of 1QHª* (Atlanta, GA: Society of Biblical Literature, 2012), 9 Appendix C comment
      on opening formulas in the Thanksgiving Hymns: "The formula אודכה ('I give you thanks')
      always indicates the beginning of a psalm; sometimes (but not always) the ברוך אתה
      'Blessed are you' formula begins a new psalm. In some places there are headings simi-
      lar to those found in the biblical Psalter, with the rubric למשכיל 'For the Maskil' (in 5:12,
      7:21, 20:7, 25:34; probably to be reconstructed in 1:1). In one place, 1QHª 20:6, a scribal mark
      in the margin seems to indicate a new section."

32   DJD 34:87–88, (1) for the righteous to understand/distinguish (להבין) the difference be-
      tween good and evil; (2) for someone, and the editors suggest God, to make the righteous
      understand; (3) to establish (להכון) a right measure between good and evil; or (4) for a
      right measure to be established (*Niphal* להכון) between good and evil.

33   DJD 34:83, 87 transcription follows 4Q416 (להב֯י֯ן); however, they are not committed to
      this reading. Rey, *4QInstruction*, 229 and Goff, *4QInstruction*, 43 reconstruct 4Q416 1 להב֯י֯ן
      צדק בין ("[...]to make a righteous person understand the difference ..."); Qimron, *Dead
      Sea Scrolls*, 2:147 comments that להבין צדיק is the clearer reading. Tigchelaar, *To Increase
      Learning*, 175–176 transcribes 4Q416 1 15 as "to establish" (להב֯ו֯ן), although he translates "to
      let the righteous understand."

Puech's transcription and translation of 4Q416 1 14–15:[34]	Harrington & Strugnell's transcription and translation of 4Q416 1 14–15:[35]
14 בכל קצי עד כי אל אמת הוא ומקדם שני[עולם הכין הכול וגלה אוזן משכיל[15 [להבין צד(י)]ק בין טוב לרע לה[כי]ר כל משפ[טיהם(?)............................כיא[	14 בכול קצי עד כי אל אמת הוא ומקדם שנ[י] עולם [ל 15 להבֿין צדק בין טוב לֹרֹעֿ לֹ[ ]רֿ כל משפֿ[ט א]
14 dans tous les temps éternels, car Il est le Vrai Dieu. Depuis les temps anciens, les années[*d'éternité, Il a disposé toute chose, et Il a instruit l'oreille du sage*] 15 pour expliquer au juste à distinguer le bien du mal, pour faire[connaître] tous [les (?)] jugemen[ts (/de ...) ... car	14 in all periods of eternity. For He is a God of fidelity. And from *of old* (*from*) *years* of[eternity] 15 So that *the righteous may distinguish* (?) between good and evil, *So that* ... every *judgem[ent ...]*

While others have not followed Puech's reconstruction of line 14b (*"He uncovered the ear of the sage* to cause the righteous ones to understand ...") and a reference to a *maśkîl*, justification for this possibility is given by Tigchelaar who comments that:

> One may speculate, on the basis of the wording of other texts, that the lacuna in 4Q416 1 14 refers to the appointment by God of the sage or sages. They are to teach the righteous the difference between good and bad, to teach simpletons ... It is not clear whether this is presented as the task of the presumed instructor, or of the addressees of the text ...[36]

If 4Q416 1 14–15 were to refer to the role of a sage instructing students in third-person forms, then this needs to be accounted for alongside the theory that first-person, self-referential speech opens the column. These two forms of speech need not be seen to be in conflict with one another, a *maśkîl* speaking in the first-person about his own activity before describing the role a *maśkîl* in third-person forms (i.e., passive speech "God uncovered the ear of the *maśkîl*") accords well with the assessment below that there are multiple *maśkilîm* in 4QInstruction.

---

34   Puech, "Les fragments," 90.

35   DJD 34:81–83.

36   Tigchelaar, *To Increase Learning*, 193.

In addition to finding first-person singular pronouns in frgs. 222 + 221, Tigchelaar also observes the series of infinitives in them, of particular note is להו[ס]יף לקח למבינים ("to increase learning for the understanding ones"), which is "strongly reminiscent of the beginning of the Two Spirits (1QS III 13) and 1QHa V 12–14."[37] He concludes that one should "allow for the possibility that the beginning of the composition introduced a משכיל who had to increase learning for the מבינים, 'understanding ones.'"[38]

4Q418 frgs. 222 + 221, Transcription and Translation (see figs. 5–6 in plate section):[39]

frag. 222

‏[ב]֗ל[בב דברתי ‏°°°לֿכ]‏[40	] 1
שמ]עה רוחי ומזל שפתי א]ל	] 2
להוכיח פושעים ולהֿבֿיֿ]ן	] 3
דעוֿ]ֿ ‏[ ]° [ ]° כֿ֗א בֿ]	] 4
]°[ ]֗ל[	] 5

frag. 221

ה֗מה ולוֿא֗] פ]י֗	] 1
‏ נ֗בֿיאים ולהבין כֿוֿל פֿותיים]	] 2
להו]ֿסֿ֗יף לקח למבינים vacat	] 3
נא ֗זדעו משפטיֿ ואז תבדֿ֗לו בֿ]יֿן	] 4
וֿ]תתבוננו לדעת טוב]	] 5

bottom margin

---

37   Tigchelaar, *To Increase Learning*, 245–246; note that in the Community Rule the "sons of light" are taught while here both "simple ones" and "understanding ones" are instructed: למשכיל להבין וללמד את כול בני אור 1QS III 13.

38   Tigchelaar, *To Increase Learning*, 246.

39   Cf. Tigchelaar, "Wisdom and Counter-Wisdom," 187.

40   l. 1 Before דברתי the editors read]בֿנֿ[ה֗] and having examined the fragment along with Torleif Elgvin, with the use of an electronic miscroscope and infrared imaging, have been able to rule out this reading. The remains of a diagonal stroke from the top left down and to the right where the *heh* should be suggests rather the possibility of a *shin* or *samek*. The word to follow is not בנ for several reasons: (a) the bottom horizontal stroke is too long and there is the trace of ink at the top of the line that appears to be the remains of an upper horizontal line, this indicates that either בכ or בב are to be read here; (b) the space that follows these two letters appears to be a long *vacat* due to the absence of ink traces where they would be expected; (c) in the liklihood that this is a *vacat*, the scribe who copied 4Q418 is highly skilled and there are no instances of him using a *nun* where a *final nun* is required. The space between the first remaining letter of this line and the *beit* may be a break or possibily a *lamed*; 4Q418 204 2 preserves בלבב, which is possible here.

1   [   ]in the heart. *vac* I spoke and ... [
2   [he]ar *my* spirit and the outpouring of *my* lips, do not[
3   [   ]to reprove transgressor and to gain understand[ing
4   [   ] know[   ] [ ] for in [
1   [   ] them, and no [   ]mouth of/my mouth[
2   [   ] prophets, and to give insight to all the simple ones[
3   [and to] increase learning for the understanding ones *vac* [
4   [   ].. and know *my* judgments, and then you will distinguish betwe[en
5   [and] you will understand to know good[*and evil*
                         bottom margin

Although Harrington and Strugnell comment that first-person speech does not occur in 4QInstruction, other than in the indirect statements (i.e., 4Q418 55 and 69 ii), on this occasion they nearly make an exception when adjudicating whether 4Q418 222 1 could be a *maśkîl*'s self-referential statement when he addresses the understanding ones.[41] The assessment of 4Q418 55 above strengthens the possibility that first-person forms are found here.

The three substantives to which the possible first-person singular pronominal suffix is attached, i.e. 4Q418 221 (משפט) and 4Q418 222 (שפה, רוח), only occur together elsewhere in 4QInstruction in 4Q418 77 + 4Q416 7 (hereafter 4Q418 77), fragments that are returned to in Chapter 2 (§ 2.5.). Another important similarity between 4Q418 77 and frgs. 222 + 221 is that this the only other place in the document where the root נזל and שפה occur together. The *mēvîn* in 4Q418 77 is instructed: (1) to understand the mystery of existence and "grasp the nature [תולדות] of man" (l. 2);[42] (2) to discern judgment (l. 3); (3) to listen to the "outpouring of his lips" (l. 4 מזל שפתיו); and (4) to do this "according to his spirit" (l. 4 לפי רוחו). "Outpouring of lips" and "spirit" combine in 4Q418 77 and are instrumental in grasping the mystery of existence, which may be similar to their context here in 4Q418 222.

The phrase מזל שפתי is not found in the Hebrew Bible; however, like משפטי it is also found in both recensions of the Self-Glorification Hymn (4Q471ᵇ frgs.

---

41   DJD 34:437–438 "No certain uses of the 1st sing. verb or suffix in 4Q415ff. except in statements of others quoted in *oratio recta*; they might, however, be acceptable in self-reference to the משכיל who is addressing the בן מבין." Although they translate suffixes as third-person.

42   cf. 4Q417 1 i 3 תֽוֹלֽדֽוֹת ברז נהיה ומעשי קדם למה נהיה ומה נהיה ("... history, and by the mystery of existence, and deeds of old, what was, and what will be"). The editors reconstruct וֽהֽבֽטֽ instead of תולדות, with the use of new imaging techniques תולדות can be deciphered.

1–4 5–6; 4Q491ᶜ i 10; 4QHᵃ 9).[43] This composition is composed in first-person speech and an exalted figure, whose identity is a matter of debate, boasts of his place among the angels.[44] The elevated status of this individual, who shares in the heavenly realm, allows him to assert: "I have been instructed, and there is no teaching comparable to my teaching" (4Q491ᶜ i 9b–10a). With a wordplay between the roots שפה and שפט, the author asks in first-person (4Q491ᶜ i 10b): "Who can endure the utterance of *my lips*? Who will challenge me and com-

---

43   There are four witnesses to the Self-Glorification Hymn and they have frequently been discussed as comprising two different recensions: Recension A (4Q427 7, 1QHᵃ xxv 34–xxvii 3, and 4Q471ᵇ + 4Q431 1); Recension B (4Q491ᶜ i = 4Q491 frg. 11 col. 1). Recension A are three portions of the Thanksgiving Hymn mss., Recension B was originally thought to be part of the War Scroll; cf. Brian Schultz, *Conquering the World: The War Scroll (1QM) Reconsidered*, STDJ 76 (Leiden: Brill, 2009), 375–376: Joseph Angel, "The Liturgical-Eschatological Priest of the Self-Glorification Hymn," *RevQ* 96/1 (2010): 585–605. Émile Puech suggests in a recent article an alternative to recensions, see his "L'hymne de la glorification du Maître de 4Q431," in *Prayer and Poetry in the Dead Sea Scrolls and Related Literature*, ed. Jeremy Penner, Ken M. Penner, & Cecilia Wassen, STDJ 98 (Leiden: Brill, 2012), 377–408.

44   Identified as (1) Archangel Michael: Maurice Baillet, *Qumran grotte 4.III (4Q482–4Q520)*, DJD 7 (Oxford: Clarendon Press, 1982); Florentino García Martínez, "Old Texts and Modern Mirages: The 'I' of Two Qumran Hymns," *ETL* 78 (2002): 321–339; (2) Various exalted human figures: (Herod the Great:) Morton Smith, "Ascent to the Heavens and Deification in 4QMᵃ" in *Archaeology and History in the Dead Sea Scrolls*, ed. Lawrence H. Schiffman, JSPS 8 (Sheffield: JSOT Press, 1990), 181–188; Devorah Dimant, "A Synoptic Comparison of Parallel Sections in 4Q427 7, 4Q491 11 and 4Q471B," *JQR* 85 (1994): 157–161; Esther Eshel, "The Identification of the 'Speaker' of the Self-Glorification Hymn," in *The Provo International Conference on the Dead Sea Scrolls: Technological Innovations, New Texts, and Reformulated Issues*, ed. Donald W. Parry & Eugene Ulrich, STDJ 30 (Leiden: Brill, 1999), 619–635; Martin Abegg, "Who Ascended to Heaven? 4Q491, 4Q427, and the Teacher of Righteousness," in *Eschatology, Messianism, and the Dead Sea Scrolls*, ed. Craig Evans & Peter Flint (Grand Rapids: Eerdmans, 1997), 61–73; Israel Knohl, *The Messiah Before Jesus: The Suffering Servant of the Dead Sea Scrolls*, trans. D. Maisel (Berkeley, CA: University of California Press, 2000), 15–21; John C. O'Neill, "'Who Is Comparable to Me in My Glory?': 4Q491 Fragment 11 (4Q491C) and the New Testament," *NovT* 42 (2000): 24–38; specifically as sage (instructor): Émile Puech, *La Croyance des Esséniens en la vie future: immortalité, résurrection, vie éternelle*, 2 vols. (Paris: J. Gabalda, 1993) 2:494; as exalted priestly figure (Teacher of Righteousness): John J. Collins, *The Scepter and the Star: The Messiahs of the Dead Sea Scrolls and Other Ancient Literature*, ABRL (New York, NY: Doubleday, 1995), 146–149; Esther Eshel, "Self-Glorification Hymn," in *Qumran Cave 4.XX, Poetical and Liturgical Texts, Part 2*, E. Chazon, et al., DJD 19 (Oxford: Clarendon Press, 1999), 421–436; as eschatological-priestly figure: Angel, "Liturgical-Eschatological," 604–605. (3) Menahem Kister, "Divine and Heavenly Figures in the Dead Sea Scroll," presented at the *Fourteenth International Orion Symposium, May 28–30*, considers that Wisdom speaks in the Self-Glorification Hymn.

pare with *my judgments* (משפטי)?" Indeed, it is not only that both terms occur in the hymn, but also that they are closely related to one another. 4Q471ᵇ frgs. 1–4 lines 5–7a read:

מי כמוני באלים [מי יגודני בפתחי פי ומזל] שפתי מי יכיל מי [בלשון יודעני וידמה
במשפטי כי אני] ידיד המלך רע לקד[ושים

> Who is like me among the angels? [Who will oppose me when I open my
> mouth? and the flow] of my lips endure? Who can match me in [speech
> and compare with my judgment? For I] am a friend of the king, and of
> angels ...

The similarity of these rare expressions found in both the Self-Glorification Hymn and in 4Q418 222 + 221 suggests that this language relates to the acquisition of heavenly knowledge. These are terms found in other *maśkîl* texts and need not be seen as exclusive to the Yaḥad. In 4QSongs of the Sage an exalted *maśkîl* speaks to his audience and describes his own speech with the expression מזל שפתי ("outpouring of my lips" 4Q511 63–64 ii 4).[45] Similarly, in the Rule of the Blessing (1QSb III 22–27) are words of invocation belonging to an Instructor (דברי ברכה למשכיל); here, the *maśkîl* blesses the Sons of Zadok, the priests, and expresses hope that God will establish them "in the midst of the holy ones" (בתוך קדושים, 1QSb III 26–27). In this context, קדושים is likely ambiguous in order intentionally to include the holy community with angelic beings. The place of the priests in the "holy habitation" (במעון קודש) provides the context for the *maśkîl* to describe them as judging the nobles and ministers of the people by the "outpouring of your lips" and "your deeds" (במעשיכה ישפוט כול נדיבים וממזל שפתיכה כול שרי עמים). That this expression is found only on these occasions and in relationship to exalted figures suggests that the expression in 4Q418 is similarly related to a sage.

It is not unusual for *maśkilîm* to derive their authority vis-à-vis access to the heavenly realm. As part of a broader assessment of 4QInstruction as a composition expressing the speech of a sage, the relationship of the teacher and addressee to angelic beings is treated near the conclusion of this chapter. Questions have been asked about whether, to what extent, and how the addressee participates with angelic beings in the present. 4QInstruction has a lively interest into angels and participation with them may be purely future or there may be a "realized" aspect to it. John Collins calls evidence for present participation

---

45   Note the similarity with 1QS IX 4–5 ותרומת שפתים למשפט כניחוח צדק.

with the angels "less than conclusive."[46] Whereas the Thanksgiving Hymns have instances of present participation with the angels, his view is that 4QInstruction only anticipates future glory. The similarities of frgs. 222 + 221 and 238 with the Self-Glorification Hymn and other writings where a *maśkîl* speaks offer a fresh perspective from which to reassess the possibility that present participation with the angels is envisaged.

The instances of שפתי used by itself are typically found in expressions of praise. The term is found frequently in 1QS X, for instance "fruit of eulogy and a portion of my lips" (1QS X 8; cf. X 9, 14) are a substitute for sacrifice. In 4Q512 (Ritual of Purification) 1–4 the author proclaims that God "placed on my lips [שפתי] a fount of praise," which is equated with having been given in his "heart the secret of the start of all human actions and the completion of the deeds of the perfect ones of the path." Knowledge imparted to the author allows him to judge all the works done by others in order to vindicate the just and pronounce the wicked guilty. In these passages praise is not only a part of a response when receiving revelation, but also praise can be given and is a source for understanding.

When the author of 4QInstruction uses first-person singular suffixes in frgs. 222 + 221 the expression "outpouring of my lips" refers to sharing knowledge with the *mēvîn*. In contrast, in the Self-Glorification Hymn the author expresses that this is his domain alone. 4Q418 77 associates the opening of lips with pursuing the mystery of existence, and in 4Q418 81 + 81a 1 the speaker instructs the *mēvîn* to open his lips as a spring to bless the holy ones. The act of blessing angelic beings has venerative connotations and may also be seen as an activity related to participating in the heavenly realm and accessing revelation.[47]

Frag. 221 2 is the only reference to prophets found in 4QInstruction. Given the role the author has in imparting knowledge, and exhorting the addressees to seek mysteries, this line may find some life alongside expressions in 1QpHab VII 2–8. In this passage, Hab 2:2 כְּתוֹב חָזוֹן וּבָאֵר עַל־הַלֻּחוֹת לְמַעַן יָרוּץ קוֹרֵא בוֹ ("write the vision; make it plain on tablets, so that a runner may read it") finds its interpretation, unsurprisingly, in the Teacher of Righteousness "to whom God made known all the mysterious revelations of His servants the prophets" (אשר הודיעו אל את כל רזי דברי עבדיו הנבאים).[48] Following this, Pesher Habakkuk

---

46 Collins, "The Eschatologizing of Wisdom," 57.

47 *Maśkîlîm* have been appreciated for their liturgical and poetical qualities by Bilhah Nitzan, *Qumran Prayer and Religious Poetry*, STDJ 12 (Leiden: Brill, 1994), 265–272 (Hebrew original: תפילת קומראן ושירתה [Jerusalem: Bialik Institute, 1996]).

48 William H. Brownlee, *Midrash Pesher of Habakkuk* (Atlanta, GA: Scholars Press, 1979) first suggested that this may be a purposeful pun between רץ ("run") and רז ("mystery").

interprets Hab 2:3 ("prophecy is for a specific period, it testifies of that time and does not deceive"), which is explained as a reference to the end days that are longer than the prophets had said, and follows this with the refrain: "for the mysteries of God are wonderful!" (יארוך הקץ האחרון ויתר על כול אשר דברו הנביאים כי רזי אל להפלא).[49] If 4QInstruction similarly evokes the prophets, then the role the speaker conceives for himself is as one sharing the mysterious revelations of "His servants the prophets" to the simple ones (l. 2); in this fragment, the sage is wise and venerable in contrast to his pupils.[50]

Noted above, "my judgments" in frag. 221 4 may be read alongside both recensions of the Self-Glorification Hymn (4Q471[b] frgs. 1–4 6; 4Q491[c] i 10; 4QH[a] 10). Less likely is that "my judgments" find a parallel in the hymn of praise in the Rule of the Community (1QS X 9–XI 22) where the speaker's own "judgments" are referred to twice (1QS XI 12–14; cf. par. 4Q264 i 1).[51] In these lines of the Rule of the Community the speaker expresses thankfulness for God's mercies, stating that He is his salvation when he stumbles. When the speaker falls in the sin of the flesh, the just and eternal God is said to be the place of "my judgment" (משפטי). In times of distress God delivers the speaker and he thus proclaims that: "by kindnesses set in motion" is "my judgment" (משפטי).[52] "My judgments" in the Rule of the Community is a term that evokes God's mercy, while in the Self-Glorification Hymn it infers that the speaker's authority is unparalleled.

If משפטי rather than משפטו is read in frg. 221, then the sage is making an appeal to the simple ones to understand his "judgment" in order to distinguish between good and evil. It is not likely that the speaker is referring to God's mercies, in keeping with the use in 1QS XI, but rather the context suggests that the speaker is appealing to his privileged position as a maśkîl. The "I" of the Self-Glorification Hymn enjoys a special status; the common terms

---

49   Cf. 1QSb I 27 "all the ages of [His] servant[s the prophets]"; in later Ethiopian tradition Enoch is called the "first born of prophets," Michael A. Knibb, "The Book of Enoch in Light of the Qumran Wisdom Literature," in *Wisdom and Apocalypticism in the Dead Sea Scrolls and in the Biblical Tradition*, ed. Florentino García Martínez, BETL 168 (Leuven: Peeters, 2003), 193–210, at 196.

50   In 1QH[a] V 12 begins, "[A song for the ma]śkîl to fall before God" and continues at the end of the line, "to make the simple [פותאים] understand."

51   On the one occasion that רז נהיה occurs in the Rule of the Community (1QS XI 3–4) this mystery is "hidden from humanity" (נסתרה מאנוש 1QS XI 6), to whom the speaker belongs (1QS XI 9 "I belong to evil humanity"), and he is rescued out of the "assembly of worms" when his lot is cast with angels and unites with them in their assembly.

52   A better translation may be "my justification" rather than "my judgment" on account of the context; here משפט has to do with deliverance and salvation.

Not a particle

in these compositions evoke authority and suggest that in 4QInstruction too the speaker accesses the heavenly realm. Frg. 238 is crucial to deciphering the identity of the speaker in frgs. 222 + 221.

4Q418 238 is a small five-line fragment and in the first line משכיל is clearly visible.

4Q418 frg. 238, Transcription and Translation (see fig. 7 in plate section):[53]

ואני [מֹשכיל וֹא]	1]
אֹ[וֹבֹמעשה]	2]
התבו[נֹן בנהיי עֹ]ולם	3]
יֹ[מֹי נצח]∘	4]
יום [ ]	5]

1 [*and I the*]maśkîl and [
2 [   ] and in deed[
3 [cons]ider by those who have been fore[ver
4 [d]ays everlasting [
5 [   ] day [

Tigchelaar suggests the hypothetical placement of 4Q418 238 (single underline) in the lines preceding 4Q416 1 1–4 (no underline) together with 4Q418 229 (double underline):[54]

[משכיל וא			01
א וֹבֹמעשה			02
[כוכבי אור	התבו[נֹן בנהיי עֹ]ולם	כֹלֹ רֹוֹחֹ]	1
ולתכן חפצֹי [צבאם לכול יֹ[מֹי נצח [] ירוצו מעת עולם			2
[ואין] [להדמות בכו]שר[55] ילכו	מועד במועד יֹום [ביום]		3
לפי צבאם לֹמֹשֹ[וֹר במשֹוֹרה ול∘			4

---

53   DJD 34:447–448.

54   Tigchelaar, *To Increase Learning*, 183 fn. 25 "These reconstructions do not perfectly fit in the presumed lacunae between 4Q418 229 1 and 2, and 4Q418 238 4 and 5." Transcription adapted from Tigchelaar and translation is my own.

55   Terms from the root כשר occur on three occasions in 4QInstruction (4Q417 1 i 11; 4Q417 2 i 2; 4Q418 77 2) and are nearly absent from other Qumran discoveries, only occurring in 4Q200 (4QTobᵉ) 1 ii 3.

Partiple of man

01   ] *maśkîl* and *a*
02   *a* and ⁱⁿ deed
1   every spirit[cons]ider by those who have been fore[ver
        ]stars of light
2   and to establish/order the good pleasure of [their hosts for all d]ays
        everlasting [] they will run from the time of eternity
3   season by season, day [by day]   [and there is nothing] to
        compare in *perf*[*ection*, they go]
4   according to their hosts to ru[le by dominion and to

The term משכיל occurs four times in 4QInstruction and may be read either as
a noun or the *Hiphil* masculine singular participle. Here it is convincingly read
as a noun referring to the instructor because it relates to first-person forms in
frgs. 222 + 221.[56] The other three occurrences of משכיל are found in: 4Q416 2 ii
15 (par. 4Q417 2 ii; 4Q418 8, 21, 22; 4Q418a), 4Q417 1 i 25 (par. 4Q418 43, 44, 45;
4Q418a 11), and 4Q418 81 + 81a 17 and are considered in detail below (§2).

The reconstruction of line 3 as עׄ[ולם] התבו[נן בנהיי is supported by Strugnell
and Harrington in their comments.[57] This is the only clear occurrence in 4QIn-
struction of נהיה in construct form. In support of reconstructing עׄ[ד rather than
עׄ[ולם, the editors cite the occurrence of עד together with נהיות in CD II 10. The
evidence for reading "those who have been forever" with the word עולם is much
stronger, with two occasions outside of 4QInstruction where נהיות and עולם are
used together (CD XIII 8; 1QHᵃ XVIII 27). More importantly, the editors raise the
possibility that נהיה עולם in 4Q418 69 ii 7 is a phonetic spelling of נהיי עולם, here
a group who are eternal ones, seekers of truth, and have the task of arising (lit.
"rousing themselves") in the end time to judge the foolish (cf. אחזת עולם ינחלו
in 4Q418 55 12 likely in reference to the righteous).[58] The expression "eternal

---

56   Johann Maier, *Die Qumran-Essener: Die Texte vom Toten Meer 1–3* (München/Basel: E. Rein-
     hardt, 1995), 1:481 translates: *maśkîl*.
57   DJD 34:448; for התבונן see Jer 23:20; Job 30:20; 1QS XI 19; 1QHᵃ VII 32; 1Q27 1 i 3.
58   DJD 34:286; Émile Puech, "Apports des textes apocalyptiques et sapientiels de Qumrân à
     l'eschatologie du judaïsme ancien," in *Wisdom and Apocalypticism in the Dead Sea Scrolls
     and in the Biblical Tradition*, ed. Florentino García Martínez, BEThL 168 (Leuven: Peeters,
     2003), 140–141 views this line as referring to the resurrection of the righteous; this view
     has been convincingly rejected by Tigchelaar, *To Increase Learning*, 211; Goff, *The Worldly*,
     176–179; John J. Collins, "The Eschatologizing of Wisdom in the Dead Sea Scrolls," in *Sapi-
     ential Perspectives: Wisdom Literature in Light of the Dead Sea Scrolls: Proceedings of the
     Sixth International Symposium of the Orion Center, 20–22 May 2001*, ed. John J. Collins, Greg
     E. Sterling & Ruth A. Clements, STDJ 51 (Leiden: Brill, 2004), 49–65, at 56–57.

[handwritten annotation: Maśkîl texts verses language in other places]

ones" is used as an angelic title in the Qumran literature, particularly with the phrase הויי עולם in Songs of the Sabbath Sacrifice (4Q403 22).[59] Therefore, in 4Q418 238 are the remains of a phrase that fits well with a Leitmotif in 4QInstruction, especially 4Q418 55 and 69 ii: angelic beings are a role model and point of contemplation for the *mēvîn*. Therefore, an exhortation in 4Q418 238 3 to contemplate angels would be in keeping with the angelology of the composition.

While 4Q418 238 cannot be located in the opening column of 4QInstruction based upon overlaps with 4Q416 1, the rationale behind its theoretical placement as part of the incipit of the composition is solid. Fragments 222 + 221 use language associated with the speech of a *maśkîl*, which is known from other compositions, and frag. 238 is likely to be located in close proximity to these two fragments. Even if these fragments were not part of the first column of the composition they are nonetheless part of its discourse and cannot simply be ignored. Therefore, it is important to establish that frag. 238 does not use משכיל as a participle, not only by associating it with first-person forms in frags. 222 + 221, but also based upon the other occurrences of the term in 4QInstruction. In the next section, the other three occurrences of the term משכיל in 4QInstruction are analyzed.

2   Occurrences of משכיל in 4QInstruction

In 4Q416 2 ii, 4Q417 1 i, and 4Q418 81 + 81a the term משכיל occurs and although most translations render the term as a participle in 4Q416 2 ii and 4Q417 1 i, the possibility that in some instances it should be read as a noun are revisited in light of questions raised about the opening address of the document (4Q418 222 + 221, 238) as well as the presence of first-person plural speech in 4Q418 55. In the case of 4Q417 1 i 25 the addressee is referred to as a בן משכיל, which is an expression that differs in use from that found in Proverbs and Ben Sira and may indicate how speaker and addressee related, a pattern that may be followed in 4Q416 2 ii 15 as well.[60] In the presentation of passages below, we begin with an

---

59   Carol Newsom, *Songs of the Sabbath Sacrifice: A Critical Edition*, HSS 27 (Atlanta, GA: Scholars Press, 1985), 203 however "the phrase הויי עולם does not otherwise occur as an angelic title." DJD 34:286 the editors comment "to treat וכול נהיה עולם here as merely a chronological marker (which would have to be emended to ובכול נהיה) rather than a name for angels would be difficult."

60   DJD 34:244; cf. Prov 14:35 (עֶבֶד־מַשְׂכִּיל יִמְשֹׁל בְּבֵן מֵבִישׁ) and 17:2 (רְצוֹן־מֶלֶךְ לְעֶבֶד מַשְׂכִּיל) where משכיל is used as a *Hiphil* verb; the expression עבד משכיל is found in Hebrew Ben

assessment of משכיל in 4Q416 2 ii first because its use in reference to a sage, a likely translation that had previously gone unexplored, influences the analysis of the following two occurrences of משכיל.

2.1   Maśkîl *in 4Q416 2 i Line 22–4Q416 2 ii Line 17*

The one addressed in 4Q416 2 ii becomes an עבד משכיל (trans. either as a participle *"wise* servant" or noun in construct "servant of a *sage*") in line 15; however, in preceding line 13 this same figure is described as בן בכור ("firstborn son"), יחיד ("unique" or "only" one) and בחיר ("chosen one").[61] None of these terms in line 13 are used elsewhere, either in the Hebrew scriptures or literature of the period, to depict a "common" relationship between two people or to describe an ordinary figure; line 13 is discussed in detail here because of its significance for establishing how עבד משכיל should be translated. Lines 12b–17 have been universally read as depicting the relationship of a servant with a creditor or, alternatively, a slave and master.[62] However, as will be seen, it would truly be remarkable if the slave/servant addressed in this passage could come to be in such a relationship with an earthly master/creditor. To complicate matters, in 4Q416 2 ii both "father" and "son" are mentioned, but not to depict a relationship between two individuals (i.e., the slave/servant and master/creditor are not depicted as being in a father/son relationship). There is general agreement among translators that the very same "servant" who becomes like a "son" to someone is also like a "father" to someone (else?); the "you" of the passage is called both a "son" and a "father" and the point of disagreement is who the *mēvîn* relates to in these two familial roles.[63]

Throughout 4Q416 2 i–iv (par. 4Q417 2 i–ii; 4Q418 7, 8; 4Q418a), which is the largest single fragment of 4QInstruction, and elsewhere in the composition, it is not uncommon to find subjects in a single column alternate; therefore, care should be taken not to assume that themes or referents are monolithic

---

Sira on several occasions, see: 7:21, 10:25 "he shall love a wise servant as himself" (עבד משכיל חביב כנפש).

61   Cf. Benjamin Wold, "Is the 'Firstborn Son' in 4Q369 a Messiah? The Evidence from 4QInstruction," *RevQ* 29/1 (2017): 3–20.

62   A slave/master relationship is seen to resolve some of the abnormalities perceived in a servant/creditor one.

63   Goff, *4QInstruction*, 80–81 does not specify who the "him" is, he comments: "Lines 15–16 assert that the *mebin* can become like a father to *someone* [ital. mine]" and that "this appeal to family language should probably not be understood literally but rather as drawing upon a father-son relationship to describe the ideal worker-supervisor dynamic."

throughout any one column.[64] Because 4Q416 2 ii 12b–17 have been translated as concerned with the same subject matter as the preceding section, especially line 4 where there is a reference to a "creditor" (נושה),[65] it is noteworthy that Harrington and Strugnell comment that the "form and content [of lines 4–6] show that this material ... forms one paragraph" and that it is unclear whether what follows relates "thematically or structurally to what precedes it."[66] Moreover, the referents of the pronouns found in lines 12b–17 are difficult to identify because *waws* and *yods* are indistinguishable in this hand. When translating ambiguous pronominal suffixes in lines 12b–17 the editors and others prefer to read them as third-person, masculine, singular *waws* referring to the creditor in the preceding paragraph.[67]

In the translation below a complex network of relationships is found. While teaching about how to relate to a creditor is in view in parts of this passage, so too are instructions about how to relate to other members of the community as well as to God. These lines are returned to in chapter two (§ 2.2.).

4Q416 2 i line 22b–ii line 17 [single underline] (par. 4Q417 2 ii [double underline]; cf. 4Q418 8a, 8, 11, 21; 4Q418a 19; **overlap**), Transcription and Translation:[68]

---

64   DJD 34:172–177.

65   נושה is a rare word, among Dead Sea Scrolls it only occurs in 4QInstruction and is never used as a noun in the 11B; in 4QInstruction it is found here, in: 4Q416 2 ii 5 (comp. 4Q417 2 ii 6–7), preceding column 4Q416 2 i (par. 4Q417 2 i), 4Q416 2 i 18, and 4Q417 2 i 22, 23. Locating נושה within its socio-economic context is complicated by 4QInstruction's multivalent use of "poor," if this column were straightforwardly offering instruction about how those on the lower end of the economic scale endured debt this most commonly took the form of tenancy agreements and contracts rather than debt slavery, therefore a "creditor" is more plausible than a "master"; cf. Peter Garnsey, *Cities, Peasant and Food in Classical Antiquity: Essays in Social and Economic History* (Cambridge: CUP, 1998), esp. 134–150. Moreover, עבד in 4QInstruction is better rendered as "servant," without necessarily carrying economic connotations, than as a "slave."

66   DJD 34:96.

67   DJD 34:93.

68   Cf. Goff, *4QInstruction*, 60 who translates these lines as depicting a relationship between a slave and master: "[12b] If in his favor you hold fast to his service and the wisdom of his resources, [13] [...] you will advise him [so that you may become] for him a first-born son and he will be compassionate towards you, like a man towards his only son, [14] [for you are his slave and his chos]en one. But you, do not be (overly) confident lest you become hated and do not lie awake over your distress. [15] [Become for him an intellige]nt [slave]. And also, do not lower yourself before one who is not your equal. And then you will become [16] [a father to him ...] For what is beyond your strength do not reach, lest you stumble and your

‫... מאל] שאל טרפכה כי הוא‬   22b

‫למלא] כול מחסורי אוטו ולתת טרף‬   **‫פתח רחמיו]‬**   1

‫וא]ם יקפוץ ידו ונאספה רו]ח כול [‬   **‫לכל חי ואין‬**]○   2

‫כש]יל בה ובחרפתו תכסה פניׄכׄה ובאולת‬   ‫בשר אל תק]ח‬   3

‫מאסוֹר כמה]   [וֹ אם בהון]   ‫ה]נׄושה בו]   [מֹהר שלם ואתה תשוה בו כי כי]ס‬   4

‫צפונׄכׄהׄ פׄקׄדׄתׄ]הׄ לנושה בדׄה בעד רעוׄכה נתתׄהׄ כל חייכה בזׄ מׄהר תן אשר‬   5

‫לו וקח כ]סכה ובדבריכה אל תמעט רוחכה בכל הון אל תמר רוח קׄדׄשכה‬   6

‫כי אין מחיר שוֹה]‬   ‫אם אי]ש לא יׄטכה ברצון שחר פניו וכלשונו‬   7

‫[דב]ר ואז תמצא חפצכה מחׄרׄ]פֹתכה אל תׄ]מׄר]לו זחוקיכה אל תרף וברזיכה‬   8
‫השמר‬

‫מא]דׄה אם עבודתוׄ יפקׄיׄד לכה אל מנוח ב]נפשכה וא]ל תנומה לעיניכה עד‬   9
‫עשותכה‬

‫מצו]תיו וא]ל תוסף ואם יש להצניע   ר   מע   ואל תותר לׄוׄ אׄף הון בלׄוׄ‬   10

‫[   ]   תנׄוׄ פן יאמר בזני ונפלה א]   ‫[יׄצ]   [כה זׄראה כי רבה קנאת‬   11

‫אנוש ועקוב הלב מ]   [ׄוׄ אׄם ברצונו תחזיק עבודתו וחכמת אוטו‬   12

‫[   ]○○ **‫תיעצׄנׄוׄ** והייתה לוׄ לבן בכור וחמל עליכה כאיש על יחידו‬   13

‫[   ]   **‫כי אתה ע]**בדו ובחׄי **‫רו ואׄתׄה‬** אל תבטח למה תשנׄאׄ ואל תשקור ממדהבכה‬   14

‫[‫ואתה]**‫דמה לׄיׄ לעׄבׄד** משכיל וגם אל תשפל **‫נפשכה** לאשר לא ישוה בכה **‫ואז תהיה‬**‬   15

‫לוׄ לאׄב]‬   ‫[לאשר אין כוחכה אל תגע פן תכשל **‫וחרפתכה תׄרׄבׄה** מׄאׄדׄהׄ‬   16

‫[אל תמ]כׄוׄר נפשכה בהון טוב היותכה **‫עבד ברוׄח וחנם תעבוׄד** נוגשיכה ובמחיר‬   17

‫אל תמכור כבודכה ...‬   18

22b ... ask for your food [from God],
for He **1** has opened his mercies[...]
to fill] all that is lacking from his/its ‫אוט‬ (humble station?),[69]
and to give food **2** to all that lives,

---

shame will be very great. [17] [Do not se]ll yourself for wealth. It is good that you are a slave
in spirit and without wages you serve your oppressors. For a price [18] do not sell your glory
...."

69   ‫אוט‬ is a technical term in 4QInstruction and may be translated as the Hebrew substantive
of the adverb ‫לאט‬, meaning "gently," "slowly," or "humbly." As such it may denote a positively conceived ethical value of gentleness or humility (cf. § 2.3. below). The only other
place it is found outside of this document is in sapiential work 4Q424 1 6 ("into the hand
of lazy man do not apportion ‫אט‬"). The term has been translated in a variety of ways, as:
"inner desires," John Kampen, *Wisdom Literature*, ECDSS (Grand Rapids, MI/Cambridge:
Eerdmans, 2011), 50–51; "resource," Goff, *The Worldly*, 152–153, fn. 104 and Puech, "Les fragments," 105; Rey, *4QInstruction*, 33 writes: "Le terme se rapporte à l'humanité sans idée de
révélation particulière"; Harrington and Strugnell, DJD 34:32, consider that it is associated
with ‫חפץ‬, which is "notoriously ambiguous in it own right, and the words used in parallel
to it do not help very much." The positive description of ‫אוט‬ as "wisdom of His ‫אוט‬" (i.e.,

and there is not ○[...]
[... and i]f He closes His hand,
and gathers in the spir[it of all] 3 flesh,
do not ta[ke ...]
[... stumb]ling in it,
and in his (i.e., a debtor) shame cover your face,
and (also) in the folly of 4 imprisonment (i.e., cover your face),
how great [   ] if by wealth [...]
[... the] creditor in it[ ]quickly pay,
and you will be even with him,
for your hidden purse 5 you gave to the one lending to you,
on behalf of your neighbor you gave all of your life with it,
quickly give 6 what is his (i.e., creditor), and take your purse,
and by your words do not belittle your spirit,
and for any wealth do not exchange your holy spirit,
7 for there is no price equal [...]
[... if a ma]n (i.e., generally) is not favorably disposed,
seek his presence and according to his speech 8 [spea]k,
and you will find what pleases you rather than your own sha[m]e,
do not abandon your statutes,   *debt*
do not alter/change for him,
and by your mysteries keep 9 diligent watch,   *Slavery*
if he appoints you his servant, let there not be rest for [your soul,
nor le]t there be sleep for your eyes, until you have done 10 [his
     c]ommandments,
and do not add (to them), and if it is possible to (be) humble [...],
and let there not remain undone for him (?), even tribute money (?) 11
     [...],
lest he says, he has despoiled me, and fallen [...],
see how great is the jealously of 12 humanity, and how deceitful the
     heart, [...] if in *His* good will you hold fast
and serve *Him*, and the wisdom of *His* אוט (gentleness?),
13 [...] will you counsel *him* (i.e., humanity)? And you will be to *Him* as a
firstborn son, And *He* will have compassion upon you, as a man upon
     his only child;

───────────

"wisdom of God's gentleness") here precludes it from belonging to the creditor. Pursuing
wisdom elsewhere in the composition is associated with אוט and may be in reference to
one's place within a hierarchy: human beings are in a modest place and lack (l. 1), but God
acts out of the wisdom of his אוט (l. 12).

14 For you are [*His*] servant and [*His* chos]en one, and do

not trust in what you hate, and do not be concerned about (stay on
   watch for) your own destruction,

15 [And you], be like *me*, a servant of a *maśkîl*,

And also, do not lower your soul to one not equal with you,

And then you will be **16** to *him* as a father (i.e., the one not equal to you),

[   ] to one who has not your strength do not strike,

lest you stumble and multiply your shame greatly,

17 [do not se]ll your soul for wealth, it is good for you to be a servant in
   the spirit,

and to serve your oppressor freely,

and for a price **18** do not sell your glory ...

There are several reasons that the relationship implied in lines 12b–17 is difficult to explain as that of the addressee to a creditor. In order to justify the extraordinarily intimate, and even familial relationship, expressed with the terms "firstborn son," "unique child," and "chosen one" requires viewing the creditor in a positive light. When borrowing is described in the preceding lines it is, demonstrably, not between members of the community, but rather between the addressees and a figure external to the *mēvîn*'s community. Indeed, if the *mēvîn* does not repay the creditor in good time it leads to him being flogged (par. ms. 4Q417 2 i 21–25).[70] In the translation of lines 12b–17 proposed, the only reference to a "creditor" is found in line 17 where he may be referred to as an "oppressor" (נוגש). That a master/creditor is an "oppressor" and that one can become like an only son to him is difficult to reconcile. Moreover, the descriptions of the creditor are not what one would expect to be applied to someone within the community; the relationship between the addressee and the creditor is tense and corporal punishment is a threat. If borrowing were taking place between members of the same group, then it is surprising that there is no instruction directed to the wealthy on lending to brethren who are impoverished; instead, there is insistence that the addressee is poor, which seems to preclude that there are wealthy among them.[71] Therefore, it is highly proba-

---

70   4Q416 2 ii 6 also warns not to exchange one's holy spirit when dealing with wealth (see
        below).

71   4Q416 2 ii 4–6 are the closest 4QInstruction comes to teaching about the use of wealth; the
        addressee uses his "purse" (כיס) to bail out a member of his community. Rey, *4QInstruction*, 266 sees 4Q418 126 ii 11–16 as interested in the excess or wealth of the addressees; however, this is speculative and based upon a translation of אוט, as well as a reconstruction of ambiguous l. 15. That the addressee is instructed about this-worldly wealth while

makes sense

ble that the creditor does not belong to the *mēvîn*'s community. To become a "firstborn son" to someone outside of the community would be, in the language of 4QInstruction, to enjoy a positive relationship with someone whom those within the community call "fleshly spirit." Indeed, the one addressed in 4Q418 81 + 81a 4–5 is called God's "firstborn" (see further below) and is separated from the "fleshly spirit" and instructed to keep apart from everything that God hates (ll. 1–2).

One of the most difficult pronouns to render in this passage of 4Q416 2 ii is found in the broken hemistich in line 13a translated here as: "[...] will you counsel *him*?" The author of 4QInstruction is known to use rhetorical questions elsewhere and if one occurs here, the pronoun could refer to deceitful humanity in the preceding lines (ll. 11–12).[72] That is, the speaker asks the question, "if you faithfully pursue wisdom will you then advise wicked humanity?" to which there is an implied "no" before proceeding to describe that the addressee will enjoy a special relationship with God. As a rhetorical question with an implied negative response the pronoun could, in theory, also refer to the creditor (i.e., you will not counsel him). If this is a statement rather than a question, the pronoun is difficult to make sense of because it cannot be read in reference to God.[73] As a statement, if the pronoun refers to the creditor, not only does the servant become a firstborn, unique and chosen one to him, but is also his counselor.[74] In summary, each of the options is problematic and by process of elimination the only plausible translation is that line 13a is part of a rhetorical question.

Harrington and Strugnell translate line 15a as "But become thou to him like a wise servant" and they comment that "the expression [עבד משכיל] might [also]

---

reminded of his literal poverty is unconvincing, regardless, 4Q418 126 ii does not mention borrowing and lending. In 4Q418 103 ii 9 wealth is described as coming to an end when the days of one's life end (וג]ם הונכה עם בשרכה [כתום ימי] חייכה יתמו יחד); Goff, *Worldly and Heavenly*, 158, comments that "4QInstruction's business teachings presuppose that the addressee has something to trade, implying that he has a stable means of support. None of its trade instruction, however, seems designed for someone who is wealthy."

72   A series of rhetorical questions occur in 4Q418 55 with two constructions: הלוא (ll. 5, 12) and אם לא (l. 8).

73   The average number of letter spaces in each line of this column is about 62, indicating that about half of the line is missing.

74   DJD 34:103 "תיעצנו excludes the possibility of an interpretation concerning the sage's relationship with God—here the sage's superior must be an earthly one (cf. the next two hemistichs)." This is the only occurrence of יעץ in 4QInstruction.

mean 'servant of an intelligent man.'"[75] In order to determine which of these is the better translation, the immediately preceding דמה needs to be rendered. דמה לי may be understood as an imperative, that is an exhortation or, as some have rendered it, a participle. If this were a participle the orthography expected in this scroll would instead be דומה. Whether לו or לי should be read here can only be adduced from the context.[76] If it is לו, assuming that the creditor is not in view, the option remaining is that God is the referent. The *mēvîn* has already been told that he is a servant (l. 14), therefore an admonition to be a wise servant would not be out of place if it were not for the comparison in the following line. If in lines 15–16 the pronoun refers consistently to the creditor, then the addressee is encouraged to "be a wise servant to him" (l. 15) and then "become to him a father." Unconvincing is that the *mēvîn* would relate either to a creditor or to God as both a wise servant and a father. One solution is to read a first-person pronoun in line 15 and a third-person pronoun in line 16. The expression עבד משכיל could be translated as "servant of an *intelligent man*" or "servant of a *maśkîl*" and the exhortation in these lines would, then, be for the addressee to become a wise sage like the speaker, which is complimented by his identity as firstborn son, only child, and chosen one. Indeed, this would conform with the proposal above that from the outset of 4QInstruction a *maśkîl* addresses the understanding ones. If this is the case, the speaker of 4QInstruction teaches his disciples about the "mystery of existence"; faithful pursuit of truth and obedience to God allow the *mēvîn* to become a sage.

In line 15 the *mēvîn* is instructed about one who is not equal to him. In line 16 he is exhorted how to behave towards someone who does not have his strength. Both figures appear, from the context, to be community members (cf. helping an indebted neighbor l. 5; resolving disputes with others l. 7). By relating appropriately to others during times of hardship (i.e., not striking them or lowering himself to their level) the addressee becomes like, or relates as, a father to them. When the following line 17 turns to the subject of wealth, instruction occurs about how to relate to one's financial oppressor. Therefore, in becoming

---

75   DJD 34:244; cf. § 2.2 below, Tigchelaar, "Towards a Reconstruction," 123 states that בן משכיל may be an expression for the sage himself; cf. the alternative view of Charlotte Hempel, "The Qumran Sapiential Texts and the Rule Books," in *The Wisdom Texts from Qumran*, 277–296 at 287. Cf. Prov (14:35; 17:2) and Ben Sira (7:21; 10:25) where עבד משכיל is found, and on these occasions משכיל is used as a *Hiphil* participle ("wise servant"), see fn. 60.

76   Cf. DJD 34:244 where the editors comment that "4Q417 2 ii 19 read probably דמה לו but דמה לי could be possible too." There are many instances in these lines where the letters *waw* and *yod* are ambiguous, in the immediate preceding context of 4Q416 2 ii see l. 10 בלו; l. 11 תנו, בזני, וראה; and even אוטו.

[handwritten annotation in top margin: "Reads this against predominet des slavery reading & reference spiritual instead"]

as a firstborn son to God the addressee relates to weaker members of his community as a father by modeling the appropriate way of dealing with financial affairs.

The term בן בכור ("firstborn son") occurs twice in 4QInstruction/1QInstruction (4Q416 2 ii 13; 1Q26 3) and elsewhere in the Scrolls is only found on three occasions: (1) 4QWords of the Luminaries (4Q504 1–2 iii 5–6) where "Israel" is God's firstborn son;[77] (2) 4QNarrative A (4Q458 15 1) where the context is too fragmentary to determine how it is used; and (3) the so-called "Prayer of Enosh" (4Q369 1 ii 6) where it is debated whether it is a future, royal Messiah or the nation Israel.[78] "Firstborn" (בכור), without being modified by "son" (בן), occurs in the Scrolls elsewhere about twenty times.[79] In the Hebrew Bible, בן בכור occurs in Exodus 4:22 (בְּנִי בְכֹרִי יִשְׂרָאֵל) in reference to Israel. Among biblical

---

[77] Cf. Jub. 2:19–20 ("Israel is God's firstborn"); Sir 17:17–18 ("Israel is the Lord's portion; whom, being his firstborn, he brought up with discipline"), 36:17, 44:23; Pss. Sol. 18:3–4 ("your love is upon the seed of Abraham, the sons of Israel; your discipline is upon us as upon a firstborn, and only son"); 4 Ezra 6:58 ("but we are your people, whom you have called your 'firstborn'").

[78] Among those that translate the predicates of 4Q369 1 ii as future and referring to an eschatological and royal figure are John Strugnell & Harold Attridge, "4Q369 '4QPrayer of Enosh,'" in *Qumran Cave 4, VIII: Parabiblical Texts, Part 1*, ed. J.C. VanderKam, DJD 13 (Oxford: Clarendon Press, 1994), 353–362, at 358; Craig A. Evans, "A Note on the 'First-Born Son' of 4Q369," *DSD* 2/2 (1995): 185–201; Andrew Chester, *Messiah and Exaltation*, WUNT 207 (Tübingen: Mohr Siebeck, 2007), 237–238; Marc Philonenko, "De la 'Prière de Jesus' au 'Notre Père': (Abba; targoum du Psaume 89,27; 4Q369, 1,2, 1–12; Luc 11,2)," *RHPR* 77/1 (1997): 133–140; Géza G. Xeravits, *King, Priest, Prophet: Positive Eschatological Protagonists of the Qumran Library*, STDJ 47 (Leiden: Brill, 2003), 93–94. Alternatively, James Kugel translates the predicates in the past tense and argues that the firstborn son in line 6 is "Israel" in, "4Q369 'Prayer of Enosh' and Ancient Biblical Interpretation," *DSD* 5/2 (1998): 119–148. See most recently Wold, "Is the 'Firstborn Son' in 4Q369 a Messiah?"

[79] Used in a literal sense are: the curse of Josh 6:26 (4Q175 1 22; 4Q379 22 ii 8); Manasseh as Joseph's firstborn (4Q368 2 12); halakhic issues/consecration of firstborn (4Q251 10 5; 4Q270 2 ii 8; 4Q368 2 12; 11Q19 LII 7, LX 2); plague on Pharaoh's firstborn son (4Q222 3 3; 4Q222 3 12); and an analogy (1QHᵃ XI 8). Figuratively "firstborn" is used several times of Israel (4Q216 VII 11; 4Q252 IV 3; 4Q504 1 2 iii 6 *recto*). Two noteworthy occurrences of possible figurative uses of בכור are found in: (1) 11Q19 3 3 (בכור הולד כי נבכדים) where there is interest into angelic beings; George W.E. Nickelsburg, *1 Enoch 1: A Commentary on the Book of 1 Enoch. Chapters 1–36; 81–108*, Hermeneia (Minneapolis, MN: Fortress Press, 2001), 77 suggests that 1Q19 (Book of Noah) is influenced by Enochic literature; (2) 4Q426 (4QInstruction-like work) 1 ii 2 "a firstborn I will raise" (בכור ארים) and if this firstborn is the subject of the lines to follow he will "pay attention to the deeds of men" (cf. §2.2. below).

figures only David is called a firstborn (בְּכוֹר), in Psalm 89:28, but not explicitly firstborn "son."[80] The reference to "firstborn son" in 1QInstruction (1Q26
3) occurs in a fragment with only two partially preserved lines; line 2 reads:
כי אתה לו לבן ב]כור ("for you are to him a firstborn son"). These lines do not
correspond to 4Q416 2 ii 13 where "firstborn son" is also used (see discussion
below).[81] In regard to "firstborn" without "son," 4Q423 3 is a six-line fragment
that overlaps with 1Q26 2 2–4 and the reference to "firstborn" here may occur
in close proximity to 1Q26 3. In DJD 34, Torleif Elgvin offers substantial theoretical reconstructions of 4Q423 3 based upon several passages of the Hebrew
Bible (Exod 13:12–15; Num 3:12–13; Deut 15:19–20, 28:11). The words that actually remain on the fragment are: ראשית פרי בטנכה ובכור כל ("]first fruits of your
womb and firstborn among all of["). The specificity of "first fruits of your womb"
indicate that "firstborn" here is to be taken literally and likely in reference to
dedication.[82] The exalted figure in 4Q418 81+81a 4–5 (par. 4Q423 8 4) is "placed"
(שים) as a "firstborn" to God; this line reads: you are a "most holy one for all the
earth" and "among the [a]ng[els] He cast your lot and exceedingly multiplied
your honor and set you for himself a firstborn [וישימכה לו בכור]."[83] Therefore,
the occurrences of "firstborn" in 4QInstruction indicate that one can be called
(or "set as"; cf. 4Q369 1 ii) a "firstborn" or literally be a "firstborn."

---

80   In the HB the noun בכור is used literally for the "firstborn" of mothers and fathers as well
      as to animals, figuratively it is used two ways: "Israel is the first-born of Yahweh among
      the nations Ex 4:22 cf. Je 31:9; and the seed of David among dynasties ψ 89:28" see Francis
      Brown, S.R. Driver, and Charles A. Briggs, *The Enhanced Brown-Driver-Briggs Hebrew and
      English Lexicon* (Peabody, MA: Hendrickson, 1994), 333.
81   1Q26 3 1 reads: קדושי החים [.
82   בטן is used as an appellation for one's "wife"; the speaker refers to "your womb" and "his
      womb" (4Q423 3a 3 בטנו).
83   DJD 34:305 comment on 4Q418 81+81a 5 that "[t]o identify the maven with God's בכור is
      a little surprising," and that "the text seems clearly to have used one of the metaphors for
      adopting someone as a first-born child"; Tigchelaar, *To Increase Learning*, 233 summarizes
      the view of Elgvin, *Analysis*, 143–144 writing that "Elgvin argues that the terminology of
      divine sonship was democratized in the second century B.C.E.," and that בכור in 4Q418
      81+81a 5 "there is a tension between the corporate and the individual." Torleif Elgvin,
      "Priestly Sages? The Milieus of Origin of 4QMysteries an 4QInstruction," in *Sapiential Per-
      spectives*, 81–82 points to Babylonian inscriptions that call the king his father's "firstborn
      son" and "princely priest," and in the same materials he is portrayed as God's beloved,
      called by God's name, intercessor, seeker of wisdom, guardian of the people, and punisher
      of the unjust; see Stephen Langdon, *Die neubabylonischen Königsinschriften* (Leipzig: Hin-
      richs, 1912).

"Firstborn son" in 4Q416 2 ii 13 cannot be understood in the literal sense of a relationship of the addressee to his creditor (or "master"); figurative uses in early Jewish literature are limited to Israel, David's royal descendant, and perhaps an exalted figure in 11Q19 3 3 and/or 4Q424 1 ii 2. When "firstborn son" is coupled with יחיד (l. 13) this further elevates his status beyond what one would expect could potentially be enjoyed with a creditor (or "master"). The only other occurrence of יחיד in 4QInstruction is in the column immediately preceding 4Q416 2 ii (i.e., 4Q416 2 i), the first lines of which are preserved in parallel manuscript 4Q417 2 i 1–6; these manuscripts are presented in composite form in DJD 34 (cf. Ch. 2 § 2.1.). In line 6 is the incomplete interrogative: "for how unique is he among every creature" (כיא מה הואה יח'ד בכול מעשה), which appears to refer to an exalted figure who is similar to the addressee (i.e., he is "righteous like you" 4Q417 2 i 5). In this passage, just before the subject is described as יחיד (4Q417 2 i 6) a figure is said to be שר בש[רים ("prince among pri[nces"). Having compassion upon the *mēvîn* as a יחיד in 4Q416 2 ii 13, given the connotations of this term in the immediately preceding column, indicates a special status is to be associated with it.[84]

The coupling of "firstborn son" and "only son," noted above (fn. 77), is used for Israel in Psalms of Solomon 18:3–4 (ὡς υἱὸν πρωτότοκον μονογενῆ). יחיד in the Hebrew Bible occurs on a dozen occasions and may mean literally "only" child (e.g., Jepthah in Judg 11:34), or figuratively "unique"/"priceless" (Pss 22:21; 35:17).[85] In the Akedah Isaac is called Abraham's יחיד on three occasions (Gen 22:2, 12, 16) and yet he is not literally his "only" son. This tradition of referring to Isaac as יחיד is continued in 4QPseudo-Jubilees (4Q225 2 i 11). The LXX translates the יחיד of Genesis 22 with ἀγαπητός ("beloved"); however, the book of Hebrews (11:17) refers to Isaac as μονογενής, a term that reflects the Hebrew יחיד. Tensions between rendering μονογενής in John's Gospel (John 1:14, 18; 3:16, 18) as "only" or "unique" are well known. In the New Testament, the notion of "begetting" (γεννάω) is not used to designate a literal father and son relationship, and in the Fourth Gospel "son" is reserved for the "son of God" alone (John 1:34, 49; 3:18;

---

84   Goff, *4QInstruction*, 81 "The assertion that the *mebin* will become like an only son may indicate that he is the only slave possessed by his master. While 4QInstruction contains no explicit evidence for this view, it is suggested by Ben Sira. Normally the sage [i.e., Ben Sira] takes a rather harsh attitude towards slaves … However, if the owner has only one, the tone is much more positive (Ben Sira 33:31)." Sir 33:31 is only partially extant in MS E (אחד עבדך), Sirach reads: Εἰ ἔστιν σοι οἰκέτης, ἔστω ὡς σύ ("if you have a slave, let him be as you").

85   Mss. of Tobit use יחיד to designate Sarah as literally an only child (4Q196 6 10; 4Q200 1 i 12).

5:25; 10:36; 11:4, 27; 17:1; 19:7; 20:31) and is never used to describe a believer's relationship with God the father.[86] Therefore, in John's Gospel, μονογενής is likely applied to Jesus to describe a "unique" relationship with God.[87]

The Damascus Document describes the Teacher of Righteousness as יחיד on three occasions, all in the same column: CD XX 1 מורה היחיד ("unique teacher"); CD XX 14 האסף יורה היחיד ("the gathering in of the unique teacher"); and CD XX 32 אנשי היחיד ("men of the unique one"). In the Damascus Document the Teacher of Righteousness, as a "unique one," is explicitly differentiated from the messiah (CD XX 1 "the unique teacher until there arises the messiah out of Aaron and Israel").[88] The teacher as an idealized priest resonates with the image of Levi in Isaac's blessing (Deut 33:8; Jub. 31; cf. 4Q174 6–7 5; 1QSb III 22–24). Indeed, the eschatological priest found in 4QApocryphon of Levi[b] ar (4Q541) is described as one who understands the depths and enigmas of wisdom. Jub. 31:11–17 depict Isaac's blessing of Levi and his descendants, which is an exclusive election of them alone as priests. James Kugel discusses how Levi is chosen as God's special servant and ends up with the priesthood when this would normally belong to the firstborn (Exod 13:13–15; Num 18:15).[89] One explanation for this relates to the notion of "human tithe"; that is, counting backwards Levi is the tenth child, and as such he was substituted as firstborn because of

---

86   See Dale Moody, "God's Only Son: The Translation of John 3:16 in the Revised Standard Version," *JBL* 72/4 (1953): 213–219; at 219 Moody comments that even Ps 2:7 is a coronation idea and not a conception idea.

87   Christ is called πρωτότοκος ("firstborn") twice in the New Testament when identifying him with personified "Wisdom." The hymn in Col 1:15–20, widely regarded as composed prior to Colossians and originally applied to Wisdom, Christ as personified Wisdom is pre-existent and plays a role in creation: "the image of the invisible God, the firstborn of all creation (πρωτότοκος πάσης κτίσεως)" (1:15); in the first line of the second stanza of this hymn Christ is "the beginning, the firstborn of the dead" (Col 1:18b); cf. Wisdom as the "image" of God's goodness in Wis 7:26; Philo, *Alleg. Interp.* 1.43; see "firstborn mother of all things" in Philo, *QG* 4.97; Wisdom as the agent through which God creates see Prov 3:19; Wis 8:4–6; Philo, *Worse* 54. Col 1:16 "in him all things are created" see Ps 104:24 (= LXX 103:24) "in Wisdom you have made all things." Christ is an archetype of God's wisdom and 1:16 does not necessarily mean that Christ was active in creation, but that there is continuity between God's creative power and Christ, who is its clearest expression. Within the Wisdom Christology of Col. 1:17 Christ is "before all things and in him all things hold together"; cf. Prov 8:27–30; Philo, *Heir* 199; Sir 43:26; Heb 1:3 ("son" is radiance of God's glory, cf. Philo, *Planting* 18; Wis 7:26). Wisdom Christology and Christ as "firstborn" also combine in Heb 1:1–3, 6.

88   Cf. James VanderKam, "Jubilees and the Priestly Messiah of Qumran," *RevQ* 13 (1988): 353–365.

89   James Kugel, "Levi's Elevation to the Priesthood in Second Temple Writings," *HTR* 86/1 (1993): 1–64.

Reuben's sin with Bilhah.[90] Therefore, the language of uniqueness and firstborn have priestly connotations vis-à-vis Isaac's blessing of Levi in, especially, post-biblical tradition. Also noteworthy is that in the Testament of Levi 4:2 Levi says to his sons: "The Most High has given heed to your prayer that you be delivered from wrongdoing, that you should become a son to him [γενέσθαι αὐτῷ υἱὸν], as minister [θεράποντα] and priest in his presence [λειτουργὸν τοῦ προσώπου αὐτοῦ]."[91] That this is priestly language is clear from the following verses (4:3–5) and the cultic connotations of the words θεράπων and λειτουργός in 5:2.[92]

The phrase (4Q416 2 ii 14) "you are His servant and His chosen one" is par-tially a theoretical reconstruction based upon Isaiah 45:4 (עַבְדִּי יַעֲקֹב וְיִשְׂרָאֵל בְּחִירִי) and has been accepted in all transcriptions.[93] In 4QInstruction, the only other time "chosen" occurs is in 4Q418 69 ii 10 where the faithful are called "those who choose truth" (בחירי אמת).[94] The attribution "chosen" (בחיר) is not frequent in the Hebrew Bible, occurring only thirteen times, and on nine of those occasions "Israel" is God's "chosen one" (Isa 43:20; 45:4; 65:9, 15, 22; Pss 105:6, 43; 106:5; 1Chr 16:13). Of the remaining references in the Hebrew Bible four individuals are referred to as "chosen," these are: Saul (2Sam 21:6), the Ser-vant in Isaiah (Isa 42:1), David (Ps 89:4), and Moses (Ps 106:23). In many of the documents found at Qumran the "chosen" or "elect" are not straightforwardly "Israel," but rather the remnant and true Israel.[95] There is no application of

---

90 Kugel, "Levi's Elevation," 13–14.

91 Translation by Howard Clark Kee in *Old Testament Pseudepigrapha: Apocalyptic Literature and Testaments*, vol. 1, ed. James H. Charlesworth (New York, NY: Doubleday, 1983), 789.

92 Tigchelaar, *To Increase Learning*, 233 makes this observation on 4Q418 81+81a 5 in refer-ence to Harm Wouter Hollander & Marinus de Jonge, *The Testament of the Twelve Patri-archs: A Commentary*, SVTP 8 (Leiden: Brill, 1985), 142.

93 Proposed in DJD 34:90; Tigchelaar, *To Increase Learning*, 46; Rey, *Sagesse*, 65; Qimron, *Dead Sea Scrolls*, 2:154.

94 Goff, *4QInstruction*, 81 only comments that the language of "chosen one" "emphasizes that the supervisor appreciates the labor of the *mebin*."

95 Whereas in the Hebrew Bible Israel is "my chosen people" (e.g., עַמִּי בְחִירִי Isa 43:20) in 4QFlorilegium 1 2 i 19 are the "chosen of Israel" (בחירי ישראל), which expresses an elect group out of Israel; CD has the "chosen of Israel" who are explicitly the Sons of Zadok (CD IV 3; cf. 1QS IX 14); Cave 1 Rule of the Community refers to the chosen as a "holy of holies" and "true planting" (1QS VIII 6; cf. 1QS XI 16; 4Q212 1 iii 19; 4Q374 2 ii 5), in a variant ms. from Cave 4 are "chosen ones of the way" (4QSᵇ XVIII 1; 4QSᵈ VIII 2; cf. 1QS IX 17–23); the Wicked Priest persecutes and pursues God's chosen ones (1QpHab IX 12; cf. X 13); "men of truth" and "chosen ones of righteousness" are synonymously parallel in the Thanks-giving Hymns (1QHᵃ VI 13, 26; X 15); 4QBarki Nafshiᵉ (4Q438) 3 2 God's "noble ones" and "chosen ones" appear to be synonymous.

בחיר, in either the Hebrew Bible or among Qumran discoveries, to individuals or communities in a daily life context. When used of individual figures among Qumran texts it refers to: Enoch,[96] the figure referred to in 4Q534 (4QElect of God ar or Birth of Noah ar),[97] and possibly a messianic figure in 4Q580 1 i 10 (בחיר לשקט) and 4Q558 (תמיניא לבחיר).[98] If the servant in 4Q416 2 ii 14 is truly a laborer and slave then the ascription "chosen," if this reconstruction is correct, is highly unusual.

In summary, the internal and external textual evidence point to 4Q416 2 ii 12b–17 as depicting the addressee becoming, figuratively, God's firstborn son, unique child, and chosen one by dint of discipline (i.e., l. 12 holding fast to God's good will and serving Him and His wisdom). The one addressed in 4Q418 81+81a 5 also becomes a firstborn to God.[99] In light of the assessment here, when these two passages are read together a clearer idea about how the fig-

---

96   4QEnoch[g] ar (4Q212) 1 ii 23 (= 1 En. 92:1) has Enoch describing himself as: [וח]כים אנושא וּבחיֹן [ר בֹּנֹי] ארעא ("wisest among men and the chosen one of the sons of the earth").

97   בחיר אלהא ("chosen one of God" 1 i 10) is a figure who possesses unrivaled wisdom and understands mysteries and has been interpreted as: (1) the Messiah [Jean Starcky, "Un texte messianique araméen de la Grotte 4 de Qumrân," in *Mémorial du cinquante-naire de l'Ecole des langues orientales de l'Institut Catholique de Paris* (Paris: Bloud et Gay, 1964), 51–66; Jean Carmignac, "Les horoscopes de Qumran," *RevQ* 5/18 (1965): 199–207; Michael O. Wise, Martin Abegg & Edward Cook, *The Dead Sea Scrolls: A New Translation* (San Francisco, CA/London: HarperCollins, 1996), 427–429; Chester, *Messiah and Exaltation*, 255–256.]; (2) Noah [Joseph Fitzmyer, "The Aramaic 'Elect of God' Text from Qumran Cave 4," *CBQ* 27 (1965): 348–372; Jean Starcky retracts his identification and accepts Fitzmyer's in "Le Maître de Justice et Jésus," *Le Monde de la Bible* 4 (1978): 53–55; Florentino García Martínez, *Qumran and Apocalyptic: Studies on the Aramaic Texts from Qumran*, STDJ 9 (Leiden: Brill, 1992), 43–44. The view that the figure is Noah remains the most popular to date.]; (3) Melchizedek [Jonas C. Greenfield, "Prolegomenon," in *3 Enoch or the Hebrew Book of Enoch*, ed. H. Odeberg (New York, NY: Ktav, 1973), xx–xxi]; and (4) Enoch redivivus [André Caquot, "4QMess ar 1 i 8–11," *RevQ* 15/57–58 (1991): 145–155]. James R. Davila, "4QMess ar (4Q534) and Merkavah Mysticism," *DSD* 5/3 (1998): 367–381 suggests 4Q534 is a "prototype of the Merkavah mystics" and, although he argues that the "chosen one" is anonymous, he observes that the figure is still compatible with other interpretations of 4Q534. See also the *editio princeps* by Émile Puech, *Qumrân Grotte 4. XXII: Textes araméens partie, 4Q529–549*, DJD 31 (Oxford: Clarendon Press, 2001), 117–120.

98   Émile Puech, *Qumrân Grotte 4. XXVII: Textes araméens, deuxième partie, 4Q550–4Q575a, 4Q580–4Q587 et appendices*, DJD 37 (Oxford: Clarendon Press, 2009).

99   Tigchelaar, *To Increase Learning*, 233 commenting on 4Q418 81+81a 5 "One has to assume that since the community may have been addressed as sons of God, each individual elect belonging to that community could have been called a son of God."

ure in 4Q418 81 + 81a comes to enjoy this exalted status is found. The speaker of 4QInstruction appears to be a *maśkîl* who addresses "understanding ones" who aspire to grow in their knowledge of, and faithfulness to, wisdom. The *mēvîn* has the potential to serve as a sage himself, 4Q416 2 ii 12b–17 preserve a description of this potentiality, and 4Q418 81 + 81a 1–14 instruct in the ways of a *maśkîl*. The one addressed in 4Q418 81 + 81a, discussed in detail below, variously: blesses the holy one and praises God's name (ll. 1, 12); has authority over God's inheritance (ll. 3, 6, 9); is appointed as a most holy one over the earth (l. 4); has his glory magnified and is set among angels (ll. 4–5); understands and seeks justice from his opponents (ll. 7, 9); is given insight (l. 9); and plays a role turning wrath away from "the men of good pleasure" (l. 10). This community leader certainly enjoys an elevated status and would relate to his community in a fatherly way.[100]

In Chapter 2 4QInstruction's emphasis on "spirit," and concern to guard one's spirit, is returned to. In the well-known Vision of Hagu passage (4Q417 1 i 13b–18a) "spirit" features in the creation of humanity (i.e., "humanity with spirit") and even the wicked are described, oxymoronically, as "fleshly *spirit*." In 4Q416 2 ii (par. ms. 4Q417 2 ii) 6–7 the exhortation occurs that: "by your words do not belittle your spirit, and for any wealth do not exchange your holy spirit, for there is no price equal" (cf. Ch. 2 § 2.2.). Here the *mēvîn* is taught to take precautions, the way that one exchanges or belittles spirit is not straightforwardly about trading it for wealth, but rather how one attends to a relationship with a fellow member of the community when dealing with wealth and poverty. Indeed, the frequent reminder in sections of 4QInstruction that "you are poor" may not be so much about poverty as about wealth; rhetorically their function may be to remind the addressee not to pursue material benefit, especially at the expense of other members of the community (cf. "you cannot serve both God and mammon" in Matt 6:24; Luke 16:13), and to value humility.[101]

As we have seen in this sub-section (§ 2.1.), the student addressed in 4Q416 2 ii is able to become like his teacher, who himself is a servant of a *maśkîl*. The *mēvîn*'s status and station is not static, but rather by living in accordance with revealed wisdom he may progress along a scale from novice to master. We now turn to a second occurrence of משכיל in 4QInstruction.

---

100 Cf. Paul in 1 Cor 4 describes his role as an apostle in terms of being a servant and steward of God's mysteries (1 Cor 4:1), he describes living in hardship, poverty, and humility before declaring (1 Cor 4:15b–16): "For I became your father in Christ Jesus through the gospel, I urge you, then, be imitators of me."

101 The similarities with the Beatitudes in Matt 5 are striking, the "poor in spirit" (5.3) and "meek" (5.5) respectively have the kingdom of heaven and inherit the earth. In 4Q418 81 + 81a 14 the exalted sage "inherits the land" (ארץ).

2.2   Maśkîl *in 4Q417 1 i Lines 18b–27*

4Q417 1 i is a 27-line column. The lines of concern in this section are located in a distinct paragraph, indicated by the address ואתה בן מבין ("and you, son of an understanding one"), which follows the Vision of Hagu passage (4Q417 1 i 13b–18a). 4Q417 1 i 11–18a are discussed in Chapters 2 (§1.1.1.; §1.1.2) and 3 (§2.1.). Most of lines 18b–27 are poorly preserved with only a few words of each line remaining.[102] Line 25 is of particular interest because the *mēvîn* is called בן משכיל ("son of a *maśkîl*" or "wise son").

4Q417 1 i lines 18b–27 (4Q418 43–45 [single underline]; 4Q418a 11 [double underline]; **overlap**), Transcription and Translation:[103]

[טו]ב̇ לרע כמשפט [ר]וח̇ז̇ז̇] vacat [ואתה בן מבין הבט̇ vacat ברז נהיה ודע	18
[נתיבו]ת̇ כול חי והתהלכו ופקוד על̇ מ̇עש̇[יהמה [ל]]ה̇ ז̇עז̇]ל [ל̇]	19
[הב]י̇ן בין רוב למעט ובסודכמה]	20
[דרוש חפ[צ̇יכה ברז נהי̇ה̇]	21
[י כול חזון ד̇ע ובכ̇ול]	22
כיא כול היגע] ו̇ת[ת]ח̇ז̇ק̇ תמיד אל ת̇גע בעולה̇]	23
ואתה] בה לא ינקה כפי נחלתו בה יר]שע	24
בן̇ משכיל התבונן ברזיכה ובא̇ז̇ש̇]יכה	25
י̇]ז̇סד̇ז̇ בכה ◦]מע[ש̇יהן עם פעולת̇ז̇]	26
ואחרי	
ל̇ז̇א תתרו אחר]י̇] ל̇ב̇בכמ̇]ה[ ]י̇{ז̇}עי[נ]י̇כמה̇]	27
bottom margin	

18 [goo]d and evil according to the judgment of his [sp]irit[ ]
vac
And you, son of an understanding one,
gaze *vac* upon the mystery of existence,
    and know **19** [the path]s of all that live,
    and the manner of their walking,
    and examine (them) based upon [their] deeds [...]
20 [under]stand the difference between great and small,
and in your counsel[...]

---

102   The subject matter and sequence of thought in these lines is difficult to follow. The editors comment that the "surviving section of text is surrounded by lacunae of three or four times the width of the preserved text" DJD 34:168.

103   DJD 34:151–152; Tigchelaar, *To Increase Learning*, 52; Rey, *4QInstruction*, 279; Goff, *4QInstruction*, 138; Qimron, *Dead Sea Scrolls*, 2:148.

21 [seek] your [de]sires by the mystery of existence[

22 [ ] every vision know,

and in every[…]

23 and always b[e s]trong,

do not be contaminated by wickedness

[… for all who touch] 24 it will not be clean,

according to his inheritance in it he will be *deemed* wi[cked

… and you,] 25 son of a *maśkîl*, understand by your mysteries,

and by [your] foundation[s …]

26 their (i.e., truth's) [de]eds are established in you,

together with the reward of[…]

27 you will not follow after yo[ur] heart {and} ᵃᶠᵗᵉʳ your e[y]es[…]

The injunction for the addressee to understand the "mystery of existence" is followed by an admonition to distinguish the ways of all creatures (l. 19). In the translation and transcription here, "[their] deeds" (מעשיהמה) in line 19 is reconstructed rather than "[his] deeds" (מעשיו) because "their walking" (התהלכו) in the preceding stich is plural.[104] In lines 19–20 "knowing the paths of all that live" and "understanding the difference between great and small" appear to be synonymously parallel. Here, in contrast to other translations, two other parallel stichs are found in line 19, the second of which is an exhortation to differentiate between them by "examining" (פקוד) their deeds.[105] Except for Qimron, others transcribe and translate the verb הפקוד in the passive as "appointed" (i.e., "the way one should go he appointed upon [his] deeds"), which then has highly deterministic connotations. It is difficult to justify the transcription of a *heh* when the infrared image is set alongside the color photograph, especially when there are examples of *hehs* and *waws* in the immediate context for comparison. What has been taken as a downward stroke on the left in the color image (see

---

104   DJD 34:166 "[t]he end of מֹעֹשֹ is uncertain; perhaps a trace of the final letter (in מעשיהמה or מעשיו) can been seen."

105   DJD 34:166 "[w]hether הפקוד or הפקיד be read, it must be taken as a passive participle rather than as a noun." DJD 34:155 translate l. 19b as "And the manner of his walking that is appointed *for* [his] deed[s]." The word פקוד could be read as an imperative: "and examine by their deeds," cf. 4Q417 1 ii 11 ופקוד כול דרכיבה; 4Q423 5 5 פקוד מועדי הקיץ; alternatively, one might read the imperfect יפקוד "and the manner of their walking he will examine by their deeds," cf. 4Q416 2 ii 9 אם עבודתו יפקוד לכה; 4Q423 5 4 ובנים לאבות יפקוד. Cf. 4Q416 2 iii 6 and הפקיד where the editors speculate that it means "to take charge of something" or "deposit, interest" DJD 34:115. In the passive, it occurs only in 4Q418 81+81a 9 in the Pual, "and a true ephah *has been* la[id" (ואיפת אמת פיקד[ה). As a noun, פקד is frequent.

figs. 11–12 in plate section) is clearly damage to the parchment. Therefore, this use of פקוד is similar to the Rule of the Community (1QS v 24; cf. 4Q258 11 3) "they will examine their spirit and their deeds" (פוקדם את רוחם ומעשיהם) and the Damascus Document (CD XIII 11) "he will be examined on his deeds and his understanding" (יפקדהו למעשיו ושוכלו). In Chapter 2 it is argued that the immediately preceding section (i.e., Vision of Hagu) emphasizes the creation of all humanity, bestowing meditation universally, and that insider/outsider status is based upon personal ethics and merit. The rendering of פקוד rather than the passive participle הפקוד in this passage has significant ramifications for the study and critique of determinism found in Chapter 2.[106]

The theoretical reconstruction in line 21 of the imperative דרוש חפציכה follows Qimron and is left unconstructed in other transcriptions.[107] In these lines is an unusual interest into "your [de]sires" (l. 21), "your mysteries" (l. 25), "[your] foundations" (l. 25), and positively denoted "deeds" (perhaps "truth's deeds" because of the feminine plural pronoun), which are established "in you" (l. 26).[108] These instances of "your" and "you" relate to the addressee being strong and remaining righteous (l. 23). How one should understand the possession of "desires," mysteries, and foundations of truth is unclear; is it that the addressee has somehow been imbued with these? The concern not to become wicked is also connected to the *mēvîn*'s person; in line 27 "your heart" and "your eyes" lead the addressee astray. Therefore, there are a series of "yours" ("desires," mysteries, foundations) that are positive and these are contrasted with other "yours" (heart, eyes) that are untrustworthy. Among the series of

---

106   4Q426 (4QInstruction-like work) 1 ii 2 has "a firstborn I will raise" (בכור ארים) and if this firstborn is the subject of the lines to follow he will "pay attention to the deeds of men" (l. 4 אנוש) and "take possession of it (fem., perhaps "truth")" (l. 6); Adam S. van der Woude, "Wisdom at Qumran," in *Wisdom in Ancient Israel: Essays in Honour of J.A. Emerton*, ed. John Day, Robert P. Gordon, Hugh G.M. Williamson (Cambridge: CUP, 1995), 244–256 at 249 fn. 10 comments on this line that "the noun [בכור] means 'first-born' (which makes no sense in the context)." If the firstborn in 4Q426 is similar to 4QInstruction then the activity of paying attention, which is in the first-person form, to the deeds of men may also be similar.

107   DJD 34:30, 84 the word חפץ is frequent in 4QInstruction (24×), occurring nearly as often in this one composition as in all the other Qumran discoveries combined (23×). In postbiblical Hebrew it has several meanings: "desire," "delight," humanity's "pleasure," God's "good will" and in this last sense is similar to רצון. The activity of "seeking" (דרש) "desires" (חפץ) is common place in 4QInstruction (4Q418 81 + 81a 18; 4Q418 102 a+b 4; 4Q418 103 ii 5; 4Q418 126 ii 4, 12; 4Q418 158 3).

108   DJD 34:168 the editors note that the second-person masculine suffix qualifying רז "is most strange" and conclude that these must be mysteries concerning the *mēvîn*.

positive "yours," both mysteries and foundations are external to a person while "desires" would be internal. If it is indeed accurate to translate חפץ as "desire," then they are internal. Line 21 exhorts the addressee to seek "your desires" by the mystery of existence. "Your" חפץ are those that have been searched out by the mystery. The term חפץ rendered as "desire" would then present a contrast between trusting and relying upon what is outside of oneself in order to understand one's own interior and distrusting exterior members of one's physical self. These are admonitions directed to the "son of a *maśkîl*."

Elsewhere in 4Q416 2 ii 8, discussed above (§ 2.1.), a series of "yours" also occurs: "speak (in the right way) and you will find your *desire* [חפצכה];" "keep diligent watch by your mysteries [רזיכה] for your own soul;" and "do not abandon your statutes [חוקיכה]." These parallel hemistichs clarify one another.[109] Both uses of the second-person masculine suffix qualifying רז and חוק indicate that these terms are associated with how the *mēvîn* should go about his affairs. 4Q416 2 ii 8 is the only other place in 4QInstruction where רז occurs with the second-person singular possessive "your."[110] Moreover, the "your" in 4Q416 2 ii was seen in the preceding section to refer to an addressee who is being instructed in the ways of a *maśkîl*.

Attention to חפץ elsewhere in 4QInstruction further illuminates its use in 4Q416 2 ii and, in the likelihood that Qimron's reconstruction is correct, 4Q417 1 i too. 4Q416 1 2, which is the opening column of the document, has לתכן חפצי; the verb תכן can mean to "weigh," "regulate," "set in order," "apportion," or "be sct straight," but without context it is difficult to determine its meaning there. The pronominal suffix could be *waw* ("his") or *yod* which could be first-person ("my") or a plural in construct with a following noun (cf. § 1.2.). If it is in the third-person, then it would likely refer to God and in first-person to the speaker.[111] If it is correct to locate 4Q418 222 + 221 and 238 at the beginning of 4QInstruction, then this may support the translation "my pleasure/good will" in reference to the *maśkîl*. In fact, among the twenty-four occurrences of חפץ in 4QInstruction there is no unambiguous use of the term where a pronoun refers to God (i.e., "God's good will"), but rather only to that of human figures. Indeed, the verb תכן occurs with חפץ on two other occasions in this composition. 4Q418 88 1 has the instruction that "you will prepare all your *desires* (?)" (תכין לכול חפציכה). 4Q418 127 5 has "God made all the *desire* (?) *of* אוט and established them in truth" (אל עשה כול חפצי אוט ויתכנם באמת), a statement that is in

---

109   Cf. 4Q417 1 i 14 חֻרֹות הֿחוקכה ("your ordinances are engraved").

110   Cf. the only other occurrence with a possessive pronoun: 4Q418 177 7a דֹע רֻזֹיֿ.

111   Qimron, *Dead Sea Scrolls*, 2:147 reconstructs חפצי אוט, cf. § 3.3 below.

parallel to God weighing out measurements justly (l. 6).[112] In this context, חפץ would seem to refer to one's "portion" or perhaps even "reward" rather than "desire."

4Q418 103 ii also helps to clarify the meaning of חפץ in 4QInstruction. This fragment is concerned with agriculture and laws of diverse kinds, in reference to Lev 19:19 ("You will not let your animals breed with a different kind; you will not sow your field with two kinds of seed; nor will you put on a garment made of two different materials"). In describing harvest time (lit. gathering in of baskets) the addressee is exhorted to "compare a season with the season of their seeking" (l. 4a, ישוה עת בעת דרושם). After a half-line lacuna, the beginning of line 5 then reads: "for all of them will seek according to their season and a man according to his *desire* (?)" (כי כולם ידרשו לעתם ואיש כפי חפצו). 4Q418 103 ii reinforces that observing the created order, whether it is times and seasons or nature generally, is intertwined with understanding one's חפץ, perhaps here as "portion" or "reward" rather than "desire." This theme continues in 4Q418 126 ii 3–4 where God uses a "true *ephah*" and a "correct weight" when making judgments; God has "spread out" (פרשם) and "placed" (שמם) this order (cf. 4Q417 1 i in Ch. 2 § 1.1.1.). We also read here that "those who *delight* (?) in them, th[ey] seek[...]" (ולחפציהם ידרשו). In the same column, the addressee is admonished to walk in truth along with other seekers of understanding (l. 11). The *mēvîn* is told in line 12 that "in your hand are its אוט" and "from your basket he will seek its/his *desire* (?)" (ומטנאכה ידרוש חפצו). The sense of these lines is not entirely clear, but the impression is that the addressee's status within the hierarchy of the community, his exalted position as a sage, is a resource that members of the community may draw upon (i.e., he is a font of wisdom). Moreover, the language of חפץ and אוט appear to have economic connotations, again perhaps as "portion."

Another passage important to our understanding of חפץ is 4Q418 102 a+b. That there is a hierarchy in the community and some of those addressed draw upon their superiors, or alternatively inferiors draw upon the addressee, appears to be part of 4QInstruction's discourse. In 4Q418 102 a+b are two occurrences of חפץ, these lines read (cf. § 2.3):

> 2 [...] good *pleasure* (?) [חפץ] and righteous truth [in] all his works [מעשיו], and [...] 3 [and you], who understands truth, *through all of your actualized wisdom* [מיד כול חכמת ידיסכה] 4 [...] in your ways (lit. walking), and then

---

112   Cf. comments on אוט in fn. 68.

he will seek your good will for all those seeking it/requesting him (?) [ואם
ידרוש חפצכה לכול מבקשיו 5 [...] [from the] iniquity of abomination you
will be clean [מעוון תועבה תנקה], and in the joy of truth you will [...].

Harrington and Strugnell translate both occurrences of חפץ here as belonging
to human figures, but in line 4 they translate: "And then He will *look for thy pleasure for* all those who seek it."[113] That God is the one seeking the addressee's חפץ
is unlikely. These lines are returned to below (§ 3.3.).

Continuing with an analysis of חפץ, in 4Q417 2 i 12–13 the *mēvîn* is exhorted:
"be an advocate on behalf of you own *reward/portion* (?)" (היה בעל ריב לחפצכה),
and not to let his soul be contaminated "by any of your perversities" (לכול
נעותכה). As such, this same addressee is told to "pronounce your judgments like
a righteous ruler" (דבר משפטיכה כמושל צדיק). As a result (l. 14), God's anger is
abated and he overlooks one's sins. This is intercessory activity which corre-
sponds to that of the exalted figure in 4Q418 81 + 81a 10 who turns away wrath
from the "men of good pleasure" (אנשי רצון).

In summary, חפץ is notoriously difficult to translate in 4QInstruction. It
appears to have multiple connotations, including but not necessarily limited
to one's "portion" and "reward" (in the hereafter?). The significance and yet
ambiguous use of this term comes into view again below.

Returning to 4Q417 1 i 18b–27, if the משכיל in line 25 is read as a noun, then
the expression "son of a *maśkîl*" may draw attention to the relationship that the
mēvîn enjoys with the instructor. The role of *maśkîl* is not exclusionary and to
be a son of a sage may express discipleship. Alternatively, following Tigchelaar,
בן משכיל may be an expression for the sage himself.[114] Charlotte Hempel reads
most of the occurrences of משכיל in 4QInstruction as participles and concludes
that the בן מבין ("understanding one"; cf. 4Q418 69 ii 15) and בן משכיל, which she
translates as "wise one," are synonymous.[115] Reading משכיל as a noun rather
than participle differentiates these expressions and yet, although "understanding one" and "son of a *maśkîl*" are both ways of identifying the addressee, they
are not identical expressions. In light of the possessive "your" with "mysteries," "foundations," and "*desires*," as well as similar possessives in 4Q416 2 ii, the
one addressed here may be viewed as a *mēvîn-maśkîl* who is being instructed
in the way he should conduct himself as well as differentiating other people

113   DJD 34:328.

114   Tigchelaar, "Toward a Reconstruction," 123.

115   Charlotte Hempel, "The Qumran Sapiential Texts," 287; cf. Ben Sira 47:12 where it is used
      adjectivally: "after him a wise son [בן משכיל] rose up."

according to their deeds. This disciple, as he seeks to understand the mystery
of existence, contemplates the order of creation which involves introspection
and, although he is a righteous individual, he is not without sin or blemish.[116]
Self-contemplation and actualization of wisdom are also features of the passage considered immediately below, where the final occurrence of משכיל is
analyzed.

2.3   Maśkîl in 4Q418 81 + 81a Lines 15–20

4Q418 81 + 81a is a 20-line column, the first 14 lines (cf. § 5.1 below) preserve a
passage that has been viewed as distinct from the section that follows (ll. 15–
20). In line 15 is the address "and you, understanding one," which may be used
to begin a new section, but not necessarily.[117] The remaining reference to משכיל
in 4QInstruction is found in line 17.

4Q418 81 + 81a lines 15–20, Transcription and Translation:[118]

15   ואתה מבין אם בחכמת ידים המשילכה וֹדעַ]ת
16   אוֹט לכול הולכי אדם ומשם תפקוֹד טרפכה וֹ]
17   התבונן מוֹדה ומיד כול משכילכה הוסף לקחֹ]
18   הוצא מחסורכה לכול דורשי חפץ ואז תכוֹן]
19   תמלא ושבעתה בֹּרוב טוב ומחכמת ידיכֹה]
20   כי אל פלג נחֹלֹתֹ] כוֹ[לֹ] חיֹ] וכול חכמי לב השכֹלֹוֹ]

  15 And you, understanding one,
if by *wisdom actualized* (lit. *wisdom of hands*) He has placed you in
      authority,
and knowled[ge ...]
[...] 16 אוט (humility?) to each of *the ways of* mankind (?),
and from there you are appointed your sustenance,
and [...]

---

116   On the development of self, see Carol A. Newsom, "Deriving Negative Anthropology
through Exegetical Activity: The Hodayot as Case Study," in *Is There a Text in This Cave?
Studies in the Textuality of the Dead Sea Scrolls in Honour of George J. Brooke*, ed. Ariel Feldman, Maria Cioată & Charlotte Hempel, STDJ 119 (Leiden: Brill, 2017), 258–276.

117   ואתה מבין occurs on eight occasions (4Q416 4 3; 4Q417 1 i 1, 13; 4Q418 123 ii 5; 4Q418 126 ii
12; 4Q418 168 4; 4Q418 176 3) and is often but not always the incipit of a new section.

118   DJD 34:301; Tigchelaar, *To Increase Learning*, 94; Rey, *4QInstruction*, 307–308 only discusses
the first fourteen lines; Goff, *4QInstruction*, 239–240; Qimron, *Dead Sea Scrolls*, 2:166.

[...] **17** grow in understanding exceedingly,
and from the hand of each of your *maśkil[îm]*[119] increase learning[...]
[...]**18** make your (material?) lacking evident to all who pursue good
  will,
and then you will be ready[...]
[...] **19** you will be full,
and you will be satisfied in the abundance of good things,
and from your *actualized wisdom* (lit. *wisdom of hands*) [...]
[...] **20** for God divided the inheritance of[ever]y[living thing],
and all those wise of heart we have taught (or: have gained understanding)[[120]

In other translations, these lines are seen as transitioning from an address to
an exalted figure in the preceding lines to a different figure introduced in a
separate section. According to this view, the figure in lines 15–20 serves as an
overseer of manual labor. Harrington and Strugnell translate line 15 as: "if over
the manual *artisans* He has *set thee in charge*" and they offer the, partially, theoretical reconstruction of line 19 as: "*by* thy manual craftsmanship [*thy treasuries
shall be filled*]."[121] However, the translation "manual craftsmanship" and "manual artisans" (חכמת ידים) in lines 15 and 19 respectively, a trade which in this
context is unquestionably highly esteemed, is difficult to substantiate from the
evidence.[122] Indeed, the addressee can be "set" as a firstborn son to God figura-

---

119   The plural *maśkilîm* rather than singular *maśkil* is required in the phrase "all" or "each" of
      your "teacher[s]."

120   DJD 34:311 find here in 4Q418 81 + 81a 20 a possible defective spelling of the *Hiphil*, השכלו
      i.e. instead of השכילו, and comment: "One might instead read השכלנו 'we have taught the
      wise', which meets the requirements of the traces materially, grammatically, and ortho-
      graphically; but a move to the 1st plural verb would be unexpected in this fragment."

121   DJD 34:303; cf. Goff, *4QInstruction*, 241 who translates "manual labor"; at 259 interprets this
      section of 4Q418 81 + 81a in light of his understanding of 4Q416 2 ii (cf. § 2.1); he writes that
      line 15 "refers to God's creation of food for humanity and the addressee's acquisition of his
      own provisions. The word אוט, translated here as 'resources,' is enigmatic, but is reason-
      ably understood as referring to material that has a practical benefit for the mebin (see the
      commentary on 4Q416 2 ii 1)." Cf. fn. 69, אוט is a term derived from the adverb לאט which,
      alternatively, may refer to lowliness and humility.

122   חכמה is rarely used in 4QInstruction; excluding references to חכמת ידים it occurs once in
      construct with אוט in 4Q416 2 ii 12 (par. 4Q418 8 13); twice in 4Q417 1 i 6–9 where it is by
      the mystery of existence that one can distinguish between wisdom (חכמה) and foolish-
      ness (אולת); and otherwise is theoretically reconstructed in fragmentary contexts twice
      (4Q418 126 ii 5; 4Q418b 1 4).

tively, but it is altogether another issue for God to be the agent who places the addressee in authority (המשילכה) over "manual labor" literally. In the editors' translation, this would appear to be a deterministic expression of one's occupation and place within the hierarchy of the community. In my translation, one is given authority by merit of their pursuit and "actualization of wisdom," a similar idea as "dint of discipline" discussed in § 2.1. above. One consequence of not translating חכמת ידים as referring to manual labor is that the figure in lines 15–20 cannot so easily be distinguished from the exalted sage in preceding lines 1–14.

Justification for my translation is found in a reassessment of the expression חכמת ידים. This term occurs three other times in 4QInstruction (4Q418 102 a+b 3; 4Q418 137 2; 4Q418 139 2), often with limited context available to decipher its precise sense, and elsewhere is found only twice in extant Hebrew texts (4QSapiential Text [4Q424 3 7]; Ben Sira 9:17) and one variation in Aramaic (Ezra 7:25).[123] Harrington and Strugnell are inclined to translate all the occurrences of חכמת ידים in 4QInstruction in reference to a scribe's manual skills and artisanal activity.[124] However, they comment that "[t]he attribution to the sage of artisanship (i.e., ḥokma of the hands) is paradoxical; in a wisdom text, the craftsman is usually contrasted unfavorably with the sage (Sir 38:24–34; cf. also line 15 supra, where the artisan could be understood as being subordinate to the sage)." How did the editors come to the conclusion that "wisdom of the hands" refers to the skill of an artisan? The answer is found in the Greek translation of Ben Sira. Hebrew Ben Sira uses the term "wisdom of hands" in 9:17: בחכמי ידים יחשך ומושל עמׁו חכם ("those wise in hand will uncover straightness, and he who rules over his people is wise"). Note that in 4Q418 81 + 81a 15 "wisdom of hands" is also associated with "ruling" (משל). There is nothing in Ben Sira 9:17 that refers to manual labor. The association of manual artisans or artisanship with חכמת ידים appears to have slipped into the translation of 4QInstruction vis-à-vis Greek Sirach 9:17, which reads: ἐν χειρὶ τεχνιτῶν ἔργον ἐπαινεσθήσεται ("A work is praised for the skill of the artisan").

The two occurrences of חכמת ידים outside of 4QInstruction do not substantiate the editors' translation either. In 4QSapiential Work (4Q424 3 5–8) a slothful man is contrasted with a wise man: if a man with a "fat heart" and "drowsy spirit" is sent to find wisdom, lines 6–7 read that כי נסתרה חכמת לבו ולוא ימשול

---

123   4Q418 137 2 has the incomplete חכׁ[מ]ת ידים יוסף לכהׁ, which Harrington and Strugnell, DJD 34:366 translate as: "manual [sk]ill let Him increase for thee." 4Q418 137 preserves parts of only four lines and, like 4Q418 81 + 81a 15–20, recompense is associated in some way with the "wisdom of the hands" (4Q418 137 3 "]righteousness in thy wages, For to thy labour[").

124   Cf. DJD 34:311, 328 for comments on חכמת ידים.

ב[...] חכמת ידיו לא ימצא ("for the wisdom of his heart is hidden and he is not able to rule over[...] he will not find the wisdom of his hands"). In contrast to this "fat hearted" person: איש שכל יקבל בינה ("a wise man receives understanding").[125] Gershon Brin draws attention to two types of wisdom reflected in these lines of 4QSapiential Work: (1) wisdom of heart (חכמת לבב), and (2) wisdom of hands (חכמת ידים). For the course-hearted individual not to find the wisdom of his hands is "to not realize or *actualize* his inner talents" and, Brin writes, it is "because of his dullness the wisdom of his heart is hidden and he does not find the wisdom of his hands."[126] It is significant that in 4Q418 81 + 81a "wisdom of hands" (ll. 15, 19) and "wise ones of heart" (l. 20) also occur paired together as found in 4QSapiential Work. The notion of "ruling" (משל) is associated with this actualization of wisdom in each instance, in: 4Q4Q418 81 + 81a 15, 4Q424 3 7, and Ben Sira 9:17. Like 4QSapiential Text, "wisdom of the hands" in 4QInstruction, and probably Ben Sira too, relates to "actualizing" or living out wisdom.[127]

The one addressed in 4Q418 81 + 81a 15–20 is placed in a position of authority because he has attained a level of understanding. Despite being placed in authority, the addressee is impoverished (l. 18, he lacks materially). How do we understand lines 15–16? The Hebrew term אוט may express the ways of humankind as being humble. Some translators render אוט here as a "storehouse" and it is "from there" (משם) that they are given their sustenance. This understanding of אוט is adduced from the context, one that mistakenly refers to artisanal labor rather than living out wisdom. Based upon the translation of *ḥokma* of the hands here, the reference of "from there" (משם) is more likely the position to which this sage has been appointed. That is, the *maśkîl*'s needs are met in this role as sage.

Although the contexts are fragmentary, we may also make limited observations about how חכמת ידים is used elsewhere in 4QInstruction.[128]

---

125   Gershon Brin, "Studies in 4Q424, Fragment 3," *VT* 46/3 (1996): 271–295.

126   Brin, "4Q424," 288 italics mine; "wisdom of heart" is also found in Exod 35:25 and Sir 45:26 ויתן לכם חכמת לב למען לא ישכח טובכם ("and He will give to you wisdom of the heart so that you will not forget your good things").

127   When Ezra (7:25) is addressed in the first-person he is told: "And you, Ezra, according to the God-given wisdom that is in your hand" (כְּחָכְמַת אֱלָהָךְ דִּי־בִידָךְ). This wisdom in his hands is used to appoint magistrates and judges who know the laws of God and to teach these laws to those who do not know them.

128   4Q418 139 2 only preserves בחכמת ידיכה and nothing more, notable is that the preposition ב- and the second-person singular possessive pronoun are used similarly to 4Q418 81 + 81a 15 and 19.

4Q418 102 a+b, Transcription and Translation (cf. § 2.2):[129]

]ה בשחתׄ[○]   [1

[○וׄ מעשיו]□[כול] צדק זׄ חׄפׄץ וׄאמת   [2

[וׄאתה]מׄבין באמת מיד כול חכמת ידיֹסׄכׄהׄ]   [3

[הת]הׄלככה ואז ידרוש חפצכה לכול מבקשיו]   [4

[מׄ]עׄוׄׄון תועבה תנקה ובשמחת אמת תשת]   [5

bottom margin

1   [   ] in the pit[

2   [   ]desire and righteous truth []are all his deeds[

3   [and you], who truly understands, through all of your *actualized wisdom*[

4   [   ]your ways, and then he will seek your *portion* for all those seeking it (requesting him?)[

5   [from] guilty abomination you will be clean and in joy of truth you will[

Harrington and Strugnell translate line 3 as "And as for thee,] O thou who undertandest truth, Through all the *cunning of thy hands*[."[130] However, חכמה and ידים as two nouns in construct with a possessive pronoun "your" are better translated in light of the occurrences observed above. The other second-person singular possessive relationships (i.e., the other "yours") further elucidate "*ḥokma* of your hands" here, these are: רזיכה ("your mysteries"), התהלככה ("your ways"), and חפציכה ("your *portion* (?)"). The subject of the verb "seek" (ידרוש) in line 4 is taken by the editors as God (i.e., "He will seek your *desire*"); however, why God would seek the addressee's חפץ is difficult to make sense of, especially in light of observations made about חפץ above where it at times alludes to one's "portion" or "reward." Here, one who has attained understanding, as a sage, is a (re)source sought after by other wisdom seekers. Other members of the community seek the *maśkîl's* חפץ.

4Q418 137 2 has the fragmentary sentence חכ]מת ידים יוסף לכהׄ[, which Harrington and Strugnell translate as: "manual [sk]ill let Him increase for thee."[131]

---

129   DJD 34:327; cf. Qimron, *Dead Sea Scrolls*, 2:169. Note: Tigchelaar, *To Increase Learning*; Goff, *4QInstruction* (2013); Rey, *4QInstruction* do not offer transcription and translation or otherwise comment on the content of this fragment.

130   DJD 34:328, italics mine.

131   DJD 34:366.

4Q418 137 preserves parts of only four lines and, like 4Q418 81 + 81a 15–20, recompense and sustenance may be associated with the "wisdom of the hands," but the line is too fragmentary to determine context (4Q418 137 3 "]righteousness in your wages, for to your labour["). When יסף ("increase") is used in 4QInstruction it is most often within a negative imperative (אל תוסף; e.g., 4Q416 2 ii 10; 417 2 i 18, 20) and less frequently with the conditional conjunction "lest" (פן יוסיף על רישכה in 4Q416 2 iii 6). Here in 4Q418 137 "to increase" is positive and as such this verb is only similarly used in regard to increasing wisdom: הוסף לקח (4Q418 81 + 81a 17; 4Q418 221 3). חכמת ידים and לקח appear to be closely related terms for "wisdom" in 4QInstruction and both are to be increased.[132]

The one addressed in 4Q418 81 + 81a 15–20 is placed in a position of authority because he has attained a level of understanding. Despite being placed in authority, the addressee is one who lacks, a situation he is to make apparent to others, an idea that reflects a type of *Armenfrömmigkeit*. This sage is reassured (l. 16, 19) that from "אוט to all the ways of mankind" he is apportioned his sustenance. 4Q418 81 + 81a 17 refers to multiple *maśkilîm* and, identical to the *maśkîl*-speaker in 4Q418 221 3, they increase the addressee's learning (cf. 4Q298 3–4 ii 5; Prov 1:5, 9:9, 16:23).[133] This reference to learning from other teachers, in light of the preceding analysis, requires contextualization: this address is not to someone of lesser stature who is an overseer of manual labor, but rather to a *mēvîn* whose actualized wisdom results in being placed in authority. Indeed, the addressee in these lines is a peer of the *maśkilîm* in line 17 and instruction to learn from them is focused specifically on issues of sustenance, lacking, and poverty. On the one hand side, understanding may be gained from other sages about how to live rightly in these difficult economic conditions (l. 17); on the other hand, the addressee himself is to make his lacking apparent to others who seek wisdom (l. 18 דורשי חפץ). This is a posture of humility and piety he adopts from his teachers and which is to be demonstrated to others. The same notion of poverty is to be found in teaching about, and relating to, family members (4Q416 2 iii 15–18 "in your poverty" parents should be honored).

In this section (§ 2.) of Chapter 1 our focus has been on the three occurrences of משכיל in 4QInstruction. Previous studies recognized that on one occasion (4Q418 81 + 81a 17) משכיל refers to a teacher or sage. In another instance (4Q417 1 i 25), the term בן משכיל ("son of a *maśkîl*") is predominately translated as a "wise son," whereas a strong case may also be made that this is a designation

---

132   The noun לקח itself denotes the concrete activity of "taking" learning or teaching as reflected in its relationship to the verbal counterpart.

133   DJD 34:303 translate משכילים as "teachers"; so too Goff, *4QInstruction*, 241.

highlighting a student-sage relationship. 4Q416 2 ii 15 refers to an עבד משכיל and I argue that this is not a "wise servant," as translators have consistently rendered the term, but rather a "servant of a *maśkîl*." 4Q416 2 ii is particularly important because it yields valuable information about the process of becoming a sage and the way that hierarchies and divisions operate in 4QInstruction. When this understanding of the student-sage relationship in 4Q416 2 ii is read alongside 4Q418 81 + 81a (§ 4. below), it becomes much clearer who the exalted figure in 4Q418 81 + 81a is and how he came to that position.

We turn now to other occurrences of משכיל in Qumran discoveries with two main objectives. First, the sage figure in 4QInstruction can be contextualized among other *maśkilîm*, allowing us to see how this position in 4QInstruction compares with other compositions that are interested in a *maśkîl*. Second, the specific vocabulary associated with these other *maśkilîm*, when compared with terms occurring in conjunction with משכיל in 4QInstruction, strengthen arguments that debated fragments of 4QInstruction are indeed concerned with the same or similar topic.

3   *Maśkîl* in Qumran Discoveries

In addition to משכילים in Daniel 12, other models are available for understanding the role of a *maśkîl* in early Jewish literature, particularly in compositions discovered at Qumran.[134] *Maśkîl* may refer generally to someone who understands, but more frequently the *maśkîl* plays a particular role, function, or office. In the Rule of the Community the *maśkîl* is charged with instructing and guiding members of the community (1QS IX 12; cf. CD XII 20–21, XIII 22).[135] In the Treatise on the Two Spirits the *maśkîl* teaches the Sons of Light about the character (תולדות) and fate of humankind (1QS III 13–14). Some of the 4QS material suggests that the Rule of the Community began with reference to the *maśkîl* (4QS^d 1 i 1, מדרש למשכיל).[136] A technical role for the *maśkîl* is also clear

---

134   A designation that is used in several ways at Qumran, see Torleif Elgvin, "משכיל, *maśkîl*," *ThWQ*, vol. 2; Newsom, "The Sage in the Literature of Qumran," 373–382; cf. Shane A. Berg, "An Elite Group within the Yaḥad," in *Qumran Studies: New Approaches, New Questions*, ed. Michael T. Davis & Brent A. Strawn (Grand Rapids, MI: Eerdmans, 2007), 161–177 at 174–175.

135   For an in-depth review of the role of the *maśkîl* in the *Rule of the Community* see: Armin Lange, *Weisheit und Prädestination: Weisheitliche Urordnung und Prädestination in den Textfunden von Qumran*, STDJ 18 (Leiden: Brill, 1995), 144–165.

136   Sarianna Metso, *The Textual Development of the Qumran Community Rule*, STDJ 21 (Leiden: Brill, 1997), 112 and concludes that the "first line of 1QS is thus restored ל[משכיל ללמד את

in the Rule of the Blessing where he blesses priests and the community (1QSb I 1; III 22; V 20). The *maśkîl* is the instructor several times in the Thanksgiving Hymns (1QHª V 12, VII 21, XX 7, 14). Just as the *maśkîl* instructs the simple ones in 4Q418 221 2 (פּוֹתיים בֹּוֹלֹ ולהבין), so too in 1QHª V 12–13 (פּ'תאים להבין).[137] In both 1QHª V 12 and VII 21 an identical expression is found: "a psalm for the instructor" (מזמור למשכיל).

In 1QHª XX 14–16 a first-person proclamation is made that "I, the *maśkîl* [ואני משכיל], I know you my God, by the spirit you have placed in me." The instructor claims to have listened to God's wondrous secrets (פלאכה סוד) and gained knowledge through the mystery of His wisdom (רז שכלבה). This is not the only place where the *maśkîl* refers to himself with the first-person "I." In Songs of the Sage (4Q510 1 4–5) the same self-identification occurs (משכיל אני) and the speaker proclaims God's glorious splendor (ותפארתו הוד) in order to exorcise demonic beings.[138] Although the words preceding *maśkîl* ([משכיל) in 4Q418 238 1 are not extant, the reconstruction משכיל ואני is probable in light of the first-person pronouns in 222 + 221.

The Self-Glorification Hymn has several important parallels not only with 4Q418 222 + 221 and 238, but also with 4Q418 81 + 81a 1–14. Moreover, in the Thanksgiving Hymns this recension begins with a reference to a *maśkîl* (1QHª XXV 34; i.e., "Recension A").[139] Michael Wise comments on the function of the *maśkîl* in this recension; he observes that determining whether the *lamed* ("to a *maśkîl*") is datival or auctorial creates a false dichotomy.[140] The first line of this recension may well have been redacted by a *maśkîl* and the phrase "to a *maśkîl*" includes other *maśkilîm* who use the hymn. Wise suggests that each

היחד סרך ספר לחיו שים[אנ 'For the wise leader, to instruct the men for (during?) his life, the book of the order of the community.'" Cf. Jean Carmignac, "Conjecture sur la première ligne de la Règle de la Communauté," *RevQ* 2 (1959): 85–87.

137   Carol Newsom, Hartmut Stegemann & Eileen Schuller, *Qumran Cave 1.III: 1QHodayot a, with Incorporation of 4QHodayot a-f and 1QHodayot b*, DJD 40 (Oxford: Clarendon Press, 2009), 75.

138   For a current discussion and assessment of this *maśkîl* alongside the Rule of the Community see Joseph L. Angel, "Maskil, Community, and Religious Experience in the *Songs of the Sage* (4Q510–511)," *DSD* 19/1 (2012): 1–27.

139   Wise, "באלים כמוני מי," 204 reconstructs 1QHª XXV 34 as לרנה ברכוהו מזמ]ור למשכיל; see the reconstruction by Puech, "L'hymne de la glorification," 377–385 offers a composite text with 4Q431 frgs. 1–2; which consists of 4QHᵉ I–II–[III 18/9] = 4Q431 1a-d-2++: 1QHª xxv 34–xxvii 3, 4Q427 3–7, 4Q428 21 and reconstructs this line as אל להללבה שיר מזמ]ור למשכיל עליון; cf. Eshel, "The Identification," 620–625; Baillet, *Qumran grotte 4.III (4Q482–4Q520)*, 26–27. Schuller & Newsom, *The Hodayot*, 76 ל שיר מזמ]ור למשכיל.

140   Wise, "A Study of 4Q491ᶜ," 205, 207.

maśkîl would have used the hymn in their own communities, at their own discretion, and that these meetings would have been interactive. He points to 1QHᵃ V 12–14 where the hymn to the *maśkîl* is followed by several infinitives, each of which is related to increasing learning and worship. Wise comments that these lines in column V may not describe precisely *how* the משכיל was to use the poem for worship and instruction; however, they emphasize *that* he is to instruct and worship.[141] Wise also comments on the term מזמור ("a psalm" or "hymn"), emphasizing that it should be taken in its full etymological sense; as such, the hymn was to be performed aloud in the form of song or chant. 4Q491ᶜ ("Recension B") material in particular supports this view because of its many liturgical elements and terms.[142]

The *maśkîl* of 4QInstruction does not share in the hubris of the speaker of the Self-Glorification Hymn, but the speakers of these two documents may share other similarities with one another, namely that at some level authority is derived by appealing to angelic beings. Among the contributions that Joseph Angel makes in his assessment of the Self-Glorification Hymn is an observation on the possession of glory and the speaker's position among angels.[143] The speaker of the Self-Glorification Hymn frequently boasts of his own glory (4Q491ᶜ 13, 14, 15, 18; cf. 1QHᵃ XXVI 7; 4Q471ᵇ 7, 8; 4Q431 I 6), he regularly exults that his place is among the angels (e.g., 4Q471ᵇ 1; 4QHᵃ 10), and his "glory" relates directly to this theme when he states that (4Q491ᶜ 15–16): "everything precious to me is in the glory of the holy [hab]itation" (כול יקר לי בכבוד [מע]ון הקודש).[144]

In the section to follow, 4Q418 81 + 81a 4–5 are assessed to determine if they are similar to the Self-Glorification Hymn when God casts the addressee among all the angels and magnifies his glory greatly.[145] 4Q418 81 + 81a portrays the addressee as having his lot cast among the angels, and it is debated whether this is solely future or presently realized. In the Self-Glorification Hymn the *maśkîl*'s authority relates to his place among the angels. If the addressee in 4Q418 81 + 81a is instructed on how to become a *maśkîl*, then placement among angelic beings

---

141   Wise, "A Study of 4Q491ᶜ," 207, italics mine.

142   It is legitimate to argue that the earlier material helps understand the later and many now view that versions of Recension B are preserved in Recension A.

143   Angel, "The Liturgical-Eschatological," 595–596.

144   Eshel, "The Identification," 621–622.

145   Angel, "The Liturgical-Eschatological," 596 comments: "Similarly, Jubilees 31:14 reads: 'May the Lord give you and your descendants extremely great honor ... The descendants of your sons will be like them [the angels of the presence and the holy ones] in honor, greatness and holiness.' The word 'honor' in this verse may with certainty be retroverted to the original Hebrew." Cf. the transformation of Paul's readers "from glory to glory" in 1 Cor 3:18.

would be an aspect of arriving to this privileged station and practicing wisdom.[146] Indeed, in light of the assessment of the "firstborn son" (§ 2.1.), where the addressee is seen as becoming a sage by dint of discipline, 4Q418 81 + 81a may be interpreted as an address to a *mēvîn* who has become a *maśkîl*.

Words of the Maskil to All the Sons of Dawn (4Q298), edited by Stephen Pfann and Menahem Kister, is written in a cryptic (i.e., esoteric) Hebrew script.[147] There is one exception: the first line of the first column, directed to a *maśkîl*, is not in cryptic script. The editors suggest that the small size of the scroll allowed it to be carried and concealed while traveling. In the case that it was lost, the title ("Words of the Maskil") was legible and its finder could return it without being able to read the rest of its content.

4Q298 1–2 i lines 1–4, Transcription and Translation:[148]

[דבר]⁰ משכיל אשר דבר לכול בני שחר האזי[נו לי כ]ול אנשי לבב   1

[ורוד]פֿי צדק הבי[נ]וֹ במלי ומבֿקֿשי אמונה שׁ[מעُ]וֹ למלי בכול   2

[מ]וֹצא שפٰתٰ[י וי]דّעים דרֹ[ש]וֹ[ן א[לֹה וٰ]שיבֿ[ו לאורח [חיים אٰ[נשי]   3

רצו[נ]וٰ וٰ[אור [עולמֹ]ם לאין] חקר בֿ]   4

1 [*Word*]*s of a Maskil which he spoke to all Sons of Dawn.*
Lend your ear to me, a]ll men of understanding;
2 [and you who pur]sue righteousness, do understa[n]d my words;
and you who seek truth, li[st]en to my words in all 3 that [is]sues from [my] lips.
[And those who k]now, have pur[s]ued [the]se things,
and have turn[ed to the way] of life.
O m[en of] 4 His [wi]ll, and etern[al light beyond] comprehension [

In this scroll the role of the *maśkîl* and his relationship to his audience are closely associated with the Yaḥad texts and perhaps also in some regards to

---

146 Stuckenbruck, "Pseudepigraphy and First Person Discourse," 324 "Whatever merit there might be in supposing that an individual like the Teacher of Righteousness or other community expressed themselves through some of the *Hodayot*, the texts remain without any formal identification. The same can be said about the so-called 'self-glorification hymn' (מי כמוני באלים, 'who is like me among the elim?') … in which a writer, with himself in mind, is getting carried away!"

147 Torleif Elgvin, et al., *Qumran Cave 4 XV: Sapiential Texts, Part 1*, DJD 20 (Oxford: Clarendon Press, 1997), 1–30.

148 DJD 20:20–21.

4QInstruction.[149] Pfann and Kister understand this document as addressed to "novices" who are "dawning" out of darkness and into the light.[150] They suggest parallels with 1QS (cf. VI 13) and conclude that these are initiates in their probationary period. Hempel notes that while this is possible there is no clear justification for the interpretation of the "sons of Dawn" (בני שחר) as a designation for initiates.[151] She concludes that "sons of Dawn" relate to "sons of light" without necessarily denoting the process of initiation into the community.[152]

After the opening title of 4Q298 the *maśkîl* follows a pattern of first-person speech. He appeals to the authority of his speech when he admonishes his audience to take heed of all that issues forth from his lips (l. 3). In the only other large fragment of this scroll (3–4 ii) first-person speech continues (ll. 8–10) when the *maśkîl* says that he will recount the appointed times (ימי תעודה) so that the addressees might know the end of the ages (קץ עולמות) and former things (קדמוניות). In 4Q298 3–4 ii, as seen in 4QInstruction, the "wise ones" and "men of understanding" are encouraged by a *maśkîl* to "increase learning" (הוסיפו לקח).

Another composition concerned with a *maśkîl* is the Songs of the Sabbath Sacrifice. This document consists of thirteen songs that were to be used in a liturgical cycle. As a liturgical document, the *maśkîl* is depicted as leading praise in the heavenly sanctuary and blessing the angels; the sage and his community enter into heavenly worship around the throne of God. Although a number of qualities are associated with angelic beings, knowledge is the most prominent. Newsom describes that the "superiority of angelic praise arises from their more exalted understanding of divine mysteries."[153] Although the Self-Glorification Hymn and the Songs of the Sabbath Sacrifice do not depict

---

149   DJD 20:18 the editors label of 4QInstruction as "sectarian" which is misleading: "this section echoes in both style and content other sectarian works such as 1 and 4QMysteries, 1 and 4QInstruction, and 4QSapiential Works B–C, as well as several hymns in 1 and 4QHodayot." משכיל appears in Yaḥad literature as the title of the instructor of the Sons of Light in 1QS I 1; III 13; IX 12, 21; 1QM I 1; 4Q421 ("Ways of Righteousness") 1 ii 10; in CD XIII 7–8 the overseer of the camp "enlightens" the community in God's ways (המבקר למחנה ישכיל את הרבים במעשי אל).

150   DJD 20:17.

151   Hempel, "The Qumran Sapiential Texts," 293.

152   Equally as possible is that "sons of Dawn" relates to their liturgical practices, see Josephus (*War* 2:128) "before sunrising they speak not a word about profane matters, but put up certain prayers which they have received from their forefathers, as if they made a supplication for its rising"; cf. Hippolytus (*Philos.* 9.21), Philo on the Theraputae (*Contempl. Life* 3.27).

153   Newsom, *Songs of the Sabbath Sacrifice*, 30.

the *maśkîl's* relationship to angels in the same way, they both find access to revelation and authority vis-à-vis their relationship to them. 4QInstruction possibly understands a *maśkîl* accessing revelation and mysteries by participating in the heavenly realm in the present, similarly to the Songs of the Sabbath Sacrifice.

The one addressed in 4Q418 81 + 81a is seen as one who mediates on behalf of men in his community as well as one who blesses holy angels; such intercession and participation is indicative of a *maśkîl's* role. Newsom describes the Rule of the Community as a document designed to assist the *maśkîl* as he readied himself for the role of instructing community members.[154] At the end of the Rule of the Community the duties and spiritual profile of the *maśkîl* are presented. She describes the *maśkîl* as "a figure who can be described not only as an apotheosis of sectarian selfhood but of the sect itself."[155] As such, he is a model for sectarian identity and master of revealed wisdom and knowledge. He embodies the values and commitments expressed and he is a template for the other members.

Joseph Angel builds upon Newsom's insights about the *maśkîl* in his research on the Songs of the Sage (4Q510–511). This composition is introduced as an exorcistic text and, Angel notes, that while the *maśkîl's* speech serves to ward off demons, it also functioned to "transmit vital knowledge *about* ritual participants *to* ritual participants."[156] For Angel too the *maśkîl* is a "*template* with which the worshipers were to identify" and the embodiment of their ideals.[157] Instruction to an exalted figure in 4Q418 81 + 81a may be more than an expression of identification with the *maśkîl*, it may be the application of a "template" by the speaker to other members of the community. Moreover, the distinction between "teacher" and "student" by the terms, respectively, משכיל and מבין, may also be misleading as the boundaries between these two are seen as somewhat permeable.[158]

---

154 Newsom, *The Self as Symbolic Space*, 187.
155 Newsom, *The Self as Symbolic Space*, 189.
156 Angel, "Community," 26, italics his.
157 Angel, "Community," 26, italics mine.
158 Leo G. Perdue, "Mantic Sages in the Ancient Near East, Israel, Judaism, and the Dead Sea Scrolls," in *Prophecy after the Prophets? The Contribution of the Dead Sea Scrolls to the Understanding of Biblical and Extra-biblical Prophecy*, ed. Kristin De Troyer & Armin Lange, CBET 52 (Leuven: Peeters, 2009), 166–174 argues that mantic sages (נבון, מבין, משכיל חכם) in Qumran literature pass along God's mysteries to members of the community.

3.1 Summary of Maśkîl *in 4QInstruction and Other Qumran Discoveries*

A comparison of terms found in 4Q418 222 + 221 and 238 with other documents from Qumran that are interested in a *maśkîl* further demonstrates the likelihood that 4QInstruction begins with first-person speech identified with a *maśkîl*.

Maśkîl & related terms in 4QInstruction (4Q418 222 + 221, 238)	Terms related to Maśkîl in other Qumran texts (+ Hymnic texts)[159]
משכיל in opening address	4QSᵇ 1 i 1 (מדרש למשכיל) 1QHᵃ XXV 34 (למשכיל מזמור) ["Recension A"] 4Q298 1–2 i 1 (דברי משכיל)
משכיל + first-person pronouns	4Q510 4 (אני משכיל) 1QHᵃ XX 14–16 (אני משכיל) cf. 4QHᵃ 8 ii 17
להבין כול פותיים	1QHᵃ V 12–13 (להבין פ'תאים) 4Q381 1 2 (ולפתים ויבינו?) 11Q5 XVIII 2–3 להודיע עוזו ותפארתו (לכול פותאים) [11QPsalmsᵃ]
מזל שפתי (cf. 4Q418 81 + 81a 1)	4Q511 63–64 ii 4 (דעת ותרומת מזל שפתי) 4Q491ᶜ i 10 (מזל שפתי מיא יכיל)
משפטי + מזל שפתי (cf. 4Q418 77)	4Q471ᶜ frgs 1–4 5–7
להוסיף לקח (cf. 4Q418 81 + 81a 17)	4Q298 3–4 ii (הוסיפו לקח) 4Q436 1 i 2 (יוסיפו לקח להתבונן) [Barki Nafshiᶜ]

In 4QInstruction, the *maśkîl's* relationship with the understanding ones is somewhat fluid, not exclusionary, and less hierarchical than that of the exalted speaker in the Self-Glorification Hymn. Similarities between the sage-speaker of 4QInstruction and that of the Self-Glorification Hymn may be explained as relating to the derivation of authority (i.e., the heavenly realm and a place

---

159   The parallel column here is exhaustive, no composition discovered at Qumran is excluded because they are not "*maśkîl*" or *hymnic* (ital.) texts.

among the angels); however, whereas this appeal to accessing wisdom allows the speaker in the Self-Glorification Hymn to ask, "who is like me?" in 4QInstruction the addressee can become like the speaker—a *maśkîl*. The place of a sage within 4QInstruction's community is starkly different than in the Self-Glorification Hymn: (1) when 4QInstruction's speaker identifies himself with his audience, this indicates that he shares common characteristics with them (4Q418 55 3–4); (2) this inclusivity is also apparent when a student may become a sage himself (4Q416 2 ii 12b–17); and (3) underscoring these points is that there are multiple *maśkilîm* (4Q418 81 + 81a 17).

Alex Jassen analyzes Yaḥad literature and describes various "arenas in which sapiential revelation was experienced." Particularly relevant here are CD and the Teacher Hymns (1QHᵃ) where the Teacher of Righteousness is identified "as the most prominent practitioner of sapiential revelation." In the Rule of the Community the *maśkîl* seems to be placed in a similar context as the Teacher. However, in contrast to the Treatise on the Two Spirits, the Community Hymns "underscore the democratization of sapiential revelation" in that the Sons of Truth are also recipients. Jassen observes that the Community Hymns are particularly important because they may reflect more general tendencies within the Yaḥad community and represent the "theological ethos of the community at large."[160] This study of 4QInstruction is concerned not only with questions about who has access to sapiential revelation, but also how one becomes a prominent practitioner of it. The view of the would-be student-sage emerging here provides the opportunity to assess 4QInstruction's own "democratization of sapiential revelation" alongside CD's, the Teacher Hymns', and the Rule of the Community's own. The degree to which 4QInstruction is inclusive, a term preferred to "democratic," becomes even more prominent in the conclusions of Chapters 2 and 3 where determinism and revelation are studied.

In the preceding three sections, we explored first-person speech as it relates to a *maśkîl*, this was followed by an analysis of other occurrences of *maśkîl* in 4QInstruction, and finally we examined how the *maśkîl* in 4QInstruction compares with other *maśkilîm* found in Qumran discoveries. 4Q418 81 + 81a 1–14 never refer to the exalted figure explicitly as a *maśkîl*; however, these lines are the most substantive in 4QInstruction that detail the activities of a sage. While this column is already discussed as relating to a sage's activities, the description of becoming a sage with the designation "firstborn" in 4Q416 2 ii and the appointment of the figure in 4Q418 81 + 81a as "firstborn" establish how this figure came to be a *maśkîl*.

---

160   Alex P. Jassen, *Mediating the Divine: Prophecy and Revelation in the Dead Sea Scrolls and Second Temple Judaism*, STDJ 68 (Leiden: Brill, 2007), 374.

4   Addressee as *Maśkîl* in 4Q418 81 + 81a Lines 1–14

4Q418 81 + 81a 1–14 form a distinct unit and are written, mostly, in direct speech
that may be organized into six stanzas, each beginning with the statement
"and you." Line 5 of this pericope came into focus in § 2.1. where the "firstborn
son" and "only child" of 4Q416 2 ii are seen to relate to the *mēvîn*'s potential
to become a *maśkîl*. In light of that relationship, 4Q418 81 + 81a 1–14 may be
returned to as a passage addressed to a figure who is a sage and is instructed in
this role. Moreover, in § 2.3. the final lines of this fragment (4Q418 81 + 81a 15–
20) were considered because multiple *maśkilîm* are mentioned. That the one
addressed in lines 15–20 is no longer the same figure as in preceding lines has
been adduced by the change from simply ואתה ("and you") to אתה מבין ("and you
understanding one," l. 15). Such a transition, or at least one so stark, is unlikely to
occur. The mis-translation of "wisdom of hands" as referring to manual labour
has contributed significantly to the perception that this is a different *mēvîn*.

First-person forms occur in line 6, which have been accounted for in critical editions as speech attributed to God. Rey and Qimron offer theoretical
reconstructions of the beginning part of this speech in the lacuna at the end
of line 5. However, neither the speech found at the beginning of line 6, nor
the reconstructions of Rey and Qimron, are a citation of scripture; indeed, in
4QInstruction there are no instances of scriptural citation with the exception
of one unconvincing theoretical reading in 4Q416 2 iii 21–iv 1.[161] Instead of an
instance of scriptural citation this is indirect speech, which affirms the status of
the addressee by divine voice. Third-person singular subjects of verbs in line 5
transition to first-person speech where God assures the firstborn and most holy
one that "I will give my good things to you."

4Q418 81 + 81a lines 1–14 (4Q418 81a [single underline]; comp. 4Q423 8 1–4 [dou-
ble underline], **overlap**), Transcription and Translation:[162]

[במזל]   0

שפתיכה פתח מקור לברך קדושים ואתה כמקור עולם הלל שׁ[מו מא]זֿ הבדילכה   1
מכול

רוח בשר ואתה הבדל מכול אשר שנא והנזר מכול תעבות נَפֿَשׁ] כי[אֿ הוא עשה כול   2

---

161   See Benjamin Wold, "Genesis 2–3 in Early Christianity and 4QInstruction," *DSD* 23/3 (2016):
         329–346.
162   See esp. DJD 34:300–301; Tigchelaar, *To Increase Learning*, 230–231; Goff, *4QInstruction*,
         239–240; Rey, *4QInstruction*, 307–310 כי אמר אברככה (ll. 5b–6 "[*for He said, 'I will bless
         you*] and my good things I will give to you'"); theoretical reconstruction in ll. 5–7 here are
         those of Qimron, *Dead Sea Scrolls*, 2:166.

ויורישם איש נחלתו והוא חלקכה ונחלתכה בתוך בני אדם ובנ֗חלתו המשילכֿה ואתה 3

בזה כבדהו בהתקדשכה לו כאשר שמכה לקדוש קודשים163 לכול תֿבל ובכול] 4
מ[לֿ]אכיו[

הפיל גורלכה וכבודכה הרבה מואדה וישימכה לו בכור164 ב[ניו ויואמר] לֿ[כה בכורי 5
אתה[

וטובתֿי לכה אתן ואתה להלוא לכה טוֿבֿ ובאמונתו הלך תמיד] והוא יברך את כול] 6

מעשיכה ואתה דרוש משפטיו מיד כול יריבֿבֿה בכול מוֿ[ם]○] בכול לבבכה[7

אהבהו ובחסד עוֿלֿם וברחמים על כול שומרי דברו זֿקנאתו[8

ואתה שכֿלֿ] פֿ[תח לכה ובאוצרו המשילכה ואיפת אמת פֿ'קד]ה 9

אתכה המה ובידכה להשיב אף מאנשי רצון ולפקוד עֿלֿ] 10

עמכה בֿטֿרֿם תקח נחלתכה מידו כבד קדושיו ובט[רם 11

פתח] מ[קֿ]וֿר כול קדֿוֿשים וכול הנקרא לשמו קדושיֿ]ם 12

עם כול קצֿים הדרֿ֗ פארתו למטעת עוֿ]לם 13

[○ תבֿלֿ בֿוֿ יֿתהלכו כול נוחלי ארץ כי בשמ]ים 14

o [... by the pouring out of] 1 your lips open up a spring to bless the holy
ones.

And you, as an everlasting spring, praise His [name,
sin]ce He separated you from every 2 fleshly spirit;

And you, keep separate from everything that He hates,
and keep apart from all the abominations of the soul;
[Fo]r He has made everyone,
3 and has given to each man his own inheritance,
but He is your portion and your inheritance among the children of
mankind,
[and over] His [in]heritance He has set you in authority.

And you, 4 honor Him in this: by consecrating yourself to Him,
just as He has appointed you as a most holy one [over all the] earth,
and among all [His a]n[gels] 5 He has cast your lot,
and has magnified your glory greatly,
He has appointed you for Himself as a first-born among [his sons,]
[and He said] to [you: "you are my firstborn] 6 and I will give my good
things to you."

---

163   4Q423 8 3 has variant reading: לק[דֿש קודשים ("to sanctify the holy ones").

164   Par. 4Q423 8 4 appears to read: כבכור ("as a firstborn"); DJD 34:525 this word looks more
like כבוכך, the first scribe likely wrote כבוד which was later corrected to כבור because
there is no scribal mark (dot) to cancel the first *kaf*.

And you, do His good things not belong to you?
In faithfulness to Him walk continually,
[and He will bless all your] 7 your deeds.

And you, seek His justice from the hand of each of your opponents,
and with all [... with all you heart] 8 love Him,
and with eternal loving-kindness,
and with mercy for all those who keep His words,
and his zeal [   ]

9 And you, He has [op]ened up insight for you,
and He has placed you in authority over His treasure,
and a true measure is appoint[ed
[   ] 10 are with you,
and it is in your hand to turn away anger from the men of good pleasure,
and to appoint upon[   ] 11 Your people.

Before you take your inheritance from His hand, glorify His holy ones,
and bef[ore   ] 12 open [a spring *of* all the ho]ly ones,
and everyone who is called by His name,
holy [ones   ] 13 during all periods,
the majesty of His glory for an ever[lasting] plantation
[   ] 14 [   ] of the world,
in it all those who will inherit the land walk,
for in he[aven   ]

The elevated status of the addressee is evident throughout these lines, he is: (1)
a liturgical leader who blesses "holy ones" (l. 1, 12); (2) separated out from the
"spirit of flesh" and told that God is his portion and inheritance (ll. 2–3, 11); (3)
in authority over both the "sons of *adam*" (l. 3) and God's "treasure" (l. 9); (4)
appointed לקדוש קודשים (l. 4 "most holy one");[165] (5) a firstborn to whom God
gives his best things (ll. 5–6); and (6) an intercessor who turns wrath away from
those in his community (l. 10).[166]

---

165   Goff, *4QInstruction*, 248–249 "The exact spelling of the phrase occurs nowhere else in the
      Hebrew Bible or Second Temple Jewish literature" and the phrase קדוש קודשים of line 4
      is reasonably understood as a variant spelling of קודש קדשים. Elgvin, "Analysis," 136 com-
      ments that it is best understood with a superlative sense "most holy one."

166   Tigchelaar, *To Increase Learning*, 235 "the statement that 'you can turn away anger' from
      the אנשי רצון, 'the men of good pleasure', may indicate that the addressee of this section
      is some kind of intercessory leader of a community."

The third stanza, in which the addressee is placed as a firstborn to God, and thus becomes a sage by merit of faithful pursuit and observance of the mystery of existence, also relates to other appointments the addressee holds, ones that occur in four parallel hemistichs that are complimentary and to some extent synonymous. In this stanza, the one addressed should consecrate himself to God (l. 4a) because he: (1) is appointed a most holy one (l. 4b); (2) has his lot cast among angelic beings (ll. 4c–5a); (3) has his glory multiplied (l. 5b); and (4) is made a firstborn (l. 5c), which is then reinforced vis-à-vis indirect speech (l. 5d). While reconstructions of line 4c differ they all agree that a reference to angels occurs here, other proposed reconstructions of this line, other than the one above, are: ובכול]א[ל]ים ("among all the gods [= angels]"),[167] and ובכול]מ[ל]אכים ("among all the angels").[168] If being set among angels is similar to becoming a firstborn and most holy one, then this is not a statement limited to assurances of future glory with them, but rather about an aspect of the sage's present occupation.[169]

Assessing how this *maśkîl* relates to angelic beings is crucial to situating him alongside *maśkilîm* in other compositions. In 4Q418 81+81a 4c–5a the addressee's "lot" (גורל) is "cast" (root נפל) with the angels. 4QInstruction is distinctively uninterested in the term גורל with only one occurrence elsewhere (4Q418 86 2), which is preserved with no remaining context.[170] Being placed among the angels is expressed with the *Hiphil* perfect of נפל (lit. "he caused you to be set"); in the previous hemistichs the addressee is "placed" (שים *Qal* perf.) as a most holy one; his glory is "multiplied" (הרבה *Hiphil* perf.); and he is again "placed" (וישימכה *Qal* waw cons.) as a firstborn. Therefore, verbal forms straightforwardly make these actions past and completed; moreover, the activity of blessing angels in the present further reinforces the view that the practice of venerating is taking place now.[171] However, if "lot" were to be read in light

---

167   DJD 34:300; Qimron, *Dead Sea Scrolls*, 2:166.

168   Rey, *4QInstruction*, 307; Goff, *4QInstruction*, 239. Following here Tigchelaar, *To Increase Learning*, 231 בכול]מ[ל]אכיו].

169   Collins finds little evidence for "realized eschatology" in 4Q418 81+81a and is convinced that participation with the angels is solely future oriented, see Collins, "The Eschatologizing of Wisdom," 58; cf. Angel, *Otherworldly and Eschatological*, 77.

170   DJD 34:314 comment that "גורל is of course one of the frequent components of the Qumran vocabulary but is extremely rare in 4Q415ff. (only two times, in contrast with the eighty-one instances elsewhere in the 1–11Q texts)" and this suggests that 4QInstruction generally has "no especially sectarian or predestinarian affinities."

171   Goff, *4QInstruction*, 250 "The term 'lot' reflects a deterministic mindset, asserting that this dispensation is part of the inheritance God established for him" and (250, fn. 32) that this

of the Treatise on the Two Spirits, then it may be seen to refer to divisions of humanity and one's predetermined place among either the Sons of Light or Darkness (1QS IV 26 להפיל גורלות לכול חי). However, neither "light" and "dark" nor any other juxtaposed binary categories feature in 4QInstruction, this composition is commonly understood not to belong to the Yaḥad, and "lot" does not shape a deterministic outlook in this composition. Nonetheless, there is an intriguing parallel between 4Q418 81 + 81a 4c–5a and the Rule of the Blessing (1QSb). When the *maśkîl* in the Rule of the Blessing blesses the sons of Zadok (1QSb III 22) there is clearly a future orientation, which sets the context soon thereafter (1QSb IV 25–26) when they are said to serve in the "temple of the kingdom" and their "lot is cast with the angels of the presence" (ומפיל גורל עם מלאכי פנים).

Unlike the Rule of the Blessing III–IV, neither the context of 4Q418 81 + 81a 4–5 nor the verbs reflect future orientation. Therefore, an interpretation of line 4c may be better informed by three other passages: 1QHᵃ XIX, 1QHᵃ XIV, and 4Q511 2 i (4QSongs of the Sageᵇ). In the Thanksgiving Hymns having one's lot cast with the holy ones expresses becoming part of the children of God's good favor to whom are revealed the secret counsel of God's truth, 1QHᵃ XIX 12–18 read.[172]

> 12 but in your goodness is abundant forgiveness, and your compassion is for all the children of your good favor [בני רצונכה]. Truly, you have made known to them the secret counsel of your truth [בסוד אמתכה] 13 and given them insight into your wonderful mysteries [רזי פלאכה]. For the sake of your glory you have purified a mortal from sin, so that he may sanctify himself 14 for you from all impure abominations and from faithless guilt, so that he might be united with the children of your truth [בני אמתך] and in the lot with 15 your holy ones [ובגורל עם קדושכה], so that a corpse-infesting maggot might be raised up from the dust to the council of [your] t[ruth] [לסוד אמתכה], and from a spirit of perversion to the understanding that comes from you, 16 and so that he may take (his) place [ולהתיצב במעמד] before you with the everlasting host [צבא עד] and the [eternal] spirit[s], and so that he may be renewed together with all that i[s] 17 and will be and with those who have knowledge in a common rejoicing [ועם ידעים ביחד רנה]. *vac* [...] 18 [And, as for me,] I thank you, O my God, I exalt you, O my rock.

---

is similar to "[t]he highly deterministic Treatise on the Two Spirits" where "God has 'cast the lots' of all people (1QS 4:26)" as well as 1QS XI 7–8 (cf. 4Q258 XII 4) where God "has given them an inheritance in the lot of the holy ones" (ינחילם בגורל קדושים).

172   Schuller & Newsom, *The Hodayot*, 60–61.

To be in the lot of the holy ones is to be lifted from dismal, sinful, fleshly mortality (cf. separation from the "fleshly spirit" in 4Q418 81 + 81a 1–2) to a place with the righteous community to whom are revealed knowledge of truth and wonderful mysteries. In 1QHᵃ XIX 14–15 being united with the children of truth is to be placed with the holy ones with whom they have knowledge in common. Being lifted from sin and set with the holy ones is a present condition with eternal consequences and the psalmist rejoices on both counts. Indeed, elsewhere in the Thanksgiving Hymns a time is described when God will raise up "a remnant in your inheritance" (1QHᵃ XIV 11) who are survivors from among his people. In this period of restoration, the "people of God's counsel" are in the midst of humankind and recite God's wonderful deeds without ceasing (1QHᵃ XIV 14), which results in the nations acknowledging God's truth. In 1QHᵃ XIV 16 the people of God's counsel have a "common lot with the angels of the presence, without an intermediary between them" (כול אנשי עצתכה ובגורל יחד עם מלאכי פנים ואין מליץ בנים). This instance of "lot" may communicate assurance of eternal life, but it is also about what it means to be a holy congregation who enjoys a place in God's "secret counsel" (1QHᵃ XIV 15; סודכה) where there is no intermediary between the righteous remnant, who ceaselessly praises God, and the heavenly throne room. Indeed, in 4Q417 1 i 20–21 (cf. § 2.2.) it is within their counsel (סוד) where the mystery of existence is pursued.

4QSongs of the Sageᵃ⁻ᵇ (4Q510–511) are a Yaḥad collection of magical hymns addressed to a *maśkîl* who, Bilhah Nitzan expresses, "wages war against evil by singing God's praises."[173] In 4Q511 35 2–3 the earthly community is correlated with the heavenly temple: "Among the holy ones God makes (some) hol[y] for himself like an everlasting sanctuary" (ובקדושים יקדי[ש] אלוהים לו למקדש עולמים). Angel observes in these lines a "homology between heavenly and earthly worshippers."[174] Indeed, in 4QSong of the Sage "the brilliance of God's knowledge is shared with the heavenly being and select humans." This divine knowledge shines in the *maśkîl*'s heart (4Q511 18 ii 7–8), it is placed within him (4Q511 28–29 3), and it is by this knowledge that the sage terrifies bastard spirits and demons (4Q510 1 4–5).[175] Several highly fragmentary passages indicate that this *maśkîl* dwells in the shelter of Shaddai (4Q511 8), righteous individuals are described as angelic priests (4Q510 1 8–9; cf. 4Q403 1 i), and the earthly community (i.e., "Israel") join the "lot" of God with the angelic beings (4Q511 2 i 7–8): "[God] placed [I]srael in [t]welve camps of [his] holy ones [so that they

---

173 Nitzan, *Qumran Prayer*, 237.

174 Joseph Angel, *Otherworldly and Eschatological Priesthood in the Dead Sea Scrolls*, STDJ 86 (Leiden: Brill, 2010), 127.

175 Angel, *Otherworldly*, 124–125.

may walk and come into] the lot of God with the ang[els of] the luminaries of

his glory" (שם [י]שראל [בש[נים עשר מחנות קדוש]יו ל[ה]תה[תה]ל[ד ולבוא ב]גורל אלוהים

עם מלא]כי [מאורות).[176] Having one's lot cast with angels is part of a much more complex depiction of a conjoined community of righteous humans and angelic beings.

Acquisition of mysteries and knowledge, as well as liturgical practices and worship, often involve notions of heavenly ascent and/or participation with the angels, not only in discoveries from Qumran such as the Rule of the Community (cf. 1QSa II 8–9; 1QSb IV 25–26), Thanksgiving Hymns, the War Scroll (1QM VII 4–6), and especially the Songs of the Sabbath Sacrifice, but also in "pseudepi-graphical" literature (e.g., Asc. Is. 8:17; 9:28, 33; Apoc. Abr. 17; Apoc. Zeph. 8:3–4), and early Christian literature (e.g., Col 2:8–23; Eph 4:8–10). In 4QInstruction God shares his knowledge with humans and angels (4Q418 55 8–9; cf. §1.1.) and the *maśkîl* in 4Q418 81 + 81a venerates angelic beings presently as superior pursuers of wisdom. To be seated among the angels in the present is for the sage to receive God's good things (l. 5d) and for insights to be opened to him (l. 9). Therefore, it is not unreasonable to interpret lines 4c–5a as the addressee participating with the angels presently, as do *maśkilîm* in the literature of the period (esp. Self-Glorification Hymn), as part of sharing God's knowledge.

Puech first reconstructed the beginning of 4Q418 81 + 81a as [במזל] שפתיכה פתח מקור, which is justified not only by the combination of מזל ("outpouring") and שפה ("lips") elsewhere in the document (4Q416 7 3; 4Q418 222 + 221) but also in several other texts from Qumran, including ones that are interested in a *maśkîl* (4Q511 63–64 ii 4; 4Q471[b] 1–4 5–6; 4Q491[c] i 10). Outside of these occurrences, the "opening of lips" is only found elsewhere in the Thanksgiving Hymns (1QH[a] XVI 37; XIX 8, cf. XXVI 5), in the Rule of the Blessing (1QSb III 27), and in nearly every passage discussed above where one's lot is cast with angels (1QH[a] XIV 11–16; XIX 12–18; 1QSb III–IV; excluding 1QH[a] XXVI).[177] The particu-larities of the first-person speech in 4Q418 222 + 221 and 238 are ascribed to the "you" of 4Q418 81 + 81a. However, one may question whether פתח in line 1 is used as an imperative, as it is in line 12; if it is, then it would be an admonition to open a spring by a speech act.[178] In regard to the opening of lips, Stuckenbruck ques-

---

176 Following the transcription and translation of Angel, *Otherworldly*, 126; cf. reconstruction of Nitzan, *Qumran Prayer*, 261.

177 Puech, "Les fragments," 110; cf. Rey, *4QInstruction*, 307.

178 Cf. Philo (*Sacrifices* 64) where God is a spring who gives understanding: "those men know who give to their pupils arts, and lessons in arts: for their case is not like that of men who pour water into a vessel, they are not in a moment able to fill their minds with the lessons which have been brought before them. But when the fountain of wisdom, that is to say,

tions whether the word כול in line 12 (פתח מקור כול קדושים) should be read as "open a spring *for* all of the holy ones" or "*of* all the holy ones."[179] He convincingly concludes that it is the latter and as such "the community is allowed to receive or participate in the fountain which belongs to the angels."[180] In line 1b the addressee is also called an "eternal spring" (מקור עולם; cf. "eternal planting" l. 13); the elevated figure joins with the angelic community in the present and looks forward to eternal life and the continuation of these activities.[181] Line 11 admonishes the addressee to honor the holy ones before taking his "inheritance," and according to line 3 God is his "portion" and "inheritance." Since God cannot be inherited, the synonymous coupling of "portion" (חלק) with "inheritance" (l. 3) offers some clarification: the exalted addressee is apportioned a place with God in his domain.

When 4Q418 81 + 81a 1–14 describe the addressee as "holy" and a "son," this is language that, at times, carries priestly connotations.[182] While several suggestions about the possible movement and milieu behind 4QInstruction have been suggested, there is no convincing evidence that priests or priestly concerns are widespread in the document.[183] Strugnell and Harrington consider

---

God (ἡ πηγὴ τῆς σοφίας, ὁ θεός), gives knowledge of the sciences to the race of mankind, he gives it to them without any limitation of time. But they, as being disciples of the only wise Being, and being competent by nature, quickly accomplish the discovery of the things which they seek to understand."

179 Loren T. Stuckenbruck, "'Angels' and 'God': Exploring the Limits of Early Jewish Monotheism," in *Early Jewish and Christian Monotheism*, ed. Loren T. Stuckenbruck & Wendy E.S. North, JSNTSup 263 (New York/London: T & T Clark, 2004), 45–70 at 65.

180 Stuckenbruck, "'Angels' and 'God,'" 65; cf. Angel, *Otherworldly*, 77 who also agrees with Stuckenbruck.

181 Stuckenbruck, "'Angels' and 'God,'" 66. Note similarities of this stanza (ll. 11b–14) with Matthew's Sermon on the Mount, esp. Matt 5:5 describes that "the meek shall inherit the earth" and line 14 also refers to inheriting the earth/land. Cf. the Book of Watchers (1En. 5:7) where the righteous likewise "inherit the earth." "Inheritance" in these lines of 4QInstruction is used in relationship to reward and apportioning of a place within a community.

182 Armin Lange, "The Determination of Fate by the Oracle of the Lot in the Dead Sea Scrolls, the Hebrew Bible and Ancient Mesopotamian Literature," in *Sapiential, Liturgical and Poetical texts from Qumran: Proceedings of the Third Meeting of the International Organization for Qumran Studies, Oslo 1998, Published in Memory of Maurice Baillet*, ed. Daniel K. Falk, Florentino García Martínez & Eileen M. Schuller, STDJ 35 (Leiden: Brill, 2000), 39–48 at 40, finds other priestly connotations in the expectation that the addressee praises God at an everlasting spring in l. 1 (40 n. 5 cites Ezek 47:1–12; Pss 36:10; 46:5; 65:10). He also finds priestly connotations in the use of the term נזר (l. 2), which he takes as an allusion to the motif of priestly praises of God in the Temple at an eternal well.

183 As indicated by Lange, *Weisheit und Prädestination*, 45–92 suggests a temple setting; cf.

4QInstruction to be directed to Judean society in broad terms.[184] Tigchelaar views 4QInstruction as directed to different groups in society and possibly some among the understanding ones were priestly descendants.[185] Goff similarly concludes that some among the community may have been priests, but this is not a community of priests.[186] Elgvin is explicit that the addressee in 4Q418 81+81a is not actually a priest.[187] Angel views the priestly privileges in 4Q418 81+81a as "non-literal and spiritualized."[188] The ones addressed in 4QInstruction do not form a monolithic group of students who all enjoy the same status and this is exemplified most clearly in the unique stature of the addressee in 4Q418 81+81a. Reading 4QInstruction as an address to a variety of students who vary in standing, each having it within their remit to become sages themselves, resolves the unique address in 4Q418 81+81a. This column offers instruction specifically to those at the pinnacle of their pursuit of wisdom. The speaker is concerned with a spectrum of pupils, from this elevated fig-

---

John J. Collins, *Jewish Wisdom in the Hellenistic Age*, OTL (Louisville, KY: Westminster, 1997), 117–127 views that the community consists of initiates to a movement.

184   DJD 34:36 "The word is addressed, then, not to any closed community like that at Qumran, nor to any earlier theologically cognate population, but to a typical junior sage (מבין) who receives advice appropriate for his needs in every stage of his life (e.g., the priesthood, administration, marriage) and in various professions." Cf. DJD 34:20–21 where the priestly or quasi-priestly authority of the addressee in 4Q418 81+81a is discussed, the editors question: "Is it literally an Aaranoid status which is intended here, or just something analogous to the special lot of the Aaronoids?"

185   Tigchelaar, *To Increase Learning*, 236, 248 summarizes the difference between his view and that of the editors: "the מבינים [for the editors] are all of priestly decent but of various social standing and function" whereas for Tigchelaar "the מבינים could be anyone in society, and that the text addresses different addressees; amongst which priests"; cf. Tigchelaar, "The Addressees of 4QInstruction," 62–75.

186   Goff, *4QInstruction*, 247; cf. Matthew J. Goff, *Discerning Wisdom: The Sapiential Literature of the Dead Sea Scrolls*, VTSup 116 (Leiden: Brill, 2007), 38–39 comments that ritual purity and liturgical prayer are absent in the document; however, there is interest in cultic and halakhic issues in it. He finds in 4Q418 103 ii 3 and 4Q423 3 4–5 evidence that the *mēvîn* is encouraged to participate in the Temple cultus, although one might speculate why 4QInstruction never uses the tetragram, which may indicate heightened reverence in light of abuse.

187   Elgvin, "Priestly Sages?" 82–83 addresses Lange's claims that cultic practices are present in 4QInstruction. Torleif Elgvin, "The Mystery to Come: Early Essene Theology of Revelation," in *Qumran Between the Old and New Testaments*, ed. Frederick H. Cryer & Thomas L. Thompson, JSOTSup 290 (Sheffield: Sheffield Academic Press, 1998), 113–150, argues for a similar milieu to 1 Enoch.

188   Angel, *Otherworldly*, 77.

ure down to "simple ones" and even the foolish who are firmly enjoined not
to give up on the arduous task of living wisely. However, the feminine address
in 4Q415 2 ii, which at times is cited in support of 4QInstruction as an address
to a diverse audience, is probably, in light of the composition's misogyny, an
instance of indirect speech within instruction on how a community leader
should teach women.

Community members in 4QInstruction are to strive scrupulously after the
mystery of existence, acquisition of these mysteries is to be lived out, and when
actualized wisdom is achieved, one joins the ranks with other *maśkilîm*. These
community leaders and teachers are exemplars who model community ideals. When priestly language infrequently occurs it does not necessarily indicate
priestly descent, other explanations are available such as the usurpation of
priestly privileges, which would align with the inclusionary and relatively non-
hierarchical views found in 4QInstruction. Armin Lange first drew attention to
the priestly connotations of 4Q418 81 + 81a by focusing on the use of Num 18:20
in lines 3b–5a.

Num 18:20	4Q418 81 + 81a 3
וַיֹּאמֶר יְהוָה אֶל־אַהֲרֹן בְּאַרְצָם לֹא תִנְחָל וְחֵלֶק לֹא־יִהְיֶה לְךָ בְּתוֹכָם אֲנִי חֶלְקְךָ וְנַחֲלָתְךָ בְּתוֹךְ בְּנֵי יִשְׂרָאֵל	ויורישם איש נחלתו והוא חלקכה ונחלתכה בתוך בני אדם ובנחלתו המשילכה
Then the LORD said to Aaron: You will have no allotment in their land, nor will you have any share among them; I am your share and your possession among the Israelites.	He has given to each man his own inheritance, but He is your portion and your inheritance among the children of mankind, [and over] His inheritance He has set you in author-ity.

Lange suggests that interest in Aaron and Aaronite priests in Num 18:20 indicates that 4QInstruction too is describing, perhaps metaphorically, the election of such priests.[189] The non-explicit use of Num 18:20 may echo priest-

---

189 Lange, "Determination of Fate," 41; cf. Armin Lange, "In Diskussion mit dem Tempel: Zur
Auseinandersetzung zwischen Kohelet und weisheitlichen Kreisen am Jerusalemer Tempel," in *Qohelet in the Context of Wisdom*, ed. A. Schoors, BETL 136 (Leuven: Peeters, 1998),
139 where he discusses l. 7 as a command to an elected one who is to interpret God's law,
and is thus a priestly function.

hood, but in fact this allusion in 4Q418 81 + 81a 3 transforms its meaning. First, when 4QInstruction uses Num 18:20 the phrase "sons of Israel" is replaced with "sons of mankind." Second, whereas Num 18:20 is concerned to address why the Levites have not received a portion and inheritance like the other tribes (i.e., "sons of Israel"), 4Q418 81 + 81a 3 is interested in the addressee's inheritance among "humanity." Finally, there are priestly connotations found in the addressee becoming קדוש קודשים ("most holy one"), which likely alludes to holy of holies, and yet this is in the whole "world" (תבל).[190] 4Q418 81 + 81a pushes boundaries: the *maśkîl* in these lines may draw upon priestly language, but unlike an Aaronite priest who is elected as representative of the sons of Israel, it is by merit that this sage has become a most holy one with authority extending to all peoples.[191] Indeed, this reworking of Numbers functions to universalize the role of the sage. By reinterpreting priestly election the role of the *maśkîl* is extended, in theory, even to the nations.[192] Harrington and Strugnell pose a series of questions about what this transformation of Num 18:20 means:

---

190 Lange, "Determination of Fate," 40 translates the phrase as "the holiest of holy things," and interprets it as describing the election of Aaron or Aaronite priests. The majority prefer to translate לקדוש קודשים in the superlative sense "most holy" (cf. fn. 165) and there is some agreement that it likely alludes to the holy of holies; cf. Tigchelaar, *To Increase Learning*, 231; Goff, *The Worldly and Heavenly*, 106; Rey, *4QInstruction*, 318–319; Angel, *Otherworldly and Eschatological*, 65; see Elgvin who considers the possible translation of this as an infinitive "to sanctify the holy ones" in *Analysis*, 136 (criticized by Tigchelaar, *To Increase Learning*, 233); cf. Elgvin's translation "set you as holy among the holy ones" in "Priestly Sages," 81; DJD 34:302 "He has appointed thee as a *Holy of Holies* [*over all the*] *earth*" although they comment on their preference for the superlative translation.

191 Rey, *4QInstruction*, 318 "Ce qui exprimait en Nb 18,20 l'élection particulière du lévite par rapport à l'élection plus globale d'Israël devient en 4QInstruction l'élection particulière du sage par rapport à toute l'humanité. Ce n'est plus "l'élu" au milieu d'Israël, mais "l'élu" au milieu de l'humanité. Le texte déplace la frontière de l'élection qui était jusqu'alors entre les fils d'Israël et les lévites vers une frontière qui se situe désormais entre tous les fils d'Adam et un "tu" qui est le lecteur." DJD 34:305 "[חלק ונחלה] need not imply a special privilege for the maven because of any priestly role of his (such a priestly role for him is not impossible, but only a few passages in 4Q415 ff. point that direction); certainly, the חלק ונחלה was related to his role as sage and had its effects for all humanity …". Cf. Ben Sira 3:20 ff. (e.g., in 3:22 "in that which you inherited/received understand and do not occupy yourself with hidden matters" [במה שהורשית התבונן ואין לך עסק בנסתרות]) seems to criticize apocalyptic visionaries. Truth for Ben Sira is fundamentally what one inherited (the ideal scribe in Sir 38:34–39:2 studies the scriptures intensively), for 4QInstruction one's inheritance relates to the רז נהיה.

192 Karina M. Hogan, *Theologies in Conflict in 4 Ezra: Wisdom Debate and Apocalyptic Solution*, JSJSup 130 (Leiden: Brill, 2008), 54.

And what does it signify that the sage's authority is no longer 'among the children of Israel' but 'among the sons of Adam/among mankind'? This *prima facie* remarkably bold claim to the universality of the maven's authority and to his authority in the international courts in which he is often described as serving—does this mean what on the surface it is saying? Nothing suggests a more minimalistic interpretation.[193]

The editors' emphasis on this bold claim finds its mark, but how it relates to "international courts" is questionable. His authority, and any judicial language surrounding it, probably refers instead to the intermediary function of the sage between: (1) "children of *mankind*" and "men of good pleasure," and (2) the heavenly realm. There is no sense that any of the *mᵉvinîm* or *maśkilîm* have authority in any secular sense. Questions about the universal character of 4QInstruction are also central to the chapters to follow. In Chapter 2 the universality of creation is argued: all of humanity is created with the ability to distinguish between good and evil as opposed to being created separately and predetermined as two peoples. Chapter 3 is concerned with the absence of thematized Torah in 4QInstruction and the universal character of the mystery of existence as revelation of the created order. In terms of hierarchy and authority, how the relationship between Torah and mysteries is understood has implications for evaluations of inclusivity and exclusivity and is a crucial component when viewing universality in this composition.

4.1   The Mēvîn's Place among Angels in 4Q416 2 iii Lines 8–12

4QInstruction exhibits a lively interest in angelic beings with at least eight different epithets used for them: קדושים (4Q417 1 i 17; 4Q418 81+81a 1, 12), צבא (4Q416 1 6–7), מלאכי קודש (4Q418 55 8), אילים (4Q418 69 ii 15), בני שמים (4Q418 69 ii 12–13), נוראים (4Q417 1 i 2), נדיבים (4Q416 2 iii 11), and perhaps אדונים (4Q416 2 iii 15). The addressee of 4Q418 81+81a presently has a place among the angels and partakes of the same spring as the holy ones. Human beings and angels both pursue knowledge and the steadfast nature of angelic beings is held up as a model (4Q418 55; 4Q418 69 ii). The Vision of Hagu passage (4Q417 1 i 13b–18; cf. Ch. 2 §1.1.2.) states that: "according to the pattern of the holy ones [קדושים] is *humanity's* fashioning" (l. 17). Despite different translations and interpretations of this pericope, in large part related to debates about whether all of humanity or just a "spiritual people" were created in this likeness, there is some consensus that this line refers to angelic beings taking part in creation in reference to

Genesis 1:26 ("come, let *us* make man in *our* image and in our likeness") and are, therefore, co-creators with God.[194] Therefore, the *mēvîn* is created in the likeness of angels, reveres them for their superiority, and participates with them in the act of seeking after knowledge and wisdom. This likeness also explains the affinity of human beings with angels and desire to emulate and join with them.

The term נדיבים is used in 4Q416 2 iii 11 where the addressee is said to have his head lifted from poverty and made to dwell with "noble ones." 4Q416 2 iii 8–12 preserve a distinct paragraph, although the theme of poverty is shared with other passages in the immediately surrounding context (4Q416 2 i–iv). In these columns are frequent reminders to the *mēvîn* that he is poor, admonitions that at times refer to material lacking, but also at times serve to remind him to remain humble and reject greedy pursuit of material gain (cf. § 2.3.).[195] At other times poverty functions as metaphor for the *mēvîn*'s own struggles to perfectly pursue wisdom in relationship to angelic beings.[196] The speaker draws attention to the addressee's poverty in this fragment, beginning in 4Q416 2 ii 20 and following. These reminders are formulated as: ואתה ראש ("you are poor," 4Q416 2 ii 20), אביון אתה ("you are poor," 4Q416 2 iii 8, 12), and זכור כי ראש אתה ("remember that you are poor," 4Q416 2 iii 2). There is one conditional state-

---

194   See esp. the original articulation by John J. Collins, "In the Likeness of the Holy Ones: The Creation of Humankind in a Wisdom Text from Qumran," in *The Provo International Conference*, 609–618.

195   Goff, *4QInstruction*, 2–27 at 26, "[t]he refrain 'you are poor' means not simply that he is materially poor but also that he should live in a way which is humble, simple and reverent"; Tigchelaar, "The Addressees," 62–65 considers "you are poor" as conditional; cf. Benjamin G. Wright III, "The Categories of Rich and Poor in the Qumran Sapiential Literature," in *Sapiential Perspectives*, 125–140; Heinz-Josef Fabry, "Die Armenfrömmigkeit in den qumranischen Weisheitstexten," in *Weisheit in Israel: Beiträge des Symposiums "Das Alte Testament und die Kultur der Moderne" anlässlich des 100. Geburtstags Gerhard von Rads (1901–1971), Heidelberg, 18.–21. Oktober 2001*, ed. David J.A. Clines, Hermann Lichtenberger & Hans Peter Müller, ATM 12 (Münster: Lit-Verlag, 2003), 163–209; Catherine M. Murphy, *Wealth in the Dead Sea Scrolls and in the Qumran Community*, STDJ 40 (Leiden: Brill, 2001), 163–210. Cf. Greco-Roman tradition where poverty is equated with freedom, William D. Desmond, *The Greek Praise of Poverty: Origins of Ancient Cynicism* (Notre Dame, IN: University of Notre Dame, 2006), esp. 143–168.

196   How poverty language is used metaphorically is presented in two different ways; Goff, *4QInstruction*, 25–26 sees this metaphorical sense as an encouragement for the *mēvîn* to "act like a 'poor' or 'humble' man" and that this is an "ethical ideal"; alternatively, Benjamin G. Wold, "Metaphorical Poverty in *Musar leMevin*," *JJS* 58/1 (2007): 140–153 I view some instances of poverty as a metaphor for the fatigable nature of human beings.

ment that likely refers to literal povery: ואם רש אתה ("if you are poor," 4Q416 2 iii 19). In column iii the twice occurring exhortation אביון אתה demarcates this pericope.

4Q416 2 iii lines 8–12 (par. 4Q418 9–10 lines 6–13 [single underline]), Transcription and Translation:[197]

8   שמׄחה <i>vacat</i> אביון אתה אל תתאו זׄוׄלׄתׄ נחלתכה ואל תתבלע בה פן תסיג

9   גבולכה ואׄם] [יׄשיבכה לכבודׄ בה התהלׄךׄ וברז [נ]הׄיׄה דרוש מולדיו ואׄז תדע

10 נחלתו ובצדק תתהלׄך כׄי יׄגׄיׄה אל ת[אר]הׄו בכׄיׄל דרכיכהׄ למכבדיכה תן הדר[198

11 ושמו הׄלׄל תמיד כי מראש הרים ראׄשכה ועם נדיבים הושיבכה ובנחלת

12 כבוד המשילכה רצׄונו שחר תמׄידׄ אביון אתה אל תאמרׄ רש אני ול[וא]

8 joy

vacat

You are poor, do not desire anything except your inheritance,

and do not be confused by it,

lest you move 9 your boundaries,

and if He has restored you to glory, walk in it,

and by the mystery of existence seek its origins/birthtimes,

and then you will know 10 its inheritance,

and in righteousness you will walk,

for God will shine His a[ppearance] in all of your ways.

To the ones honoring you give splendor,

11 and always praise His name,

for from poverty He lifted your head,

and with the nobles He made you to dwell,

and in the inheritance 12 of glory He placed you in authority,

diligently seek His good will always

vacat

You are poor, do not say, "I am poor and will n[ot] ..."

The term "nobles" (נדיבים) occurs five times in the manuscripts of 4QInstruction (here in 4Q416 2 iii 11; par. ms. 4Q418 9 11; 4Q415 2 i + 1 ii 7; 4Q418 149 2; 4Q418 177 5), and yet despite these other occurrences there is little material

---

197   DJD 34:110; Tigchelaar, *To Increase Learning*, 47–48; Rey, *4QInstruction*, 92; Goff, *4QInstruction*, 239–240; Qimron, *Dead Sea Scrolls*, 2:156.

198   In 4Q418 9 10 occurs dittography of line 9 in its entirety, the scribe erases it.

to help decipher the meaning of this word. No immediate context is available in 4Q415 2 i + 1 ii 7 and 4Q418 149 2.[199] 4Q418 177 5 preserves three words that may capture the same conundrum found in 4Q416 2 iii, namely being "poor" and "nobles," all that remains of this line is:]י אתה רש ונדיבים[∘ ("]you are poor and nobles ... ["). Another highly fragmentary occurrence is in 4Q416 6 2 where three words are preserved: אביון א[ת]ה ומֹלֹכֹ[ים] ("y[o]u are poor and king[s").[200] One may only conjecture whether 4Q418 177 and 4Q416 6 present the *mēvîn* as being lifted from poverty and enjoying a place among the nobles and kings in the same way that 4Q416 2 iii 11 does.

4Q416 2 iii 8–12 allude to 1Sam 2:8 (מֵקִים מֵעָפָר דָּל מֵאַשְׁפֹּת יָרִים אֶבְיוֹן לְהוֹשִׁיב) Ps 113:7–8 (מְקִימִי).[201] (עִם־נְדִיבִים וְכִסֵּא כָבוֹד יַנְחִלֵם כִּי לֵיהוָה מְצֻקֵי אֶרֶץ וַיָּשֶׁת עֲלֵיהֶם תֵּבֵל) recount Hannah's (מֵעָפָר דָּל מֵאַשְׁפֹּת יָרִים אֶבְיוֹן לְהוֹשִׁיבִי עִם־נְדִיבִים עִם נְדִיבֵי עַמּוֹ) thanksgiving (1Sam 2:8) and reformulates the expression that the poor are seated with the nobles.[202] Both of these passages share remarkable similarities with this passage of 4QInstruction. Targum Pseudo-Jonathan on this prayer, an Aramaic translation that has been described as an "apocalypse," may preserve an earlier exegetical tradition that interprets "nobles" as angelic beings.[203] Pseudo-Jonathan on 1Sam 2:8 reads:

---

199 DJD 34:118 the editors state that נדיבים is "a term frequent in 4Q415 ff.," which is true relative to other compositions from Qumran. Cf. Ben Sira 11:1, Victor M. Asensio, "Poverty and Wealth: Ben Sira's View of Possessions," in *Der Einzelne und seine Gemeinschaft bei Ben Sira*, ed. Renate Egger-Wenzel & Ingrid Krammer (Berlin: de Gruyter, 1998), 151–178 at 158, comments on this verse: "the poor man who directs his life to the search of wisdom does not have to feel lower than powerful people. At any rate, even if this is the correct interpretation (the imaginative value of נדיב), did Ben Sira share the probably generalized conviction of the social superiority of the rich?"

200 4Q415 6 partially preserves the first few words of seven lines, among them reference to סוד אנשים (l. 6), a phrase not found elsewhere in 4QInstruction but that may resonate with the hapax סוד אילים in 4Q418 69 ii 15. DJD 34:486 discuss סוד אמת (cf. the expression נחלת אמת, e.g. 4Q415 2 i + 1 ii 6; 4Q416 4 3).

201 1Sam 2:8 "He raises up the poor from the dust; he lifts the needy from the ash heap, to make them sit with princes and inherit a seat of honor" (NRSV).

202 Ps 113:5–9 "5 Who is like the LORD our God, who is seated on high, 6 who looks far down on the heavens and the earth? 7 He raises the poor from the dust, and lifts the needy from the ash heap, 8 to make them sit with princes, with the princes of his people. 9 He gives the barren woman a home, making her the joyous mother of children. Praise the LORD!" (NRSV).

203 Daniel J. Harrington, "The Apocalypse of Hannah: Targum Jonathan of 1Samuel 2:1–10," in *Working with no Data: Semitic and Egyptian Studies Presented to Thomas O. Lambdin*, ed. David M. Golomb & Susan T. Hollis (Winona Lake, IN: Eisenbrauns, 1987), 147–152.

He raises up the poor [מִסְכֵּינָא] from the dust, from the dunghill he exalts the needy one [חֲשִׁיכָא], to make them dwell with the righteous ones [צַדִּיקַיָּא], the chiefs of the world [רַבְרְבֵי עָלְמָא]; and he bequeathes to them thrones of glory [כָּרְסֵי יְקָרָא], for before the Lord the deeds of the sons of men are revealed. He has established Gehenna below for the wicked ones. And the just ones—those doing his good pleasure, he established the world for them.[204]

The "chiefs of the world" may also be the "chiefs of eternity" and the inheritance of thrones of glory has heavenly connotations. Ben Sira 11:1 describes wisdom raising the poor from their station to be among the social elite: חכמת דל תשא ראשו ובין נדיבים תשיבנו ("the wisdom of the poor lifts up his head, and between the nobles he is seated"). Sirach 11:1 translates דל with ταπεινός: "The wisdom of the humble lifts their heads high, and seats them among the great" (σοφία ταπεινοῦ ἀνυψώσει κεφαλὴν αὐτοῦ καὶ ἐν μέσῳ μεγιστάνων καθίσει αὐτόν). The difference between wisdom in Ben Sira, where it is thematized, and 4QInstruction, where wisdom and Torah are never explicitly associated and Torah is never thematized, is the subject of Chapter 3. Whereas wisdom changes the status of the poor in Ben Sira, in 4QInstruction being seated with the "nobles" is to be lifted from the humble condition of "poverty." 4Q416 2 iii 11 is probably similar to having one's lot cast with holy ones (4Q418 81 + 81a) in order to share divine knowledge with them.

Other discoveries from the Qumran caves use "nobles" in noteworthy ways. In the Damascus Document VI 4 and 8 the "nobles of the people" (Ps 113:8) are "returners of Israel" who pursue the Torah. CD VI 2–5a read:[205]

2 But God remembered the covenant of the forefathers *vacat* and he raised from Aaron men of knowledge and from Israel 3 wise men, and made them listen. And they dug the well: "A well [באר] which the princes [שרים] dug, which 4 the nobles of the people [נדיבי העם] delved with the staff [במחוקק]" (Num 21:18). The well is the law [תורה] and those who dug it *vacat* are 5 the returners of Israel [שבי ישראל].

In CD VI 7 the "staff" (המחוקק) is identified as "the interpreter of the law" (דורש התורה) and lines 8–9 further elucidate who these nobles are and their activi-

---

204   Translation by Daniel J. Harrington & Anthony J. Saldarini, *Targum Jonathan of the Former Prophets*, The Aramaic Bible, vol. 10 (Edinburgh: T&T Clark, 1987), 106.

205   García Martínez & Tigchelaar, *DSSSE*, 1:559 (modified).

ties: "the nobles of the people are those who came to dig the well with the staves that the scepter decreed" (נדיבי העם הם הבאים לכרות את הבאר במחוקקות אשר חקק המוקק). The "nobles of the people" in the Damascus Document are associated with seeking Torah with the assistance of "seekers of the Torah" (= staves); in 4QInstruction positively conceived "nobles" are present, but Torah is absent. Moreover, in the Damascus Document the "staff" or "decree" (מחוקק) is related to a person, or people, whereas in 4QInstruction the "decree" (מחוקק) is what is written before God and given to humanity to meditate upon (4Q417 1 i 13b–18; cf. Ch. 2 §1.1.1.). Therefore, language of "nobles" and "decrees" in the Damascus Document relate to the people and pursuit of Torah, but when this language is found in 4QInstruction, which has a different view of revelation, this common language finds an alternative configuration. However, "noble ones" in both the Damascus Document and 4QInstruction relate to figures who are exceptional in their pursuit of revelation.[206]

The term נדיבים is also used negatively for earthly rulers. In the Rule of Blessing III, discussed previously in regard to having ones lot cast with holy ones and the pouring out of lips, "nobles" are synonymous with "princes of the nations." In 1QSb III 27–28 the words of blessing from the *maśkîl* to the sons of Zadok are: "May he j[udge al]l the nobles by your works and by what issues from your lips all the [princes of] the nations" (ובמעשייכה יש[פוט כו]ל נדיבים וממזל שפתיכה [כול [שרי] עמים).[207]

The Self-Glorification Hymn shares common characteristics with 4Q416 2 iii 11. In 4Q491[c] the "company of the poor" are also seated in an eternal counsel (l. 4). However, the "nobles" (l. 5) are earthly rulers who cannot compare with the counsel of angels. The speaker in this hymn is given a mighty throne, which has parallels with Pseudo-Jonathan's translation of 1 Sam 2:8, and may inform interpretations of the "inheritance of glory" in 4Q416 2 iii. 4Q491[c] i 3–8 read:[208]

> **3** He established it of old (as) his tr[u]th, and the mysteries of his shrewdness [רזי ערמתו] in al[l ...] might **4** [...]*m*[...]*mym* and the company of the Poor [עצת אביונים] (will become part of) the eternal council [עדת עולמים]. And [they are to say "Blessed be God who has seated me among] the

---

206   4QBarki Nafshi[e] (4Q438) 3 2 God's "noble ones" and "chosen ones" appear to be synonymous; in 4QInstruction the addressees are "ones who choose" (4Q418 69 ii 10) and the firstborn in 4Q416 2 ii 14 is likely a "chosen one." Therefore, the act of choosing results in becoming chosen.

207   Cf. similar terms are used for earthly rulers in Ps 47:10 נדיבי עמים; Esth 3:12 שרי עם.

208   Translation by Wise, "מי כמוני באלים," 182–183.

[et]ernally 5 blameless [תמימי עולמים]–(given me) a mighty throne [כסא
עוז] in the angelic council [עדת אלים]." No king of yore [מלכי קדם] will sit
therein, neith[er] will their nobles [נדיביהמה] [(take seat) therein to judge.
No o]ne can compare 6 [to] my glory; none has been exalted save myself,
and none can oppose me. I sit on [high, exalted in hea]ven, and none 7
[su]rround (me). I am reckoned with the angels, my dwelling is in the
holy council. [My] desi[re] is not of the flesh; [rather,] my [por]tion lies
in the glory of 8 the holy [hab]itation. [W]ho has been accounted con-
temptible like me, yet who is like me in my glory? Who ... 9 [like] me? Who
has born[e] afflictions like me, yet who compares to me for [la]ck of evil?
Never have I been instructed, yet no teaching compares 10 [to m]y [teach-
ing.] Who can assail me when I op[en m]y [mouth], the utterance of my
lips [מזל שפתי], who can endure? Who can challenge me and so compare
with my judgment [ידמה במשפתי]? 11 [None compares to me, fo]r [my]
stati[on] is with the angels [אלים]. My [g]lory abides with the sons of the
King [בני מלכים].

The speaker in this recension of the Self-Glorification Hymn is unique in his
glory, making claims that he laughs at sorrows and is preeminently suited to
bear evil (l. 9, ומיא יסבו[ל רא הדמה ביא). He is unequalled and no one would
dare call him to judgment (l. 10). He is reckoned with the angels and his place
among them is likened to being seated with the "sons of the king" (l. 11). Morton Smith concludes, in reference to this statement, that "in glory he ranks
with the king's sons" which is "another absurd anticlimax" of the passage.[209]
4Q491ᶜ uses "nobles" and "king of yore" derisively in order to emphasize how
utterly incomparable his own station and glory are. The statement that the
speaker dwells with the "sons of the king" may be either an anticlimax or perhaps it draws a contrast with preceding royal language. The Self-Glorification
Hymn expresses that corrupt kings and nobles, likely at the Jerusalem temple, are to be contrasted with a heavenly throne; this would certainly be a
reaction to those earthly leaders who exalt themselves in the city (i.e., Has-
moneans, Romans, Parthians, Herodians). Smith comments that "the speaker
still thinks it worthwhile to contrast himself with them [corrupt kings]," and
may be correlated to the reign of specific kings such as Herod.[210] Smith finds
in 4Q491ᶜ the speaker boasting that "[t]he status of a holy temple" has been
attributed to him (cf. 4Q418 81 + 81a 4), which further reinforces the view that

209   Smith, "Ascent to the Heavens," 186–187.
210   Smith, "Ascent to the Heavens," 186.

the speaker's exaltations are in reaction to corrupt earthly leadership.[211] However, if the statement about being given glory like the "sons of the king" is in
reference to earthly princes, then the statement is rather absurd. In fact, it
would seem to work against the speaker's polemic; instead, "sons of the king"
should be interpreted as parallel to אלים ("angels") in the same line. The significance of the Self-Glorification Hymn for 4QInstruction then is not that it uses
"nobles" in the same way, indeed it is opposite, but rather that royal language
and sonship are associated with angels and the speakers place among them.
In 1QH³ XXVI (= Self-Glorification Hymn) line 6 royal language is used for God
when the speaker describes himself as "beloved of the king" (ידיד המלך) and a
"friend to the holy ones" (רע לקדושים); as such, no earthly glory compares with
his heavenly exaltation.

Finally, 4Q416 2 iii 12 describes the addressee as having been placed in
authority, with the *Hiphil* perfect conjugation, over an inheritance (ובנחלת כבוד
המשילכה); this is nearly an identical expression to that found in 4Q418 81+81a
3 (ובנ]חלתו המשילכה). If royal language is used here for angelic beings with the
term "nobles," then the language of sonship to describe the function of a *maśkîl*
would further emphasize his place among them.[212] That 4QInstruction only
envisages a future with the angels is unlikely, and the consequences of misin-
terpreting the relationship of the addressee to angelic beings effects how one
understands the pursuit and acquisition of wisdom in the document and the
role of the sage.[213] The evidence points to the conclusion that present participation with the angels is a feature of this composition and integral to the role
of a *maśkîl*. In 4Q416 2 iii a metaphorically "poor" *maśkîl* is lifted from this con-

---

211   Smith, "Ascent to the Heavens," 184; Wise, "מי כמוני באלים," 183 translates in lines 7–8 "my
      [por]tion lies in the glory of the holy [hab]itation."

212   Cf. Rom 8:15 "you have received the spirit of sonship (υἱοθεσίας), when we cry, 'Abba,
      Father!'" υἱοθεσία is used in Romans in reference to adoption into a divine family (Rom
      8:23, 9:4; Gal 4:5; Eph 1:5).

213   Jonathan T. Pennington, *The Sermon on the Mount and Human Flourishing: A Theological
      Commentary* (Grand Rapids, MI: Baker Academic, 2017) translates Matt 5:3 as "Flourishing
      are the poor in spirit because the kingdom of heaven is theirs," a statement rather than a
      conditional followed by apodosis (i.e., "if ... then"); furthermore, he comments at 156–157
      "The reason Jesus can boldly claim that the poor in spirit are truly flourishing is *because*,
      despite appearances, these lowly ones are actually possessors and citizens of God's heav-
      enly kingdom ... What is radical and unique about Jesus's macarism is the unexpected
      eschatological twist that human flourishing is now found amid suffering in the time of
      waiting for God to bring his just reign from heaven to earth (see the Lord's Prayer)." More-
      over, "heaven is theirs" is present tense. Cf. Christopher Rowland, "Apocalyptic, the Poor,
      and the Gospel of Matthew," *JTS* 45 (1994): 504–518. See also fn. 181 above.

dition when he is seated among angelic beings, which is an exaltation that the sage enjoys presently, similar to 4Q418 81 + 81a.

5   Conclusions

That a *maśkîl* addresses his audience in first-person speech, and that the fragments where this address occurs may be the incipit of 4QInstruction, was first suggested by Tigchelaar. Puech also reconstructs a reference to a *maśkîl* in the opening column of 4QInstruction, although not in the opening lines nor in first-person form. Tigchelaar's suggestion that 4Q418 frgs. 222 + 221 and 238 should be located at the top of 4Q416 1, the opening column of the composition, cannot be substantiated by overlaps; however, it may be established that these fragments use first-person forms in close proximity to the occurrence of "*maśkîl*." One may reasonably conclude that first-person forms, rather than third-person, are used in frgs. 222 + 221 and 238. Where these fragments were located in the composition is secondary to the observation that a *maśkîl* speaks in 4QInstruction. The beginning of this chapter is devoted to demonstrating the probability that a sage speaks to his audience by two means. First, attention is given to first-person speech throughout the composition to assess whether it would be out of place, to such a degree, as to discount Tigchelaar's hypothesis. While first-person forms are not frequent, they do occur; moreover, there are several ambiguous pronouns in 4QInstruction that may also be read as first-person forms rather than third-person ones. Second, there are other instances of the term משכיל in 4QInstruction and each of these are analyzed. One of these occurrences (4Q418 81 + 81a 17) is already widely translated as referring to a "sage," and not as a participle, and upon careful scrutiny it was argued that the other instances are more convincingly read as nouns too. These two approaches to contextualizing frgs. 222 + 221 and 238 strongly support the transcription and translation of first-person forms.

In the process of adjudicating the plausibility that a *maśkîl* speaks and refers to himself in 4QInstruction, observations are made about the character of the sage and his relationship with the addressees. Most significantly, those within the community may also, by actualizing wisdom (i.e., *ḥokma* of the hands) and living faithfully to truth's ways, also become *maśkilîm*. The language of becoming a sage in 4Q416 2 ii is to become a firstborn son, which is also the description of the elevated figure in 4Q418 81 + 81a. The translation and interpretation of 4Q416 2 ii, one that had not previously been argued, transforms how 4Q418 81 + 81a, a much discussed and debated column, is interpreted. 4Q418 81 + 81a instructs the addressee about the station, status, and role of a *maśkîl*; furthermore, this column may not present two distinct sections (ll. 1–14; 15–20) as previously thought, a conclusion that others came to based upon a mistaken translation of "*ḥokma* of the hands" as a reference to manual labor rather than the actualization of wisdom.

Tigchelaar's suggestion that frgs. 222 + 221 and 238 are the incipit of 4QInstruction is based upon similar language used in the opening of other compositions discovered at Qumran that mention a *maśkîl*. This study returns to Tigchelaar's observation only after the characteristics and role of the *maśkîl* are more specifically elaborated upon. Language found in close proximity to references to *maśkilîm* throughout 4QInstruction further reinforce the conclusion that a *maśkîl* speaks in the opening column. Moreover, by setting 4QInstruction's sage alongside other *maśkilîm* from Qumran one is able to make comparisons with them. Angel's description of the *maśkîl*, in Songs of the Sage, as a template with which worshipers were to identify resonates with 4QInstruction. To become a sage is an ideal and, to borrow and adapt Newsom's conclusions, he is the apotheosis of the community and model to those who seek revealed wisdom and knowledge. However, the conclusions of the chapters to follow help establish that 4QInstruction, as a non-sectarian composition, does not understand mastering revealed knowledge as part of the formation of sectarian selfhood or the sect itself. The values that this composition presents respond to other values and may serve to perceive better its purpose and function. A less hierarchical and more inclusive perspective on who may acquire wisdom is suggested by the presentation of the sage in 4QInstruction. Whether this is in reaction to alternative views of a *maśkîl*, such as the Self-Glorification hymn, or perhaps authoritarian structures related to scribes at the temple, is unknown.

One result of this study is a different perspective on 4QInstruction's teaching about financial matters. The translation and reassessment of 4Q416 2 i–ii here does not change the viewpoint that the addressees live in difficult financial circumstances, are at times materially poor, and struggle with debt; however, the relationship of the addressee to his oppressors/creditors is more distant than sometimes suggested. Moreover, in 4Q416 2 i–ii, the most substantial section where instruction about financial issues occurs, the theme of daily life economics and figures related to it are not monolithic throughout; a number of relationships are in view, not just between the addressee and creditor, but also the *mēvîn* and other *mevinîm*, the *mēvîn* and God, and the *mēvîn* and *maśkîl*. These relationships are of greater import for the author than a relationship with a creditor. One "sells themselves for wealth" (4Q416 2 ii 17) if they do not respect their neighbor when helping them out of their debt and its consequences.

Another text that has been viewed as reflecting the economic situation of the addressee is 4Q418 81 + 81a 15–20 where many translations understand "*hokma* of the hands" as depicting an overseer of "manual labor" or "artisanship." We have seen that this is the result of mistakenly reading Greek Sirach 9:17 (ἐν χειρὶ τεχνιτῶν) instead of Ben Sira 9:17 (בחכמי ידים). 4QInstruction, like 4QSapiential Text (4Q424), presents two types of wisdom: (1) wisdom of heart (חכמת לבב), and (2) wisdom of hands (חכמת ידים). The internal *hokma* of the heart is contrasted with lived out wisdom, expressed with exterior action: *hokma* of the hands. In early Christian wisdom tradition, namely the letter of James 1:22, a similar idea is found in the exhortation "be doers of the word, not only hearers." To be a sage in 4QInstruction is to be one who actualizes wisdom in their daily lives. The erroneous translation of "*hokma* of the hands" as manual labor influences the translation of אוט as "storehouse" when in fact it should be translated in reference to "gentleness" (e.g., 4Q416 2 ii 12 "wisdom of God's *gentleness*") or "lowliness" (e.g., 4Q418 81 + 81a 16 "lowliness of all the ways of mankind") as a noun related to the adverb from the root אט.

Previous translations and interpretations of 4Q416 2 ii and 4Q418 81 + 81a 1–20 led to the perception that the addressee was invested in economic trade and at times even a slave. These passages were then associated with the *topoi* of poverty, borrowing, and debt within the broader context of ancient wisdom and the economy of the ancient world. Such simplistic approaches to 4QInstruction's economic teachings are the results of several highly problematic translations. The translations proposed here place the emphasis of instruction on attaining wisdom and living it out in relationship to several figures. The broader discourse about debt in 4Q416 2 ii is ultimately about one's relationship with God and how that then effects relationships with other people in the community.

Some instances of poverty in 4QInstruction are metaphorical and refer to the fatigable nature of human beings. An important passage in this regard is 4Q416 2 iii 11–12a ("For out of poverty He has lifted up your head, and with the nobles he has made you to be seated"). As we have seen, this statement relates to the addressee participating with the angels in the present time. Reminding one about their metaphorical poverty (i.e., "you are poor" found several times in 4Q416 2 i–iv) does not exclude a view of the speaker and his audience as experiencing literal impoverishment. As metaphor, reminding one of their poverty is similar to being told that human beings easily weary in their pursuit of wisdom, which stands in contrast to angelic beings who are models to be emulated (4Q418 69 ii). Being seated with "nobles" relates to participating with angels presently, similar to 4Q418 81 + 81a where the exalted figure likewise participates with angels. How poverty language functions as metaphor is presented

in different ways, it may be used to encourage the *mēvîn* to adopt the character of a poor and humble person as an ethical ideal.[214] Alternatively, poverty
may not be an ideal, but rather "poverty" is a cipher for the human condition
and the proper response to it is a pious, humble attitude. In both of these interpretations, "poor" is equated with humility and the difference is whether the
metaphor of "poverty" is the ideal, or living humbly in response to one's own
shortcomings as a human being is the ideal. That the latter is the case is clear
from 4Q416 2 iii 11–12a. Being lifted from poverty and seated with the "nobles" is
unquestionably positive and reserved for those who pursue wisdom; therefore,
if "poverty" were the ethical ideal, then the expectation of being raised out of
it is contradictory.

The speaker of 4QInstruction is concerned with the various stages of his students as they pursue and seek to actualize wisdom. The social structures the
speaker shapes for his audience involve clear hierarchies and divisions. The
maśkîl teaches: how to live wisely within family relationships, how the *mēvîn*
should understand his place within his community, how the faithful community is to relate to those outside and to keep separate from them, the place
of humankind within a hierarchy that includes angelic beings, and ultimately
what an ideal relationship with God is.

---

214   Goff, *4QInstruction*, 25–26.

Spirit and Flesh

The divisions and hierarchies that concerned us in Chapter 1 related to the speaker and addressee as teacher and pupils within the pedagogical environment of a community. In this chapter, our focus shifts to divisions among humanity. The separation of "spirit" and "flesh" at the point of creation has been viewed by some as dividing humanity into two distinct groups. One consequence of this interpretation is that revelation, expressed as both רז נהיה and Hagu, is only accessible to the elect, chosen, and pre-determined few. This dualistic view of humankind, as elect and non-elect, also results in a hierarchical and exclusionary understanding of revelation and access to wisdom.

The speaker-sage discussed in Chapter 1 addresses a community of students who desire to grow in knowledge and diligently pursue the mystery of existence. Ideally, practitioners of wisdom may themselves become a maśkîl and indeed multiple maśkîlîm are referred to in 4QInstruction. This composition envisages a spectrum of pupils at varying levels.[1] Not everyone addressed will necessarily become a sage, but the pinnacle of learning and living out wisdom is expressed as becoming like your teacher. Merit plays a role within the hierarchy of the community, namely one's place within it is dependent upon acquisition of wisdom ("ḥokma of the hands").[2] The urgent exhortations to seek understanding, and warnings to the lazy about their foolishness, indicate that not all pupils are equally disciplined and faithful. The relationship of speaker to addressee is inclusive with emphasis on humility and awareness of the challenges present in the perpetual and yet arduous pursuit to actualize wisdom. The sage was not, from the beginning, a firstborn and most holy one, but is only placed as such through constant care and piety. In light of these divisions and hierarchies within the community, an exclusionary and deterministic view of humankind, if that is an accurate view, would stand in sharp contrast.

---

1 In our own time, "differentiated teaching and learning" is an approach that accounts for a variety of skill and knowledge levels within a single classroom environment and, in this regard, 4QInstruction has commonalities. However, differentiated teaching and learning places emphasis on instructional *strategies* whereas 4QInstruction is sparse, at least in the extant fragments, in providing details about how precisely a student actualizes wisdom.

2 Cf. 1En 99:10 where righteousness is determined not by election but by understanding and observing wisdom.

In this chapter I am interested in asking about who among humanity has, or had, access to wisdom. An integral aspect of this question is how the separation between the just and unjust, the righteous and wicked, is conceived in 4QInstruction.[3] The path to revelation, according to some interpreters of 4QInstruction, is paved only for an elect group while the non-elect are barred from it. In this view only the predetermined "spiritual people," found in the Vision of Hagu passage, were bestowed meditation on revelation while the "fleshly spirit" were not. That a dualistic anthropology frames deterministic ideas in the composition is challenged here; in this chapter it is argued that all of humanity shares in the same creation and from the beginning "meditation" (i.e., on revealed wisdom) was given to all.[4] However, it is also recognized that free will and determinism in the Scrolls, and beyond, are not incompatible.[5] The driving question is how faithful and unfaithful pursuit and adherence to "revealed wisdom"— a merit based system—serve to categorize groups in 4QInstruction.[6] Indeed, if one's place within the hierarchy of the community is by virtue of an individ-

---

3   The significance of 4QInstruction for assessing the compositional history of the hypothetical source Q is only in its infancy; indeed, how one sets the Saying Source within early Jewish literature is the subject of the recent collection: Markus Tiwald (ed.), *Q in Context I: The Separation between the Just and Unjust in Early Judaism and in the Saying Source* (Göttingen: Vandenhoeck & Ruprecht, 2015).

4   Cf. Benjamin Wold, "The Universality of Creation in 4QInstruction," *RevQ* 102/1 (2013): 211–226.

5   Jonathan Klawans, "Josephus on Fate, Free Will, and Ancient Jewish Types of Compatibilism," *Numen* 56 (2009): 44–90, at 45, writes that "[f]or philosophers, the term 'compatibilism' refers to the varied efforts to maintain that determinism and free will are not contradictory, but compatible. In particular, the term often refers to the position that holds that a strict determinism can still allow for the possibility that individuals make free and unrestrained decisions, and are therefore responsible for their actions, despite the fact that the decisions and their consequences are determined in advance." Even the highly deterministic Treatise on the Two Spirits intertwines determinism and free will, see Miryam T. Brand, "Belial, Free Will, and Identity-Building in the Community Rule," in *Evil, the Devil, and Demons: Dualistic Characteristics in the Religion of Israel, Ancient Judaism, and Christianity*, ed. Benjamin Wold, Jan Dochhorn & Susanne Rudnig-Zelt, WUNT 2.412 (Tübingen: Mohr Siebeck, 2015), 77–92.

6   Florentino García Martínez, "Wisdom at Qumran: Worldly or Heavenly?" in *Qumranica Minora II: Thematic Studies on the Dead Sea Scrolls*, ed. Eibert J.C. Tigchelaar, STDJ 64 (Leiden: Brill, 2007), 171–186, at 185 "I do not know whether we can use the term 'apocalyptic wisdom' in the case of 4QInstruction ... in my opinion, it's author tries to present the knowledge he wants to communicate not as simple human knowledge (as in biblical wisdom tradition) but as 'revealed' knowledge, as heavenly wisdom. Therefore, I think we can answer the question posed in a different way to how Goff answered it. Qumran wisdom is not worldly *and* heavenly wisdom, it is revealed wisdom, and thus thoroughly heavenly."

ual's acquisition of insight, actualization of wisdom, and dint of discipline, then there is reason to suspect that the same holds true when assessing humanity and who is part of the righteous community and who is outside of it.

A sub-question arises in this chapter about how inclusive 4QInstruction's outlook is when referring to "humanity"; or more to the point, if the creation of humanity and bequeathing of revelation is universal, then this would, seemingly, include not just Jews but gentiles too. Alternatively, perhaps the expression "humanity," as will be considered, is not literally all of humankind and the author's horizon simply does not extend to the nations. What is clear in 4QInstruction is that the label "fleshly" is used to categorize a segment of humankind, but when does this division occur, at creation or sometime post-creation, and if it is the latter who are the divisions among: (1) faithful Israel and wayward Israel, or (2) faithful humanity and wicked humanity?

1   "Spirit" and "Flesh"

To date, there is a near consensus that 4QInstruction's anthropology is dualistic and deterministic; this is derived mainly vis-à-vis a particular translation and interpretation of the Vision of Hagu passage (4Q417 1 i 13b–18a) that finds the creation of two types of people expressed as: (1) a "spiritual people" (עָם רוח) and (2) a "spirit of flesh/fleshly spirit" (רוח בשר).[7] According to this interpretation, these two peoples were created separately and the group described as רוח בשר never enjoyed access to revealed wisdom. In the following sections the people categorized as רוח בשר are evaluated by giving attention to language of "flesh" more broadly in the document before comparing the expression רוח בשר with similar occurrences in the Thanksgiving Hymns.

---

7 Collins, "In the Likeness," 609–618 first suggested that the vision of Hagu passage is based upon an interpretation of two contrasting creations in Gen 1–2. The two different humanities created are found in: (1) אנוש, interpreted as the first man Adam, who relates to the "spiritual people" (l. 16); and (2) the "fleshly spirit" (l. 17). The first creation of Adam and the spiritual people is described as a fashioning in the likeness of angelic beings. A well attested exegesis of Gen 1:27 ("come let us make man in our image and likeness") is as an address by God to angels to share in the creation of humanity. According to this view, a similar exegesis is to be found in the vision of Hagu. The second creation, that of the fleshly spirit, is according to the earthly creation of Gen. 2. In this interpretation, the spiritual people share in the likeness of the holy ones whereas the spirit of flesh do not.

1.1   *"Flesh" in 4QInstruction*

Early on in the study of 4QInstruction, Torleif Elgvin noted a number of unique terms shared with the Thanksgiving Hymns.[8] Distinctive among these commonalities are descriptions of "flesh." In the hymns, the expression יצר בשר ("vessel of flesh") occurs twice (1QHᵃ XVIII 25; XXIV 6) and while the fragmentary context leaves conclusions uncertain, the words יצר בשר also occur in the opening column of 4QInstruction (4Q416 1 16; par. 4Q418 2 + 2a 8) in close proximity to רוח בשר. Excluding 4QInstruction and the hymns, no extant references to יצר בשר or רוח בשר are to be found in ancient Jewish literature.[9] In the hymns, רוח בשר occurs three times (1QHᵃ IV 37; V 15, 30) and so too in 4QInstruction (4Q416 1 12, par. 4Q418 2, 2 a–c 4; 4Q417 1 i 17; 4Q418 81 + 81a 2). In light of these observations, the point of departure here is an exploration of how these two expressions—יצר בשר and רוח בשר—are used in these documents in order to view better how "flesh" language serves each document's anthropology and perspective on revelation.[10]

Already acknowledged is that 4QInstruction does not share the pessimistic view of human nature with the hymns and yet both use רוח בשר to refer to

---

8   Elgvin, *An Analysis*, 160–163 also notes: כבוד עולם (4Q418 126 ii 8; 1QHᵃ V 23; XI 5) and רזי פלא (4Q417 1 i 2, 13; 1QHᵃ VI 13; IX 23; X 15; XV 30; XIX 13); Matthew J. Goff, "Reading Wisdom at Qumran: 4QInstruction and the Hodayot," *DSD* 11/3 (2004): 263–288 adds to this: סוד אמת (4Q417 1 i 8; 1QHᵃ X 12; XIII 11, 28) and אל אמת (4Q416 1 14; 1QHᵃ VII 38 where אל is written in paleo-Hebrew). Lange, *Weisheit und Prädestination*, 204–232 discusses the shared language of "engraving" (חרות), "statutes" (חקוק), and "memorials" (זכרון) found in 1QHᵃ IX and 4Q417 1 i 15–18. In 1QHᵃ IX 21 the psalmist extols God for "opening my ears" to wonderful mysteries (גליתה אוזני לרזי פלא), this language of revealing mysteries is remarkably similar to that found in 4QInstruction (1Q26 1 4; 4Q416 2 iii 17–18 [= 4Q418 10 1]; 4Q418 123 ii 4; 4Q418 184 2; 4Q418 190 2). In 1QHᵃ IX, while his ears are uncovered to mysteries, he can also state that "nothing is hidden" (l. 27), the reason for this is that seasons, years, and appointed times are known from all eternity; indeed, the author says that "everything is inscribed before You with an engraving of remembrance" (ll. 25–26; הכול חקוק לפניכה בחרת זכרון). The language of "engraving" and "inscribing" is positively used of the design of the cosmos in 4QInstruction and the hymns and relates to judgment and serves as a memorial. See also Tigchelaar, *To Increase Learning*, 203–207.

9   Cf. Num 16:22; 27:16 for יצר בשר.

10   The most distinctive term in 4QInstruction, רז נהיה, does not occur in the hymns; רז נהיה occurs only in 1Q/4QMysteries (1Q27 1 i 4; par. 4Q300 3 4) where the wicked "do not know the mystery of existence [רז נהיה], nor understand ancient matters"; and in 1QS XI 3–4, "and with his just acts he cancels my iniquities. For from the source of knowledge he has disclosed his light, and my eyes have observed his wonders, and the light of my heart the mystery of existence [רז נהיה]. What always is, is support for my right hand ..." Translation from DSSE 1:97.

humanity or segment of humankind. Harrington and Strugnell comment that
רוח בשר in 4QInstruction "scarcely has any connection with the רוח בשר" in the
Thanksgiving Hymns "where the meaning is 'a fleshly spirit.'"[11] *Pace* the editors,
if רוח בשר is not language for one group of humanity created separately from
another, then comparisons with the expression in the hymns become much
more meaningful.

1.1.1   4Q417 1 i Lines 1–13
While 4QInstruction refers to both "spirit" and "flesh" there is no spirit/flesh
dichotomy where they function as binary opposites. In disagreement with this
view are those who translate and interpret the Vision of Hagu as depicting the
creation of two types of humanity, one fleshly and the other spiritual.[12] For
those who hold this view, the Hagu pericope is an expression of deterministic theology similar to, but less developed than, the Treatise on the Two Spirits;
indeed, interpreting this pericope through the lens of the Treatise contributes
to conclusions that a spirit/flesh dichotomy is at play in the composition as
a whole. In the two opposing groups (i.e., "spiritual people"/"spirit of flesh")
that the majority find in this passage, the proposed עַם רוח would be a *hapax
legomenon* not only in 4QInstruction, but the whole of ancient Hebrew literature too. Moreover, the suggested contrasting people are referred to with, in
the words of Carol Newsom, a "wonderfully oxymoronic" term that describes
spirit as fleshly; therefore, how one understands divisions in humanity is by no
means straightforwardly between spirit and flesh, but rather between different
types of spirit.[13] Even if the translation that finds two predetermined peoples
who are created seperately is correct, this would be the only occasion in 4QIn-
struction when these two peoples are explicitly mentioned and set in contrast
with one another.

A distinctly separate section immediately precedes the Vision of Hagu pericope. In the first line of column 4Q417 1 i only three words are preserved: "and
you, understanding one." 4Q417 1 i 1–13a are fragmentary and share a common
interest with the following Hagu paragraph (ll. 13b–18a) by emphasizing the
pursuit of revealed wisdom. The importance of not reading lines 13b–18a in

11   DJD 34:95.
12   For a bibliography on treatments of this pericope see esp. Eibert J.C. Tigchelaar, "'Spiritual
      People,' 'Fleshly Spirit,' and 'Vision of Meditation': Reflections on 4QInstruction and 1 Co-
      rinthians," in *Echoes from the Caves: Qumran and the New Testament*, ed. Florentino García
      Martínez, STDJ 85 (Leiden: Brill, 2009), 103–118 at 103–104.
13   Carol A. Newsom, "Spirit, Flesh, and the Indigenous Psychology of the Hodayot," in *Prayer
      and Poetry in the Dead Sea Scrolls*, 339–354 at 344.

isolation from this preceding passage is found in the following observations: (1) lines 13b–18a are concerned with meditation on a vision and in line 6 the verb "meditate" is used explicitly with the mystery of existence as the object; (2) when lines 1–13a mention רז נהיה the surrounding descriptors clarify the meaning and scope of revelation; and (3) even though lines 1–13a do not use "spirit" or "flesh" in relationship to humanity they are nonetheless interested in humankind similarly to the Hagu pericope.

These lines are returned to in Chapter 3 (§ 2.1.) where attention is given to the significance of this paragraph for revelation and Torah (see fig. 13 in plate section).

4Q417 1 i 1–14 (comp. 4Q418 43 1–10 [single underline]; overlap [double underline]), Transcription and Translation:[14]

ו]אתה מב̊ן]י̊[	1
○○○ הֿבֿט̊ ו]ב̊רֿזֿי פלאי אל הנוראים תשכיל ראש ○	2
ל̊ז בפ̊ן]כֿה ○○○ ו̊הֿבֿט̊ ברז נהיה ומעשי] קדם למה נהיה ומה נהיה	3
בנ̊ן ו]○○○○○○○עו]ל̊ם לחש̊ו	4
הז̊א ול̊מ̊]ה]נהיה במה̊ן] ○ ב̊כו̊ל̊ן	5
יומם ו]לילה הגה ברז נהיה {ו}דורש תמיד̊ ואז תדע אמת ועול חכמה	6
ואול̊[ת ת̊[ב̊י̊ן] דע מֿעֿשֿי̊הם]ב̊כול דרכיהם עם פקודת̊ם לכול קצי עולם ופֿקודֿת	7
עד ואז תדע בי̊ן]טו̊[ב ל̊[רע כ̊]מֿעֿש̊י̊]הם [כ̊י̊א אל הדעות סוד אמת וברז נהיה	8
פֿרש אֿת אֿושֿהֿ ומֿעֿשֿי̊ה ○○○]לכול חכ]מה ולכול ע̊[רמה יצרה וממשלת מעשיה	9
לב̊[ו]ל̊○○למ̊ה ול̊כו̊ל̊ א̊[ת ב̊[ו]ל̊○○בא̊[ו]ש[פ̊]רש למ̊[ב̊]ינ̊תם לכול מ]עשי̊]ה̊ להתהלך	10
ביֿצר מבֿי̊נ̊תֿם ו̊פֿרש לא̊[נוש]○[ ]רֿיֿה ובכוֿשׂ̊ מבֿי̊נות נ̊ו̊דֿ]עו נ̊ס̊[תֿרֿי	11
מחשבתו עם התֿהֿלֿכֿו̊ז̊] ת̊[מ̊ם̊ן בכול מ]עֿשֿיו אלה שחר תמיד והתבוננן בכו]ל̊	12
תוצאותֿמֿה ואז תדע בכבוד עֿ]חֿו עֿ[ם רזי פלאו וגבורות מעשיו ו̊א̊ת̊ה̊	13
מבין ...	14

1 [and] you underst[an]ding one[

2 [   ] gaze,   *or feastful*

[and] by the mysteries of the wonders of the God of the awesome ones gain insight,

the beginnings of [   ]

3 [   ] to him in your [   ]

14   DJD 34:151; Tigchelaar, *To Increase Learning*, 52; Rey, *4QInstruction*, 278; Goff, *4QInstruction*, 137–138; Qimron, *Dead Sea Scrolls*, 2:148; Menahem Kister, "ספרות החכמה בקומראן," in מגילות קומראן—מבואות ומחקרים / *The Qumran Scrolls and Their World*, 2 vols.; ed. Menahem Kister (Jerusalem: Yad ben-Zvi, 2009), 1:299–320 at 308 [Hebrew].

[   ] and gaze [upon the mystery of existence
and the deeds of] ancient times,
to what is and what will be,
4 in what [   ]
[eter]nity to [   ]
[   ] to what 5 was and to wh[at]will be,
in what [   ] in all [   ]
[   ] deed and dee[d]
6 [day and] night meditate on the mystery of existence,
seek always and then you will know truth and iniquity,
wisdom 7 [and foolishne]ss [understand],
know [their] dee[ds] in all their ways with their punishments,
for all periods of eternity, and eternal punishments,
8 and then you will know between [goo]d and [evil according to their
    ]deeds,   *Hud*
for the God of knowledge is the foundation of truth,
and by the mystery of existence 9 He has spread out the foundation of
    its (i.e., truth's) deeds,
[... with all wis]dom and with all [cu]nning He fashioned it (i.e., truth),
and the domain of its (i.e., truth's) deeds 10 for a[l]l [...]
He expounded for their un[der]standing, with all of its d[ee]ds,
to walk 11 in the inclination of their understanding,
and He expounded to h[umanity (?) ...],
and in the *abundance* of understanding were made kn[own the se]crets
    of 12 His plan,
together with how they should walk [pe]rfectly[in all] His [d]eeds,
These things always *seek early* (i.e., diligently),
and understand[all] 13 their consequences,
and then you will know about the glory of [His] mi[ght wi]th His mar-
    velous mysteries,
and the might of His deeds.

And you 14 understanding one ...

Most striking in this section are the exhortations to seek the רז נהיה because
this mystery is supplemented in ways that clarify its scope, which ranges from
Urzeit to *Endzeit*. In lines 1–2 the addressee is admonished to "gaze" (הבט) upon:
(1) the רזי פלאי אל הנוראים ("mysteries of the wonders of the God of the Awesome
Ones"); and (2) the רז נהיה which appears to be synonymous with the מעשי קדם
("deeds of old"). That the *mēvîn* is to understand the past and future is found in

the expressions: ראש ("beginning"), and the qualification of "deeds of old" with למה נהיה ומה נהיה ("what was and what will be"). How these mysteries relate to the notion of meditation (הגה) in the following paragraph is crucial; as will be seen, both meditation and mysteries are closely associated with creation and the ordering of the cosmos. In line 8, it is according to "their deeds" (כמעשיהם) that the addressees know the difference between good and evil (אז תדע בין טוב לרע); the notion of "deeds" is returned to in lines 10 and 12–13 which, respectively, refer to "truth's deeds" and "God's deeds." "Deed" and "plan" (cf. l. 12) are similar to one another and relate to cosmology; moreover, there is emphasis on deeds in connection with the knowledge of good and evil and in lines 12–13 diligent pursuit to understand deeds and their "consequences" probably refers to punishment and reward for foolish or righteous behavior.

In lines 9–11 a play on the two verbs פרש ("spread out") and פרש ("separate," "make distinct," "expound") occurs: in line 9 by the mystery of existence God "spreads out" truth's foundation (בְּרָז נָהָיה פרש את אושה); in lines 10–11 God "expounds" to them all of truth's deeds so that they might walk in the inclination of their understanding (פרש למבינתם לכול מעשיה להתהלך ביצר מבינתם).[15] "Truth" (אמת) is frequent in 4QInstruction, occurring forty-five time in the different manuscripts, and is a term closely associated with God's order of the cosmos.[16] The term פרש only occurs elsewhere in 4QInstruction in 4Q418 126 ii 4 (cf. §2.4. below) where, despite limited context, it appears that God's creative activity is also expressed: "[He]spread them out, in truth He established them, and by those that delight in them they are studied" (פרשם באמת הוא שמם ולחפציהם ידרש[ו). The "them" in 4Q418 126 ii likely refer to "all of their hosts" (כול צבאם l. 1), by which God has established justice and order: "by a true *ephah* and right weight God established everything" (l. 3 באי[פ]ת אמת ומשקל צדק תכן אל כול).[17]

---

15   L. 11 is the broken, undiscernible phrase וֹפרש לא[; 4Q417 14 4 God appears to "separate out" names (שמות פרש אל). For weights and measures at creation, cf. Sir 16:25–27 "I will impart discipline precisely and declare knowledge accurately. When the Lord created his works from the beginning, and, in making them, determined their boundaries, he arranged his works in an eternal order, and their dominion for all generations. They neither hunger nor grow weary, and they do not abandon their tasks." Note than in Ben Sira Wisdom is a way of speaking about God ordering creation and design for humanity in the Torah, which is not the case in 4QInstruction (cf. Ch. 3).

16   John Kampen, "Wisdom in Deuterocanonical," 109, observes how important אמת is in 4QInstruction and interprets "truth" as a designation for "the desired knowledge to be appropriated by the son(s) of discernment."

17   "Spreading out" in the Scrolls may be used of an eagle literally spreading out its wings or as a metaphor (cf. 1QHᵃ III 26 "the snare of wickedness is spread out").

When truth's ways are expounded to "them" in 4Q417 1 i 10–11 there are good reasons to conclude that they are "humanity." First, the foundation of the cosmos is what is expounded upon and it is from this that one knows good and evil; therefore, it would make sense that creation, as the beginning point of wisdom, is knowable to humanity.[18] Second, "He expounded" occurs twice, once in line 10 and again in line 11 ("to h[umanity]"); although the reconstruction in line 11 is only theoretical, Harrington and Strugnell read "for m[an."[19] The options of who could be given understanding is restricted to a word beginning with the letter *aleph* and while אדם is possible אנוש is more likely.[20] Third, "expounding to humanity" is supported by the giving of meditation to humanity in the following pericope (l. 16), which also uses the same preposition (-ל) as found in line 11 (לאנוש).

In line 10, God expounds to all "מבינתם," which is translated here, following the editors, as for "their understanding."[21] However, it is debated whether 4Q417 1 i 11 should be read as God expounding truth's ways so that they should walk in "His *yēṣer*" (יצר מבינתוֹ) or in "their *yēṣer*" (יצר מבינתֹם).[22] This is the only

---

18   Matthew J. Goff, "The Mystery of Creation in 4QInstruction," *DSD* 10/2 (2003): 163–186, at 170, comments on ll. 8–9 that "God is the foundation of the world because he created 'its foundation and its work …' In *4QInstruction* one can use the mystery that is to be to understand the natural order in a more comprehensive way because God used the mystery to create the world." In Goff's view the natural order is not revelation, but rather mysteries enable the elect to comprehend the created order.

19   DJD 34:154 no commentary is offered and the Hebrew is not reconstructed; however, they translate ll. 10a–12b "He [ex]*pounded* for their un[der]standing every d[ee]d/cr[eatu]re So that *man* could walk in the [fashion (inclination) of *their/his* understanding, And He will/did *expound* for m[an …] And *in abundance/property/purity* of understanding *were made* kn[own the se]crets of his (man's?) plan …"

20   Among the seven occurrences of אדם three occur in the expression בן אדם (4Q418 55 11; 4Q418 81+81a 3; 4Q423 8 2) in reference to "humanity"; the remaining instances always occur in construct form and are never introduced with the preposition -ל: "generations of man [אדם]" (4Q418 77 2); "inher]itance of man" (4Q418 251 1); "hand of man [האדם]" (4Q423 13 4); "ways of mankind (?)" (4Q418 81+81a 16).

21   DJD 34:159 "The suffix [of למֹ[ב]ינתם] may indicate that להתהלך had implicitly a personal subject which referred to several persons (e.g. the righteous, the sages *vel sim.*); but in למֹ[ב]ינתם לכול מ]עשי[ה, the suffix תם- could alternatively be non-personal, prospective to לכול מעשים in a periphrastic construct."

22   Supporting מביֹנתֹם are DJD 34:151, 159 "Considerations of space may equally permit תֹ-, but the mark on the line would perhaps stand in the wrong place for מבינתוֹ" and "in line 11 this reading מבינתוֹ, with a singular suffix, is uncertain; מבינתֹם] is as possible, and perhaps preferable"; Rey, *4QInstruction*, 279; and Kister, "ספרות החכמה בקומראן," 308. Alternatively, those reading ל- are Tigchelaar, *To Increase Learning*, 52; Goff, *4QInstruction*, 138; Qimron, *Dead Sea Scrolls*, 2:148.

reference to a "*yēṣer* of understanding" in 4QInstruction, and the only other occurrence in early Jewish literature is in 1QHᵃ XXIII 12 (par. 4Q428 14 1 = 4QHᵇ): "for a *yēṣer* of his understanding, and to interpret by these to dust like me" (ליצר מבינתו ולמליץ באלה לעפר כמוני). However, in the Vision of Hagu passage all of humankind has a *yēṣer* (i.e., "fashioning" rather than "inclination") like the holy ones (i.e., angelic beings), which indicates that human beings are created with the capacity to understand similar to angels (cf. Ch. 1 § 4.1.), and this preceding section anticipates the *yēṣer* mentioned next. If it is correct to transcribe a third person plural pronominal suffix, then this stands out among typically second person address; as such, this line expresses interest in more than just the *mēvîn* and his community; humanity is fashioned to understand the created order and to live accordingly (i.e., distinguishing between good and evil).

1.1.2   4Q417 1 i Lines 13–18

The address "and you, O understanding one" at the end of line 13 marks the beginning of the Hagu passage; a similar expression "and you, son of an understanding one" (l. 18; cf. Ch. 1 § 2.2.) marks the end of this passage and beginning of a new one. These lines are in relatively poor material condition and interpreters often find little agreement about their meaning (see figs. 9–10 in plate section).

4Q417 1 i lines 13–18 (4Q418 43 11–14 [single underline]; overlap [double underline]), Transcription and Translation:[23]

... וֹאתהֹ	13
מבין רוֹש²⁴ פעלתכה בזכרון הֹ[ ]∘ [בא²⁵ חֹרוֹתֹ החוק/ʰחוק}כה{ וֹחקוק כוֹל הפקוֹדהֹ	14
כי חרות מחוקק לאל על כול ע[/לילות]בני שוֹת וספר זכרון כתוב לפניו	15

---

23 DJD 34:151; Tigchelaar, *To Increase Learning*, 52; Puech, "Apports des textes," 137–139; Rey, *4QInstruction*, 278–289; Goff, *4QInstruction*, 137–138; Qimron, *Dead Sea Scrolls*, 2:148.

24 Reading רוש as a participle (cf. 4Q416 2 ii 20); this phrase may be read in relationship to the insistence in the document that the *mēvîn* is "poor," a motif that relates to material poverty and his character. If פעלה is taken as "reward" rather than "work" or "deeds," then one is compelled to translate רוש as an unusual and unattested form of "inherit" (ירש); cf. DJD 34:161–162.

25 Puech, "Apports des textes," 137–139 reconstructs הקֹ[ף כי בא; the letter following *heh* may be the semi-circular stroke of a *qof*, there are several in the immediate context for comparison; however, in the bottom leftward stroke the ink may be too heavy when one would expect it to taper; in DJD 34:151 the reconstruction הֹשׁ[לום כי בא] is too long; Tigchelaar, *To Increase Learning*, 52 reconstructs הֹעֹ[בא].

לשמרי דברו[^26] והי֯אה חזון ההגו[^27] לספר זכרון וינחילה֯[^28] לאנוש עם רוח ‏ע[י]א‎   16

כתבנית קדושים יצרו ועוד לוא נתן[^29] הג֯ו֯[^30] לרוח ב[ש]ר כי לא ידע בין   17

[טו]ב̇ לרע כמשפט [ר]וחו֯]   *vacat*   ] ואתה בן מבין ...   18

And you, **14** O understanding one,
inherit your reward,
by the remembrance of [   ]come.
Engraved is {your} the statute and every punishment inscribed,
15 for engraved is the decree by God,
against all w[antonness of] the sons of perdition,
and a book of memory is written before him,
16 for those who keep His word,
and this is a vision of *meditation* to a book of memorial,
and He made humanity, a people ᵂⁱᵗʰ a spirit, to inherit it (i.e., the
     vision?),
for **17** according to the pattern of the holy ones is *humanity's* fashioning,
and no longer is *hagu* given to a f[le]shly spirit,
because it *did not know* the difference between **18** [goo]d and evil,
according to the judgment of his [sp]irit
     vacat and you, O son of an understanding one ...

The three words עם רוח ‏ע, found in line 16, may be read either as the creation
of אנוש who are "a people with a spirit," or אנוש "with a spiritual people."[^31]

---

[^26]: The phrase לשמרי דברו here may be an allusion to Mal 3:16 לְיִרְאֵי יְהוָה וּלְחֹשְׁבֵי שְׁמוֹ where a book of remembrance is found; 4QInstruction likely understands the heavenly book to be "for those who keep his word," as opposed to a predetermined list of names, and is closely associated with the "vision of Hagu."

[^27]: Rey, *4QInstruction*, 279 reads ההגו֯ת ("une vision *de la méditation*"), a possible reading; however, under infrared I have not been able to decipher traces of a *tav*.

[^28]: DJD 34:163–164 suggest that וינחילה was later changed to וינ֯חיל֯ו֯נ֯י; cf. Tigchelaar, "Spiritual People,'" 111.

[^29]: Reading as *Niphal* נִתַּן.

[^30]: Puech, "Apports des textes," 137–139 reads החֹזֹון rather than הגו֯; the *gimel* appears in some photographs to have a right downward stroke that is too vertical for the expected diagonal stroke of a *gimel* in this hand; under infrared the diagonal stroke is clearer. Cf. the *gimel* in line 23.

[^31]: Eibert J.C. Tigchelaar, "Dittography and Copying Lines in the Dead Sea Scrolls: Considering George Brooke's Proposal about 1QpHab 7:1–2," in *Is There a Text in This Cave*, 293–307 at 306–307 writes that the "repetition of עם ... is almost universally seen as the correction of an erroneous haplography ..." and "the first hand of 4Q417 repeatedly omitted words,

Cana Werman suggests reading the first עַם ("people") as the attributive of אנוש, rather than the preposition "with," and the second עַם ("with") as the preposition.[32] In support of her suggestion, we may observe a similar combination of "with spirit" in the Thanksgiving Hymns: "And you cast for a person an eternal lot with the spirits of knowledge (עם רוחות דעת)" (1QHᵃ XI 23–24).[33] If this is the correct way to translate line 16, then there is no "spiritual people" and instead the emphasis is on humanity possessing a spirit and a segment of humanity (i.e., רוח בשר) is wayward and dispossessed of revealed wisdom. Further below we will return to "spirit" in 4QInstruction where this emphasis on "with spirit" comes into focus again. In line 17 the "fleshly spirit" are "no longer" (ועוד לוא) given Hagu, which implies that they once had it. Therefore, there is no ontological and predetermined distinction between spiritual and fleshly people in 4QInstruction; in fact, there are no "people of flesh," only a *spirit* that is labeled "fleshly."

If the רוח בשר had been created separately, then they would never have possessed Hagu and it would not be possible to state that they "no longer" (l. 17) have it. The "fleshly spirit" is so designated because they are corrupted humanity, and humankind is a people with a spirit. In line 17 the phrase ועוד לוא has too often been glossed over. Harrington and Strugnell comment that the temporal sense is likely "and no more" and Goff also states that this is a reasonable rendering of the expression.[34] If the editors' suggestion is followed, then the

---

which were then added by a second hand." The first hand reading then is: וינחילה לאנוש עם רוח ("He made humanity, with a spirit, to inherit it"). However, Tigchelaar concludes that "an examination of the additions by the second hand ... shows that none of those unambiguously correct a mistaken text, but rather propose, as indicated in the translations of DJD 34, different readings. But if the second hand actually aimed at improving the first, then the possibility should at least be considered that the attempt at correction introduced the mistake." A first hand reading of this phrase as "spiritual people" without "with" makes no sense (i.e., אנוש *is* a "spiritual people?"); as "with spirit" it is explained immediately: "for according to the pattern of the holy ones is humanity's fashioning" (cf. Gen 3:5, 3:22 where knowing good and evil is to be like God and angels).

32   Cana Werman, "What Is the Book of Hagu?" in *Sapiential Perspectives*, 125–140 at 137; cf. Cana Werman, "The 'תורה' and the 'תעודה' Engraved on the Tablets," *DSD* 9/1 (2002): 75–103 at 92.

33   Unless otherwise indicated English and Hebrew references to the Thanksgiving Hymns are from Schuller and Newsom, *The Hodayot* (*Thanksgiving Psalms*).

34   Following DJD 34:166; Goff, "Adam, the Angels," 17 further notes that עוד is a constituent adverb and when used with a finite verb, in this case נתן, has a temporal sense. Harrington and Strugnell rule out a future sense "not yet." The temporal sense of ועוד לוא has been glossed over in many translations, cf. Lange, *Weisheit und Prädestination*, 53 "Doch

[handwritten: Adam & humanity not opposed to each other]

claim of line 17 is that Hagu is "no longer" given to the fleshly spirit, and this then means that the fleshly spirit once possessed this revelation. If this is the case, then the reason for distinguishing between the righteous community and those outside of it must be found somewhere other than the creation of a spiritual people, on the one hand, and the creation of fleshly people, on the other, in which this latter segment of humanity is ontologically different and excluded from revelation.

How אנוש is translated is as important as how the consecutive עם עם are rendered. אנוש has been translated as: (1) the antediluvian figure "Enosh" son of Seth (Gen 4:26);[35] (2) the first man "Adam"; and (3) "humanity." That "Enosh" is in view here is unconvincing, in part because it is argued on the basis of line 15 referring to "Seth" when in fact בני שׁות is best read as "sons of perdition" (Num 24:17).[36] That אנוש means "Adam" is justified vis-à-vis 1QS III 17–18 (והואה ברא אנוש לממשלת תבל), although this reference actually makes explicit that "humanity" and not just "Adam" are tasked with ruling over the world. Some have found a tautological problem with the translation "humanity"—which arises only when עם עם רוח is translated as "with a spiritual people"—since it would be nonsensical to describe the creation of all humanity together with a sub-section of humankind.[37] אנוש is well attested at Qumran and in particular 4QInstruction (4Q416 2 ii 12; 4Q418 77 3) as a designation for humankind.[38]

In the case of both רוח בשר and עם רוח the author's emphasis is on spirit. The *mēvîn* and his community are imperfect in their pursuit of revealed wis-

---

die Erklärung wurde nicht dem Geist des Fleisches gegeben"; Puech, "Apports des textes," 138 "mais n'a pas encore été donnée la vision à un esprit de chair"; Rey, *4QInstruction*, 281 "Mais il n'a pas donné la vision à un esprit charnel"; Goff, *The Worldly and Heavenly*, 84 "Moreover, he did not give Hagu" changes translation in "Adam, the Angels," 13 to "But no more." Cf. 4Q418 201 where the broken phrase "]and it will be closed (ויסגר) to all the sons of in[iquity" may refer to meditation being withdrawn.

35 George J. Brooke, "Biblical Interpretation in the Wisdom Texts from Qumran," in *The Wisdom Texts from Qumran*, 201–222.

36 See Goff's persuasive discussion that בני שׁות should be read in relation to Num 24:17 and "refers to the wicked whose punishment is determined but not yet fully realized" Goff, *The Worldly and Heavenly Wisdom*, 92. Rey, *4QInstruction*, 297 comes to the same conclusion.

37 Matthew J. Goff, "Recent Trends in the Study of Early Jewish Wisdom Literature: The Contribution of 4QInstruction and Other Qumran Texts," *CBR* 7/3 (2009): 376–416 at 385 comments that "[t]he core problem with the 'humanity' reading, as Strugnell and Harrington point out (1999: 165), is that it is 'tautological'—it would not make sense for the text to state that the vision was given to all of humanity and to the spiritual people, since the latter term presumably denotes one category of humankind."

38 Rey, *4QInstruction*, 281 translates line 16: "Et voici une vision de la méditation du livre mémorial: il l'a donnée en héritage à l'homme comme [peuple] spirituel."

All spirit [spiritual → flesh]

dom and are concerned with all that threatens their acquisition of it. As will be seen below, in 4QInstruction people should take care of their spirit because it is possible for it to become displaced. The Vision of Hagu passage is crucial for understanding whether all of humanity or only a specific group is revealed wisdom. However, whether "humanity" (אנוש) is as all-encompassing as first appears requires further scrutiny. 4QInstruction designates some of humanity as "fleshly spirit" because they did not differentiate between good and evil when access to meditation enabled them to do so (l. 17). 4QInstruction is interested to describe those who had been tasked with pursuing revealed mysteries, failed in their pursuit, and had this privilege removed. On the one hand, this may suggest a polemical context between fellow Jews and an accusation that some had gone astray (e.g., CD I 13); in this case, even though אנוש is translated "humanity," the author may not think beyond Israel. On the other hand, 4QInstruction may reflect a wisdom universal to all humanity, namely revelation of the created order and cosmos, and an inclination (*yēṣer*) to understand, as expressed in preceding paragraph 4Q417 1 i 1–13a (cf. "the pattern of the holy ones" in l. 17).[39] Whatever the case, in 4QInstruction the ability to gain insight begins with "spirit," which itself was given from creation; possessing "spirit" is equated with having access to Hagu and when not maintained through observing and practicing truth it may become corrupted (cf. 4Q416 2 iii 6–7) leading to the wayward being designated as "fleshly spirit."

1.1.3   "Fleshly Spirit" in 4Q418 81 + 81a Lines 1–3

The focus on 4Q418 81 + 81a 1–14 in Chapter 1 (§ 4.) is on the speaker and exalted status of the addressee. The first two lines of this section begin with a description of a figure who has been separated from the רוח בשר. While this has been taken at times as reinforcing the view that there are two groups of humanity predetermined from creation, this interpretation is much less convincing in light of a reassessment of the Hagu passage.

---

39   Similarly, in Jubilees the idolatry of the Gentiles is not derived from an innate nature, but is a problem that is explained as a blindness resulting from the work of evil spirits. General revelation goes unheard, cf. Ps 19:1–6; Rom 1:19–20 (see §1.1.5 below), "ever since the creation of the world his invisible nature ... has been clearly perceived." According to Ellen Birnbaum, *The Place of Judaism in Philo's Thought: Israel, Jews, and Proselytes*, BJS 290 (Atlanta: Scholars Press, 1996), 1–14 there are two types of divine-human relationships in Philo, the particularism of God's covenant with Israel ("the position that only Jews can participate in these relationships") and a universal quest to see God ("the position that anyone can participate in these relationships"). Greg Schmidt Goering, *Wisdom's Roots Revealed: Ben Sira and the Election of Israel*, JSJSup 139 (Leiden: Brill, 2009), seeks to demonstrate that Ben Sira distinguishes between general wisdom revealed to all humanity and a special wisdom revealed only to Israel.

Singular

I see this as actualizing what God already has done

4Q418 81 + 81a lines 1–3

[... by the pouring out of] your lips open up a spring to bless the holy
    ones.
And you, as an everlasting spring, praise His [name,
sin]ce He separated you [הבדילך] from every 2 fleshly spirit [רוח בשר];

And you, keep separate [ואתה הבדל] from everything that He hates,
and keep apart from all the abominations of the soul;
[Fo]r He has made everyone,
3 and has given to each man his own inheritance,
but He is your portion and your inheritance among the children of
    mankind,
[and over] His [in]heritance He has set you in authority.

Descriptions of the elevated status of the addressee in Chapter 1 depict a member of the community serving in a special role as *maśkîl*. This column is not concerned with an ontological distinction and separation. There is no ontological division between who can pursue wisdom and who cannot in 4QInstruction, but rather members of a community and segments of humanity are distinguished along ethical lines, namely between those who are either faithful or unfaithful differentiating between good from evil and living accordingly. An uncorrupted spirit (i.e., holy spirit) permits this *maśkîl* to serve as an intercessor, pursue revealed wisdom, as well as to participate with and venerate angelic beings (l. 1); what separates the addressee from the "fleshly spirit" is his actualization of wisdom (i.e., "*ḥokma* of the hands" or "dint of discipline") and, in his position as sage, he keeps separate from the wicked.

In assessing the addressee's separation from the רוח בשר, the singular subject "you" (ואתה) should not be overlooked. Unlikely is that this singular address is a statement reflecting anthropology broadly. Given the characteristics of the addressee here, the second person singular form does not apply to all within the community; indeed, a variety of people in different positions are addressed in 4QInstruction. The "first-born" and "most holy" individual in 4Q418 81 + 81a 1–14 may, using the *Hiphil* followed by *Niphal* verb from the root בדל, be used to describe being "distinguished," and less so "separated," from "fleshly spirit." To be "distinguished" from others underscores that the addressees in 4QInstruction do not all share an identical "lot" or "inheritance," instead they acquire revealed wisdom to different degrees.[40] 4QInstruction's urgent exhortations to

---

40   The universalizing of 4Q418 81 + 81a in its use of Num 18:20 is discussed in Chapter 1 (§ 2.3.);

seek the רז נהיה, as well as genuine concern that one may succumb to fatigue in the process, are well known. Angelic beings are held up as superior in pursuing mysteries and therefore models to be emulated. The distinguishing of the one addressed in 4Q418 81 + 81a from the "fleshly spirit" reinforces his special status and superior acquisition of revelation in comparison to other members of the community.

1.1.4   "Fleshly Spirit" in 4Q416 1 Line 12

4Q416 1 preserves part of the opening column of the document (cf. Ch. 1 §1.2.), which is evident from the wide right margin, and here we find references to both the רוח בשר and יצר בשר.

4Q416 1 lines 10–16 (comp. 4Q418 1, 2, 2a, 2b, 2c, 208, 209 218, 212, 217, 224), Transcription and Translation:[41]

[	בֹּשֹׁמים ישפוט על עבודת רשעה וכל בני אמֹתֹו ירצוֹ לֹ[	10
[ממקומה]42	קצה ויפחדו וירֹזעו כל אשר התגללו בה כי שמים ירֹאוֹ[ן וארץ תרעש	11
ביום]	יֹ[מֹים ותהמות פחדו ויתערערו כל רוח בשר ובני חשמיֹ[ם	12
[סלם ooo	מֹשֹ[פֹטה וכל עולה תתם עודֹ43 יֹשלם קץ האמֹ]ת	13
[ל	בכל קצי עד כי אל אמת הוא ומקדם שנֹ[י] עולם	14
[א	להבֹֹין צדק בין טוב לֹרֹעֹ לֹ[ ]רֹ כל משפֹֹ[ט	15
[ל ל	יֹ[צר בשר הֹזֹאה ומבינוֹן]תֹ44	16

Tigchelaar, *To Increase Learning*, 232 comments on the use of the verb הבדיל here that line 3 quotes the promise of Num 18:20. "In Num 8:14 and 16:9 the same verb הבדיל is used with regard to the Levites, where it is said they have been separated from the midst of the Israelites, or the congregation of Israel. Deut 10:8–9 combines these concepts: … 'at the time the Lord set apart the tribe of Levi' for several cultic tasks, followed in verse 9 by" reference to inheritance. "Just as בני אדם in line 3 replaces the biblical בני ישראל, so רוח בשר replaces בני ישראל or עדת ישראל in this phrase. In other words, רוח בשר and בני אדם seem to be synonymous in this fragment."

41   Tigchelaar, *To Increase Learning*, 42–43 and 175–181; cf. DJD 34:81–88; Rey, *4QInstruction*, 229–230; Goff, *4QInstruction*, 43–44; Qimron, *Dead Sea Scrolls*, 2:147.

42   Theoretical reconstruction, Qimron, *Dead Sea Scrolls*, 2:147.

43   Reading עד.

44   DJD 34:558 in the concordance reconstruct: כיא בור[א יצר בשר הואה ומביני; cf. DJD 34:88 and the editors' comment: "Who or what is being described as יצר בשר? If, as 4Q418 might suggest, א[לו, כי]א, or הלו[א preceded יצר, then הואה could refer to man or his sinful *yeṣer* (cf. the emphasis in the surrounding text on man's knowledge). However, if a longer phrase preceded it (e.g., schematically, בורא יצר בשר הואה), then in that case הואה would refer to God (cf. 1QHᵃ X 23) as the *creator* (?) of the יצר בשר." Tigchelaar, *To Increase Learning*, 176

New reading

10 in heaven he *declares* judgment upon wicked works,
and all the sons of his truth will hasten to […]
11 […] its end.
And they will feel dread,
and all who wallowed in it will cry out,
for the heavens will fear [and the earth shake from its place]
12 [the s]eas and the depths fear,
and the fleshly spirit will be made destitute,
and the sons of heave[n …]
and in the day of 13 its [ju]dgment,
and all iniquity will be completed,
until the period of tru[th] is fulfilled
∘lm∘∘∘
14 in all periods of eternity,
for he is the God of truth and from before the years of[eternity …
15 to understand righteousness,
between good and evil to *l*[ ]*r* every judgmen[t …
16 fleshly [v]essel is he,
and understanding[…

4Q416 1 describes the order of the cosmos (ll. 1–9) before turning to the theme
of judgment. While judgment upon the רוח בשר is described in line 12, where
they are "stripped" or "made destitute" (ערער), they are never contrasted with
a righteous group of humanity.[45] In line 10 the בני אמתו cannot be assumed to
be a group of righteous and elect human beings, but rather may be heavenly
beings. If the verb at the end of line 11 is read as יְרָצוּ, then this is a depiction
of angelic beings hastening to judgment.[46] The בני השמים ("sons of heaven") in
line 12 is more straightforwardly a designation for heavenly beings.[47] These sons

---

reads יֵצֶר בשר הואה ומבינ∘[and translates: "[incl]ination of the flesh is he/it. And from
understanding (?) [."

45   In Ch. 1 (§1.2.) 4Q416 1 15 (par. 4Q418 2) was considered in detail because it has been
reconstructed by Puech as referring to a sage causing the righteous to understand. L. 15
may begin a new section; cf. DJD 34:83 translate l 15 "So that *the righteous may distinguish* (?) between good and evil"; Tigchelaar, *To Increase Learning*, 176 has "to let the
righteous understand (the distinction) between good and evil." Here, the righteous would
be instructed to draw upon the lesson of judgment in the preceding lines.

46   Tigchelaar, *To Increase Learning*, 180.

47   DJD 34:290 בני שמים "is usually a non-metaphorical epithet for a group of heavenly beings."
Cf. 1QS IV 22; XI 8; 1QHᵃ XI 23; XXIII 30; XXVI 36; 4Q181 1 2.

of heaven are not likely set in contrast with the "fleshly spirit," but rather serve as instruments of judgment upon them, similar to line 10.

In 4QInstruction בני שמים is only found here and in 4Q418 69 ii 13 where a rhetorical question is posed whether human beings are like angelic beings who do not tire. In 4Q418 69 ii, future judgment on the wicked is contrasted with reward for the righteous (cf. eschatological judgment in 4Q418 126 ii). 4Q418 69 ii does not refer to the רוח בשר, but rather the wicked are the "foolish of heart," "sons of iniquity," and most importantly of all "ones who hold fast to evil" (l. 8). By contrast the righteous are those who "seek understanding" and "watch over all knowledge" (ll. 10–11). These expressions for the righteous and wicked root reward and judgment in human activity. The author justifies judgment on the wicked by asking another rhetorical question: "what good is justice for what has not been established?" (ומה משפט ללוא נוסד) and then answers this question with, "... you were fashioned [נוצרתם], but to eternal destruction you will return" (ll. 4–6). These lines underscore, like the Vision of Hagu pericope, that the wicked were originally fashioned and established to pursue wisdom. This resonates well with the description of judgment upon the רוח בשר in 4Q416 1, which begins with a pronouncement against their "evil works" (l. 10) and upon those who "wallowed" in wickedness (l. 11).

The words יצר בשר הוא in 4Q416 1 16 could refer to an "earthly vessel" (יֵצֶר בָּשָׂר) as an epithet for a base human condition (i.e., "he/it is an earthly vessel") or to a fleshly inclination. Theoretically one could read יָצַר בָּשָׂר ("He fashioned flesh") but would the הוא refer to God as the subject? One justification for reading this as a fleshly *yēṣer* is found in 4Q417 1 ii 12 where this fragmentary phrase is preserved: אל תפתכה מחשבת יצר רע ("do not be *enticed* by the thought of an evil inclination").[48] Tigchelaar mentions line 12 briefly, commenting that the context is too fragmentary to determine whether this is a reference to the *yēṣer ra'* or more specifically a sexual desire.[49] Kister notes this line and does so within a broader treatment of *yēṣer* in Qumran literature without giving

---

[48] Depending on how one reconstructs and reads different passages, there are as many as three different "inclinations" in 4QInstruction: יצר בשר ("inclination of the flesh"), יצר רע ("evil inclination"), and יצר מבין ("inclination of understanding"). Excluding overlaps, the noun יצר *may* occur as many as 6 times; 5 times with at least some discernible context (4Q416 1 16; 4Q417 1 i 9, 11, 17; 4Q417 1 ii 12) and once without any meaningful context (4Q418 217 1).

[49] Tigchelaar, "The Evil Inclination," 350 and makes no further comment on 4QInstruction. The use of יצר רע as "sexual desire" is likely a later development as there is no clear attestation to this meaning in the earliest traditions.

explicit attention to other possible *yĕṣerîm* in 4QInstruction.[50] Notably, Ishay Rosen-Zvi refers to this use of יצר רע as "innovative," describing it as "an active agent that can entice people to evil."[51] Moreover, in his assessment the *yēṣer* is not yet reified and yet it features "in a demonological semantic field" even if its precise meaning is rather fluid.[52]

In 4Q417 1 ii 12 is the use of an imperative form of the verb פתה to exhort the addressee to avoid the thought of an evil inclination. Few commentators have offered substantial comment on the יצר רע in line 12.

4Q417 1 ii lines 12–14 (par. 4Q418 123 i 1–2), Transcription and Translation:[53]

[	אל תפתכה מחשבת יצר רע] 12
אל תעש דבר[54]	לאמת תדרוש אל תפתכה מ̇[◦] 13
	צוה
[	בלוא נבונות בשר אל תשגכ]ה 14

12   do not let the thought of an evil inclination entice you[
13   by truth you will seek, do not [let the thought of an evil inclination (?)]
     entice you [and do not do anything]
14   without ^{His commanding.} By understandings of the flesh, do not be lead
     as[tray

How the *Piel* verb from the root פתה is translated has significant impact on our understanding of the יצר רע. Moreover, the expression "thought" (מחשבה) in construct with the *yēṣer*, were it to occur without פתה, would seemingly locate the inclination within the interior of a human being. For פתה I offer the translation "enticed" although it could be rendered as "mislead," "deceived," or even "seduced." In 4QInstruction the *Piel* verb occurs only here, and in *Qal* form is

50   Menahem Kister, "'Inclination of the Heart of Man,' the Body and Purification from Evil," in *Meghillot: Studies in the Dead Sea Scrolls VIII*, ed. Moshe Bar-Asher & Devorah Dimant (Jerusalem: Bialik Institute & Haifa University Press, 2010), 243–286 at 252 [Hebrew], where he comments on the positive *yēṣer* in 4Q417 1 i.

51   Ishay Rosen-Zvi, *Demonic Desire: Yetzer HaRa and the Problem of Evil in Late Antiquity* (Philadelphia, PA: University of Pennsylvania Press, 2011), 46.

52   Rosen-Zvi, *Demonic Desires*, 48.

53   DJD 34:169; Tigchelaar, *To Increase Learning*, 54; Goff, *4QInstruction*, 173–174; Qimron, *Dead Sea Scrolls*, 2:149.

54   DJD 34:170 the editors offer the translation "[...] thou shalt *faithfully* seek. Let not the th[ought of an evil *inclination*] mislead thee[...]."

well known as a description for "being simple" (4Q418 221 2). In *Piel*, פתה is
used in the Qumran literature only twice, in: (1) 4Q184 1 17 ("Wiles of the
Wicked Woman"), and (2) the Temple Scroll (11Q19 LXVI 8; par. 4Q524 15 22).[55]
In 4Q184 the seductress "entices" human beings, and in the Temple Scroll a
man "seduces" a virgin. In the early 1990s Joseph Baumgarten suggested that
the woman of 4Q184 is a demonic figure[56] and, in this regard, there have
been several supporting and competing views put forward.[57] If the seductress
is demonic in 4Q184, then this only strengthens the argument that the verb
פתה functions in a demonological semantic field in 4QInstruction. The activity ascribed to the evil inclination in line 12 makes it an alien and independent
force. This is likely similar to the use of יצר רע in the Plea for Deliverance and
Barkhi Nafshi where the cause of evil also begins to move from an internal to
external force.[58] However, as an alien threat it refers to demonic forces whose
field of play is the human mind, emotions, and perceptions; this is particularly
threatening because one can no longer trust one's self.[59] Moreover, reflected in
this mechanism is the generation of a more highly attuned sense of interior-
ity. The warning for the righteous not to be led astray further demonstrates the
concern about falling away and urgency to remain vigilant.

While there is an active, evil *yēṣer* in 4QInstruction it seems unlikely that
the יצר בשר in 4Q416 1 16 is a synonym for it. The presence of the pronoun following this language (יצר בשר הוא) indicates that it is not an active agent and
the translation "fleshly vessel" is preferred. Therefore, although this is not an

---

55   Not a frequently used term, it occurs several other times in mostly *Pual* forms (e.g., 1QHª
     XII 17, XIV 22, XXII 27).

56   Joseph M. Baumgarten, "On the Nature of the Seductress in 4Q184," *RevQ* 15 (1991–1992):
     133–143.

57   Matthew J. Goff, "A Seductive Demoness at Qumran? Lilith, Female Demons and 4Q184," in
     Evil, the Devil, and Demons, 59–76; Michael J. Lesley, "Exegetical Wiles: 4Q184 as Scriptural
     Interpretation," in *The Scrolls and Biblical Traditions: Proceedings of the Seventh Meeting
     of the IOQS in Helsinki*, ed. George J. Brooke et al., STDJ 103 (Leiden: Brill, 2012), 107–142;
     Jacobus A. Naudé, "The Wiles of the Wicked Woman (4Q184), the Netherworld and the
     Body," *JSem* 15 (2006): 372–384; Armin Lange, "Die Weisheitstexte aus Qumran: Eine Ein-
     leitung," in *The Wisdom Texts from Qumran*, 3–30; Yiphtah Zur, "Parallels between Acts of
     Thomas 6–7 and 4Q184," *RevQ* 16 (1993): 103–107.

58   In the Qumran literature, the set phrase is found on five occasions, in: the Plea for Deliv-
     erance (11QPsª/11Q5 XIX 15–16); 4QInstruction (4Q417 1 ii 12); Barkhi Nafshi (4Q436 1 i 10);
     and the so-called "4QSectarian Text" (4Q422 i 12).

59   4Q416 2 iii 13–15 have exhortations to tend to "your thoughts" (DJD 34:113 suggest "refine"
     your thoughts) as part of understanding and seeking the mystery of existence.

identical description for the wicked as the רוח בשר, it is closely aligned with it because it uses "flesh" language for them.

1.1.5   Excursus: 4QInstruction and Romans

One of the consequences of this translation of the Hagu passage is that 4QIn-struction's relationship to Paul's use of "spirit" and "flesh" language changes.[60] Jörg Frey and Matthew Goff have each dedicated studies on the relationship of 4QInstruction to Pauline passages; Frey makes explicit his interest in Romans 8:5–8 and Galatians 5:17 whereas Goff focuses on 1 Corinthians 3 and 15.[61] When discussing passages in Paul's writings, both Frey and Goff hold a dualistic and deterministic reading of the Vision of Hagu passage.[62] In their assessments of "spirit" and "flesh" they propose that Qumran sapiential tradition influences Paul's anthropology. Along with, especially, the Thanksgiving Hymn and Rule of the Community, Frey describes them as "the earliest documents from Early Jewish tradition in which the term 'flesh' is used in a strongly negative sense," and that "[s]uch a negative usage of 'flesh' can also be seen ... in the letters of the Apostle Paul."[63] Goff comments that "as Frey advocates" the "flesh-spirit dichotomy in Paul is reasonably read as shaped by Palestinian traditions attested by 4QInstruction."[64] Frey's emphasis on the negative use of "flesh" as a shared characteristic between some Pauline letters and 4QInstruction is con-

---

60   Early in the study of the Scrolls noted by John Pryke, "'Spirit' and 'Flesh' in the Qumran Documents and Some New Testament Texts," *RevQ* 5 (1965): 345–360.

61   Jörg Frey, "Die paulinische Antithese von "Fleisch" und "Geist" und die palästinisch-jüdische Weisheitstradtion," *ZNW* 90/1 (1999): 45–77; "The Notion of 'Flesh' in 4QInstruc-tion and the Background of Pauline Usage," in *Sapiential, Poetical and Liturgical Texts*, 197–226; "Flesh and Spirit in the Palestinian Jewish Sapiential Tradition and in the Qum-ran Texts: An Inquiry into the Background of Pauline Usage," in *The Wisdom Texts from Qumran*, 367–404; Matthew J. Goff, "Being Fleshly or Spiritual: Anthropological Reflection and Exegesis of Genesis 1–3 in 4QInstruction and First Corinthians," in *Christian Body, Christian Self: Concepts of Early Christian Personhood*, ed. Clare K. Rothschild & Trevor W. Thompson, WUNT 284 (Tübingen: Mohr Siebeck, 2011), 41–59; cf. Tigchelaar, "'Spiritual People,'" 113–118.

62   See also the recent publications by Robert L. Cavin, *New Existence and Righteous Liv-ing: Colossians and 1 Peter in Conversation with 4QInstruction and the Hodayot*, BZNW 197 (Berlin: Walter de Gruyter, 2014), 200–209 and Nicholas A. Meyer, *Adam's Dust and Adam's Glory in the Hodayot and the Letters of Paul: Rethinking Anthropogony and Theology*, SNT 169 (Leiden: Brill, 2016), 41–42; both assume the dichotomy of "spirit" and "flesh" in this passage and an anthropology that consists of two predetermined peoples.

63   Frey, "Flesh and Spirit," 367.

64   Goff, "Being Fleshly or Spiritual," 58.

vincing. Indeed, Paul, like 4QInstruction, associates "flesh" with sin when he writes in Rom 7:5 "while we were living in the flesh, our sinful passions, aroused by the law, were at work in our members." Moreover, "flesh" in both Paul and 4QInstruction is the source of corruption and sin and has cosmic dimensions including quasi-demonic powers. The negative use of בשר in 4QInstruction is important for the study of σάρξ in Pauline language; however, the emphasis in 4QInstruction is not on dualities, but rather on the importance of distinguishing types of spirits.[65]

Although it is not the exact language of 4QInstruction, "no longer" being given meditation on Hagu has similarities with the darkening of the mind in Rom 1:21.[66] Paul is interested in a knowledge of God that is universal to all people available through the natural world.[67] Indeed, in Rom 3:19 he writes, so that "the whole world may be held accountable to God." Humanity enjoys a universal perception and is able and accountable (Rom 1:20 "without excuse") to understand God's existence and his nature.[68] The invisible attributes of God are observable since the world's creation.[69] Within the rhetorical framework of

65   Loren T. Stuckenbruck, "The Dead Sea Scrolls and the New Testament," in *Qumran and the Bible: Studying the Jewish and Christian Scriptures in Light of the Dead Sea Scrolls*, ed. Nora Dávid & Armin Lange, CBET 57 (Leuven: Peeters, 2010), 131–170 at 167; Benjamin Wold, "'Flesh' and 'Spirit' in Qumran Sapiential Literature as the Background to the Use in Pauline Epistles," *ZNW* 106/2 (2015): 262–279.

66   Rom 1:18–21: "18 For the wrath of God is revealed (ἀποκαλύπτεται) from heaven against all ungodliness and wickedness of those who by their wickedness suppress the truth. 19 For what can be known about God is made visible/plain (φανερόν) to them, because God has shown it (ἐφανέρωσεν) to them. 20 Ever since the creation of the world his eternal power (ἡ ἀΐδιος αὐτοῦ δύναμις) and divine nature (θειότης), invisible though they are, have been percieved (νοούμενα) and seen (καθορᾶται) through the things he has made. So they are without excuse; 21 for though they knew God, they did not honor him as God or give thanks to him, but they became futile in their thinking (ἐματαιώθησαν ἐν τοῖς διαλογισμοῖς), and their senseless hearts were darkened (ἐσκοτίσθη ἡ ἀσύνετος αὐτῶν καρδία)."

67   In contrast with Wis 13:1 where humanity is unable to understand God: "For all people who were ignorant of God were foolish by nature; and they were unable from the good things that are seen to know the one who exists, nor did they recognize the artisan while paying heed to his works." Both Rom 1 and Wis 13 are focused on condemning idolatry within the context of the Creator and his natural order. Cf. H.P. Owen, "The Scope of Natural Revelation in Rom. i and Acts xvii," *NTS* 5 (1959): 133–143; Morna D. Hooker, *From Adam to Christ: Essays on Paul* (Cambridge: CUP, 1990), 73–84.

68   Cf. Enochic literature where wisdom is made available to all humanity and has a universal character, Nickelsburg, *1 Enoch*, 54.

69   Joseph Fitzmyer, *Romans: A New Translation with Introduction and Commentary*, AB (New York, NY: Doubleday, 1993).

Romans this natural revelation establishes the guilt of all humanity to which Paul has a solution in Christ.[70] The association of creation with an awareness of the Creator is found frequently in early Jewish literature and uses similar predicates as found here in Rom 1. Humankind has an initial knowledge of God, however this innate ability to reason has been harmed. Because humanity did not honor God by living correctly in response to creation their "hearts" were darkened and they became futile in their reasoning.[71] Rom 1 and 4QInstruction both concieve of humanity being given an awareness of right and wrong from the created world and both texts also portray a human failure responding to it which has led to that gift being revoked.

In Rom 1 what precisely does it mean that humankind can "percieve" (νοέω) and "see" (καθοράω) God's eternal power and divine nature from creation? καθοράω ("observe," "percieve," "look down upon," "see") in the New Testament only occurs here; in LXX there are four instances: Num 24:2 "Balaam lifted his eyes and saw (וַיַּרְא) Israel"; Job 10:4 likewise translates יִרְא; Job 39:26 a hawk "spreads" its wings (יִפְרֹשׂ כְּנָפָו) to the south and in LXX a hawk "looks" [καθορῶν] to the south; and in 3 Macc 3:11 the king does not "consider" (καθορῶν) the might of the supreme God. In Classical literature, the word may denote physical seeing or mental perception.[72] Josephus uses καθοράω on a number of occasions (40×).[73] However, it is from Philo that we gain the most insights. He uses the term frequently (69×) and two associations are noteworthy here.

First, in *On the Creation of the World* humanity is able to see (καθοράω) the orderly structure of the cosmos and conclude that there is a Creator. Philo writes (*Creation* 45) that God foreknew the character of humankind, that they would trust their own conjectures rather than wisdom, and so he established the times and seasons so that no one would attribute to a created being the creation itself: "and again he knew that surveying (κατιδόντες) the periods of the

---

70   Knowledge of God for the Jews comes through the Mosaic Torah (Rom 2:18, 20), whereas here in ch. 1 Paul is interested in the responsibility of all people to know about God and the created order through the nature of the world.

71   Cf. Wis 11:15–16: "In return for their [the Gentiles'] foolish and wicked thoughts, which led them astray to worship irrational serpents and worthless animals, you sent upon them a multitude of irrational creatures to punish them, that they might learn that one is punished by the very things by which he sins."

72   Henry G. Liddell, Robert Scott & Henry S. Jones, *Greek-English Lexicon, Ninth Edition with a Revised Supplement* (Oxford: Clarendon Press, 1996), 856.

73   See esp. *Ant.* 8.106 when God's cloud enters the temple priests cannot "perceive" (καθορᾶν) one another; *Ant.* 8.168 king Solomon "shows" (καθεώρα) great wisdom; *Ant.* 9.84 the king sends out to search for the truth (κατοψομένους ἐξέπεμψεν).

sun and moon, to which are owing the summers and winters, and the alterna-
tions of spring and autumn, they would conceive the revolutions of the stars
in heaven to be the causes of all the things which every year should be produced and generated on the earth, accordingly that no one might venture either
through shameless impudence or inordinate ignorance to attribute to any created thing the primary causes of things …". This is repeated again in regard to
the ability of humanity to consider the origin of creation (*Creation* 54): "behold-
ing (κατιδοῦσα) the nature of the stars and their harmonious movement, and
the well-ordered revolutions of the fixed stars, and of the planets …".

Second, there are true laws of nature but not everyone sees (καθοράω) them.
There are those who do "not perceive (κατιδὼν) the true laws of nature" (*Drunk-
ness* 83). Like Rom 1:21 there are those who ignore truth and are now blinded:
"those, then, who have no desire for either discovery or investigation have
shamefully debased their reason by ignorance and indifference, and though
they had it in their power to see acutely (καθορᾶν) they have become blind"
(*Flight* 121). The Gentiles "rendered their own intellect blind when it might have
seen clearly (καθορᾶν)" (*Spec. Laws* 1.54).

Philo's use of καθοράω accords well with Rom 1. Romans, Philo, and 4QIn-
struction each express the view that humanity has the ability to perceive truth
from creation but that some have lost this ability in their erring.

The term νοέω (Rom 1:20) occurs 13 times in the New Testament and denotes
an inner recognition (cf. Matt 15:17; 16:9, 11; 24:15; Mark 7:18; 8:17; 13:14; John 12:40
contrasts between "seeing" (ὁράω) with the eye and "understanding" (νοέω) in
the heart; Eph 3:4, 20; 1 Tim 1:7; 2 Tim 2:7; Heb 11:3). Nearly half of the occurrences of νοέω in LXX are found in wisdom literature, and is particularly frequent in Proverbs where it is used to translate להבין (Prov 1:2, 3, 6; 8:5; 20:24;
23:1; 28:5; 29:19) and להשכיל (Prov 16:23).[74] The term also occurs twice in Sirach
where it translates בקר and דעה: (1) Sir 11:7 "do not find fault before you inves-
tigate, *examine* (νόησον) first and then criticize" is preserved in MS A and MS B
where we read בקר לפנים ואחר תזיף ("*seek/inquire* first and then criticize"); and
(2) Sir 31:15 "judge your neighbor's feelings by your own" (νόει τὰ τοῦ πλησίον ἐκ
σεαυτοῦ) is only preserved in MS B where we read דעה רעך כנפשך ("know your
neighbor as yourself").

In the first five chapters of the Book of Watchers, where the created order is
in view, we find the exhortation: "consider and know concerning all his works,
and know (νοήσατε) that a living God made them so, and he lives for all the

---

74   Liddell, Scott & Jones, *Greek-English Lexicon*, 1177–1178 νοέω is translated as (1) "perceive by
      the mind," "apprehend"; (2) "think," "consider," "reflect"; (3) "consider," "deem," "presume."

ages" (1 En. 3:1). Epistle of Jeremiah 41 is also concerned with perceiving from creation that there is a Creator, here the context is Chaldeans making idols: "yet they themselves cannot perceive (νοήσαντες) this and abandon them, for they have no sense" (cf. Philo, *Abraham* 70). In the Life of Adam and Eve the serpent speaks to Eve in the Garden of Eden encouraging her to eat from the tree of the knowledge of good and evil and to: "understand (νόησον) the value of the tree" (LAE 18:1).

The depiction of natural revelation that enables one to distinguish right from wrong in Rom 1 elucidates how creation and the created order may operate in 4QInstruction. "Flesh" in both Paul and 4QInstruction is the source of corruption and sin, which for both is a product of not living in accordance with what has been revealed to humanity.

1.2   *"Flesh" in the Thanksgiving Hymns*

The shared use of rare vocabulary in the Thanksgiving Hymns and 4QInstruction may suggest a common cultural milieu. Similar material could be explained as the work of bricoleurs gathering available materials for their own bricolage. Alternatively, a small amount of verbatim material found in 1QHᵃ XVIII and 4Q418 55 may indicate direct knowledge of the other composition.[75] Goff argues that the "Hodayot exhibits a degree of reliance on the sapiential tradition" and that "[t]heir thematic correspondences and terminological overlaps suggest a direct relationship."[76] Thematic and terminological correspondences between 4QInstruction and other traditions have been observed; when Stuckenbruck assesses 4QInstruction's relationship to Enochic authors he concludes that although they share many similar terms and phrases there is insufficient evidence to posit a direct literary relationship between them.[77] Also on the basis of observing similarities, although in Chapter 3 emphasis is on dissimilarity, Rey concludes that Ben Sira and 4QInstruction derive from the same scribal school. Whether the hymns, Enochic literature, or Ben Sira, intriguing commonalities are found and yet so too are sharp differences. If 4QInstruction is viewed as a "non-Yaḥad" composition, as opposed to a "pre-sectarian" one, then this alters the perception of a trajectory and evolutionary development toward "sectarianism"; it allows for the possibility that 4QInstruction is part of a wider pattern of religious thinking that potentially spans a

---

75   For the parallel phrase דעתם יכבדו איש מרעהו in 1QHᵃ XVIII 29–30 and 4Q418 55 10 see DJD 34:272; in the hymns, this phrase begins with לפי.

76   Goff, "Reading Wisdom," 287.

77   Loren T. Stuckenbruck, "4QInstruction and the Possible Influence of Early Enochic Traditions: An Evaluation," in *The Wisdom Texts from Qumran*, 245–261 at 260–261.

longer period of time than is often viewed. Indeed, when we turn to wisdom in the New Testament, particularly James and the Saying Source Q, we see the continuation of similar world views, language, and categories. How 4QInstruction and the hymns are related to one another, whether they draw upon a wider tradition (e.g., Enochic literature, Jubilees) or we should posit a direct literary relationship of one upon the other, remains unresolved. Differences between these compositions need to be taken into account when assessing their relationship and, as will be seen, shared language does not result in similar views on recipients of revelation and resulting authority constructs.

Discussion of the parallels between 4QInstruction and the Thanksgiving Hymns in this section have an interpretive function rather than a significant social function. The comparison is more for heuristic purposes than to assess influence. However, in both this section and the preceding one it becomes increasingly clear that 4QInstruction's relationship to Yaḥad compositions requires clarification. The *opinio communis* is that 4QInstruction pre-dates the emergence of the Yaḥad; the late first century BCE and early first century CE manuscripts of 4QInstruction suggest that the community copied and used it. Therefore, the hymns reflect a later evolution and application of common terms related to בשר ("flesh"). Therefore, chronologically, the question is not: "how does 4QInstruction relate to the Yaḥad?" but rather: "how did the Yaḥad relate to 4QInstruction?" In regard to the preceding section, the uncertain provenance and date of the Treatise on the Two Spirits makes it more difficult to assess 4QInstruction's relationship to it; in theory, it is at least possible that 4QInstruction may be reacting to the overt dualism of the Treatise.

1.2.1   יצר בשר
The majority of occurrences of יצר in the Thanksgiving Hymns are used to describe scurrilous human nature. That humanity is innately sinful in the hymns, and that this is intertwined with physical aspects of a person (e.g., the heart or eyes), has been noted since they were first studied.[78] Rosen-Zvi con-

---

78   J. Philip Hyatt, "The View of Man in the Qumran 'Hodayot,'" *NTS* 2 (1955–1956): 276–284; Mathias Delcor, *Les Hymnes de Qumrân (Hodayot): texte hébreu, introduction, traduction, commentaire* (Paris: Letouzey et Ané, 1962), 48–49; Svend Holm-Nielsen, *Hodayot: Psalms from Qumran* (Aarhus: Universitetsforlaget, 1960), 274; Gerhard Maier, *Mensch und freier Wille: Nach den jüdischen Religionsparteien zwischen Ben Sira und Paulus*, WUNT 12 (Tübingen: Mohr Siebeck, 1971), 170; Eugene H. Merrill, *Qumran and Predestination: A Theological Study of the Thanksgiving Hymns*, STDJ 8 (Leiden: Brill, 1975), 38; Denise Dombrowski-Hopkins, "The Qumran Community and 1Q Hodayot: a Reassessment," *RevQ* 10 (1981): 323–364 at 325; Newsom, *The Self as Symbolic Space*, 219–220; Miryam T. Brand, *Evil Within*

vincingly argues that to distinguish between *yēṣer* either as part of a person's nature or as a component of cosmology is to make a false distinction.[79] Indeed, in the Thanksgiving Hymns יצר is used frequently in relationship to anthropology, and yet there are occurrences that suggest it is at times reified (1QH[a] XIII 8): "you did not abandon me to the devices of my inclination [זמות יצרי]."[80] This echoes "devilish plans" (זמות בליעל) in 1QH[a] XII 14 (cf. 1QH[a] XIII 12 all those "scheming" [כל מזמותם] against the speaker; Isa 32:7 where the weapon of the wicked is "evil counsel" זמות יעץ). However, human nature does not consist of two interior parts: good and evil are not battling within. As such care should be taken not to label the cosmology or anthropology of the hymns as "dualistic," they are not identical to the Treatise of the Two Spirits where dualistic tensions between light/dark and good/evil, both internal and external, are found.[81] Rather, the hymns testify to a *yēṣer* as an external actor which serves to explain members' sinful consciousness. Referring to evil as "external" is also a bit misleading, these passages refer to something alien at work in the interior of a human being, that is "you did not abandon me to the devices of my (own) inclination." Indeed, this is similar to CD III 1–3 where Abraham keeps God's precepts and does not follow after his own "desire" (רצון).

An examination of the different ways יצר is used in the Thanksgiving Hymns further demonstrates Rosen-Zvi's observation. In 1QH[a] XV 16 ("for you yourself know the intention [יצר] of every deed") and line 19 ("you yourself know the intention [יצר] of your servant") *yēṣer* is used in reference to a neutral tendency and generic "intention."[82] יצר סמוך occurs three times in the hymns (1QH[a] IX 37; X 11, 38) and has positive connotations, denoting firmness or resoluteness in purpose (cf. יצר מבין in 4Q417 1 i 11).[83] The most frequent and well-known expres-

---

and Without: The Source of Sin and Its Nature as Portrayed in Second Temple Literature, JAJ-Sup 9 (Göttingen: Vandenhoeck & Ruprecht, 2013), 59–61.

79 Rosen-Zvi, *Demonic Desire*, 48–51.

80 Tensions are found in the hymns when the *yēṣer* is both an external actor and an aspect of human nature, one way to resolve this is source-critical: Gert Jeremias, *Der Lehrer der Gerechtigkeit* (Gottingen: Vandenhoeck & Ruprecht, 1963) made the case for distinguishing two groups in the Thanksgiving Hymns, identified as the hymns of the Teacher and the hymns of the community, and this has since been refined; Rosen-Zvi, *Demonic Desire*, 50 is right to dismiss these inconsistencies as arising from a source-critical issue.

81 *Pace* Holm-Nielsen, *Hodayot*, 296 who makes the case for a dualistic cosmology in the hymns.

82 Roland E. Murphy, "Yēṣer in the Qumran Literature," *Bib* 39 (1958): 334–344 at 343–344; cf. Rosen Zvi, *Demonic Desire*, 48.

83 יצר סמוך is found elsewhere at Qumran only in the Rule of the Community (1QS IV 5; VIII 3) and Barkhi Nafshi (4Q438 4 ii 2).

sion is יצר חמר ("vessel of clay"; 1QHᵃ III 29; IX 23; XI 24–25; XII 30; XIX 6; XX 29; XX 35; XXI 11, 38; XXII 12; XXIII 13, 28; XXV 31–32). A similar expression is found in יצר עפר ("vessel of dust"; 1QHᵃ VIII 18; XXI 17, 25, 34; XXIII 28). Describing the human "vessel" with dust, and perhaps to a lesser extent "clay" (cf. 1QS XI 22), is an allusion to the creation of man from the earth in Genesis 2 and relates to human nature.[84] The יצר אשמה ("guilty creature"; 1QHᵃ XIV 35), יצר עולה ("vessel of iniquity"; 1QHᵃ XXI 30), and יצר נתעב ("abhorrent vessel"; 1QHᵃ XXIII 37, 38) are also indicative of the psalmist's pessimistic anthropology. However, at least two other uses indicate that it is used as an "inclination," these are the יצר הוה ("destructive intention"; 1QHᵃ XV 6–7), and יצר רמיה ("deceitful inclination"; 1QHᵃ XXI 29).

In the case of יצר בשר (1QHᵃ XVIII 25; XXIV 6), Eileen Schuller and Carol Newsom's translation "vessel of flesh" rather than "fleshly inclination" makes the best sense because it would be difficult to account for an "inclination" within the context. Among the two occurrences of the term, only 1QHᵃ XVIII 25 provides context, here we read: "a vessel of flesh you have not set up as my refuge" (ויצר בשר לא שמתה לי מעוז). This description appears to be about the speaker's own corporeal being which is insufficient to protect him. Moreover, in the immediately preceding lines the speaker elaborates that he does not put his trust in wealth and unjust gain. "Vessel of flesh" in line 25 is closely related to his body and tangentially to physical luxury and possessions. In lines 28–29 all humanity is given produce from the land, which is contrasted with the sons of truth who have intelligence and an everlasting inheritance added to this.

In 1QHᵃ XXIV 6 the term יצר בשר is preserved at the end of the line without immediate context; line 6 is the first preserved line in the column. An important theme in this column is judgment upon the wicked and, although the text is only preserved in part, guilt is in some way associated with flesh: "and the mysteries of transgression to change flesh through their guilt" (ורזי פשע להשנות בשר באשמתם).[85] Column XXIV is interested in angelic beings (מלאכים, ll. 8, 11) and depicts the fall of the heavenly angels in lines 11–12: "You cast down the heavenly beings from [your holy] place" (ותכנע אלים ממכון קודשכה). Line 15 refers to the "bastards" (ממזרים) and despite the immediate context being unavailable to confirm that these are half-breed offspring from human/angel relations, the broader context makes this most probable. That "flesh" imprisons is suggested by line 13: "like a bird imprisoned until the time of your favor" (כעוף אסור עד

---

84 Murphy, "Yēṣer," 339–340.

85 Translation mine, Schuller & Newsom, *The Hodayot*, 73 translate: "and the mysteries of transgression in order that humankind be changed through their guilt."

קץ רצונכה). Therefore, "vessel of flesh" in column XXIV is not straightforwardly about human nature, but may also extend to the ממזרים. Indeed, it is interesting to note that twin spiritual and fleshly existence is typically only found in the Enochic tradition of the Giants, here in the hymns, and in 4QInstruction— human beings as רוח בשר combine what is separate elsewhere. The negative association of spirit with flesh, vis-á-vis the Giants tradition, may resonate when רוח בשר is used in 4QInstruction and the hymns; however, this is a remote possibility and likely means simply that a spirit is characterized by "fleshliness" (i.e., moral incapacity).[86]

1.2.2   רוח בשר

Although humanity is a creature who is defiled by perverted spirits (cf. 1QH[a] V 31–33 below),[87] here in 1QH[a] IV it is not entirely clear whether the psalmist views רוחות as: (1) evil spirits possessing human beings and trying to lead them astray (e.g., 4Q444 1 1–4; 2 i 4; 4Q510 1 5–6; 4Q560 1 i 2–3; 1 ii 5–6; 11QPs[a] XIX 13– 16), or (2) human tendencies. When in line 35 the speaker is strengthened to resist spirits, he is enabled to persevere by the spirits given by God (l. 29). That spirits are resisted by insight and knowledge (l. 33) may indicate that these are human tendencies rather than external evil spirits. However, in line 37 the subject who rules over the psalmist is lost to the lacuna, but given the context it is likely רוחות.

1QH[a] IV lines 35b–37

... חזק מתנ]יו לעמו[ד על רוחות	35
ולה[תהלך בכול אשר אהבתה ולמאוס בכול אשר שנאתה] ולעשות[הטוב בעיניך	36
ממ[שלתם בתכמו כי רוח בשר עבדך] *vacat* [ ] *vacat* [ ]	37

---

86   A short list of Enochic writings found at Qumran: Book of Watchers (1 En. 1–36) in 4Q201, 4Q202, 4Q204–4Q207; Astronomical Book (1 En. 72–82) 4Q208–4Q211; Book of Giants 4Q203, 1Q23, 2Q26, 4Q530–532, 6Q8; Letter of Enoch 4Q212; 4QPseudo-Enoch 4Q530– 4Q533.

87   That these "spirits" are explicitly related to the dominion of "Belial" is unlikely; Philip R. Davies, "Dualism in the Qumran War Texts," in *Dualism in Qumran*, ed. Géza G. Xeravits (London: T & T Clark, 2010), 8–19 at 8 writes that "בליעל occurs eleven times (1QH[a] x 16, 22; xi 28, 29, 32; xii 10, 13; xiii 26, 39; xiv 21 and xv 3), but in every instance is either used adjectivally, in a noun-pair, or can be interpreted as an abstract noun more readily than a personal name."

35   ... Strengthen [his] loi[ns that he may sta]nd against spirits
36   [... and that he may w]alk in everything that you love and despise every-
         thing that [you] hate, [and do] what is good in your eyes.
37   [...]their [domi]nion in his members; for your servant (is) a spirit of
         flesh. [...] *vacat*
      [...] *vacat*

In this column, and the hymns generally, God chooses those who are delivered from sin to act in accordance with God's will (1QHᵃ IV 33–34 "As for me, I understand that (for) the one whom you have chosen [בחרתה] you determine his way and through insight [... you] draw him back from sinning against you").[88] The ability to resist sin and evil may ultimately be attributed to election;[89] and yet, despite the psalmist's election and divine support he still expresses that he is a רוח בשר (l. 37).[90]

1QHᵃ V 12–VI 18 is reconstructed by Émile Puech as a hymn of the *maśkîl* and it is here that the other two uses of "fleshly spirit" are found (1QHᵃ V 15, 30).[91] A prominent theme is knowledge of the mysteries of God.[92] Mortals are רוח בשר, including the elect, and what differentiates them from the rest of humanity is the granting of true knowledge through the divine spirit.[93] In the hymns, humanity, including the author, is described as fashioned of dust and water and, as such, he asks what רוח בשר is to understand all these matters and to have insight into God's counsel; the answer is that the holy spirit placed within the elect enables them to know mysteries.

1QHᵃ V lines 12–20

[מֹעֹשֹׂי אֹל	[מזמור למ[שׂכֹּיֹל להתנפל לפֹנֹ]יֹ אל	12
[יֹ○ עולם	[ולהבין פֹּיֹתים]]○○[ ]○○[	13
[○ התהלכו	[ת○ ולהבין אנוש בֹּ○ [ ] בשר וסוד רֹוחֹי]	14
[בֹּכֹוֹח גבורתך	[ברוך] אתה אדוני ○○[ ]○○ר רוח בֹּשֹׂר בֹּבֹ[○]	15

---

88   Cf. 1QHᵃ VIII 28; XIII 5 where the psalmist also writes about his chosenness.
89   Brand, *Evil Within and Without*, 59–67.
90   Cf. the tensions of spirit/flesh in Rom 7–8; esp. 8:9 "you are not in the flesh, you are in the Spirit" and 8:24–25 and the expectation of deliverance from the body.
91   Puech, "Un hymne Essénien," 63.
92   Newsom, *Self as Symbolic*, 217.
93   Cf. 1 Cor 2:14 where "natural man" (ψυχικὸς ἄνθρωπος) does not receive the gifts of the spirit, and in 1 Cor 3:1 Paul contrasts spiritual people (πνευματικός) with fleshly ones (σαρκίνος).

לאין [חֹקר כול 16 [והמון ח[סֹֹדֹֹךֹֹ עם רוב טובךֹ] וכוס [חֹֹמֹֹתֹֹך וקנאת צמשפֹֹ]טיך

ה[כֹינותה 17 [ ]ֹֹת כול בינה וֹמֹ[וֹסר] ורזי מחשבת וראשֹֹיֹֹת]

[קֹדושיֹם 18 [ ]ֹֹ◦◦ קודש מקדם עוֹ[לם ו[לֹעוֹלמי עד אתה הוֹאֹֹ]תה

מעין [בֹינתך לא 19 [ ] וברזי פלאך הֹוֹדֹעֹ[תֹני בעֹ]בֹֹור כבודך ובעומק ◦◦

צֹֹדֹֹקֹֹ 20 [ ]אתה גליתה דרכֹי אֹמֹֹתֹ וֹמעשיֹ רֹע חוכמה ואולֹתֹ]

12 [A psalm for the In]structor, that he may prostrate himself befor[e God
...]deeds of God

13 [...]and that the simple may understand [...]◦◦[...]◦◦[...]◦y forever

14 [...]◦t and that humandkind may understand concerning [...]◦ flesh and
the council of the spirits of [...]◦ they walk.

15 [... Blessed are] you, O Lord, ◦◦[...]◦◦r a spirit of flesh *bb*◦[...]through
your mighty strength

16 [and the abundance of]your [kind]ness together with your great goodness[and the cup of]your wrath and [your] zealous judgeme[nts ...
unsea]rchable. All

17 [...]◦t all insight and in[struction] and the mysteries of the plan and the
beginning[...]you [es]tablished

18 [...]◦◦ holiness from a[ges of old [and] to everlasting ages you yourself
resolved [...]holy ones

19 [...] and in your wonderful mysteries [you] have instructed [me for the
s]ake of your glory, and in the depth ◦◦[... source of] your insight not

20 [...]you yourself have revealed the ways of truth and the works of evil,
wisdom and folly[...] righteousness

God grants the *maśkîl* of these lines insight into the mysteries of his plan. The
revelation of mysteries is intertwined with the ways of truth and evil (l. 20),
which accords well with the Vision of Hagu. Later in the same column, after
the second occurrence of רוח בשר, the means by which understanding is given
is the spirit (l. 36).

1QHᵃ v lines 31–36a

דֹ[וֹ]לֹ[יֹ]ךֹ 31 [ ]◦בכוֹל אלה ולהשכיל בסֹ[◦]◦ [ ] גדול ומה ילוד אשה בכוֹל [גֹ]דֹ[וֹ]
הנוֹ'אֹים והוא

32 מבנה עפר ומגבל מים אֹ[שמה וחט]אה סודו ערות קלוֹן וֹמֹ[קור הנֹ]דה ורוח נעוה
משלה

בו 33 ואם ירשע יהיֹהֹ] לאות עד [עֹולם ומופת דורות רחוקֹ[יֹ]ֹם לבשר רק בטובך

יצדק איש וברֹוֹב רח[מיֹך 34 [בהדרך תפארנו ותמשֹׁיֹלֹנֹ]וֹ בֹ]רֹוב עדנים עם שלום

עולם ואורך ימים כי 35 וֹ]דֹבֹרך לא ישוב אחור ואני עבדך ידעתי

ברוח אשר נתתה בי] 36a [...

30   for everlasting ages. In the mysteries of your understanding [you] appor-
      tioned all these in order to make known your glory. [But how i]s a
      spirit of flesh to understand

31   all these things and to discern *bs*○[...] great [...]? What is one born of
      woman amid all your [gre]at fearful acts? He

32   is a thing constructed of dust and kneaded with water. Sin[ful gui]lt is
      his foundation, obscene shame, and a so[urce of im]purity. And a
      perverted spirit rules

33   him. If he acts wickedly, he will become[a sign for]ever and a portent
      for dis[ta]nt generations of flesh. Only through your goodness

34   can a person be righteous, and by [your] abundant compas[sion ...]. By
      your splendor you glorify him, and you give [him] dominion [with]
      abundant delights together with eternal

35   peace and long life. For [... and] your word will not turn back. And I,
      your servant, know

36   by means of the spirit that you place in me [...] and all your deeds are
      righteousness. And your word will not turn back. ...

The רוח בשר in the Thanksgiving Hymns is equated with the obtuse part of
humanity unable to gain insight without God's spirit. As David Flusser comments, the gift of the spirit elevates the Qumran elect from the realm of the
flesh even if the psalmist still declares that he is among mortal humanity.[94]
Later in the hymns, in 1QHᵃ XIX 12–17, the psalmist exults that instruction in
truth leads to purification from sin and a place among angelic beings.

    In summary, when occurrences of רוח בשר in 4QInstruction and the Thanks-
giving Hymns are read alongside one another the following observations may
be made. For a human being to have an existence as both "flesh" and "spirit" is
rare in early Judaism; outside of these two Scrolls this notion is only found in
the Enochic tradition of the Giants. In 4QInstruction, those who are within the
community are never referred to as "fleshly," only those who are outside of it,
referring to those who have lost the ability to meditate on Hagu. In the hymns,
the elect figure is "fleshly" and the issue is how to transcend this negative condition to gain knowledge and understanding of mysteries. The directionality
found in 4QInstruction is opposite from that found in the hymns. In both 4QIn-

---

94   David Flusser, *Judaism of the Second Temple Period, vol. 1 Qumran and Apocalypticism*
      (Grand Rapids, MI: Eerdmans, 2007), 288–290. The exultations of the speaker in 1QS XI
      15–22 echo similar sentiments to the hymns: a human fashioned of clay and dust gives
      thanks for being granted knowledge.

struction and the hymns "spirit" enables one to gain wisdom, the difference is
that 4QInstruction's beginning point is not a negative anthropology, but rather
having a "spirit" which may become harmed.

2   "Spirit" in 4QInstruction

One of 4QInstruction's concerns is to maintain spirit in the present in order
to avoid judgment in the hereafter.[95] The "evil inclination" appears to be an
active threat and those who fail to "act according to the spirit" (4Q417 1 i 18),
as they were created to do, become corrupted and are "fleshly spirit." In the
garden metaphor (cf. Ch. 3 § 4.), humanity tends wisdom producing trees, the
consequence of ceasing to toil is the loss of access to meditation; thus, within
the metaphor this is to be barred from Eden. However, the mēvîn and his community are far from perfect, they too are deficient in pursuing the רז נהיה and
are deeply concerned with all that threatens their acquisition of wisdom. Even
in this state of imperfection and weakness they have not failed to pursue the
knowledge of good and evil.

4Q418 222 2 depicts a maśkîl who, in his exalted position, exhorts the addressees to "listen to my spirit." This sage is concerned with how the mēvîn is
to treat and relate to others' spirits. Not only is the addressee to distinguish
the spirits of other men (4Q417 2 i 1; 4Q418 77 3–4), but is also to rule over a
woman's spirit (4Q415 9 8; 4Q416 2 iv 6–7); apparently a groom even "weighs"
(cf. 4Q418 172 2) and "measures" a bride according to "spirits" (4Q415 11 5, 9 כי
לפיא רוחות).[96] Instruction occurs most frequently in regard to the mēvîn's spirit;

---

95   Alternatively, Goff, "Being Fleshly," 58 argues that in 4QInstruction "'spirit' language [is
      used] to assert that the elect can attain a form of existence after death that does not involve
      the flesh."

96   This reified notion of "spirit" is reminiscent of the theory of humors; i.e., Hippocrates the-
      ory that human moods, emotions and behaviors are caused by excess or lack of "humors"
      (or body fluids: blood, yellow bile, black bile and phlegm). While "spirits" may be external
      actors, such as unclean spirits or evil spirits, they are often internal, such as the Treatise
      on the Two Spirits (1QS III 18) where God places two spirits within humanity (וישם לו שתי
      רוחות להתהלך בם); cf. 1 Cor 12:10 where one of the "spiritual gifts" imparted is the abil-
      ity to "distinguish between spirits" (διακρίσεις πνευμάτων). 4QInstruction frequently refers
      to the addressee's נחלה ("portion" or "inheritance"), which may at times relate to a per-
      son's "spirit." Cf. Stuckenbruck, 1 Enoch, 422–423 comments on 1 En. 99:14 ("Woe to those
      who reject the foundation and everlasting inheritance (κληρονομίαν) of their fathers") that
      inheritance and one's place within the community is a result of pursuing wisdom or not.

such instances are found in second person singular exhortations: רוחכה ("your spirit" 4Q415 12 2; 4Q416 2 ii 6; 4Q416 2 iii 6; 4Q416 2 iv 8; 4Q418a 16b+17 2). The *mēvîn* has a "holy spirit" (4Q416 2 ii 6) and is taught that it is "good to be a servant in the spirit" (טוב היותכה עבד ברוח 4Q416 2 ii 17; 4Q417 2 ii+23 22).

2.1   Spirit in 4Q417 2 i Lines 1–6

Preserved in 4Q416 2 i–iv (par. 4Q417 2 i–ii) are several passages that are particularly important for understanding רוח. This occurrence of "spirit" is unusual among writings discovered at Qumran where it is often used in reference to God's spirit; in columns i–iv "spirit" is not used for God, but rather is limited either to the spirit of the *mēvîn* or to others in his community.[97] The first occurrence of רוח is in the first six lines of 4Q417 2 i, which is a passage that precedes the preserved text in 4Q416 2 i. These lines form a distinct unit which is indicated by the following *vacat* at the beginning of line 7 where the subject changes.[98] On two occasions in this column different kinds of people are mentioned, and these types then form themes that are used to structure sections. In line 7 the concern is with "a man of iniquity" (איש עול) and in line 10 one who is poor (רש), unfortunately, the subject of the paragraph in lines 1–6 is not preserved.

4Q417 2 i lines 1–6, Translation and Transcription:[99]

[	בֹּכֹל עת פן ישבעכה וכרֹוֹחוֹ דבר בו פן יֹ₀]	1
[	בלוא הוכח הכשר עבור לוֹ והנק שר ₀]	2
[	וגם את רוחו לא תבלע כיא בדממה דברת]ה	3
[	ותוכחתו ספר מהר ואל תעבוֹר על פשעיכה [כיא	4
סליחה]	יֹצדק כמוכה הואה כיא הואה }כיא הואה{ שר בשֹ[רים ועם	5
[	יֹעשה כיא מה הואה יחֹ'ד בכול מעשה לבלתי ₀₀]	6

1 and at all times,
lest he become fed up with you,
and according to his spirit speak to him,

---

97   Cf. Arthur E. Sekki, *The Meaning of Ruaḥ at Qumran*, SBLDS 110 (Atlanta, GA: Scholars Press, 1989), 7–69.

98   4Q416 2 i 1 preserves a few letters of the word לבלתי in 4Q417 2 i 6; otherwise this short pericope has no parallels in the mss. of 4QInstruction.

99   DJD 34:172; Tigchelaar, *To Increase Learning*, 55; Goff, *4QInstruction*, 183–184; Qimron, *Dead Sea Scrolls*, 2:152, Rey, *4QInstruction*, 42–43 does not transliterate or discuss these lines, but begins presentation at line 7.

lest he [...]

2 without a suitable reproach pass him by,

and he who is bound [...]

3 and also do not trouble his spirit,

for you have spok[en] in calmness [...]

4 and his reproof speak quickly,

and do not overlook your own iniquities [...]

5 he is righteous like you,

for he is {for he is} a prince among pr[inces (?)]

[... and with ... forgiveness] 6 he will act,

for how unique is he among all creatures without [...]

Although questions remain about the meaning of these lines, one may generally surmise that they are concerned with how the *mēvîn* is to relate to another
member of the community. The subject of this section is at points portrayed
as having a superior status, especially evident in: (1) line 1 the speaker warns
about the subject's possible dissatisfaction and for this reason cautions how
to address him; (2) line 5 the subject may be described as a "prince";[100] and (3)
line 6 the subject is "unique." However, this superiority is tempered at nearly every turn, in: (1) line 2 reproach is directed to the same subject; (2) line 4 words of
reproof are directed to the subject; and (3) line 5 the addressee is said to be like
the subject, both righteous and sharing in his elevated position as a "prince."
Therefore, the subject of these lines holds a position of authority as does the
addressee, and the concern is not just for the subject's sin, but also for his own.

    "Spirit" in lines 1 and 3 carries positive and even elevated connotations. The
warning (l. 1) to show caution toward the subject, followed by directions to take
his "spirit" into account, suggest that by "spirit" one may know another's status
or position. How the *mēvîn* is to reprove his compatriot is also marked by discretion and another warning follows, לא תבלע ("do not trouble/confound"), which
is likely used with an imperative sense.[101] On two occasions in 4Q416 2 ii (l. 6)
negative imperatives (אל) are used when instructing about spirit (see below).
One might consider that "spirit" is then similar to a disposition.[102]

---

100   A term likely part of 4QInstruction's lively interest into angels (Ch. 1 § 4.); Qimron, *Dead
       Sea Scrolls*, 2:152–153 reconstructs שר בש[רכה and notes שֵׁר ("demon"), which would be
       here a reference to "demon in your flesh" and would be the only reference to a demon in
       4QInstruction.

101   DJD 34:178 בלע according to the editors is best understood as "confound," although "swal-
       low" is well attested in 4QInstruction and elsewhere at Qumran.

102   4QHoroscope (4Q186) apparently depicts the assessment of individuals, including their

The addressee's sin and need to repent is returned to periodically in the lines that follow, which again reflect tensions between simultaneously having a high status, in these lines he is a judge, and being imperfect. In lines 12–16 is an exhortation to those who mourn, in reference to line 11 and those who inherit glory by seeking and understanding the birth times of salvation. Birth times of salvation likely refers to the structuring of the cosmos at the time of creation. Line 17 begins a new pericope indicated by a change of topic, namely the address "you are poor." The reminder that one is "poor" functions as a metaphor for fatigable human nature (cf. Ch. 1 § 5.), which is a similar theme to the *mēvîn*'s imperfection in the preceding section.

4Q417 2 i lines 12–16 [single underline] (comp. 4Q416 2 i 6–8 [double underline]; 4Q418a 22 2–4; 4Q418 7a 1–2; **overlap**), Transcription and Translation:[103]

[	ולאבליהמה שמחת עולם היה בעל ריב[104] לֹחֹפְצֹבֹה ואין[ ]○	12
[	לכול נֿעֿוֿזֿתֿיֿֿֿה דֿבֿ[ר]מֹשפטיכה כמושל צדיק אֿל תֿקֿח[	13
[105[	ואֿל תעבֹר עלֿ] פש[עיכה היה בֿאֿיֿש עֿנֿי ברֿיֿבֿך משפטֿיֿ[	14
[	קח ואז יראה אל ושב אפו ועבֹר על חטֹאֹותֹכֹֹה [רי]א לֹחֹיֿ [אֿפו	15
[לוא יעמוד כול ומי יצדק במשפטֹוֹ ובלי סליחה] אֿ[וֹכֹה [יקום לפניו כול]		16

12 and to the one's mourning among them, eternal joy,
be an advocate to those in whom you delight,
and there is not (?) [...] **13** to all your perversity,
speak your judgments like a righteous ruler,
do not ta[ke ...]
14 and do not overlook your own [si]ns,
but rather be like a humble man when you plead/dispute *my* judgment (?),
[...] **15** take,
and then God will see and His anger will be turned away,
and He will forgive your sins,

---

physical features, and describes how many parts one's spirit has; however, this is within a dualistic and deterministic framework.

103   DJD 34:173; Tigchelaar, *To Increase Learning*, 55; Rey, *4QInstruction*, 42–43; Goff, *4QInstruction*, 183–184; Qimron, *Dead Sea Scrolls*, 2:152.

104   Occurs only elsewhere in 1QHᵃ VII 22–23; DJD 34:183 find equivalence in איש ריב ("advocate" Judg 12:2; Jer 15:10).

105   DJD 34:173 בֿרֿיֿבֿך משפטוֹ[("when thou contendest for a judgement *in favour of him*") Qimron, *Dead Sea Scrolls*, 2:152 reconstructs בריבך משפט]כה מרצונכה; here following Kister, "ספרות החכמה בקומראן," 1:299–320 who reads משפטי.

> for before [His anger] **16** no one will stand,
> and who will be found righteous in His judgment?
> For without forgiveness[h]ow [will anyone stand before Him?]

The theme of advocacy and turning away wrath recall the role of the exalted figure in 4Q418 81 + 81a 10. Instructing him in the role of judge and advocate precedes 4Q416 2 ii 12b–17, a passage discussed in Chapter 1 in regard to first person speech and a reference to a *maśkîl*. In 4Q418 81 + 81a there is not concern for the addressee's sin and iniquity, which may be explained by 4Q416 2 ii 12b–17 where arrival to the position of *maśkîl* is described in terms of faithfulness to God and dint of discipline. In 4Q416 2 ii 13 the addressee is said to become like a "firstborn son" (בן בכור) and "only child" (יחיד) to God when he holds fast to God's will; the status of the figure in 4Q418 + 81a 5 (בכור) arises in a context that assumes arrival to this status. Here in 4Q417 2 i 12–16 the *mēvîn* is imperfect, and yet is commissioned to serve as judge, suggesting gradation in leadership, and that some are community leaders who may not have reached the status of the speaker.

Reading משפטי ("my judgment") would be in keeping with the use of first-person form in the following column 4Q416 2 ii 12b–17 where the voice of the speaker may be found. Moreover, in 4Q418 221 4 (cf. Ch. 1 §1.2.) the speaker also likely refers to his own judgments. The meaning of the noun ריב may be with the sense of participating in the teacher's judgment, or perhaps it is used along the same lines as in the Thanksgiving Hymns where it expresses "pleading a cause" (1QHᵃ IX 23); that is, this figure is an emissary of the *maśkîl*.

Harrington and Strugnell comment that רוח in 4Q417 2 i "could refer to any human either according to his character or, in Qumranic style, according to his share in Light or Darkness"; however, given that light and darkness are not present in 4QInstruction, nor is it "Qumranic" in this implied sense, the use of רוח here is more likely indicative of, in a general sense, a person's character, place within the community, and assessment of his actualized wisdom. The *mēvîn* is charged with evaluating and caring for others' spirits in this particular role.[106]

2.2   *Holy Spirit in 4Q416 2 ii Line 6*

In 4QInstruction, the *mēvîn* should take care of his own "holy spirit" because it is possible for it to become displaced. 4Q416 2 ii 6 (par. 4Q418 8 6) is the only ref-

---

106   DJD 34:178.

erence to a "holy spirit" in the composition.[107] In 4Q418 76 3 the broken phrase
"]and spirits of holiness[" ([]ורוחי קודש) occurs, which may be a reference to
angelic beings, similar to the Songs of the Sabbath Sacrifice[108] and 4QBless-
ings.[109] "Holy spirit" occurs several times in the Rule of the Community (1QS IV
21; VIII 16; IX 3; cf. 1QSb II 24) and somewhat frequently in the Thanksgiving
Hymns (1QHᵃ IV 38; VI 24; VIII 20, 25, 30; XVI 13; XVII 32; XX 15; XXIII 33) and
is clearly God's spirit.[110] In 1QS III 6–8 the "spirit of truth" and the "holy spirit"
are identified with one another, and it is by both these spirits that the iniquities
of humanity are atoned (ll. 7–8 וברוח קדושה ליחד באמתו יטהר מכול עוונתו).[111] The
"holy spirit" in the hymns also cleanses (1QHᵃ IV 38; VIII 30; XXIII 33); moreover,
God's holy spirit is associated with a "spirit of understanding" (1QHᵃ VIII 24–
25 רוח בינה) and it is by his holy spirit that knowledge and mysteries are made
known (1QHᵃ VI 24; XX 15).[112] The maśkîl is illumined by the holy spirit, which
has even been seen as conjuring theophanic images of the heavenly chariot.[113]

---

107   כול רוח בינה ("every spirit of understanding") occurs twice in 4QInstruction (4Q418 58 2;
        4Q418 73 1); although virtually no context survives the expression does not indicate that
        this is a spirit similar to the addressee's holy spirit.

108   Songs of the Sabbath Sacrifice has plural spirits, see esp. רוחי קודש קודשים ("spirits of holi-
        est holiness" in 4Q403 1 i 44; 4Q405 5 12) and singular spirit רוח קודש קודשים ("spirit of
        holiest holiness" in 4Q403 1 ii 1; par. 4Q404 5 1; 11Q17 9 5). The feminine plural form רוחות
        קודש קודשים ("spirits of holiest holiness") is found in contexts that evoke the chariot scene
        in Ezek 1 and these spirits appear to be angelic beings (4Q403 1 ii 6–9; 4Q405 20 ii–22 10);
        see Carol A. Newsom, Poetical and Liturgical Texts, Part 1, DJD 11 (Oxford: Clarendon Press,
        1998), 352.

109   4Q287 2 5 רוחי קודש קודשים ("spirits of holiest holiness").

110   See esp. Eibert J.C. Tigchelaar, "Historical Origins of the Early Christian Concept of the
        Holy Spirit: Perspectives from the Dead Sea Scrolls," in The Holy Spirit, Inspiration, and
        the Cultures of Antiquity (Boston, MA/Berlin: Walter de Gruyter, 2014), 167–240 who offers
        a comprehensive treatment on holy spirit(s) at Qumran; cf. Edward Lee Beavin, Ruah
        Hakodesh in Some Early Jewish Literature (Ph.D. diss., Vanderbilt University, 1961); Freder-
        ick F. Bruce, "Holy Spirit in the Qumran Texts," Annual of Leeds University Oriental Society
        6 (1966/68): 49–55; Arnold A. Anderson, "The Use of Ruah in 1QS, 1QH and 1QM," JSS 7
        (1962): 293–303.

111   Flusser, Judaism of the Second Temple Period, 1:285.

112   Jassen, Mediating the Divine, 62 fn. 73, 372–374; note that in 1QM X 10 the elect are called
        משכילי בינ]ה ("enlightened in understanding"); cf. Dan 9:22, 11:33.

113   Elliot R. Wolfson, "Seven Mysteries of Knowledge: Qumran E/Sotericism Recovered," in
        The Idea of Biblical Interpretation: Essays in Honor of James L. Kugel, ed. Hindy Najman &
        Judith H. Newman, JSJSup 83 (Leiden: Brill, 2004), 177–213 at 191.

4Q416 2 ii 6–7 is the only place in Qumran discoveries where "holy spirit" is applied to the speaker; although, on a few other occasions in the Scrolls it refers to the spirit of a human being.[114] While the speaker's spirit is not called "holy" elsewhere, holiness language is applied to him in other ways, in: (1) 4Q418 81+81a 4 the addressee is placed as a most holy one in the world; (2) 4Q418 81+81a 12 all those called by God's name are "holy"; and (3) 4Q418 76 2 is a broken reference to "men of {holiness} righteousness." The term טמא ("unclean/impure") and טהור ("pure"), typically found in liturgical contexts concerned with purity, are almost entirely absent from 4QInstruction because interest is in ethical instruction rather than liturgical purity.[115] The Damascus Document has several occurrences of "holy spirit" referring to a human being. Those who ignore commandments about sexual relations are blasphemous and, in CD V 11–12, they are said to "defile their holy spirit" (רוח קדשיהם טמאו). CD VII 1–6 are concerned with instruction about members of the community living in perfect righteousness. Keeping apart from uncleanness and fornication leads to cautions that (ll. 3–4): "a man does not detest his own holy spirit" (ולא ישקץ איש את רוח קדשיו).[116] One other occurrence of "holy spirit" merits investigation, this is in a Cave 4 fragment of the Damascus Document, lines that are not preserved elsewhere.

4QD^e (4Q270) 2 ii lines 11–14, Transcription and Translation:[117]

[פרוש]   10

בשמותם לטמא את רוח קודשו]   11

או ינוגע בנגע צרעת או זוב טמ]אה   12

[או] אשר יגלה את רז עמו לגואים או יקלל א]ת עמו   13

[או ידבר] סרה על משיחי רוח הקדש ותועה ב]   14

---

114   Tigchelaar, "Historical Origins," 198–199, 206, comments that 4QInstruction "does not use other terms of purity or impurity that would warrant the use of 'holy' here."

115   טמא never occurs, טהור occurs once (4Q418 186 2):]טהור[. In contrast to Yaḥad literature where this language of im/purity is relatively frequent.

116   Tigchelaar, "Historical Origins," 199, observes that Isa 63:10 וְהֵמָּה מָרוּ וְעִצְּבוּ אֶת־רוּחַ קָדְשׁוֹ "his holy spirit" referring to God, 1QIsa^a of 63:10 makes plural רוח קודשיו "his spirit of holinesses."

117   Tigchelaar, "Historical Origins," 199–200; cf. Joseph M. Baumgarten, The Damascus Document (4Q266–273), Qumran Cave 4, XIII, DJD 18 (Oxford: Clarendon Press, 1996).

10   [and recounted]

11   them by name, those who defile his holy spirit [...]

12   or one plagued by skin blemishes or im[pure] discharge [...]

13   [or] one who reveals the mystery of his people to gentiles or curses [his people]

14   [or speaks] falsehood about those anointed with the holy spirit and error against[...]

Justification for reconstructing ובפרוש at the end of line 10 is found from a similar use in CD II 12–13 (ובפרוש {שמו} שמותיהם) and CD IV 4–5 (פרוש שמותיהם לתולדותם). Tigchelaar points to the prohibition against swearing by foreign gods in Josh 23:7 and speculates that in line 11 "their names" may refer to swearing by the names of these gods which leads to the defilement of someone's holy spirit.[118] However, among the Scrolls שמותיהם is an expression unique to the Damascus Document, and names are either "recounted," "numbered" (CD XIV 3 יפקדו כלם בשמותיהם), or "written" (CD XIV 3 ויכתבו בשמֹותיהם); therefore, line 11 recounts the act of defiling someone else's holy spirit. The ones anointed by the holy spirit in line 14 are identified in CD II 12–13 explicitly with "seers of truth":

12   ... ויודיעם ביד משיחו (משיחי) רוח קדשו וחוזֹי

13   אמת ובפרוש שמו (שמותיהם) ואת אשר שנא התעה

12 ... and he made them known by the hand of his anointed (those anointed) with the holy spirit, and seers of **13** truth, and he recounted his name (them by name), and those he hated he caused to err.

That seers and prophets are described as "those anointed with the holy spirit" makes sense in light of the role that the gift of the holy spirit plays in the revelatory process (esp. 1QS VIII 16: כאשר גלו הנביאים ברוח קודשו "as he revealed to the prophets by his holy spirit"). While uncertain, it is possible that the seer's holy spirit is defiled in line 11, an activity that may be explained by the sin of revealing mysteries to gentiles in line 13.

In Chapter 1, 4Q416 2 i 22b–4Q416 ii 17 (par. 4Q417 2 ii+23) were presented and discussed in relationship to a *maśkîl* (§ 2.1.). The presentation here returns to these lines with the addition of the immediately preceding section of 4Q416 2 i; however, this section is best preserved in 4Q417 2 i 19–24 (= 4Q416 2 i 15–17).

---

118   Tigchelaar, "Historical Origins," 199.

In the transcription below several lines are omitted—these are 4Q417 2 i 25–28 (4Q416 2 i 18–20), which bring the column to the bottom—because only a few broken words and phrases remain. Therefore, the presentation is limited to two consecutive sections reconstructed around two manuscripts. 4Q417 2 i 19 introduces a new pericope with the conditional address "if you are in need" (image of 4Q417 2 i in plate section, fig. 8).

4Q417 2 i lines 19–24 [single underline] (par. 4Q416 2 i 15–17 [double underline]; 4Q418 7b; **overlap**), Transcription and Translation:[119]

וֹאׄם תחסר לוא מ[ב]לׄ[י]ן הׄ[ו]ן מחסורכה כיא לוא יחסר אוצרׄ[ו] על	19
פיהו יהיה כול ואת אשר יטריפכה אׄכׄוׄל ואל תוסף עׄוׄד פׄ[ן] תקציר[	20
vacat **חייכה** vacat אם הון אנשׄ[י]ׄם תלוה למחסורכה אל [	21
יומם ולילה **ואל מנוח לנפש**[כה עד]הׄשיבכה ל[נושה בכה אל תכזב[120]	22
לו למה תשה עון וגם מחרפה ל] [ולוא תאמין עׄ[ו]ד	23
ובחסורכה יקפץ ידו כחכה] [וכמוהו לוה ודע מאׄ[	24

19 And if you are in need,
your lacking is not without wealth,
for [His] treasury does not lack,
[by] 20 His mouth everything has come into being,
and He gives you food to eat,
do not gather more l[est you cut off] 21 *vacat* your life,
vacat if you borrow m[e]n's wealth when you are in need,
do not [...] 22 day and night,
and let there be no rest for [your]self [until] you repay [your creditor,
do not lie] 23 to him, why should you bear guilt, and also shame to [...]
[...] and you will not trust a[ny longer (?) ...]
24 and in your lacking he close his hand,
your strength[...]and like him borrow, and know from a[...][121]

119   DJD 34:172–174; Tigchelaar, *To Increase Learning*, 55; Rey, *4QInstruction*, 44; Goff, *4QInstruction*, 184; Qimron, *Dead Sea Scrolls*, 2:152.

120   All critical reconstructions find נושה in 4Q416 2 i 17 and אל תכזב at the end of this line in 4Q417 2 i; ל[נוׄשׄה is possible, but everything after the *lamed* is best read as a theoretical reconstruction.

121   4Q417 2 i 25–26 may set a condition of hardship befalling the *mēvîn* (ואם נגע יפגשכה) and not hiding from one's creditor.

4Q416 2 i line 22b–ii lines 1–8 [single underline] (par. 4Q417 2 ii + 23 [double underline]; 4Q418 8a, 8; **overlap/overlap**), Transcription and Translation:[122]

... מאל] שאל טרפכה כי הוא	22b
למלא] **כל מחסורי** אוטו ולתת טרף **פתח רחמיו**]	1
וא[ם **יקפוץ ידו** ונאספה רו[ח כול] **לכל חי ואין**]◦	2
כש[יל בה **ובחרפתו תכסה פניכה** ובאולת בשר אל תק]ח	3
ה[נ̇ושה בו] [מ̇הר **שלם ואתה** תשוה בו כי [ו אם בהון[123] מאסור כמה] בי]ס[	4
לנושה בדה בעד רעיכה נתת̇ה̇ כל חייכה בז מהר תן אשר צפונ̇כ̇ה̇ פקדת[ה]	5
רוחכה בכל הון אל תמר רוח ק[ד**שכה**[124] לו וקח כי̇סכה ובדברייכה אל תמעט	6
אם אי[ש לא י̇טכה **ברצון** שחר **פניו** וכלשונו **כי אין** מחיר שוה̇]	7
[דב]ר ואז תמצא חפצכה מח̇ר̇[פ]תכה אל ת̇[מ]ר **לו וחזקיכה** אל תרף ו̇תרף ו̇ברזיכה השמר	8
[מא]ד̇ה [...] 9a	

22b   ... ask for your food [from God],

for He **1** has opened his mercies[...]

to fill] all that is lacking from his/its אוט (lowly station?),

and to give food **2** to all that lives,

and there is not ◦[...]

[... and i]f He closes His hand,

and gathers in the spir[it of all] **3** flesh,

do not ta[ke ...]

[... stumb]ling in it,

and in his shame cover your face,

and (also) in the folly of **4** imprisonment (i.e., cover your face),

how great [   ] if by wealth [...]

[... the] creditor in it[ ]quickly pay,

and you will be even with him,

for your hidden purse **5** you gave to the one lending to you,

---

122   DJD 34:90–91; Tigchelaar, *To Increase Learning*, 46–47; Rey, *4QInstruction*, 64–65; Qimron, *Dead Sea Scrolls*, 2:154; Goff, *4QInstruction*, 57–58 takes a more maximalist approach offering extensive theoretical reconstruction.

123   Rey and Goff find the suffix *waw* at the end of line 3, and join 4Q418 8 1 to 4Q416 2 ii 4 to read: ובאולתו מאסיר כמהו אם בהון and Goff translates: "and with his folly (you will be covered) by an obligation like him"; however, there is no overlap and a direct join of כמה ו + seems unlikely.

124   4Q418 8 4 reads תאמר רוח קדושה כיא.

> on behalf of your neighbor you gave all of your life with it,
> quickly give **6** what is his, and take your purse,
> and by your words do not belittle your spirit,
> and for any wealth do not exchange your holy spirit,
> **7** for there is no price equal [...]
> [... if a ma]n is not favorably disposed,
> seek his presence and according to his speech **8** [spea]k,
> and you will find what pleases you rather than your own sha[m]e,
> do not alter/change for him,
> and by your mysteries keep **9** diligent watch ...

That the *mēvîn* borrows is seemingly out of keeping with the teaching in 4Q417 2 i 19–20 and 4Q416 2 i 22b that he should be satisfied with what God has given as nourishment; indeed, borrowing would seem to imply that God's mercies are insufficient. However, the *mēvîn* is not instructed about how he is to borrow money from a creditor (4Q417 2 i 21; 4Q416 2 ii 4–5), but rather how to respond to a neighbor in need. The *mēvîn* performs a gracious act by going into debt on behalf of his neighbor (4Q416 2 ii 5). This sets the context for the admonition about "exchanging," from the root מור, his own holy spirit and is language that evokes a financial transaction.[125] This warning about "spirit" is interwoven with cryptic lines where the *mēvîn* gives his "secret purse," and indeed his "life," on behalf of his neighbor. The warning not to belittle your spirit "by your words" (l. 6) may be in reference either to how he speaks with the creditor or, alternatively and more convincingly, how he treats and speaks to his neighbor in the process of coming to his financial aid. The subject in line 7 is unclear; "man" is reconstructed and yet it is ambiguous who this is. Lines 7–8 may possibly be instruction about maintaining healthy relations between the addressee and his neighbor in this undesirable and complex economic situation.

If the activity of borrowing were, in itself, prohibited and leads to exchanging one's holy spirit, then this is out of place with the very assumption of the instruction.[126] When the addressee is warned about his spirit the concern appears to be in the context of borrowing to help a neighbor who is in financial difficulty. Perhaps in lines 3–4 it is this same neighbor who is imprisoned

---

125   מור is used in 1QHᵃ II 18, 36; IV 10; XIV 20; 4Q286 7 ii 12 (4QBerᵃ) where it is consistently used in the sense of bartering one's deepest convictions and values; the fem. n. תמורה ("exchange") in the HB is used for acquiring wealth (cf. Lev 27:10; 27:33; Job 15:31).

126   If the exchange were straightforwardly "holy spirit" for "wealth" this may be read in light of the Damascus Document (CD/DD) where fornication and pollution lead to a defiled holy spirit; the three nets of Belial (CD IV 15–18) are fornication, wealth, and defilement of

and suffering shame, so that when the addressee is to "cover his face" it is as an act of respecting his dignity. If this is the case, then the passage describes a process in which the addressee deals with a creditor, as a benefactor who is himself of limited means, in order to help his neighbor. In so doing the *mēvîn* is taught to take precautions. Indeed, increasing "shame" (4Q416 2 ii 16) and covering "shame" (4Q418 177 3; 4Q418 178 4) are well known in this composition. Ultimately, the way that one exchanges or belittles spirit here is not straightforwardly about trading it for wealth, but rather how one attends to a relationship with a fellow member of the community when dealing with poverty. Preserving the dignity of one's neighbor and selflessly coming to their aid is highly valued; failure to live by these principles leads to "exchanging," a term that evokes a financial transaction, one's holy spirit.

2.3   *4Q416 2 iii Lines 17–18*

In 4Q416 2 iii 15–18, where the command to honor parents from the Decalogue is rewritten, the author is sure to emphasize that parents are the "womb that was pregnant with you" (l. 17) before a further addition to the commandment is made: God "fashioned you according to the spirit [ויצר על הרוח] so serve them (i.e., your parents)" (4Q416 2 iii 17). This statement is in synonymous parallel with the immediately following stich: "as t(he)y (i.e., your parents) uncovered your ear to the mystery of existence so honor them" (4Q416 2 iii 18; cf. Ch. 3 §2.2.). The emphasis on spirit here, similar to the Vision of Hagu, relates to access to revelation. Having "spirit" communicates an ability to seek mysteries, and here the giving of "spirit" is again emphasized as a part of the creation of humanity. The formation of humankind is by both God and angels (4Q417 1 i 17 כתבנית קדושים יצרו), spirit is connected with human parentage, and all humanity shares creation in common. The implication is that creation with spirit is universal.[127]

2.4   *4Q418 126 ii Line 8* (*+122 ii*)

4Q418 126 ii partially preserves sixteen lines; the twice occurring "and you understanding one, in truth" (ll. 2, 11) indicate a distinct paragraph in lines 2–10. 4Q418 126 ii 8 has a broken phrase that refers to a "spirit of life." This spirit may enable one to distinguish between good and evil within an allusion to Genesis

---

the temple. There would, therefore, be precedent for wealth corrupting the speaker's holy spirit here. Cf. 4Q416 2 iii 6–7: "do not let your spirit be corrupted by him/it" (ורוחכה אל תחבל בו), which relates to an interpersonal financial transaction.

127   This is reminiscent of the animation of humanity in Gen 2:7 where God forms man by the breath (נפשה) of life resulting in him having a living soul (נפש). In later Jewish tradition it is well known that by the constitution of one's soul the commandments are performed.

1–2 (esp. 1:14, 18) where there is also the infinitive construct להבדיל; this is suggested by line 9 where "children of Eve" occurs. The only other occurrences of
"spirit of life" are found in the Damascus Document and may refer to a healing angelic spirit: in 4Q266 6 i 12 (cf. 4Q272 1 i 7) the spirit of life ascends and
descends before healing a blemish and this is described (l. 13) as an ordinance
of the law of skin blemishes "to distinguish" (להבדיל) between one and another.

4Q418 126 ii (+ 4Q418 122 ii [single underline]), Transcription and Translation:[128]

וא]תה מב]ין באמת מזד כול אוט אנשים א]יפת אמת ומשקל צדק]	2
כי ב̇א̇י]פ]ת̇ אמת ומשקל צדק תכן אל כול מ̇]עשיו	3
פ̇רשם באמת הוא שמם ולחפציהם ידרש]ו	4
יסתר כול וגם לוא נהיו בלוא רצונו ומחוכ̇]מתו	5
משפט להשיב נקם לפ̇עלי̇ און ופקודת ש]	6
ולסגור בעד רשעים ולהרים ראוש דלים]	7
בכבוד עולם ושלום עד ורוח חיים להבדיל̇]	8
כול בני חזה ובכוח אל ורוב כבודו עם טובו]	9
ובאמונתו ישיחו כול היום תמיד יהללו שמו זה̇]	10

2 and y[ou understand]ing one,
in/by truth measure every אוט (humble station?) of men,
[a true] e[phah and a right weight,]
3 for by a true e[ph]ah and a right weight
God has prepared all [his] d[eeds]
4 He has spread them (i.e deeds) out (i.e. in the heavens; cf. 4Q417 1 i
   1–13a);
in truth He made them,
and to the ones delighting in them are [they] sought[...]
5 (*from those who do not seek?*) everything will be hidden,
and will they not be without His good pleasure?
and from [His] wis[dom ...] 6 judgment;
to turn away vengeance from workers of iniquity,
and punishment/visitation of [...]
7 and to lock away the wicked ones,
and to raise the heads of the poor [...]

---

128   Following Tigchelaar, *To Increase Learning*, 102–103; cf. DJD 34:349–350; Rey, *4QInstruction*,
      255–256; Goff, *4QInstruction*, 273–274; Qimron, *Dead Sea Scrolls*, 2:171, following Qimron's
      theoretical constructions; at the end of line 1 as well as reading מוד, an imperative from
      the root מדד, rather than מיד ("from the hand").

8 in everlasting honor and eternal peace,
and a spirit of life to distinguish [between ...]
    9 all the sons of Eve,
and in the strength of God,
and abundance of his mercy,
with His goodness [...]
10 and about His faithfulness they will converse all the day,
and they will always praise His name [...]

4Q416 1 4–6, the opening column of 4QInstruction, and 4Q418 126 ii 2–4 share common interests in setting judgment within a cosmological framework. In 4Q418 126 ii 4 the heavens are spread out, and there are those who delight in the created order and seek understanding and those who do not, from this latter group all things are hidden (l. 5). Qimron reconstructs the end of line 4 and beginning of line 5 as מלפניו לוא] יסתר כול ("from before Him nothing] will be hidden"); however, this does not fit with the contrast made in the context and the need for a negative subject in line 5b (i.e., who are "they"?). That "vengeance" is to be *repaid* (להשיב) to the "(*workers of*) iniquity" (l. 6), as the editors suggest, would be an unusual use of the infinitive from the root שוב.[129] Indeed, in 4Q418 81 + 81a the role of the exalted figure is to "turn away," rather than "return" or "repay," wrath (להשיב אף) from the "men of good pleasure." When the sin and iniquity of the addressee and his fellow community members came into view in 4Q417 2 i, the addressee intercedes as a judge which leads God to see, "turn his anger" (ושב אפו), and forgive sin (ll. 14–15). Line 5 is more convincingly taken in reference to hiding meditation from the wicked because they suppressed the truth (cf. 4Q201 and the broken phrase "and it will be closed"). If the addressee has a role turning vengeance away from workers of iniquity, then this underscores how problematic a dualistic and deterministic view of humankind is; indeed, 4Q418 69 ii may be revisited where direct speech to the wicked (i.e., those within the community) is found. 4QInstruction appears not to be entrenched in the opinion that the unfaithful are hopelessly wayward.

    In lines 8–9 are two rare expressions: רוח חיים ("spirit of life") and בני חוה ("sons of Eve"). As noted, רוח חיים occurs in the Damascus Document with

---

129   DJD 34:352. This is the only occasion in 4QInstruction that נקם ("vengeance") occurs, there is no extant example of the root שוב used with נקם in the Hebrew from the period. Here, following the reconstruction of Tigchelaar and Qimron who read פעלי און rather than בעלי און ("masters of iniquity"). If "masters of iniquity" this would be a *hapax legomenon* whereas "workers of iniquity" is frequent, 23× in the HB (cf. Prov 10:29; 21:15; 30:20) and in the Scrolls 4Q230 1 6 ("Catologue of Spirits").

angelic connotations (cf. Gen 7:22 "living beings"). How this relates to להבדיל in 4QInstruction is open to question; the root בדל occurs on three occasions. In 4Q418 81 + 81a 1–2 the exalted *mēvîn* is distinguished from every spirit of flesh and he is to keep separate from all that God hates. In 4Q418 221 4, discussed in Chapter 1, the *maśkîl* instructs: "know my judgment, and then you will distinguish be[tween ...". In 4Q418 126 ii 8 one possibility is that the "spirit of life" helps to distinguish between different types of people, one of them being the "sons of Eve"[130] who are compared with others and the reference to them is likely lost in the preceding lacuna.[131]

2.5   *4Q418 77*

4Q418 77 (comp. 4Q416 7 1–3) is a small five-line fragment which refers to "spirit" in a way strongly reminiscent of 4Q418 222 2: שמ[עה רוחי ומזל שפתי. This fragment may have directly preceded 4Q418 81 + 81a.

4Q418 77 [single underline] (4Q416 7 1–3 [double underline]; **overlap**), Transcription and Translation:[132]

[	] *vacat* בֹּ֯הֹ [ ]הֹ שמש[	] 1
[	ר]וֹ נהיה וקח תולדות[ו א]דם וראה בכושׂ[ר	] 2
שמעה]	ופקודת מעֹשֹיהו ואז תבין במשפט אנוש ומשקל[	] 3
[	מזל שפתיו לפי רֹוחו וקח ברז נהיה על [מ]שֹקל קצים ומדֹת[	] 4
[	]ל[ ] ◦עֹ֯דֹ[לֹ	] 5

1 [...]sun *h*[ ]*bh*   *vacat* [...]
2 [...] mystery of existence,
and grasp the nature[of m]an,
and gaze on the suitabil[ity ...] 3 [...]
and the punishment of his deeds, and then you will understand the
    judgment on humanity,
and the weighing [...]
[hear] 4 *the* outpouring of his lips according to his spirit,

---

130   In both Sir (25:24) and Paul (1 Tim 2:14; Rom 5:12–13; 1 Cor 15:21–22) are negative associations with Eve, even if not called by name. For Philo (*Heir* 52–53; *Cherubim* 57–60), Adam is the earthly mind and Eve is the outward sense.

131   DJD 34:352 interpret רוח חיים as a category of people: "And to separate the spirit of life [*from every spirit of darkness* ...]"; Rey, *4QInstruction*, 260 likewise comments: "L'expression désigne vraisemblablement la catégorie des justes en opposition aux impies."

132   DJD 34:297; Tigchelaar, *To Increase Learning*, 93–94.

and grasp the mystery of existence by the weighing of times,
and measure[of ...]
5 [...]*l*[ ] *Ed*[*en* ...]

Line 2 implores the *mēvîn* to understand the nature of man in parallel with
an exhortation to seek the mystery of existence, thereby associating the two.
Human nature and mysteries provide the source for understanding good and
evil, which form the basis of judgment. Elsewhere in 4QInstruction, insistence
that the addressee is poor, as metaphor for human nature, likewise relates to
the pursuit of the mystery of existence. Weights (l. 3) and measures are terms
used when determining "spirits" in another fragment (4Q415 11 5, 9). Line 2 may
also be elucidated by the Treatise on the Two Spirits where the *maśkîl* teaches
the sons of light about a person's character (תולדות); however, in 4QInstruction
this would not be related to the deterministic fate of humankind (1QS III 13–
14). The subject of "outpouring lips" is likely to be identified with an exalted
sage figure, as in 4Q418 81+81a 1, who opens his lips to bless the holy ones.
The appeal to "spirit" is in reference to his status, here especially in regard to
the degree to which someone is elevated by their own actualization of wisdom
and faithfulness to God. Indeed, when in 4Q418 222+221 the *maśkîl* begins his
address with an appeal to his own spirit, this is ultimately a reference to his
authority as a practitioner of wisdom. Moreover, related themes of judgment
and distinguishing are also found in fragments 222+221. Here, heeding "his"
outpouring lips may be part and parcel with seeking the mystery of existence
in the following stich (l. 4) because this language is only identified with a *maśkîl*
in 4QInstruction. Here, this is an exhortation to listen and to learn from a sage.
Line 4 hints at participation in the act of blessing angels: in 4Q418 81+81a 1 the
exalted figure is instructed "[you] open your lips [as an outpouring] to bless
the holy ones," and in 4Q418 77 6 the address is to "listen to him" (i.e., another
maśkîl). Although speculative, if Eden is to be found in the following line, the
liturgical activities of blessing and praising, as part of seeking mysteries, may
intersect with the Eden metaphor in 4Q423 1 (cf. Ch. 3 § 4.2.).

3   **Conclusions**

The Thanksgiving Hymns are particularly valuable for viewing the relationship of "spirit" and "flesh" in 4QInstruction because they share common terms,
found only in these two compositions, which shape their respective anthropologies. Both 4QInstruction and the hymns use רוח בשר to express distance
from the divine; the difference between these texts is how this distance comes

But Not every one has access to (az nihyeh

about. In this assessment of human nature, different perspectives on disclosing revelation to the elect have been in view. In the hymns, humanity is viewed as generally corrupt and spirit elevates the psalmist so that he can access myster-ies. In 4QInstruction the order of spirit and corruption is reversed. There is only one humanity in 4QInstruction, they are created with spirit and bestowed rev-elation from the outset, and the challenge is to maintain spirit through diligent pursuit of the רז נהיה and by actualizing wisdom. Whereas the psalmist begins as, and is, "fleshly spirit," in 4QInstruction it is the failure to maintain spirit that leads one to become, or to be designated, רוח בשר. Whereas 4QInstruc-tion emphasizes that the exalted *maśkîl* figure is separated from the "fleshly spirit" (4Q418 81 + 81a), in the hymns the psalmist underscores that even with the divinely granted spirit he remains "fleshly spirit." The granting of spirit in 1QHª IV is a matter of "chosenness" and "election," an idea that is strikingly absent from 4QInstruction.[133] Thus, those who receive revealed wisdom are few in the hymns, while in 4QInstruction meditation on "Hagu" and the mystery of existence is universally given.

The comparison of 4QInstruction and the Thanksgiving Hymns in this chap-ter is for heuristic purposes more than an assessment of influence. The *opinio communis* is that 4QInstruction pre-dates the hymns and is not a Yaḥad com-position. Therefore, 4QInstruction may be exerting influence on the hymns, but the hymns do not share the same view of humankind, election, or deter-minism. If the hymns are familiar with 4QInstruction, then significant changes occur in regard to who has access to wisdom. In the Thanksgiving Hymns, only an elect group is endowed with spirit in order to perceive revealed wisdom, while in 4QInstruction spirit is given to all at creation. In the hymns, not only is revelation disclosed, but also the psalmist is in an extraordinary position of authority. The theological shifts in the hymns match well with an evolution of a worldview that, perhaps because of discontent and marginalization, seeks to limit and control access to revelation. 4QInstruction does not limit access to revelation in the same way, it is interested to explain why others do not faith-fully pursue and observe it which results in them being "outside." In the hymns, the only way to rise above the continuing situation of a negative anthropology (i.e., "fleshly spirit") in order to gain understanding is God's election; in 4QIn-struction the addressees are not lifted from the "fleshly spirit," but rather if one forsakes meditation on Hagu and the study of the רז נהיה, then he corrupts his

---

133   The verb בחר occurs three times in *4QInstruction*, twice without any meaningful context
        (4Q418 45 ii 1; 4Q418 234 2) and once as an indictment on the wicked who are described
        as not choosing what God delights in: וברצון אל לוא בחרו (4Q418 55 5).

spirit. These differences reflect a dramatic shift in portraying and explaining who are part of the faithful community and who is outside. 4QInstruction may view that humans easily become weary and are imperfect, but does not share with the hymns such a profoundly negative anthropology. In both 4QInstruction and the Thanksgiving Hymns the "fleshly spirit" is ultimately the same description for the unenlightened and base human being; however, it operates within very different anthropologies. Moreover, the use of "vessel of flesh," if it is correct to translate יצר בשר this way in 4QInstruction, is a much more straightforward circumlocution for (a segment of) humanity as "flesh" than the oxymoronic "fleshly spirit."

Despite these differences, other similarities have emerged that have not received attention in other studies of these two documents. A dualistic framework for 4QInstruction is only found in an unconvincing interpretation of two creations and two peoples in the Vision of Hagu passage. Neither 4QInstruction nor the hymns are dualistic. When in the hymns רוח is used more than 60 times, most often in the plural and as an attribute of humanity or for divine beings, this is never within binary opposites (e.g., good/evil). Even when "light" and "dark" are contrasted in 1QHᵃ xx 4–10 they do not express a dualistic cosmology and they are not in opposition.[134] In 4QInstruction too opposing and antithetical categories are entirely absent, there is no "spirit" and "flesh," "light" and "darkness," nor is an evil yēṣer opposing a good yēṣer. However, both texts enter into an emerging tradition of demonizing sin and presenting alien forces at work within a human's interior. Both have a "positive" yēṣer that does not function within a binary model. There is an evil yēṣer in both, in 4QInstruction it leads one astray and away from the pursuit of wisdom, whereas in the hymns it is present from the beginning and the psalmist gives thanks for not being left to its devices.

Attention to "spirit" sheds light on observations made on the maśkîl and mēvîn in Chapter 1. Instruction to the understanding one includes exhortations to care for his own and others' spirits, and to take "spirit" into account when relating to and assessing others. The mēvîn is not necessarily superior to, or faultless in comparison with, others within his community; indeed, his own sin is a point of reflection on a few occasions. Frequent concern for spirit reflects its vulnerability; spirit is fragile and requires constant tending vis-à-vis seeking wisdom. There is a point at which the mēvîn's faithfulness raises his standing, and his role, within the community. He may become a maśkîl himself and is taught in the ways of a maśkîl. In this role, he leads liturgy that involves partic-

---

134   Davies, "Dualism," 8–9.

ipation with angelic beings, which is part of pursuing the mystery of existence. The speaker, a *maśkîl*, urges the addressee to listen to another *maśkîl*'s spirit. The speaker's voice found in the opening address of 4QInstruction ("hear my spirit and the outpouring of my lips") resonates again when he exhorts the *mēvîn* to listen to "his spirit and the outpouring of his lips." Ultimately, this reflects that someone with an elevated or superior "spirit" is concerned for others' spirits and desires to raise them up and help them to actualize wisdom. However, it is not only the *maśkîl* who intercedes and mediates on behalf of the community, the understanding ones who are themselves on the way to living out wisdom and acting in obedience are tasked with protecting one another's spirits.

In Chapter 1 it was suggested that the Self-Glorification Hymn is located at the more extreme and higher end of a spectrum (i.e., wisdom is revealed only to the one or the few) and that the Treatise on the Two Spirits and the Community Hymns (1QH^a), where the elect are also recipients of revealed wisdom, are to be located further down the scale. The combined views that practitioners of wisdom may themselves aspire to the status of *maśkîl* and that wisdom is not revealed only to an elect few, as seen here, locates 4QInstruction even further down that scale. But does the sapiential discourse of 4QInstruction really have a universal outlook, one that is inclusive to the extent that the gentiles' relationship to wisdom and revelation are part of this compositions worldview? In 4QD^e (4Q270) 2 ii 13, although fragmentary, revealing mysteries to gentiles is depicted as a wicked act. 4QInstruction is not composed for or written to gentiles, but rather meditation on right and wrong is universal at the point of creation. The theological stance of the composition is that all humanity, whether gentiles or Jews, are held to account because of their universal creation with spirit and ability to meditate on Hagu. 4QInstruction is an address from a *maśkîl* who speaks only to those who remain within the faithful community. In the words of Rom 1, those who are already fools and whose minds are darkened do not interest our sage, but rather he is concerned that others do not follow down that path. As attention now shifts to Torah and mysteries, more may be said on the topic of gentiles and the extent to which 4QInstruction is universal.

Torah and Mysteries

The defining characteristic of 4QInstruction is the frequent exhortation to pursue the רז נהיה, the "mystery of existence," a term that refers to God's ordering of the cosmos and has temporal connotations encompassing everything from creation to end-time judgment. To understand the nature of this mystery it is crucial to identify the place of Mosaic Torah in the composition as precisely as possible. How 4QInstruction conceives revelation stands at the center of interpreting this document and understanding hierarchies of authority (esp. types of revelation and their inter-relationship). There is a consensus that Mosaic Torah is not thematized in 4QInstruction and that in the extant fragments the word תורה never occurs. However, if one follows the reconstructions and translations of John Strugnell, Daniel Harrington, and Torleif Elgvin in DJD 34 then there are two references to the "hand of Moses" (ביד משה) in two separate manuscripts, these are 4Q418 184 and 4Q423 11.[1] Matthew Goff concludes that "[i]t is possible that 4QInstruction appealed to the Torah as an authoritative source," but "there is simply not enough evidence for this position."[2] Greg Schmidt Goering comments that the phrase "hand of Moses" "may suggest a concern for the Torah on the part of 4QInstruction," but "the fragmentary nature of both texts [i.e., the fragments where it is found] ... make it impossible to put the phrase into a larger context and draw such a conclusion."[3] Andrew Teeter is the most definitive, concluding that the mystery of existence "is associated with the revelation at Sinai and the meditation of Moses" and "that the רז נהיה is discernible within and accessed by means of a textual corpus the extent of which is unclear but which includes at a minimum the Torah itself."[4]

---

1 DJD 34:408–409, 527. Daniel J. Harrington, "The *Raz Nihyeh*," 552 first suggested a connection between the רז נהיה and the "hand of Moses" in 4Q418 184.

2 Goff, *Discerning Wisdom*, 28–29.

3 Greg Schmidt Goering, "Creation, Torah, and Revealed Wisdom in Some Second Temple Sapiential Texts (Sirach, *4QInstruction*, 4Q185, and 4Q525): A Response to John Kampen," in *Canonicity, Setting*, 121–145, at 128 fn. 33.

4 D. Andrew Teeter, "Torah, Wisdom, and the Composition of Rewritten Scripture: Jubilees and 11QPs^a in Comparative Perspective," in *Wisdom and Torah: The Reception of 'Torah' in the Wis-*

© KONINKLIJKE BRILL NV, LEIDEN, 2018 | DOI: 10.1163/9789004364240_005

In the first half of this chapter (§ 1.–§ 2.) negative and positive evidence is presented, which allows us to reasonably conclude that Mosaic Torah is not— and was not—part of 4QInstruction's discourse because Torah is subordinate to the רז נהיה and supplanted by the mystery of existence. The negative evidence relates to reading the "hand of Moses" in 4QInstruction without a cautious and thorough (re-)assessment of the fragments.[5] Positive evidence relates to three passages where one finds the mystery of existence standing in the traditional place of "Torah." As discussed in Chapter 2, in 4QInstruction the mystery of existence is universally imparted to humanity; in this chapter, we will further see that the mystery relates to the created order. In terms of hierarchy, a case is made that in 4QInstruction revelation at Sinai is subordinate to the revelation of the created order.

Carol Newsom's study on symbolic power describes the Torah as an ideological sign that accentuates and serves to indicate who belongs to which group.[6] The place, or absence, of "Torah" in the discourse of 4QInstruction has several important implications. Armin Lange argues that in 4QInstruction Torah is to be identified with the רז נהיה.[7] Jean-Sébastien Rey concludes that Ben Sira,

---

dom Literature of the Second Temple Period, ed. Bernd U. Schipper & D. Andrew Teeter, JSJSup 163 (Leiden: Brill, 2013), 233–272 at 252 comments that "This mystery [i.e., רז נהיה], upon which those who have understanding are to meditate day and night (4Q417 1 i 6), is associated with the revelation at Sinai and the meditation of Moses (ביד משה). It consists of 'statutes,' (4Q416 2 ii 8–9) and instructions about the keeping of appointed times ..." which "suggests that the רז נהיה is discernible within and accessed by means of a textual corpus the extent of which is unclear but which includes at a minimum the Torah itself." Cf. William A. Tooman, "Wisdom and Torah at Qumran: Evidence from the Sapiential Texts," in Wisdom and Torah, 203–232 at 206 fn. 10 excludes 4QInstruction from his treatment of Qumran sapiential texts because it, along with other compositions, does not explicitly connect wisdom to the law even if it is suggestive at points (i.e., the hand of Moses).

5   There is a continuing need to consult manuscripts and not simply rely on tools, such as Bible software programs, as presenting a definitive reconstruction and reading.

6   Newsom, Self as Symbolic Space, 3. "Torah" becomes an authoritative symbol and belongs to different symbolic universes each with a specific social production with its own history, recognition of Torah's meaning and crystallization within different symbolic constructions, understanding its history of production, is an approach elucidated by studies on social constructions of reality; see esp. Jonathan I. Kampen, "'Torah' and Authority in the Major Sectarian Rule Texts from Qumran," in The Scrolls and Biblical Tradition, 231–254, sectarian texts use "Torah" as a broad category that include lifestyle requirements. John J. Collins, "The Transformation of the Torah in Second Temple Judaism," JSJ 43 (2012): 455–474, at 458, works concerned mainly with halakhic issues arise at the time of the Maccabean revolt and grew during the Hasmonean era.

7   Lange, Weisheit und Prädestination, 58; cf. Torleif Elgvin, "Wisdom and Apocalypticism in the

who equates wisdom with Torah (cf. esp. 15:1), and 4QInstruction derive from the same scribal school.[8] Alternatively, John Kampen argues that a major distinction between 4QInstruction and Ben Sira is the absence of Mosaic Torah.[9] In addressing the place of "Torah" within 4QInstruction and how it relates to the רז נהיה at stake is the composition's location among early Jewish literature generally and other wisdom compositions specifically. For instance, within other sapiential materials discovered at Qumran is a general tendency to elevate the Mosaic Torah.[10] John Collins, among others, has observed that 4QBeatitudes (4Q525) 2 ii 3–4 equates Torah with wisdom: "Blessed is the man who obtains wisdom [חוכמה], who walks in the Torah of the most high [תורת עליון], and establishes her ways in his heart."[11] Elisa Uusimäki offers a valuable study on 4QBeatitudes and concludes that it reconfigures wisdom to cohere and resonate within its own context by introducing "Torah devotion and dualistic elements" to its discourse.[12] 4QInstruction and 4QBeatitudes formulate the relationship of wisdom to Torah much differently from one another, which raises questions about the relationship of 4QInstruction to other early Jewish sapiental traditions. Therefore, in Section 3 below, we turn to questions about the place of Torah in several traditions to view better 4QInstruction's relationship to them, these include: Enochic literature, Jubilees, the Temple Scroll, and early Christian wisdom.

Goff does not view the רז נהיה as displacing the Mosaic Torah since it is a source for instruction, but comments that 4QInstruction's "reception of the Torah is colored by an appeal to revelation beyond that of Sinai."[13] The authors

---

Early Second Century BCE: The Evidence of 4QInstruction," in *The Dead Sea Scrolls Fifty Years After Their Discovery*, 226–247, at 237, "[Lange's] assertion that an apocalyptic author identifies this mystery with the Mosaic Torah cannot be upheld. Apocalyptic circles primarily refer to esoteric secrets not contained in the Torah ... [the mystery] conveys divine revelation to man and provides the means for the right relation to God and fellow man."

8   Rey, *4QInstruction*, 334 writes: "Nous en avons conclu qu'il s'agissait de textes vraisemblablement contemporains et que ces deux auteurs auraient pu suivre une formation commune. Ils développent également des thèmes sapientiaux similaires."

9   Kampen, "Wisdom in Deuterocanonical," 96 ff.

10   Sidnie White Crawford, "Lady Wisdom and Dame Folly at Qumran," *DSD* 5 (1993): 255–266, at 365; cf. Jack T. Sanders, "When Sacred Canopies Collide: The Reception of the Torah of Moses in the Wisdom Literature of the Second-Temple Period," *JSJ* 32/2 (2001): 121–136, at 127.

11   Collins, *Jewish Wisdom*, 49. 11QPs[a] 154 explicitly identified Torah with wisdom.

12   Elisa Uusimäki, *Turning Proverbs Towards Torah: An Analysis of 4Q525*, STDJ 117 (Leiden: Brill, 2016), 268, "The Hebrew language of 4Q525 even serves as a way to extend the existing Torah, i.e., a body of teachings of some sort."

13   Goff, *Worldly and Heavenly*, 72–73.

of Enochic literature are familiar with and allude to scriptural passages and yet the Mosaic Torah is not of central importance to them nor is it thematized.[14] Jack Sanders describes well that the Mosaic Torah did not become a dominant force immediately or all at once, nor was it a foregone conclusion that it would come to dominate.[15] If 4QInstruction reflects an understanding of Torah from an era, or within a community, that did not hold it in a position of supremacy, then this is valuable when dating the composition and locating it among other traditions. One may speculate, for instance, that Torah and temple were identified in the period and that 4QInstruction is reacting to power structures in Judea and the authority of the ruling classes. In the final Section 4 of this chapter, two passages that re-write Torah are studied (4Q416 2 iii 14–19; 4Q423 1) to further understand how the authority of Sinai relates to the authority of revelation at Creation.

1   Evoking Torah? "By the Hand of Moses" in 4Q418 184 and 4Q423 11

The expression "by the hand of Moses" is one of instrumentality. In the Hebrew scriptures God "speaks" and "commands" by Moses' hand and yet the verbs צוה and דבר only immediately precede the expression on a few occasions (Josh 21:2; 1 Kgs 8:53, 8:56). The 32 occurrences of ביד משה in the HB exhibit a diverse range of expressions, formulations, and connotations. However, in the Rule of the Community (1QS I 2–3) this instrumentality is clearly used in reference to Torah (כאשר צוה ביד מושה וביד כול עבדיו). Column VIII reflects concern to describe the Yaḥad and initiation into it. At the end of line 11 and beginning of line 12 an "interpreter" (איש הדורש) is able, by studying Torah, to perceive what is hidden from Israel.[16] Entrance into the community is depicted with the language of Isaiah 40:3, and in line 15 preparing the way in the wilderness is described as "seeking of the Torah" (מדרש התורה), which is an activity "commanded by the hand of Moses" (צוה ביד מושה). Elsewhere in the Rule of the Community (1QS VI 6) is

---

14   George W.E. Nickelsburg, "Enochic Wisdom and its Relationship to the Mosaic Torah," in *The Early Enoch Literature*, 81–94 esp. 81–83.

15   Sanders, "Sacred Canopies," 122.

16   Not only is the Teacher of Righteousness the דורש התורה, but priestly leaders who are proficient in exegesis are well known in Yaḥad literature, cf. Philip R. Davies, *The Damascus Covenant: An Interpretation of the Damascus Document* (Sheffield: JSOT Press, 1982), 123–124; מדרש התורה in CD XX 6 parallels מדרש יחד in 1QS VI 24, see Joseph M. Baumgarten, "Corrigenda to the 4Q MSS of the Damascus Document," *RevQ* 19 (1999): 217–225, at 221.

instruction that among the quorum of ten there will not be absent an interpreter who seeks the Torah day and night (דורש בתורה יומם ולילה). Here the
language of Ps 1:2b is drawn upon to reinforce continuous study of Torah. The
author of the War Scroll (1QM x 6) also uses Moses' hand in reference to the
Torah; God spoke scripture, namely a passage of Numbers (10:9), by the hand
of Moses (דברתה ביד מושה).

Personal names are not typically used in 4QInstruction and indeed Moses
is not referred to elsewhere. There are only two passages, in addition to the
two fragments here (4Q418 184 and 4Q423 11), where proper names may even
occur. These are to: (1) antediluvian figures (i.e., Seth, Enosh) in the Vision of
Hagu passage (4Q417 1 i 13–18); and (2) in 4Q423 5 where "Levi" the priest and
the judgment of "Korah" are mentioned. In the case of the Vision of Hagu, as
referred to in Chapter 2, many interpreters, including myself, have not found
it convincing that these are in fact proper names. I return to the judgment of
Korah below.

The reference to Moses in 4Q418 184 occurs in a more substantive context
than in 4Q423 11. The orthography of 4Q418 184 is somewhat abnormal: typically *waw* would be used as a vowel letter in 4Q418 (e.g., און in 4Q418 123 ii 4);
therefore, one would expect מושה. There is also an unusually long gap, about a
letter length, between the *shin* and *heh* of the proposed משה (see fig. 4 in plate
section).

4Q418 184, Transcription and Translation:

א[וֹ ביד משה וֹ]   ]   1

כא[שר גלה אזנכה ברז נהיה בֹוֹֹ]¹⁷   ]   2

[שה לכה ופן ת[אכ]ל ושבעתה ○]   ]   3

[הלºººº]   ]   4

1   [wra]th by the hand of Moses and[
2   [just] as He uncovered your ear to the mystery of existence *bwy*[
3   [   ]*sh* to you, and lest y[ou ea]t and are satisfied [
4   [   ]*hl* ○○○[

---

17   DJD 34:408 read first word of this line as אשר and translate: "h]ow *He* uncovered thy ear
      about the mystery that is to come *in the day of* ["; the better reading is כאשר which is
      attested in other occurrences of the phrase in 4QInstruction (1Q26 1 4; 4Q416 2 iii 17–18).
      The final word בֹוֹֹ is highly uncertain and ביום should be taken only as a theoretical read-
      ing.

Harrington and Strugnell reconstruct 4Q418 184 1 as either צו[ה ("He commanded") or דב[ר ("He spoke") "by the hand of Moses."[18] However, there are
not even the slightest traces of either a *heh* or *resh*, i.e. the final consonants of
these two proposed reconstructions, immediately preceding the *beit* of ביד.[19]
The only letter visible before the *beit* of ביד is in fact a *pe* and it appears to be a
misshapen final form. Alternatively, it could possibly be read as a final *tsade*.[20]
The editors comment that "[t]he trace beneath the line [of their *resh* or *heh*]
... would convert this letter into a medial *pe*," and "should be dismissed as acci-
dental" (!).[21] That the letter is not in the medial form is suggested by the length
of the bottom descender which drops significantly below the line. I am not convinced that the letter *pe* should be so quickly dismissed as a scribal error. If one
looks for terms in 4QInstruction, at least in the first instance, that end in a final
pe, there are a total of ten words that may be reconstructed.[22] That among them
אף may be read is justified by several observations on Moses' hand associated
either: (a) with turning away wrath, or (b) as an instrument of judgment.

(a) In the same manuscript, an exalted figure (4Q418 81 + 81a 10) is empow-
ered "by his hand" to turn away "wrath" from the community (ובידכה להשיב
אף).[23] In 1QH[a] IV 9–15 there is an extended description of God turning
away sin and offense "by the hand of Moses" (l. 12). Although 1QH[a] does
not refer to "wrath" *per se*, Moses' hand relates generally to deliverance.
See also Num 33:1 and Ps 77:21 where "by the hand of Moses and Aaron"

---

18   Qimron, *The Dead Sea Scrolls*, 2:177, reconstructs צו[ה ביד משה.
19   If the upper horizontal stroke were from a *resh* then it would need to be to the top of the
      line and not bottom, and the final stroke should end with an upward ligature; there simply
      is no accounting for how this stroke could belong to a *heh* when it forms a horizontal to
      vertical curve consistent with a *pe*.
20   חפץ is the most frequent term in 4QInstruction ending with the letter *tsade*, but this word
      does not fit in the context here. Two other words ending in *tsade* are used in 4QInstruc-
      tion, which are immediately preceded by יד, they are: (1) אוץ ("hurry," "urge," "be in haste")
      in 4Q416 2 i 21 as *Hiphil* imperfect ידכה ("if you *hasten* (?) your hand"); and (2)
      קפץ ("close") in 4Q416 2 ii 2 as *Qal* imperfect ידו ("if he closes his hand"). Theo-
      retically, God could "hasten" or "close" *by* Moses' hand, but a direct object is missing and
      the preposition -ב indicates that it is not "hand." In 4Q418 69 ii 6 is the much discussed
      Hiphil imperfect תקיץ from the root יקץ ("awaken"); if that term occurred in this lacuna
      it may be that the account of Moses and the Amalekites (Exod 17), where Moses' hand is
      instrumental in prevailing, is retold.
21   DJD 34:408.
22   They are: אף, אסף, טרף, יסף, נגף, סוף, עיף, צרף, רדף, and רשף.
23   Cf. 4Q417 2 i 14–16 and the appeasement of God's wrath.

is used to describe deliverance from Egypt. 4Q418 184 may depict Moses
in a role that serves as a model for the exalted addressee in 4Q418 81 + 81a
10. Moreover, the notion of turning away wrath is also found in 4Q417 2 i
15 and perhaps also 4Q418 126 ii 6 (cf. Ch. 2 § 2.4.)

(b) Another way that the "hand of Moses" may be understood is in relation to Korah's Rebellion (Num 16) which is referred to in one passage of
4QInstruction (4Q423 5). Noteworthy is that the phrase כאשר גלה אזנכה
ברז נהיה occurs here in 4Q418 184 directly after "the hand of Moses" and
on five other occasions in 4QInstruction (1Q26 1 4; 4Q416 2 iii 17–18 [=
4Q418 10 1]; 4Q418 123 ii 4; 4Q418 190 2); several of these references occur
in connection to judgment, most notably in this passage about Korah who
serves as a negative example of the wicked. In Num 17:5 (= 16:40) the "hand
of Moses" is associated with Korah: "and he will not be like Korah and his
companions, just as the Lord spoke to him by the hand of Moses" (וְלֹא־יִהְיֶה
כְקֹרַח וְכַעֲדָתוֹ כַּאֲשֶׁר דִּבֶּר יְהוָה בְּיַד־מֹשֶׁה לֹו). In Numbers the association of
Moses' hand is to judgment upon Korah's followers. When Korah's rebel-
lion is alluded to in 4QInstruction (4Q423 5), the revealing of the mystery
of existence (כאשר גלה אזנכה ברז נהיה) is closely related to understanding creation (l. 3) and appointed times (l. 5). If one understands seasons
and times, by the mystery of existence, then one may distinguish between
good and evil, and between a man of understanding and a man of folly
(ll. 6–7). Elsewhere, in 1Q26 4, the phrase גלה אזנכה ברז נהיה occurs in relation to observing the created order too, here as regards marriage and agriculture, before turning to the theme of judgment against those who do
not observe the proper order. In 1Q26 4 the commissioning of judgment
is expressed as: בידו פקד משפט ("by his hand he brought judgment"). The
use of ביד elsewhere in 4QInstruction also demonstrates an instrumental
use when judging (יקפוץ ידו in 4Q416 2 ii 2; 4Q417 2 ii + 23 4; cf. 4Q417 2 i
24 where a creditor closes his hand against a debtor). The association of
Moses hand to "judgment" (i.e., משפט) is also found in Lev 26:46 and Num
36:13.[24] Although questionable, there is a theoretical reconstruction of
4QPseudo-Jubilees[a] (4Q225 1 8): משטמ]ה עומד ויקם בְּיַד[מושה ("Mastema]h
was standing, and He took vengeance by the hand of[Moses").

---

24   Cf. Exod 18:13 (and possible later traditions to the קתדרא דמשה "seat of Moses" in Mt.
      23:2–3; *Pes. de Rab Kahana*); Deut 33 Moses song is concerned with judgment (and 2 Macc
      7:6; Bar. 1:20, 2:2; Rev 15:3); John 5:38 "it is Moses who accuses you" (ἔστιν ὁ κατηγορῶν ὑμῶν
      Μωϋσῆς).

If 4Q418 184 is read in relationship to Moses as an instrument of judgment this makes sense of the following reference to the uncovering of the addressee's ear to the mystery of existence. Moreover, there are examples of Moses' hand associated with judgment elsewhere. Unless one follows the editors' choice to attribute the letter *pe* preceding "the hand of Moses" to a scribal mistake, then it needs to be accounted for, and in this regard 4Q418 81 + 81a and the association of אף with the hand of an exalted sage-addressee may also help make sense of the *pe*.[25] If 4Q418 184 1 were to be taken as a straightforward and explicit reference to "Torah" then the following line raises questions about how this accords with revealing the "mystery of existence" in the very next line. Certainly, the רז נהיה is not entirely divorced from Torah, but to evoke both explicitly, side by side, needs to be accounted for in a document that otherwise evidences no expressed interest in a thematized "Torah."

The editors also suggest reading "he commanded by the hand of Moses" in the single line fragment 4Q423 11. *Pace* the editors, in this single line fragment only a few letters are visible and there is good reason to doubt that a reference to Moses is to be found (see figs. 1–3 in plate section).[26] This fragment may be viewed in the following table:

4Q423 11, Transcription:

○ בידמ○   1

The letter before the *beit* is only a dot of ink and it cannot be determined what letter is to be read. There is no space between the *dalet* and the *mem* nor are there clear traces of a *shin* following the *mem*, and it is unlikely that a *waw* is to be read because the stroke to the left is too long and horizontal. The letter following *mem* could be a *heh*. The case against reading "hand of Moses" then is threefold: (1) between יד and משה should be a space when there is not; (2) either the letter *shin* or *waw* should follow the *mem* and this is not at all clear; and (3) neither the words דבר or צוה are visible and therefore cannot lend sup-

---

25   Another possible reconstruction is from the root רדף ("to pursue"), which occurs twice in 4Q418 69 ii 10–11 in a rhetorical statement about "pursuing knowledge" which would possibly fit with revealing mysteries in the following line.

26   The 1960 scanned infrared negative is the clearest image that remains of this fragment, in June 2012 the fragment was photographed (plate 185, frag. 13) in full spectrum color and also infrared. Unfortunately, these 2012 images display significant deterioration and the Japanese tissue paper now hold loose fragments where the *mem* was once visible.

port. One might instead see this as the expression "in their hand" (בידמה) as
found in the Temple Scroll (לוא יתפש בידמה 11Q19 LVII 11).[27] Indeed, the word
יד occurs, including overlaps, at least 38 times in 4QInstruction and often with
pronominal suffixes, although there is no extant occurrence with the third person masculine plural suffix.

In conclusion, the Torah is never mentioned in 4QInstruction, God never
speaks or commands "by the hand of Moses," and the expression ביד משה only
occurs once and not twice. Inferences made from the transcriptions of 4Q418
184 and 4Q423 11 in DJD 34 have led to confusion about how 4QInstruction sit-
uates the authority of Sinai to the authority of the mystery of existence. Three
passages in the section to follow help clarify that relationship.

2   Supplanting "Torah" with the "Mystery of Existence"

In 4QInstruction, three passages may be identified that participate in traditions
that typically reflect interest in promoting study of the Torah. However, on each
occasion 4QInstruction substitutes "Torah" with the "mystery of existence." By
giving precedence to the mystery over Torah, 4QInstruction may be seen to distance itself from Torah-centered traditions. What is clear is that the author(s)
of 4QInstruction knew Torah from Genesis to Deuteronomy; the three passages
analyzed below indicate that they were neither neutral to emerging hierarchies
of authority nor ignorant about them.

2.1   4Q417 1 i and Psalm 1:2b

In 4Q417 1 i 6 "Torah" is replaced by the רז נהיה as the focus of meditation when
Psalm 1:2b (כִּי אִם בְּתוֹרַת יהוה חֶפְצוֹ וּבְתוֹרָתוֹ יֶהְגֶּה יוֹמָם וָלָיְלָה) is rewritten.[28] This substitution in 4Q417 1 i may suggest, on the one hand, that "Torah" and the רז נהיה
are equated; or, on the other hand, that the רז נהיה is superior to Torah and,
possibly, there are even tensions between them. Noteworthy is that Sir 14:20
also alludes to Ps 1:2b when he writes: "happy is the person who meditates on

---

27   This is the typical orthography for the 3rd m. sg. pronominal suffix in this manuscript (e.g.,
        4Q418 81+81a 3).

28   Cf. Josh 1:8 and instruction to meditate on the Torah day and night: לֹא־יָמוּשׁ סֵפֶר הַתּוֹרָה
        הַזֶּה מִפִּיךָ וְהָגִיתָ בּוֹ יוֹמָם וָלָיְלָה. The reference to Torah in Ps 1:2b is likely an insertion added
        by a pious Torah observant psalter after the time of Ezra when there was a tradition of edu-
        cation in the Torah; cf. James Luther Mays, "The Place of the Torah-Psalms in the Psalter,"
        JBL 106 (1987): 3–12.

wisdom and acts wisely" (אשרי אנוש בחכמה יהגה ובתבונה יעשה).[29] Meditation on wisdom rather than Torah underscores equating law to wisdom, similar to 4QBeatitudes.[30] While the use of Ps 1:2b in Sir 14:20 reinforces that wisdom and Torah are to be identified with one another, in 4QInstruction this substitution is difficult to account for in the same way because there is no interest in Torah as a theme in its own right.[31]

4Q417 1 i preserves large parts of a 27-line column and in lines 13b–18 is the Vision of Hagu passage; this passage (ll. 1–14a) was discussed in Chapter 2 (§ 1.1.1.).

4Q417 1 i 1–9 (comp. 4Q418 43 1–10 [single underline]; overlap [double underline]), Transcription and Translation:[32]

```
[                              ]            ו[א]תה מב[ן י]ן[                      ]        1
[                ]      ○○○ הֹבֹטֹן ו[בֹרֹזֹי פלֹאֹי אל הנוראים תשכיל ראש ○        2
לֹ[ֹו בֹפֹ[  ]בֹה ○○○ וֹהֹבֹטֹן ברז נהיה ומעשי] קדם למה נהיה ומה נהיה      3
במ[ה]ה ○[ ○○○לֹם ○○○ן○○○]עֹו[ ]לֹם לתשֹן                        [למה       4
הֹזֹיא ולֹמֹ[ה ]נהיה במֹהֹ] ○ בֹֹכֹוֹלֹ[                [מֹעשֹה וֹמֹעֹ[שֹה      5  ✳
[        ]יומֹם ו[לילה הגה ברז נהיה○ {ו}דורש תמיֹד ואז תדע אמת ועול חכמה      6
ואול[ת ת]ֹ[בִֹין] דע מֹעֹשֹ[י]ֹהם ]בֹכול דרכיהם עם פקודתֹֹם לכול קצי עולם ופקודת      7
עד ואז תדע בין [טו]ֹב לֹ[רע כֹ]מֹעֹשֹי[הם ]כֹֹיֹא אל הדעות סוד אמת וברז נהיה      8
פֹרֹש אֹת אֹושֹה וֹמֹעֹשֹיֹה ○○○[לכול חכ]מה ולכול[ ע]ֹרמה יצרה וממשלת מעשיה      9
```

1 [and] you underst[an]ding one[

2 [   ] gaze,
[and] by the mysteries of the wonders of the God of the awesome ones
    gain insight,
the beginnings of [   ]

3 [   ] to him in your [   ]
[   ] and gaze [upon the mystery of existence

---

29   MS A in Pancratius C. Beentjes, *The Book of Ben Sira in Hebrew: A Text Edition of All Extant Hebrew Manuscripts and a Synopsis of All Parallel Hebrew Ben Sira Texts*, VTSup 68 (Leiden: Brill, 1997), 43; note Ps 1:1 begins: אשרי האיש אשר; cf. Sir 14:20 Μακάριος ἀνήρ, ὃς ἐν σοφίᾳ μελετήσει with LXX Ps 1:2 Μακάριος ἀνήρ … ἐν τῷ νόμῳ αὐτοῦ μελετήσει ἡμέρας καὶ νυκτός.

30   Collins, *Jewish Wisdom*, 49.

31   4Q417 1 i 12 exhorts to "always seek these things early [שחר]," which may elude to the Shema's instruction to recite these things וּבְקוּמֶךָ ("in your arising early" Deut 6:7).

32   DJD 34:151; Tigchelaar, *To Increase Learning*, 52; Rey, *4QInstruction*, 278; Goff, *4QInstruction*, 137–138; Qimron, *Dead Sea Scrolls*, 2:148; Kister, "ספרות החכמה בקומראן," 308.

and the deeds of] ancient times,
to what is and what will be,
4 in what [   ]
[eter]nity to [   ]
[   ] to what 5 was and and to wh[at] will be,
in what [   ] in all [   ]
[   ] deed and dee[d]
6 [day and] night meditate on the mystery of existence,
seek always and then you will know truth and iniquity,
wisdom 7 [and foolishne]ss [understand]
know [their] dee[ds] in all their ways with their punishments,
for all periods of eternity, and eternal punishments,
8 and then you will know between [goo]d and [evil according to their
    ]deeds,
for the God of knowledge is the foundation of truth,
and by the mystery of existence 9 He has spread out the foundation of
    its (fem. i.e. truth's) deeds ...

These lines further illustrate that the mystery of existence allows the *mēvîn* to
properly distinguish between good and evil and the activities associated with
them (l. 8). Additionally, the judgments due the wicked are also made known to
the addressee (l. 7). Unique to this passage are descriptions of the mystery that
see its revelation encompassing past, present, and future (ll. 2–4). The mysteries
in line 2 are a source of insight and they are to be taken as a further description of the רז נהיה. Line 2 is the only place in 4QInstruction where the term
נוראים occurs and is likely a reference to angelic beings.[33] In Chapter 1 reflection
upon angelic beings was seen in relation to them: (1) playing a role in creating
humanity (4Q417 1 i 17); (2) serving as a role model to be followed (4Q418 55;
69 ii); and (3) receiving veneration (4Q418 81 + 81a 1–2, 12). In the case of נוראים,
the Songs of the Sabbath Sacrifice, a composition that has increasingly been
viewed as closely related to 4QInstruction, twice uses this term for a class of
angels (4Q400 2 2; 14 i 8).[34] Moreover, 4Q440 ("Hodayot-like Text") also uses
נוראים as a class of angels (3 i 23).

---

33   DJD 34:156 "אל followed by a class of angel is frequent in Qumran literature"; although
      they do not rule out the possibility of translating here "the awesome mysteries of God's
      wonders."

34   See the recent work of Eric Montgomery, *A Stream from Eden: The Nature and Development
      of a Revelatory Tradition in the Dead Sea Scrolls* (Ph.D. dissertation, McMaster University,
      2013).

When Ps 1:2b is re-written and "Torah" is substituted with רז נהיה as the subject of continuous study, this occurs in a passage that is arguably the richest in 4QInstruction for viewing the mystery's scope. The elevation of the mystery is also seen in lines 8–9 where truth's deeds are founded by it: by the mystery of existence God spreads out the foundation of deeds. Therefore, the mystery of existence may be seen as an instrument used in establishing or creating the order of the cosmos; this is similar to 4Q418 126 ii 4 where God "spread them [i.e., the heavens] out in truth and he placed them" (פרשם באמת הוא שמם).[35] As such, line 9 recollects Prov 3:19 where God creates the world with wisdom; indeed, in the Hebrew Bible and in later Jewish tradition personified Wisdom was often portrayed as pre-existent with God (e.g., Job 28; Bar 3:9–4:4; Wis 6:12–11:1; 1 En. 42). Wisdom, *Logos*, and Spirit as bridging concepts are used to express manifestations of God's creative activities; Sir 43:26 states that "by his word all things hold together." Wisdom also pervades the whole world, in the Wisdom of Solomon 7:24 "her [i.e., Wisdom's] pureness pervades and penetrates all things" (cf. Ps 139:7). Philo writes that "the spirit ... is everywhere diffused, so as to fill the universe" (Philo, *Giants* 27) and also associates Wisdom with the *Logos* (cf. Philo, *Migration* 6). The mystery of existence in this passage is likewise a conceptual bridge that expresses God's creative acts.

Later in the column, in the Vision of Hagu passage that follows, several of the themes related to the mystery occur but without reference to the רז נהיה. This is especially the case in regard to the themes of punishment and reward which are inscribed in the heavens and are objects of meditation. In the Vision of Hagu are three passive verbs, each related to writing: "engraved" (חרות), "inscribed" (חקוק), and "written" (כתוב).[36] Each of these activities may be seen to evoke an ordering of the cosmos by way of decree.[37]

---

35 Goff, "The Mystery of Creation," 170 the mystery relates to the natural order (cf. Ch. 2 §1.1.1.); alternatively, a less convincing view that the רז נהיה is a body of teaching to transmit divine wisdom, perhaps written or oral, see Harrington "Râz Nihyeh," 552.

36 In Rabbinic literature, the two meanings of חרות as either "engraved" or "freedom" receive attention; see m. Avot 6.2 "... and it says, 'the tablets were the work of God and the writing of God, engraved upon the tablets' (Exod 32:16). Read not *haruth* [חָרוּת i.e., "engraved"] but rather *heruth* [חֵרוּת i.e., "freedom"]. For there is no free man for you but he who occupies himself with the study of the Torah ..."; cf. Lev. R. 18.3.

37 Several translators prefer חקוק as "decreed" or "ordained" and yet the important point is that the activity of ordaining or decreeing, suggested by חקק, is conducted by writing or inscribing. Cf. Prov 8:29 where the foundations of the earth are "marked out" (בְּחוּקוֹ מוֹסְדֵי אָרֶץ).

4Q417 1 i lines 13b–18 (cf. Ch. 2, §1.1.1.):

> And you, **14** O understanding one,
> *inherit* your reward,
> by the remembrance *of*[   ]come.
> Engraved [חֹרֹֽת] is {your} the statute [החוק] and every punishment inscribed [חקוק],
> **15** for engraved [חרות] is the decree [מחוקק] by God,
> against all i[*niquities of*] the sons of perdition,
> and a book of memory [ספר זכרון] is written [כתוב] before him,
> **16** for those who keep His word,
> and this is a vision of *meditation* to a book of memorial [ספר זכרון],
> and He made humanity, a people ᵂⁱᵗʰ a spirit, to inherit it (i.e., the vision?),
> for **17** according to the pattern of the holy ones is *humanity's* fashioning,
> and no longer is *hagu* given to a spirit of f[le]sh,
> because it *did not know* the difference between **18** [goo]d and evil,
> according to the judgment of his [sp]irit
>   *vacat* and you, O son of an understanding one …

The ספר זכרון of Mal 3:16 ("and a book of remembrance was written before him [סֵפֶר זִכָּרוֹן לְפָנָיו] of those who revered the LORD and thought on his name") has been convincingly read as standing in the background to the use of the term (ll. 15–16) in the Vision of Hagu pericope.[38] The only other references to a ספר זכרון in the literature of the period are in the Damascus Document (CD XX 20) and 4QPesher Malachi (4Q253a 1 i 2). While there is little to comment on in regard to 4QPesher Malachi, the Damascus Document sets the citation of Mal 3:16 within the context of instructing the addressees to help one another walk faithfully until the time of salvation. Mal 3:17–19 is interested in parents and their children, and knowing the difference between good and evil, therefore it is not

---

38   Lange, *Weisheit*, 70–79, offers an excursus on heavenly tablets in the Hebrew scriptures (Mal 3:16; Exod 32:31–33), the New Testament (Phil 4:3); and ancient Judaism (T. Lev. 5:4; T. Dan. 5:6, T. Naph. 4:19; Jub. 1:29; 1 En. 81:1–2; 93:1, cf. 4QEnᶜ 5 ii 26; 103:2–3; 108:7; 4Q504 1–2 vi 14; 4Q180 1 3; CD II 2 ff.; 4Q534 i 5; 4Q537 1 3). Florentino García Martínez, "The Heavenly Tablets in the Book of Jubilees," in *Studies in the Book of Jubilees*, ed. Matthias Albani, Jörg Frey & Armin Lange, TSAJ 65 (Tübingen: Mohr Siebeck, 1997), 243–260, outlines five ways the heavenly tablets in Jubilees may be understood: (1) Tablets of the Law (i.e., Torah of Moses); (2) Heavenly Register of Good and Evil; (3) the Book of Destiny; (4) Calendar and Feasts; and (5) New Halakhot.

surprising that Mal 3:18 is explicitly linked with the introduction to the Decalogue (Exod 20:6) in the Damascus Document. Honoring one's parents and cre-
ators comes into focus again below in the examination of re-written scripture.

On several occasions the רז נהיה is a source of revelation about seasons and
times, the created order, and the differentiation between good and evil. In the
hymn of praise to creation in the Community Rule (1QS x; cf. variant recension 4Q256 XIX) the author calls the first day of each month a "memorial"
(זכרון) and a time for praise. The author blesses God because the created order
is like an eternally engraved statute (l. 6; כחוק חרות). This is followed by further expressions of gratitude for creation (i.e., days, seasons, weeks of years,
jubilees) before he exults that: "on my tongue will the engraved statute [חוק
חרות] be!" (l. 8). In addition to this "engraved statute" referring to the created
order, as such it serves the speaker to assess his own short fallings and the measure of his own wrong doing (l. 11). Indeed, he writes that "by His law will I
convict myself" (ומשפטו אוכיח) before expressing similarly that "my sin is before
my eyes as an engraved statute" (כחוק חרות)—the association of משפט with חוק
חרות is unmistakable.

The Thanksgiving Hymns are also valuable for informing the language of
"engraving," "statutes," and "memorials." In column IX the speaker extols God
for opening his ears to "wonderful mysteries" (גליתה אוזני לרזי פלא) even though
he is but a "vessel of clay" (l. 23). The language of revealing mysteries is remarkably similar to that found in 4QInstruction and, as was raised in Chapter 2, may
indicate some kind of dependence. In this column of the Thanksgiving Hymns,
the speaker's ears are uncovered to mysteries so that he can state that "nothing is hidden" (l. 27). The reason for this is that seasons, years, and appointed
times are known from all eternity; indeed, the author says that "everything is
inscribed before You with an engraving of remembrance" (ll. 25–26; הכול חקוק
לפניכה בחרת זכרון). Not only do the Thanksgiving Hymns and hymn to creation
begin to demonstrate that this language of "engraving" and "inscribing" is positively used of the design of the cosmos, but also that that it relates to judgment
and serves as a memorial.

One final place that "engraved statutes" occurs is in the Songs of the Sabbath
Sacrifice (4Q400 1 i 5; cf. 4Q402 4 3). The address is to a *maśkîl* on the first Sabbath who is instructed to offer praise (l. 1). In the act of rejoicing the angelic
hosts are described within the heavenly realm where God "has engraved His
statutes for all spiritual deeds and the judgments of[" (חרת חוקיו לכול מעשי רוח
ומשפטי). The heavenly context of engraved statutes is also known from 4QSongs
of the Maskil (4Q511 63 + 64 ii), only here the exalted figure promises to relate
God's wonders and to engrave them as statutes for His glory (ll. 2–3; ואחורתם
חוקי הודות כבודכה).

Referees determinism but ignores it

While the "engraved statute" and the "book of remembrance" in the Vision of Hagu may refer to two different written objects, one concerned with judgment upon the wicked (i.e., "sons of perdition," l. 15) and the other reward for the righteous (i.e., "those who keep His word," l. 16), it is also possible that they are both the same basic "memorial" (cf. זכרון in l. 14). The stichs of lines 14 and 15 where the "engraved statute" and the "book of remembrance" are found appear to be expressed in synonymous parallel. As such, they are both fundamentally expressions of the order and design of the cosmos and serve as the basis of judgment and reward. Indeed, the hymn to creation (1QS x), the Thanksgiving Hymns, and the Songs of the Sabbath Sacrifice demonstrate that language for "writing" is commonly used in regard to creation. In 4QInstruction the "engraved statute" and "book of remembrance" describe an important aspect of the רז נהיה and should be viewed therefore as articulations of how God's order of the cosmos relates to humankind.[39]

Florentino García Martínez discusses heavenly tablets in Jubilees as a "heavenly register of good and evil" (Jub. 19:9, 30:19–22) as well as a "book of destiny" (Jub. 5:13–14, 16:9, 23:32, 24:33, 31:32b, 32:21–22).[40] While differentiating between these two, he comments that "[i]t is only a small step from the registration of actions as a mere record to the registration of similar actions of a predestinational character" and points to Jub. 30:19–22 as a passage that links these ideas.[41] The heavenly register is an idea that begins in ancient Mesopotamia and influences cultures for many centuries to follow, including in the New Testament and Rabbinic Literature. In Jubilees, a book of destiny records not only past acts, but also future punishment and reward are fixed and engraved forever.

Cana Werman is explicit in drawing comparisons between the Vision of Hagu and the book of Jubilees.[42] She describes the Hagu passage as referring:

---

39 Bilhah Nitzan, "The Ideological and Literary Unity of *4QInstruction* and its Authorship," *DSD* 12/3 (2005): 257–279, at 263, relates the רז נהיה to the ספר זכרון although her understanding of the vision of meditation differs from mine.

40 García Martínez, "The Heavenly Tablets," 245–248.

41 "And thus a blessing and righteousness will be written (on high) as a testimony for him in the heavenly tablets before the God of all. And we will remember for a thousand generations the righteousness which a man did during his life in all of the (appointed) times of the year. And (it) will be written (on high) and it will come to him and his descendants after him. And he will be written down as a friend and a righteous one in the heavenly tablets." Charlesworth, 2:113.

42 Werman, "The 'תורה' and the 'תעודה,'" 92.

to the march of history, which was determined prior to Creation ('memorial of time'), and to law engraved together with the 'punishment' (פקודה),
that is, the punishments preordained for whoever violates the law. There
is also a book that records 'those who keep his word,' that is, who observe
commandments. All these are conveyed by the 'meditation vision.'[43]

Thus, 4QInstruction exhorts the wise man to observe commandments, but
truly understanding God's ways is only possible through revelation, here it is
the "vision of meditation." Werman suggests that this is similar to the way the
book of Jubilees recounts the story of creation and history as a source of reflection to reveal proper halakha. Her conclusion is that just as the book of Jubilees
was given to Moses at Sinai, so the "vision of meditation" was given to אנוש in
4QInstruction. Jubilees' relationship to Torah as a point of reflection for understanding 4QInstruction will be returned to in the section to follow. However,
important to note here is that the "vision of meditation" (חזון ההגו; ll. 16–17) is
not a written object. The ספר ההגי ("book of meditation") in the Rule of the Congregation (1QSa I 6) and Damascus Document (CD X 4, XIII 2) may be related
to this vision, perhaps a later development following on from 4QInstruction,
but they are to be differentiated.[44] The vision of meditation relates to access
and ability to understand the created order and was given to אנוש ("humanity")
at creation. As seen in Chapter 2, humanity is described as possessing a spirit
as well as sharing a likeness with angelic beings (קדושים). This vision enables
humankind to act according to creation and yet some of humanity failed to distinguish between good and evil "according to their spirit" (l. 18) and, therefore,
are now denied the vision.

2.2   Decalogue-Shema Combination in 4Q416 2 iii Lines 14–19

4Q416 2 iii 14–19 are also preserved in 4Q418 frag. 9 lines 14–18 and frag. 10
lines 1–2; in this passage, the Decalogue's commandment to honor one's father
and mother is rewritten.

---

43   Werman, "The 'תורה' and the 'תעודה,'" 92.
44   Werman, "What Is the Book of Hagu?" 140, writes that "when 4QInstruction was written,
       there was no Sefer ha-Hagu. In 4QInstruction there is no reference to writings other than
       scriptures, nor does 4QInstruction rely on any previous tradition. Instead 4QInstruction
       calls on each individual to meditate both on his own life and on the course of history in
       order to learn what laws were assigned specically to him and what laws were assigned to
       humanity as a whole."

Transcription with Parallels:[45]

4Q416 2 iii 14–19 (variants in bold)	4Q418 9 14–10 1–2 (extant text underlined)	Exod 20:12	Mal 1:6
¹⁴ מחשבותיכה רז נהיה	¹⁴ מחשבתיכה ¹⁵ [רז נהיה		
דרוש והתבונן בכל דרכי	דרוש והתבונן [בכול דרכי		
אמת וכל שורשי עולה	אמת וכול שורשי עולה ¹⁶		
¹⁵תביט ואז תדע מה מר	תביט [אז תדע מה מר		
לאיש ומה מתוק לגבר כבוד	לא]יש ומה מתוק לגבר vac		
אביכה ברישכה	¹⁷ כבד אב]יכה ברישכ]ה	כַּבֵּד אֶת־אָבִיךָ וְאֶת־אִמֶּךָ	בֵּן יְכַבֵּד אָב
¹⁶ ואמכה במצעדיכה	[ואמכ]ה במצעדיכה כי		וְעֶבֶד אֲדֹנָיו
כי כאב לאיש כן אביהו	כאל לאיש כן אביהו		וְאִם־אָב אָנִי אַיֵּה כְבוֹדִי
וכאדנים לגבר כן אמו כי	¹⁸ וכאדונ]ים לגבר כן אמו כיא		וְאִם־אֲדוֹנִים אָנִי
¹⁷ המה כזר הוריכה וכאשר	ה]מ֯ה כור הוריכה וכאשר		אַיֵּה מוֹרָאִי אָמַר יְהוָה
המשילמﬣ בכה זֹיצֹר על	המשיל]כ}ם ¹ [בכה ויצר על		צְבָאוֹת
הרוח כן עובדם וכאשר	הרוח כן עובדם וכאשר		
¹⁸ גלה אוזנכה ברז נהיה	גלה או]ז֯נכה ברז נ֯]היה		
כבדם למען כבודכה וב[	כבדם למען כבודכה		
]הֹדֹר פניהמה	וב הדר ² פניהמה		
¹⁹ למען חייכה וארוך ימיכה	למען חייכה וארוד [	לְמַעַן יַאֲרִכוּן יָמֶיךָ	
vacat	ימיכה		

Translation of 4Q416 2 iii lines 14–19:

> ... your thoughts.
> **14** Seek the mystery of existence,
>   understand all the ways of truth,
>   look upon all the roots of iniquity,
>   **15** and then you will know what is bitter to a man,
>   and what is sweet for a man,
> Honor your father in your poverty,
>   **16** and your mother in your low estate.[46]

---

45   DJD 34:110–111; Tigchelaar, *To Increase Learning*, 47–48; Rey, *4QInstruction*, 92; Goff, *4QInstruction*, 91–92; Qimron, *Dead Sea Scrolls*, 2:156.

46   Following 4Q418 rather than 4Q416; במצעדיכה "your footsteps" is possible, but מצעריכה

For as God[47] is to a man, thus is his father,
>   and as lords are to a man, thus is his mother.
For 17 they are the womb of your conception,
>   and as he placed them in authority over you,
>   and fashioned you according to the spirit,
>   so you should serve them.
And as 18 t(he)y (i.e., parents) uncovered your ear to the mystery of exis-
tence,
>   honor them for your own honor,
>   and in[   ] venerate their presence,
>   19 for your life and for the length of your days. *vac*

A well-known tradition of combining the Decalogue-Shema supports the identification of an allusion to the Shema in these lines. The expression גלה אוזנכה
ברז נהיה ("he uncovered your ear by/in the mystery of existence") occurs here
and five other times in 4QInstruction (1Q26 1 4; 4Q418 123 ii 4; 4Q418 184 2; 4Q423
5 1–2; 4Q423 7 6). Whereas in Psalm 119:18 the Psalter implores God to open his
eyes so that he may gaze upon the wonders of the *tôrāh* (גַּל־עֵינַי וְאַבִּיטָה נִפְלָאוֹת
מִתּוֹרָתֶךָ), here one's eyes are opened to the רז נהיה. However, who is the one
who acts to reveal in this passage of 4QInstruction? The editors comment that
in 4Q416 2 iii 18 neither God nor any other single figure is the subject of the
verb גלה, but rather the subject is plural, which is made clear by the recipient
of honor: "and as t(he)y [i.e., your parents] uncovered your ear *by* the mystery
of existence so serve *them*" (וכאשר גלה אוזנכה ברז נהיה כבדם). A plural subject is
demanded by the "they" of the parents; the use of a singular subject גלה, when
גלו is needed here, was likely used because גלה אוזן is a fixed expression.[48] Deut
5:1 (cf. 5:16), 6:6–7 (= Shema), and 11:19 all have injunctions about educating

"in your humble condition" fits better in parallel with "poverty" and also aligns with this
motif throughout 4QInstruction.

47   "God" (i.e., following 4Q418 rather than 4Q416) is the preferred reading because of the tautological problem that arises in the statement "for as a father is to a man, thus is his father."
Cf. Goff, *4QInstruction*, 110.

48   DJD 34:122, the use of the singular subject also strengthens the analogy of parents with
God. The subject of גלה in 4Q418 123 ii 4 may be "God" or a preposition: "]His time, which
He revealed to the ear [גלה אל אוזן] of the understanding ones by the mystery of exis-
tence." 4Q418 184 2 and 4Q423 5 1–2 set this uncovering in the context of judgment. The
expression to uncover one's ears is especially frequent in the Thanksgiving Hymns (1QH[a]
IV 13; IX 23; XIV 7; XV 41; XXII 26, 31; XXIII 5) and the subject is God who reveals myster-

children, which may be echoed in this line by the activity of parents uncovering a child's ears. How the author of 4QInstruction uses this tradition, and what it possibly reflects about Torah, may be further established and elucidated by setting it alongside material that associates the Decalogue and the Shema in the Second Temple era.[49]

An interpretive rationale behind the Decalogue-Shema combination may be observed in Deuteronomy and Exodus vis-à-vis "these words" found in several passages. In the Shema (Deut 6:6), "these words" (הַדְּבָרִים הָאֵלֶּה) are to be upon one's heart and taught to one's children (Deut 6:7); there is a well-known tradition of interpreting "these words" in reference to the Decalogue in part because Exod 20:1, which introduces the giving of the law at Sinai, begins with: וַיְדַבֵּר אֱלֹהִים אֵת כָּל־הַדְּבָרִים הָאֵלֶּה ("The Lord spoke all of these words"). Moreover, Deut 11:18–20 repeats the exhortation of 6:6–9 and begins with "these words of mine" (Deut 11:18 דְּבָרַי אֵלֶּה) and came to be connected with the Shema because it repeats the exhortation to "love the Lord your God with ... your whole heart and whole soul" as well as the injunction to teach these words and bind them upon you hands. Therefore, "these words" in the Shema (Deut 6:6) could be interpreted as referring to: (1) the preceding verses (6:4–5) in a limited way; (2) the preceding Decalogue (Deut 5) and the injunction of Deut 11:18–20; or (3) the whole book of Deuteronomy.[50] "These words" have been convincingly taken by many scholars, both in contextual and reception terms, as referring to the whole of Deuteronomy.[51]

---

ies, instruction, and truth; cf. CD II 2–3 (ועתה שמעו אלי כל באי ברית ואגלה אזנכה בדרכי רשעים) and 1QM X 11 where holy angels are the ones who reveal.

49   See esp. the excellent study on the Decalogue-Shema combination by Jeremy Penner, *Patterns of Daily Prayer in Second Temple Period Judaism*, STDJ 104 (Leiden: Brill, 2012), 60 ff.

50   James L. Kugel, *Traditions of the Bible: A Guide to the Bible as It was at the Start of the Common Era* (Cambridge, MA: Harvard University Press, 1998), 830 "In context 'these words' might refer to everything that Moses had said and was about to say 'today,' that is, the day of his final address to the Israelites—in other words, virtually the whole book of Deuteronomy. But if so, was it reasonable to expect the Israelites to keep an entire biblical book 'upon your heart,' indeed, to speak of it continually and write it upon their doorposts and gates?"

51   Richard D. Nelson, *Deuteronomy: A Commentary* (Louisville, KY: Westminster John Knox Press, 2002), 91 suggests that "commanding you today" (6:6) refers to the whole of Deuteronomy; cf. Duane L. Christensen, *Deuteronomy 1:1–21:9*, WBC 6a (Nashville, TN: Thomas Nelson Publishers, 2001), 141–142, who also argues that the whole book of Deuteronomy is in view. Reuven Kimelman, "Polemics and Rabbinic Liturgy," in *Discussing Cultural Influences: Text, Context, and Non-Text in Rabbinic Judaism*, ed. Rivka Ulmer (Lanham, MD:

When seeking to establish that the Decalogue and Shema were often combined in the Second Temple era the following evidence is often presented: (1) Nash Papyri; (2) *tefillin* (phylacteries) found at Qumran; (3) LXX of Deut 6:4; (4) Letter of Aristeas (Arist. § 158–160); (5) Josephus (*Ant.* 4:212–213); (6) m. Tamid 5.1; and (7), to a lesser degree, Philo.[52] These early Jewish texts and traditions come into view below.

The Nash Papyrus, which has been understood by some as coming from a phylactery, recounts the entire Decalogue and fuses it together with the Shema.[53] LXX tradition likewise links the Shema with the Decalogue in the preface of Deut 6:4 "And these are the ordinances and judgments which the Lord commanded the sons of Israel in the day when they came out from the land of Egypt" (Καὶ ταῦτα τὰ δικαιώματα καὶ τὰ κρίματα, ὅσα ἐνετείλατο κύριος τοῖς υἱοῖς Ἰσραηλ ἐν τῇ ἐρήμῳ ἐξελθόντων αὐτῶν ἐκ γῆς Αἰγύπτου).

The degree to which religious artifacts, namely *tefillin* found at Qumran, preserve a combination of Decalogue-Shema is debated.[54] Among Qumran discoveries are 24 phylacteries, the vast majority of which are from Cave 4 (1Q13; 4Q128–148; 5Q8; 8Q3).[55] While it may be observed that parts of Deut 6 combine at times with the Decalogue in these phylacteries, the Shema is not a central focus, but rather at times only an epilogue.[56] Indeed, this combination occurs in just two phylacteries: 4QPhyl B (4Q129) and 8QPhyl (8Q3). The phylacteries

———

      University Press of America, 2007), 59–97, at 68, by the Amoraic era the Decalogue had been usurped by the Shema making recitation of the Decalogue superfluous.

52   See Daniel K. Falk, *Daily, Sabbath, and Festival Prayers in the Dead Sea Scrolls*, STDJ 27 (Leiden: Brill, 1998), 113–115, who refers to each of these, except for Philo, to establish the custom of combining the Decalogue and Shema within the context of liturgy. Falk's focus is 1QS X 9–14a and he observes that two strophes explicitly refer to the recital of the Shema and concludes that "[c]entral to the Yaḥad daily prayers is recital of the *Shema* and Decalogue morning and evening."

53   Stefan C. Reif, *Judaism and Hebrew Prayer: New Perspectives on Jewish Liturgical History* (Cambridge: CUP, 1995), 83. The Nash Papyri appear too large to have served as phylactery and there is no sign of rolling or folding; an alternative is that phylactery were copied from it.

54   Emanuel Tov, "The *Tefillin* from the Judean Desert and the Textual Criticism of the Hebrew Bible," in *Is There a Text in This Cave?*, 277–292.

55   Geza Vermes, "Pre-Mishnaic Jewish Worship and the Phylacteries from the Dead Sea," *VT* 9 (1959): 65–72; Yigal Yadin, "Tefillin (Phylacteries) from Qumran (XQPhyl 1–4)," *Eretz Israel* 9 (1969): 60–83 [Hebrew]; Józef T. Milik, *Qumran Grotte 4.II. Tefillin, Mezuzot et Targums* (*4Q128–4Q157*), DJD 6 (Oxford: Clarendon Press, 1977), 48–85.

56   George J. Brooke, "Deuteronomy 5–6 in the Phylacteries from Qumran Cave 4," in *Emanuel: Studies in Hebrew Bible, Septuagint, and Dead Sea Scrolls in Honor of Emanuel Tov*, ed. Shalom M. Paul, Robert A. Kraft, Eva Ben-David, Lawrence Schiffman & Weston W. Fields,

4QPhyl A (4Q128) and 4QPhyl J (4Q137) end at the beginning of Deuteronomy 6:3; 4QPhyl O (4Q142) appears to include Deut 6:7–9 together with an incomplete Decalogue. The majority of these texts make no explicit connection between the Decalogue and the Shema of Deut 6:4.[57] Excerpted texts found at Qumran, which include parts of Deuteronomy and Exodus (4QDeut[j,k,l,n]), have also garnered attention, particularly by Moshe Weinfeld, who observes that in some of these fragments is an affinity of the Decalogue and Shema, namely in 4QDeut[n] (= 4Q41) and 4QDeut[j] (= 4Q37).[58]

The Letter of Aristeas (Let. Aris. §158–160) is mainly concerned to instruct about observing the Shema and is our earliest witness to Jewish practice of using phylacteries. The Letter of Aristeas §158 describes the use of the *mezuzah* and *tefillin* as: "upon our garments he has given us a symbol of remembrance, and in like manner he has ordered us to put the divine oracles [τιθέναι τὰ λόγια] upon our gates and doors as a remembrance of God." Shortly after this statement Aristeas explicates Deut 6:7 (Let. Aris. §160): "He commands humans also, when lying down to sleep and rising up again, to meditate upon the works of God, not only in word [οὐ μόνον λόγῳ], but by observing distinctly the change and impression produced upon them, when they are going to sleep, and also their waking, how divine and incomprehensible the change from one of these states to the other is." Benjamin Wright observes that while the LXX of Deut 6:9 enjoins "write" (γράφω) these "words" (ῥῆμα) upon the doorposts of your homes, Aristeas expresses to "place" (τίθημι) these "sayings" (λόγια) upon them.[59] The term τὰ λόγια is more ambiguous than the LXX's τὰ ῥήματα

VTSup 94 (Leiden: Brill, 2003), 57–70 at 68–69, discusses the connection of the number of phylacteries at Qumran and emphasis on teaching and studying in many Scrolls.

57   See Penner, *Patterns*, 63–64 who makes this observation based upon the charts of Emanuel Tov, "Excerpted and Abbreviated Biblical Texts from Qumran," *RevQ* 16 (1995): 581–600, at 587.

58   Moshe Weinfeld, "Grace after Meals at Qumran," *JBL* 111/3 (1992): 427–440, at 428, comments that in 4QDeut[j] that parts of Deut 5–6 should be equated with a Decalogue-Shema combination; these precise sections found in 4QDeut[j] are: Deut 5:1–11, 13–15, 21, 22–33; 6:1–3; 8:5–10; 11:6–13; 11:21; Exod 12:43–44; 12:46–13:5; Deut 32:7–8. Penner, *Patterns*, 60, rightly notes that a "number of scrolls found at Qumran contain excerpted passages from Deuteronomy ... although none of them contain the Shema passages."

59   Benjamin G. Wright III, "Three Ritual Practices in Aristeas §158–160," in *Heavenly Tablets: Interpretation, Identity and Tradition in Ancient Judaism*, ed. Lynn LiDonnici & Andrea Lieber, JSJS 119 (Leiden: Brill, 2007), 13–21 at 14; LXX Deut 6:9 καὶ γράψετε αὐτὰ ἐπὶ τὰς φλιὰς τῶν οἰκιῶν ὑμῶν καὶ τῶν πυλῶν ὑμῶν, the antecedent of αὐτὰ is found in 6:6 (ῥῆμα).

ταῦτα.[60] Wright points to several translations of τὰ λόγια in the Letter of Aristeas § 158, these are: (1) "the chapters" as a clearly delineated group of texts;[61] (2) "words" in reference to the Jewish Law;[62] and (3) "les divines Paroles."[63] Wright explores several uses of the noun λόγιον in Aristeas and concludes that the plural use of τὰ λόγια in § 177 is the best match. In § 177 the translators of the LXX are sent by Eleazar and received by the king in Alexandria; the king takes deep interest in the scrolls brought by the scribes and penitentially gives thanks, stating: "I thank you, O men, and even more the one who sent you, but mostly the God whose λόγια these are." Wright comments that "[i]n this instance, the Greek phrase almost certainly refers to the entirety of the Jewish law written on the scrolls brought by the prospective translators."[64] His final conclusion is that τὰ λόγια is best translated as "the saying" or "utterances" and that Aristeas understood this as Jewish Law originating in an act of divine speech.[65] Wright considers whether τὰ λόγια in § 158 refer to the whole of the Jewish Law, which he finds hard to believe, or to a smaller collection, which he finds difficult to define in any precise way. In light of Wright's research, as well as the conclusions of André Pelletier, τὰ λόγια are, most likely, used in § 158 in reference to texts from Deuteronomy and Exodus, especially "these words" found in the Decalogue and Shema (Exod 20:1; Deut 6:6; cf. Deut 11:18).

Josephus (Ant. 4.212–213) associates the giving of Torah with the phylacteries of the Shema: "let all acknowledge the gifts (τὰς δωρεάς) which God bestowed upon them at their deliverance out of the land of Egypt" (4.212); "they are also to inscribe the principal blessings (τὰ μέγιστα) they have received from God upon their doors, and show the same remembrance of them upon their arms; as also they are to bear on their forehead and their arm those wonders which

---

60   The word ῥῆμα in LXX Deut is used for spoken words (cf. Deut 4:10, 13, 36); in Hebrew דברים may be spoken word or a collection of sayings.

61   Moses Hadas, *Aristeas to Philocrates* (Philadelphia, PA: Dropsie College, 1951), 163.

62   R.J.H. Shutt, "Letter of Aristeas," in *Old Testament Pseudepigrapha*, Vol. 2, ed. J.H. Charlesworth (Garden City, NY: Doubleday, 1985), 7–34 at 23.

63   André Pelletier, *Lettre d'Aristée a Philocrate*, SC 89 (Paris: Les Éditions du Cerf, 1962), 177 fn. 5 writes: "C'est le plus ancien exemple de τὰ λόγια pour designer l'ensemble de la Loi."

64   Wright, "Three Ritual," 16; other similar occurrences are noted, e.g., LXX Num 24:16; LXX Deut 33:9–10; LXX Ps 18:14 (MT 19:14); LXX Ps 118:148 (MT 119:148); Philo (*Contempl.* 25; *Rewards* 1); Josephus (*War* 6.311): Rom 3:2; Acts 7:38; Heb 5:12.

65   Wright, "Three Ritual," 19, Aristeas understands "Jewish Law to originate as acts of divine speech—in this sense they are oracular—even though he consistently attributes the origination of the law to Moses, the lawgiver. Interestingly, nowhere in Aristeas does the author talk explicitly of God giving the Law to Moses verbally at Sinai in the form of divine utterances."

declare the power of God" (4.213). In studies on liturgical practices, Josephus'
Antiquities 4.212–213 has been discussed together with Mishnah Tamid 5:1 as
an earlier witness to the tradition of a morning and evening recitation of the
Shema with the Decalogue (m. Tam. 5.1 "He said to them: 'Say one blessing,' and
they blessed. They recited the Ten Commandments [Exod 20:2–13; Dt. 5:6–17],
'Hear,' [Deut 6:4] 'and it will be, if you hear,' [Deut 11:13–21] 'and the Lord spoke,'
[Num 15:37–41]").[66]

Of particular importance here is William Horbury's study on the meaning
of δωρήματα ("gift") in Ezekiel the Tragedian §106 in which he concludes that
"gift" is "a post-biblical Jewish theological idiom of some significance for the
ideas of covenant and grace."[67] Another significant occurrence of the term is
in Ezekiel the Tragedian §35 where Moses recounts, in first person speech,
his upbringing as a prince of Egypt when he was told everything "regarding
my ancestral race and of the gifts of God" (γένος πατρῷον καὶ θεοῦ δωρήματα),
which refers to national privileges. Such an idiomatic use of "gift" is also found
in the New Testament and Philo. Paul, in his letter to the Romans, uses χάρισμα interchangeably with several other words for "gift," including δώρημα (Rom
5:15–16). Therefore, in Rom 11:27–29 when covenant and patriarchs (cf. Rom 9:4)
are closely associated with "gift" (χάρισμα) this reflects on gift language more
generally.[68] When Jesus speaks with the Samaritan woman at the well in John
4:10 he says, "if you knew the gift of God (τὴν δωρεὰν τοῦ θεοῦ) and who is the
one speaking with you," using "gift" in a distinctive way for a Jewish national
privilege. Indeed, "the gift of God" in John 4:10 is paraphrased in 4:22 as "the
salvation of the Jews" (ἡ σωτηρία ἐκ τῶν Ἰουδαίων).[69] Philo uses "gift" for God's
benefits to the nation (*Rewards* 79; *Spec. Laws* 2.219) and in *On the Change of
Names* writes that "covenants are written for the benefit of those who are worthy of the gift (δωρεὰ), so that a covenant is a symbol of grace" (*Names* 52).

Horbury observes that the noun "gift" is used by Josephus for: (1) special
graces afforded to Israel at the exodus (δωρεαί, *Ant.* 3.14, 4.212); and (2) the law
(δωρεὰ, *Ant.* 3.78, 223). The prescriptions for morning and evening prayer in

---

66   Falk, *Daily, Sabbath*, 114; cf. Reuven Hammer, "What did they Bless? A Study of Mishnah
     Tamid 5.1," *JQR* 81/3–4 (1991): 305–324; Reuven Kimelman, "The Šěma' and its Blessing:
     The Realization of God's Kingship," in *The Synagogue in Late Antiquity*, ed. Lee I. Levine
     (Philadelpia, PA: Eisenbrauns, 1987), 73–86.

67   William Horbury, "Ezekiel Tragicus 106: δωρήματα," *VT* 36/1 (1986): 37–51, at 37.

68   John M.G. Barclay, *Paul and the Gift* (Grand Rapids, MI: Eerdmans, 2015), treats divine gift
     in Second Temple Judaism in relationship to Paul at 194–330.

69   Horbury, "Ezekiel," 38–39, also refers to 1 Clem. 32:1–2 where "'gifts' are identified as the
     personages whose calling signifies covenanted mercy."

Antiquities 4.212 are, according to him, linked by Josephus with the Shema and the "gifts" in this passage are "the benefits to Israel recalled in a prayer perhaps to be identified as an early form of the benediction *Ge'ullah*, which now follows the Shema. Thus, a summary of a prescribed prayer, which might be expected to follow the Pentateuchal pattern just noted, instead describes the national privileges as gifts."[70] Ezekiel the Tragedian and Josephus use "gift" in a similar way: a connection is made with the exodus rather than the patriarchs and yet these two are frequently and closely linked in the Pentateuch. In summary, the use of "gift" in Josephus and several other writings of the period expresses God's favor to his people and at times refers to the law.[71]

Naomi Cohen makes a case that in Philo's *Special Laws* (4.137) the context of teaching about *tefillin* indicate that both the Shema and Decalogue were contained in it ("The law says, it is proper [τὰ δίκαια, φησὶν ὁ νόμος] to lay up justice in one's heart, and to fasten it as a sign upon one's head, and as frontlets before one's eyes").[72] Indeed, Philo uses νόμος and variations of it to refer to Torah and the context here is convincingly taken as referring to written law.[73] However, Hindy Najman studies the paradoxical nature of "revealed law" and "the law of Moses," which are synonymous for Philo.[74] At the heart of this paradox is the question about a written copy of the law of nature; what is the relationship of: (1) unwritten laws of nature about how one should live, and (2) a written code of precepts? Najman suggests two possible resolutions for Philo, that: (1) both laws may have the same source, and (2) Moses' laws and the created cosmos are structurally similar.[75] The enigmatic nature of these two laws is particularly

---

70   Horbury, "Ezekiel," 41.

71   Not noted by Horbury is Wis 7:14 where "gift" (δωρεὰ) is closely associated with preeminent wisdom: "for it [wisdom] is an unfailing treasure for mortals; those who get it obtain friendship with God, commended for the gifts that come from instruction (διὰ τὰς ἐκ παιδείας δωρεὰς συσταθέντες)." Cf. Barclay, *Paul and the Gift*, 198–201 on Wisdom as the ultimate gift in Wis. 6:12–10:21.

72   Naomi G. Cohen, "Philo's *Tefillin*," *WCJS* 9/A (1985): 199–206.

73   Adele Reinhartz, "The Meaning of *nomos* in Philo's Exposition of the Law," *SR* 15 (1986): 337–345, at 337; cf. Alan F. Segal, "Torah and Nomos in Recent Scholarly Discussion," *SR* 13 (1984): 19 27.

74   Hindy Najman, *Past Renewals: Interpretive Authority, Renewed Revelation and the Quest for Perfection in Jewish Antiquity*, JSJSup 53 (Leiden: Brill, 2010), 108, fn. 3.

75   Najman, *Past Renewals*, 113–114; she explores this further, asking: "But what needs to be clarified is how the law of Moses could be a copy of the natural law, so that fulfilling the former is at the same time fulfilling the latter!" and suggests that "[o]ne might think that there are two exclusive alternatives: either conceive the law of nature as a code of rules

important when Philo comments on the commandment to honor parents and connects this to parents as teachers. In *Special Laws*, Philo depicts parents as co-creators who are like God and uses this idea to provide a rationale for why children should honor them. Directly after discussing the "Fifth Commandment" (*Spec. Laws* 2:225–226) Philo transitions to parents' role as instructors (2:228): "and they stand in the light of teachers, inasmuch as all that they know themselves they teach to their children from their earliest infancy, and they not only exercise and train them in the supernumerary accomplishments, impressing reasonings on the minds of their children when they come to their prime, but they also teach them those most necessary lessons which refer to choice and avoidance, the choice, that is to say, of virtues, and the avoidance of vices, and of all the energies in accordance with them." When parents impress upon children "reasonings" and "virtues," this is in essence guiding them how to behave in accordance with the law of nature; thus, we find here the complex and paradoxical relationship of both laws.

Philo's *Special Laws* are particularly important for the study of 4Q416 2 iii 15–18. On the one hand, both root the commandment to honor parents in the notion that parents are co-creators with God. On the other hand, 4QInstruction, similarly to Philo, appears to struggle with tensions between written Torah and some other type of "law." While in Philo this is the "natural law," in 4QInstruction it is the רז נהיה, which is closely associated with cosmology and creation. Torah and cosmology are not in tension with one another in 4QInstruction, indeed they are highly complementary; however, in the end the author appears to operate with one having precedent over the other. What then does it mean for parents to uncover their children's ear ברז נהיה ("in" or "by" the mystery of existence)? Easier to determine is what the parents do not teach, namely Torah.

When the Decalogue-Shema combine in early Jewish literature this happens in a multiplicity of different ways and yet we can summarize three basic patterns: (1) collecting/transmitting/fusing relevant passages from Exodus and Deuteronomy; (2) the Shema is the point of departure and the teaching may be about the Decalogue/law/divine oracles; and (3) the Decalogue is the beginning focal point and alludes to the Shema vis-à-vis the notion of teaching. Whether following the pattern of points (2) or (3) it is not necessary for the whole of the "Torah" or the even the "Torah" itself to be in view in order to identify a Decalogue-Shema combination. Indeed, especially in the case of the

which can be written down, or else conceive it as exemplified by the disposition of the sage. But these are not exclusive alternatives for Philo."

Letter of Aristeas and Philo, a great deal may be learned about how "Torah" is not used; so too in 4QInstruction.

2.3   *"To Dig" Torah—4Q418 55 Line 3*

4Q418 55 3 states that "we are digging its (fem.) ways [נכרה דרכיה]." In Chapter 1 (§1.1.), the proposed translation is that the feminine pronoun refers to "truth's ways" (אמת ll. 6, 9) or perhaps "understanding's ways" (בינה ll. 6, 9). The Damascus Document (VI 3–4) refers to those who "dig it" (כרוה), the "it" (fem.) is explicitly said to be the well of the Torah (הבאר היא התורה). The ones who dig a "well" of Torah are the righteous remnant, literally "returners of Israel" (שבי ישראל), who reside in Damascus during an age of wickedness (CD VI 5). 4QBeatitudes (4Q525 5 12) uses the term "dig" as an activity pursuing wisdom: "the shrewd will dig out its (i.e., wisdom's) ways" (ערומים יכרו דרכיה). Uusimäki demonstrates that 4Q525 reflects a Torah-inclined wisdom, integrating Torah into wisdom discourse, and that there is an overlap between wisdom, Torah, and ritual.[76] Nonetheless, the "her" of 4Q525 5 12 is clearly feminine "wisdom" (חכמה). 4QSapiential Text (4Q424 3 6) warns not to send an undiscerning man to dig out thoughts (אל תשלח לכרות מחשבות). 4QSapiential Text does not thematize "Torah" and תורה never occurs in this composition; "thoughts" here relate to the actualization of wisdom as discussed in relationship to the "wisdom of the heart" and "wisdom of the hands" in Chapter 1 (§2.3.). The feminine pronoun in 4Q418 55 3 does not refer to "Torah," but rather this language is used in reference to "truth" which is an important term in 4QInstruction for the creation and ordering of the cosmos (4Q417 1 i). Indeed, "truth" in 4QInstruction is instrumental in creation.

2.4   *Summary*

The compositional date of 4QInstruction is typically given as the mid-second century BCE. As we have seen in this section, Torah is supplanted with the mystery of existence in 4QInstruction, but what is the author(s) reacting against? 4QInstruction stands in contrast to the Torah-centered Yaḥad compositions and yet the provenance of these different documents means that ("pre-sectarian") 4QInstruction is not reacting against these later (so-called) "sectarians." The manuscripts of 4QInstruction are written in middle (1–25 CE) and early Herodian hands (50–25 BCE).[77] If members of the Yaḥad copied and used

---

76   Uusimäki, *Turning Proverbs*, 263–268.

77   Paleographic analysis indicates that 4Q423 and 1Q26 are the earliest copies and 4Q416 is likely the latest.

4QInstruction, then how does one resolve their conflicting views on Torah? One response is to observe that among Qumran discoveries are diverse compositions that reflect a variety of views on Torah. In the following section an overview of the place of Torah in different traditions is discussed with the aim to identify 4QInstruction's cross-talk and interpretative function. Excluding the early Christian literature (§ 3.4.), each of these traditions are represented among Qumran discoveries.

3   Mosaic Torah in Early Jewish Literature

Since 4QInstruction first became available for study a great deal has been written about its relationship to wisdom traditions and the phenomenon of "apocalypticism." Often times these studies take as their focus the themes of revelation, eschatological judgment, future reward, dualism, and determinism as they relate to sapiential discourse. The conclusions reached in Chapter 2, that 4QInstruction is not a deterministic and dualistic document, already begin to re-situate it among world views of the Second Temple era. The absence of thematized Torah and non-explicit appeals to scripture also provide valuable clues regarding how 4QInstruction relates to other theological discourses. When 4QInstruction supplants "Torah" with the "mystery of existence" it still recognizes Torah as authoritative, only these two authority constructs exist within a hierarchy of authorities. In this section, we seek parallels and insights from Enochic literature, the book of Jubilees, the Temple Scroll, early Jewish wisdom literature, as well as the hypothetical Saying Source Q.

3.1   *Enochic Literature*
Gabriele Boccaccini has offered detailed studies that seek to differentiate two competing Judaisms in the second century BCE: one Torah-centered and the other Enochic.[78] Other scholars, notably Józef Milik and Paolo Sacchi, have also stressed the absence of "Torah" in Enochic literature concluding that this is indicative of "a form of Judaism centred around the figure of Enoch which, while not outright rejecting the Mosaic law, minimises its significance as the core of Jewish tradition."[79] However, there is one explicit reference to the Mosaic Torah in 1Enoch 93:6 vis-à-vis the description of the ark of the

---

78   E.g., Gabriele Boccaccini, *Middle Judaism: Jewish Thought, 300 B.C.E. to 200 C.E.* (Minneapolis, MN: Fortress Press, 1991), 80.

79   Loren T. Stuckenbruck, *1Enoch 91–108*, CEJL (Berlin/New York: de Gruyter, 2007), 107.

covenant. Stuckenbruck, in his commentary of the Apocalypse of Weeks (1 En. 91–108), concludes that "this verse and its integration—along with the rest of the Apocalypse—into the 1 Enoch materials at a very early stage (i.e., at least the copying of 4QEnoch[g] ca. the mid–1st cent. BCE) means that such a differentiation should not be pressed too far, that is, this does not mean that the postulated groups were in open ideological (and social) conflict with one another."[80]

Nonetheless, except for 1 Enoch 93:6, Enochic literature never adopts the Torah of Moses in an explicit way as found, particularly, in Ben Sira. In this regard, 4QInstruction is similar to the Enochic writings: they are both familiar with the Torah (and the prophets) but they never thematize it.[81] 4QInstruction most often alludes to and rewrites Genesis 2–3 (see esp. 4Q416 2 iii–iv; 4Q423 1).[82] Additionally, and noted previously, are allusions to Korah's Rebellion in Num 16, the book of memorial in Mal 3:16, and the commandment to honor one's parents in Exod 20 and Deut 5. Uses of Numbers and Deuteronomy are found in: (1) references to a wife (Num 30:6–15 in 4Q416 2 iv; Deut 27:16 in 4Q416 2 ii 21; Deut 13:7, 28:54 in the expression אשת חיקכה) and, (2) halakha related to agriculture (Deut 22:9; cf. Lev 19:19 in 4Q418 103 ii 6–7).[83] George Nickelsburg has written extensively on the relationship of Enochic literature to the Mosaic Torah and offers a summary of non-explicit uses of Torah by its authors.[84] Nickelsburg makes two observations about Enochic literature

---

80   Stuckenbruck, 1 Enoch, 107.

81   Andreas Bedenbender, "The Place of the Torah in the Early Enoch Literature," in *The Early Enoch Literature*, 65–80.

82   See Benjamin Wold, *Women, Men and Angels: The Qumran Wisdom Document Musar leMevin and its Allusions to Genesis Creation Traditions*, WUNT 2.201 (Tübingen: Mohr Siebeck, 2005).

83   Brooke, "Biblical Interpretation," 207–210; cf. Daniel J. Harrington, *Wisdom Texts from Qumran* (London/New York, NY: Routledge, 1996), 59 writes: "[In 4Q418 103 ii] the biblical ruling is adapted to the format of the wisdom instruction and used as a consideration (without appeal to the authority of the Torah) in sapiential advice."

84   1 En. 1–5 use wording from Deut 33:1–3 and Num 24:15–17; 1 En. 6–11 revise Gen 6:1–4, and parts of the Flood narrative; 1 En. 12–16 begin with paraphrase of Gen 5:24; 1 En. 14–15 rely on Ezek 1–2; 1 En. 22:5–7 allude to Gen 4:10 (22:5–7); 1 En. 32:6 to Gen 2:4–3:24; 1 En. 37–71 use Isa 11; Ps 2; Dan 7; 1 En. 85–90 know Gen 2; 2 Kgs; 1 En. 93:1–10 briefly follows the order of biblical history, see Nickelsburg, "Enochic Wisdom," 81–82; cf. his "Revealed Wisdom as a Criterion for Inclusion and Exclusion: From Jewish Sectarianism to Early Christianity," in *To See Ourselves as Others See Us: Christians, Jews, Others in Late Antiquity*, ed. Jacob Neusner & Ernest Frerichs (Chico, CA: Scholars, 1985), 73–91; "Enochic Wisdom: An Alternative to the Mosaic Torah?" in *HESED VE-EMET: Studies in Honor of Ernest S. Frerichs*, eds. Jodi Magness & Seymour Gittin, BJS 320 (Atlanta, GA: Scholars Press, 1998), 123–132.

that hold true of 4QInstruction as well. First, despite use of material from the Torah, the Sinaitic covenant and the Mosaic Torah are not of central importance to Enochic authors.[85] Second, rather than Mosaic Torah, "revealed wisdom" embodies "the double notion that God has revealed the divine will to humanity and will reward and punish right and wrong conduct."[86] Nickelsburg makes another observation about how Enochic literature relates to Torah, he describes that "Wisdom is a comprehensive category in 1 Enoch's theology" and elaborates that it encompasses the revealing of "God's will expressed in commandments and laws ... the coming judgment in which God will reward and punish those who obey or disobey these laws; and the structure of the universe that is both the arena and facilitator of this judgment."[87] While this also describes wisdom to a great extent in 4QInstruction, Nickelsburg further elaborates that "wisdom" is evoked within Enochic writings at times as a "designation for the corpus itself" and, at this point, commonalities cease.

The mystery of existence in 4QInstruction is a comprehensive category; however, the composition itself is not a book of revelation, but rather had a pedagogic function within didactic settings over an extended period of time. On this point another dissimilarity is found, namely the process of revelation. On the one hand, 4QInstruction gives no indication that like Sir 24 and Bar 3:9–4:4 the Mosaic Torah is the presence of real heavenly wisdom; on the other hand, it also does not align with 1 Enoch where the "descent of wisdom" begins with the ascent of the primordial seer Enoch. Once Enoch receives wisdom in heaven, he then transmits it in written form to Methuselah and his sons for later generations. 4QInstruction does not portray Torah as the embodiment of wisdom, but rather the רז נהיה enjoys this status. Moreover, present participation with the angels may be found in 4QInstruction, but unlike Enoch the *maśkîl*, as seen in Chapter 1, is not explicitly depicted as ascending into the heavens, he is not named, nor does he possess and then transmit revelation in a written form. Despite the lack of attention to Mosaic Torah in Enochic literature, Nickelsburg does not see this as evidence of an "anti-Mosaic bias or polemic."[88]

85   Nickelsburg, "Enochic Wisdom," 82.

86   Nickelsburg, "Enochic Wisdom," 83.

87   Nickelsburg, "Enochic Wisdom," 85.

88   Nickelsburg, "Enochic Wisdom," 88; Helge S. Kvanvig, "Enochic Judaism—a Judaism without the Torah and the Temple?" in *Enoch and the Mosaic Torah: The Evidence of Jubilees*, ed. Gabriele Boccaccinni & Giovanni Ibba (Grand Rapids, MI/Cambridge, UK: Eerdmans, 2009), 163–177 at 172–173, writes: "I think Nickelsburg is basically right when he emphasizes that it is the special character of the Enochic revealed wisdom that makes it different from Mosaic Judaism, rather than the lack of Torah, at least at this point of the Enochic

Indeed, the use and reinterpretation of Torah indicate respect for it; therefore, Nickelsburg's conclusion, as well as Stuckenbruck's, also hold true of 4QInstruction. The non-explicit use of Torah in 4QInstruction does not serve to anchor the composition's instruction in the giving of Torah at Mt. Sinai. When Mosaic tradition appears in Enochic literature it is clearly recognized that the authority of instruction is based upon an appeal to tradition far older than Mosaic tradition and may even be derivative.[89] The Enochic tradition is, in this respect, comparable with Mosaic tradition in 4QInstruction because appeals are made to the mystery of existence, and the ordering of the cosmos, and Torah is secondary to it.[90]

Elgvin addresses the relationship of Mosaic Torah to the רז נהיה. He observes that in apocalyptic tradition "the ultimate wisdom of God is not what is revealed to all Israel through the Torah," but rather wisdom is concealed and its secrets are made known to both sages (e.g., Adam, Enoch, Noah, Abraham) and an elect end-time community (e.g., in the Apocalypse of Weeks, 1 En. 93:10; cf. 4QEnoch[g] ar IV 12–13, where at the close of seven weeks the elect righteous "receive sevenfold instruction concerning all His creation").[91] Elgvin concludes that Enochic literature and 4QInstruction share this view of hidden wisdom; furthermore, he associates the notion of remnant and end-time restoration, also found in apocalyptic tradition, with 4QInstruction. *Pace* Elgvin, while a faithful community is described in 4Q418 81 + 81a as an "eternal planting," there is no hope expressed for a restoration or renewal of Israel in the end-time.[92] Moreover, in 4QInstruction the רז נהיה is never said to be concealed and pursuing it does not result in the disclosure of secret knowledge. The root סתר ("conceal" or "hide") only occurs with any discernible context on three occasions in

<hr>

89   writings." Cf. Heinrich Hoffmann, *Das Gesetz in der frühjüdischen Apokalyptik* (Göttingen: Vandenhoeck, 1999), 125–126.

89   Stuckenbruck, *1 Enoch*, 159.

90   Samuel I. Thomas, *The "Mysteries" of Qumran: Mystery, Secrecy and Esotericism in the Dead Sea Scrolls*, EJL 25 (Atlanta, GA: SBL Press, 2009), 156 "The רז נהיה is not equivalent to the Torah, but, like much of the early Enoch literature, is ostensibly compatible with it." Thomas follows Collin's and Goff's view in regard to the location of the mystery in a deterministic framework: "[the רז נהיה] is esoteric insofar as it is available only to the members of the elect group envisioned in the text—a group that should not be identified with the Yaḥad but that shares important ideological and religious values with it."

91   Elgvin, "Wisdom and Apocalypticism," 238.

92   For a discussion on this and other terms found in Enochic literature and 4QInstruction see Stuckenbruck, "4QInstruction and the Possible Influence of Early Enochic Traditions." "Eternal planting" signifies a remnant of Israel in other contexts, in 4QInstruction it is open to question how "Israel" fits within the author's theology.

the composition, in: (1) 4Q416 2 i 18 is an exhortation not to conceal something from one's creditor; (2) 4Q417 1 i 11 is a statement about making known a person's concealed thoughts; and (3) 4Q418 126 ii 5 is a partially preserved phrase, within the context of judgment, about future concealment from the wicked. In 4Q418 126 ii 4–5 it appears that God creates right measures and establishes the world in truth, which is studied by those who delight in them, and wisdom "will be" (יסתר כול) concealed from the wicked (cf. "uncover" as a counterpart to "concealing" in §2.2. above), which aligns with meditation "no longer" being given to the spirit of flesh because of their failure to live rightly. Indeed, as previously discussed in Chapter 2 (§1.1.1.), truth's deeds were expounded to humanity and an "inclination" and "spirit" given in order to understand.

3.2 Jubilees and the Temple Scroll

The Temple Scroll, and to a lesser extent Jubilees, call into question the unchallenged authority of Torah in the second century BCE.[93] The popularity of "rewriting" Torah is well known, but in the case of the Temple Scroll it appears that its aim was not so much to supplement scripture but to supplant it; indeed, it presents itself as the Torah and is so audacious that the speaker is portrayed as God himself.[94] That both the Temple Scroll and Jubilees are found among the Qumran caves suggests either that the community inherited them from another group or composed them fairly early in the history of their community (c. 135 BCE). 4QInstruction's provenance remains open to question, the suggestion that it was written in the mid-second century BCE is based upon views about its relationship with, especially, Ben Sira. As noted from the outset, it is

---

93 Sidnie White Crawford, *The Temple Scroll and Related Texts* (Sheffield: Sheffield Academic Press, 2000), 24 summarizes views on the date of the Temple Scroll, Jubilees dates to the 160s. On the *status quaestionis* of "canon" in this period see Eugene Ulrich, "Pluriformity in the Biblical Text, Text Groups, and Questions of Canon," in *Madrid Qumran Congress: Proceedings of the International Congress on the Dead Sea Scrolls*, 2 vols., ed. Julio T. Barrera & Luis V. Montaner, STDJ 11 (Leiden: Brill, 1992) 1.23–41; "The Canonical Process, Textual Criticism, and Latter Stages in the Composition of the Bible," in *Sha'arei Talmon: Studies in the Bible, Qumran, and the Ancient Near East Presented to Shemaryahu Talmon*, ed. Michael Fishbane, Emanuel Tov & Weston W. Fields (Winona Lake, IN: Eisenbrauns, 1992), 267–294.

94 Shaye J.D. Cohen, *From the Maccabees to the Mishnah*, 2nd ed. (Louisville, KY: Westminster John Knox Press, 2006), 177; cf. Crawford, *The Temple Scroll*, 18–20. For an excellent philological treatment of the Temple Scroll's techniques in pseudepigraphy see Bernard M. Levinson, *A More Perfect Torah: At the Intersection of Philology and Hermeneutics in Deuteronomy and the Temple Scroll*, CSHB 1 (Winona Lake, IN: Eisenbrauns, 2013).

commonly accepted that 4QInstruction is not a Yaḥad composition, with some preferring to describe it as "pre-sectarian." 4QInstruction may demonstrate reverence for Torah vis-à-vis intertextuality, but should the substitution of "Torah" with the רז נהיה be interpreted as supplanting it similar to the Temple Scroll and Jubilees which also interprets Torah? Like Jubilees, 4QInstruction indicates by its substitution that the Torah has limitations.

Martha Himmelfarb summarizes that Torah in the book of Jubilees is identified with the tablets of the law, while Jubilees itself is the transcript of revelation at Sinai.[95] Several other scholars have devoted studies to working out the relationship of Jubilees to Torah, among them is Ben Zion Wacholder who draws upon the Hebrew fragments of Jub. 1 (4Q216) to distinguish between the תעודה ("testimony") of Jub. 1:8 (4Q216 II 5) and לתורה ולתעודה in Jub. 1:26 (4Q216 IV 4). He suggests that תורה and תעודה are in contrast and that Jubilees sees itself as תורה תעודה ("Torah-Admonition") while standard Torah is תורה מצוה ("Torah-Commandment").[96] Himmelfarb convincingly argues against Wacholder's view that Jubilees represents itself in this way, as "super-canonical."[97] Instead, she describes that Jubilees "demotes the Torah by undermining its claim to uniqueness and completeness," and conceives of a "distribution of labor between itself and the Torah."[98] Jubilees is concerned with the divisions of times, and reveals this information as of first importance. Himmelfarb concludes that:

> unlike the Temple Scroll or any other text I know that implicitly challenges the authority of the Torah, Jubilees offered an account of its relationship to the Torah that provides a place for both works. Jubilees' claim to authority alongside the Torah was clearly quite persuasive to some readers. Not long after Jubilees was written, the Damascus Covenant cited it as an authoritative work. The fourteen manuscripts of Jubilees found at Qumran suggest that the community there shared the opinion of the Damascus Covenant. The only works better attested at Qumran

---

95   Martha Himmelfarb, *Between Temple and Torah: Essays on Priests, Scribes, and Visionaries in the Second Temple Period and Beyond*, TSAJ 151 (Tübingen: Mohr Siebeck, 2013), 49.

96   Ben Zion Wacholder, "Jubilees as the Super Canon: Torah-Admonition versus Torah-Commandment," in *Legal Texts and Legal Issues: Proceedings of the Second Meeting of the International Organization for Qumran Studies, Cambridge 1995, Published in Honor of Joseph M. Baumgarten*, ed. Moshe Bernstein, Florentino García Martínez & Jonathan Kampen, STDJ 23 (Leiden: Brill, 1997), 195–211.

97   Himmelfarb, *Between Temple*, 58.

98   Himmelfarb, *Between Temple*, 58.

are Psalms (thirty manuscripts), Deuteronomy (twenty-five manuscripts), Isaiah (nineteen manuscripts), and Genesis and Exodus (fifteen manuscripts each).[99]

Although the רז נהיה in 4QInstruction is not written revelation, its concern with cosmology and creation indicates that there is an aspect of undermining Torah's claim to completeness. Scripture has an authoritative status in 4QInstruction, but perhaps of a somewhat different kind than is associated with Mosaic Torah in other Jewish traditions of this era. Attention to the way that Jubilees works out its relationship with Torah, and the reception of its views, demonstrates that viewpoints present among Qumran discoveries accommodated various and complex presentations of revealed wisdom as more complete than Torah. Indeed, a reasonable conclusion is that the substitution of "Torah" with רז נהיה indicates the demotion of Torah.

3.3   Sapiential Literature

Sapiential literature from early Judaism reflects a diverse range of ways that wisdom and Torah relate to one another. Nonetheless, there is some continuity between Ben Sira, the Wisdom of Solomon, and sapiential literature discovered at Qumran when they incorporate aspects of Torah into their compositions while simultaneously maintaining wisdom's preeminence.[100] What sets 4QInstruction apart from Ben Sira/Sirach, Wisdom of Solomon (2:12, 6:4, 16:6), and other Qumran sapiential literature (e.g., 4Q525 2 ii 3–4; 4Q185 II 8–11) is that Torah, or its Greek equivalent νόμος, is not part of its discourse.[101]

Ben Sira's relationship to Torah is particularly important on account of assessments that locate 4QInstruction within the same scribal school or circles. Unlike 4QInstruction, Ben Sira is not terribly interested in interpreting Torah, he never cites it, preferring instead to write in the form of proverbs.[102] Ben Sira is well known for equating Mosaic Torah with wisdom (15:1, 24:8, 24:23); the Praise to the Fathers (chs. 44–50) is the well-noted exception where legal aspects of the Torah are subsumed under traditional wisdom. Jack Sanders summarizes Ben Sira's relationship to the Torah, that "he simply assumes that it supports his traditional sapiential morality" and that he "could not conceive

---

99   Himmelfarb, *Between Temple*, 58–59.

100   Sanders, "Sacred Canopies," 129.

101   "Torah" may be present in 4Q424 3 8–9 (Instruction-like composition).

102   Nickelsburg, "Enochic Wisdom," 91; Collins, *Jewish Wisdom*, 55 observes that Ben Sira 3 exhorts to honor parents and yet even on this occasion does not quote the Decalogue.

that its morality could be other than his traditional sapiential morality."[103] Daniel Harrington stresses that the identification of wisdom with Torah is not one of perfect equivalence, if it were Ben Sira would have simply repeated Torah when instead he writes his own wisdom book in which "legal, prophetic, and historical strands of Israel's tradition" are integrated.[104] Moreover, Collins views that Ben Sira "grounds all wisdom, including the law, in the order of creation" which I would contend is a commonality shared with 4QInstruction.[105]

Ben Sira is a devout student of the Torah and gives attention to the traditions of Israel. Collins draws attention to Sirach's preface of his Greek translation where he emphasizes that his grandfather devoted himself to reading the "Law and the Prophets and the other books of our ancestors."[106] Ben Sira's attention to Israel's scriptures sets him in sharp contrast to the biblical wisdom books of Proverbs, Qohelet, and Job, which are distinctive for not referring to Israel's traditions. Collins explains that "[w]hen Sirach identifies wisdom and the law … he is in effect introducing the Torah of Moses into the wisdom school, and thereby attempting to combine two educational traditions."[107] To pursue wisdom one may acquire it in the company of the wise (6:36), or meditate on the commandments (6:37).[108] Therefore, Ben Sira considers Torah as a source of wisdom, even if wisdom overshadows its authority. 4QInstruction is concerned to interpret the Torah, evidences no interest in Torah as a theme in its own right, and instead places emphasis on mysteries as the source of wisdom. While this does not negate the many commonalities shared between Ben Sira and 4QInstruction, dissimilar views on Torah are a substantial wedge between them.

The relationship of Ben Sira/Sirach to Enochic literature has been addressed by Randall Argall and Benjamin Wright.[109] Argall's approach is to compare

---

103   Sanders, "Sacred Canopies," 124; cf. Joseph Blenkinsopp, *Wisdom and Law in the Old Testament: The Ordering of Life in Israel and Early Judaism, second edition*, OBS (Oxford: OUP, 2003), 163, writes "As much as he insists on the observance of the commandments, it is clear that the category which dominates his thinking is not the law but wisdom."

104   Harrington, *Wisdom Texts*, 28.

105   Collins, *Jewish Wisdom*, 55.

106   Collins, *Jewish Wisdom*, 44.

107   Collins, *Jewish Wisdom*, 54–55.

108   Ben Sira MS A 6:37 והתבוננת ביראת עליון ובמצותו והגה תמיד והוא יביך לבך ואשר איות יחכמך; cf. Sir 6:37 "Reflect on the statutes of the Lord (ἐν τοῖς προστάγμασιν κυρίου), and meditate at all times on his commandments (ἐν ταῖς ἐντολαῖς αὐτοῦ), it is he who will give insight to your mind, and your desire for wisdom (ἡ ἐπιθυμία τῆς σοφίας) will be granted".

109   Randall A. Argall, *1Enoch and Sirach: A Comparative Literary and Conceptual Analysis of the Themes of Revelation, Creation and Judgment* (Atlanta, GA: Scholars Press, 1995); Ben-

three common themes (revelation, creation, judgment) and concludes that Sirach and 1 Enoch are in an adversarial relationship and each of these themes is formulated over and against the other.[110] Wright is interested in the polemicizing passages in Sirach (esp. Sir 34:1–8; 3:21–24 "what is hidden is not your concern") and concludes that Ben Sira is opposed to critics of the temple priests such as the author of the Book of Watchers. Argall's choice to focus on common themes for his study is one point of departure for assessing the relationship of these writings; however, more may be said about differences and, particularly, the way they appropriate and conceive of biblical traditions.[111] The focus on the authority of the Torah in Enochic literature and in Ben Sira here is one step in this direction.

The book of Baruch is mainly concerned with the salvation of Israel based upon wisdom. Baruch's identification of Torah with wisdom (3:9–4:4) is likely influenced by Ben Sira.[112] This second or first century BCE composition describes knowledge being given to Israel and appearing on the earth where she dwells with humankind (3:35–37), and in Bar 4:1 wisdom is identified with the book of the commandments and the law (αὕτη ἡ βίβλος τῶν προσταγμάτων τοῦ θεοῦ καὶ ὁ νόμος ὁ ὑπάρχων εἰς τὸν αἰῶνα).

The Wisdom of Solomon, in contrast to Ben Sira, mentions the law only in passing (2:12, 6:4, 16:6, 18:4) and when Moses is referred to he is a leader in the wilderness and a prophet (10:15–11:4), but not the lawgiver.[113] In the Wisdom of Solomon wisdom is never equated with Torah. Wisdom and instruction are not derived simply from biblical laws, but rather wisdom is a cosmic principle. Much of the Wisdom of Solomon's instruction is rooted in Stoicism, particularly the idea of the world-soul where wisdom stretches across the earth and orders all things.[114] Wis 7:24–26 expresses wisdom as "pervading all things" and is the "breadth of the power of God." When in chapters 10–19 biblical history is recounted from creation to the exodus, Blenkinsopp describes wisdom

---

jamin G. Wright III, "'Fear the Lord and Honor the Priest': Ben Sira as Defender of the Jerusalem Priesthood," in *The Book of Ben Sira in Modern Research*, ed. Pancratius C. Beentjes, BZAW 255 (Berlin/New York: de Gruyter, 1997), 189–222.

110   Argall, *1 Enoch and Sirach*, 8.

111   See review by Hindy Najman, *Hebrew Studies* 40 (1999): 347–348; another important distinction between these compositions is that Enoch receives revelation whereas Ben Sira does not.

112   Blenkinsopp, *Wisdom and Law*, 167.

113   Blenkinsopp, *Wisdom and Law*, 169; Wis 18:4 refers to the Torah as the: "imperishable light" that was "given to the world" (τὸ ἄφθαρτον νόμου φῶς τῷ αἰῶνι δίδοσθαι).

114   Blenkinsopp, *Wisdom and Law*, 170.

as a "principle of interpretation or reinterpretation" and that the author is "sapi-entializing" sacred history.[115] Torah, in the Wisdom of Solomon, is brought in only to the degree that its laws are made wisdom's laws, thus maintaining the preeminence of wisdom, similar to Ben Sira.[116]

3.4   *Saying Source Q and James*

According to many assessments of the Saying Source Q Jesus' wisdom is con-frontational because it rejects family ties and undermines religious traditions by stressing the imminence of God's kingdom; moreover, unlike many sapien-tial writings in the period Torah is never thematized in Q.[117] This leads Mar-cus Borg to set up a contrast between teachers of "conventional wisdom" and those of "another way," concluding that Jesus chose the latter and taught an alternative wisdom.[118] In Borg's view, Jesus' wisdom appears to have taken well-known sapiential forms, such as proverbs and parables, but used them to teach counter-cultural wisdom, which was highly critical of social conventions.

Q-tradition has been studied at times with emphasis on its sapiential charac-teristics, so Stephen Patterson who comments that "even with all of its radical-ity [Q] is still best described as wisdom," even if "in many ways it defies what we have come to expect of wisdom."[119] Other studies focus on prophetic features. An important example of this approach is Richard Horsley who suggests that Q represents a genre of prophetic sayings.[120] How this unusual material in the

---

115   Blenkinsopp, *Wisdom and Law*, 172.

116   Sanders, "Sacred Canopy," 129.

117   John Kloppenborg, *Excavating Q: The History and Setting of the Sayings Gospel* (Philadel-phia, PA: Fortress Press, 2000), 385–388.

118   Marcus M. Borg, *Conflict, Holiness and Politics in the Teaching of Jesus* (New York, NY/Lon-don: Continuum, 1984).

119   Stephen J. Patterson, *The Gospel of Thomas and Christian Origins: Essays on the Fifth Gospel* (Leiden: Brill, 2013), 160. See also Ronald A. Piper, *Wisdom in the Q-Tradition: The Aphoris-tic Teaching of Jesus*, SNTSMS 61 (Cambridge: CUP, 1989); Helmut Koester, "One Jesus and Four Primitive Gospels," in *Trajectories Through Early Christianity*, ed. James M. Robinson & Helmut Koester (Philadelphia, PA: Fortress Press, 1971), 158–204 at 160, "[t]he behavior which Jesus requests is a demonstration of the kingdom's presence, i.e., of a society which is governed by new principles of ethics. This not only ascribes a kerygmatic quality to the ethical demands of Jesus, it presents Jesus as a prophet rather than a teacher of wisdom. Although formal claims of Jesus to prophetic authorization, such as a vision of a calling or the introductory formula 'thus says the Lord,' are missing, the prophetic role of Jesus is evident in the address of these ethical demands to a community, not just to individual followers."

120   Eugene M. Boring, *Sayings of the Risen Jesus: Christian Prophecy in the Synoptic Tradition*,

Q-tradition has been accounted for varies. Unclear is what material found in Q should be attributed to the historical Jesus and what should be seen as the work of scribes and redactors. One view put forward is that of Burton Mack, who differentiates strata in Q and suggests that "wisdom" and "apocalyptic" developed in layers and that "the languages of wisdom and apocalyptic assume different views of the world."[121] John Kloppenborg does not delineate between strata, but rather understands Q as a radical form of wisdom and that when apocalyptic language is found it "is used creatively to dramatize the transfiguration of the present."[122] A particularly interesting line of questioning relates to scribalism. William Arnal and Richard Horsley posit different literate scribal classes behind Q who would have left their mark on this source; Horsley views Q-scribalism in terms of Judean scribes who produced apocalyptic texts.[123]

How both Q and James relate to one another and participate in the wisdom of the Second Temple era is another critical stream of inquiry and is overdue for a fresh assessment in light of 4QInstruction.[124] Similar to Q, within the sapi-

---

SNTS 46 (Cambridge: CUP, 1982), 180–181, suggests that Q is closer to Jeremiah than to Proverbs; Richard A. Horsley, "Logoi Prophētōn: Reflections on the Genre of Q," in *The Future of Early Christianity: Essays in Honor of Helmut Koester*, ed. Birger A. Pearson (Minneapolis, MN: Fortress Press, 1991), 195–209; Risto Uro, "Apocalyptic Symbolism and Social Identity in Q," in *Symbols and Strata: Essays on the Sayings Gospel Q*, ed. Risto Uro (Göttingen: Vandenhoeck & Ruprecht, 1991), 67–118; Arland D. Jacobson, "Apocalyptic and the Synoptic Sayings Source Q," in *The Four Gospels: Festschrift Frans Neirynck*, ed. F. Van Segbroeck, et al., BETL 100 (Leuven: Peeters, 1992), 403–419.

121   Burton Mack, *The Lost Gospel: The Book of Q and Christian Origins* (San Francisco, CA: HarperSanFrancisco, 1993), 37–38.

122   John S. Kloppenborg, "Symbolic Eschatology and Apocalypticism in Q," *HTR* 80/3 (1987): 287–306, at 304; cf. idem, *Trajectories in Ancient Wisdom Collections* (Harrisburg, PA: Trinity Press International, 1981, reprint 1999), 322–325.

123   Views on the theory that Q was produced by a literate class (as opposed to the Jesus movement) see William E. Arnal, *Jesus and the Village Scribes: Galilean Conflicts and the Setting of Q* (Minneapolis, MN: Fortress Press, 2001); Alan Kirk, *The Composition of the Saying Source: Genre, Synchrony, and Wisdom Redaction in Q*, NovTSup 91 (Leiden: Brill, 1998), 399; Richard A. Horsley, *Revolt of the Scribes: Resistance and Apocalyptic Origins* (Minneapolis, MN: Fortress Press, 2009), 8–14.

124   John S. Kloppenborg, *The Formation of Q: Trajectories in Ancient Wisdom Collections* (Minneapolis, MN: Fortress Press, 1987), 263–316, 329–341 sets Q sayings alongside a host of ancient collections of sayings; however since the publication of 4QInstruction Q scholarship has not given sustained attention to this composition. See Matthew J. Goff, "Discerning Trajectories: 4QInstruction and the Sapiential Background of the Sayings Source Q," *JBL* 124/4 (2005): 657–673, who forges new ground in bringing 4QInstruction into dialogue with Q-tradition.

ential discourse of James Torah is also not thematized, indeed whether and how James refers to Torah is debated; moreover, there are several curious characteristics that break with (the problematically termed) "traditional wisdom." One of the most striking features of James' paranesis is the nature of wisdom as revealed (Jas 1:5) and given by God from above (Jas 3:15); a feature that indicates an apocalyptic transcendence by deriving understanding from the heavenly realm as opposed to the earthly. James' teaching about wisdom has an eschatological aspect and the consequences for wise and ethical behavior are not only found in the here and now, but also reward and punishment are future. However, James may not simply be setting wisdom paranesis within an eschatological framework, as Darian Lockett and Todd Penner suggest, but rather the shift in the wisdom paradigm extends beyond eschatologizing wisdom. 4QInstruction shares a number of notable commonalities with James, including revealed wisdom, eschatology, and a cosmological framework.[125] The first column of 4QInstruction (4Q416 1) describes the heavenly hosts, God's rule over the cosmos, future reward for the righteous, punishment for the wicked, and humanity's responsibility to live rightly in light of how the cosmos has been ordered. Reading Q and James in light of 4QInstruction provides the opportunity to appreciate the relationship of cosmology to the sapiential teaching of James.

Matthew Goff has offered an important study on the significance of wisdom literature found among the Dead Sea Scrolls for the study of the Saying Source Q.[126] The reason that 4QInstruction has changed our understanding of wisdom is that it presents wisdom as obtained through revelation, the righteous and wicked receive reward and punishment in the hereafter, and other worldly beings (i.e., angels) are acknowledged throughout. Yet, the sapiential discourse of 4QInstruction also uses well-known wisdom forms, including paranesis, admonitions and poetic parallelism. In 4QInstruction, as in Q, wisdom is not explicitly identified with Torah, nor is wisdom personified and related to any particular figure. In light of these observations, Goff demonstrates that within sapiential trajectories from the second century BCE onward "sapiential" and "apocalyptic" strata cannot be distinguished. However, studies subsequent to Goff's often times do not even acknowledge 4QInstruction's exis-

---

125   Darian Lockett, "The Spectrum of Wisdom and Eschatology in the Epistle of James and 4QInstruction," *Tyndale Bulletin* 56/1 (2005): 131–148; Todd Penner, *The Epistle of James and Eschatology: Re-reading an Ancient Christian Letter*, JSNTSSup 121 (Sheffield: Sheffield Academic Press, 1996). On Q and James see Patrick J. Hartin, *James and the Q Sayings of Jesus*, JSNTSup 47 (Sheffield: JSOT Press, 1991), esp. 45–81.

126   Goff, "Discerning Trajectories."

tence.[127] 4QInstruction is significant not only because it redraws categorical lines and notions of stratification, but also because it problematizes assessments of Q as a radical form of wisdom, a conclusion that is made against the backdrop of assumptions about "mainstream" or "traditional" wisdom in the period. In the same way that 4QInstruction informs the Q-Source and James, the absence of Torah in the latter may also hold insights into the former; at the very least, together they represent trajectories in early Jewish sapiential thought.

3.5   *Summary*

In 4QInstruction Torah is never thematized, Wisdom is not personified, and Torah is never identified with Wisdom; in these ways, it may be differentiated from and contrasted with the sapiential teachings of, especially, Ben Sira. Indicative of the gulf between Ben Sira and 4QInstruction is the way Ben Sira 14:20 and 4Q417 1 i 6 rewrite Psalm 1:2b; in Ben Sira "wisdom" is substituted for "Torah" and in 4QInstruction "Torah" is substituted with the רז נהיה. The book of Jubilees demonstrates that it is not anathema among Qumran discoveries to view the Mosaic Torah as insufficient; indeed, it and several other traditions, including apocalyptic ones, appeal to revelation as a way to complete Torah. The Enochic literature shares commonalities with 4QInstruction in that Torah is interpreted, but does not make Torah an explicit theme in its own right. By appealing to an older, even *urzeitlich*, and more encompassing form of wisdom while still acknowledging Torah vis-à-vis non-explicit uses, it may be questioned what 4QInstruction is reacting to. By using the mystery of existence as an all-encompassing category of wisdom one may attribute this to polemicizing by demoting "Torah." However, even if this were the conclusion reached, 4QInstruction maintains a very high regard for Torah by frequently alluding to and re-writing it. Therefore, this use of scriptural tradition is the topic of the following section.

127   4QInstruction has not influenced assessments of Q in recent scholarship, see Sarah E. Rollens, *Framing Social Criticism in the Jesus Movement: The Ideological Project in the Sayings Gospel Q*, WUNT 2.374 (Tübingen: Mohr Siebeck, 2014), written under the supervision of John Kloppenborg, who compares the aphoristic wisdom of Q alongside Sentences of Sextus, Wisdom of Solomon, and even the *chreia* collections of Diogenes Laertius but does not refer to 4QInstruction once.

4   Re-written Torah

On several occasions in the extant manuscripts of 4QInstruction are moder-
ately substantial (i.e., in terms of giving sustained attention) instances when
Torah may be described either as being "rewritten" or alluded to continually.
One of these is 4Q416 2 iii 14–19 where the commandment to honor parents
from the Decalogue occurs and was discussed previously in this chapter (§ 2.2.).
Other instances are a running allusion to Genesis 2 in 4Q416 2 iii 20–iv 13 and
the retelling of the Garden of Eden in 4Q423 1.

4.1   4Q416 2 iii Lines 14–19
When Lange identifies the רז נהיה with the Mosaic Torah he does so on the basis
of 4Q416 2 iii 14–19. Lines 14–15a introduce the commandment with the exhortation: "study the mystery of existence, and understand all the ways of truth,
and all the roots of iniquity you will see" (רז נהיה דרוש והתבונן בכל דרכי אמת
וכל שורשי עולה תביט). The connection of contemplation on the mystery to the
commandment leads Lange to conclude that: "Bei der Aufforderung, Vater und
Mutter zu ehren, liegt es nahe, an das Gebot gleichen Inhalts aus dem Dekalog
zu denken (Ex 20,12; Dtn 5,16) und רז נהיה mit der Thora zu identifizieren."[128]
Not only is this conclusion unconvincing within the larger context of the composition, but also when in line 18 parents play a role uncovering their children's
ears to the mystery of existence, this supplants Torah, which is evident in the
use of a well-established Shema-Decalogue combination (§ 2.2.).

   When the author(s) of 4QInstruction adapts this commandment of the
Decalogue, the newly interpreted version introduces several new features. One
significant change is the addition of "poverty," which is in parallel with "low
estate" (ll. 15–16), to describe the condition of the addressee.[129] A simile is also
introduced which offers a rationale behind the command to honor mother
and father (ll. 15–16a), namely parents' role as co-creators similar to God and
"lords."[130] The comparison of mother and father with co-creators in 4Q416 2 iii

---

128   Lange, *Weisheit und Prädestination*, 58.
129   Note that 4Q416 2 iii 16 may read "in your going forth" rather than "low estate."
130   For opposing views on the meaning of "lords" (אדונים) see Wold, *Women, Men, and Angels*,
      149–155 where I argue that it is a reference to "angelic beings" (cf. angelic participation
      in creation in 4Q417 1 i 17 "according the pattern of the holy ones," which may allude
      to the interpretation of "us" in Gen 1:26 as God and angels); Rey, *4QInstruction*, 183–184
      and Goff, *4QInstruction*, 110 take אדונים as synonymous with אל ("God") and the plural of
      majesty citing קדושים in Prov 9:10; 30:3, however there is no example of אדונים as such.
      The discrepancy between mss., i.e. "God" (4Q416 2 iii 16) and "father" (4Q418 9 17), may

offers a reason not only for honoring them, but also venerating their presence (l. 18).[131] The description in line 17 that the addressee is fashioned "according to the spirit" emphasizes a concern shared by the Vision of Hagu passage and the preoccupation with spirit in several other passages of 4QInstruction (cf. Ch. 2 § 2.3.). The mystery of existence in the context of honoring and venerating parents relates to understanding the created order, which is a key theme in the following lines on marriage.[132] What then does this use of scriptural tradition, one that reworks the commandment to derive a deeper and even multivalent meaning, indicate about the relationship of Torah to the mystery of existence? Najman in her work on Mosaic discourse describes re-writing Torah as a way of "seconding Sinai"; the inverse seems to be the case in 4QInstruction, the Torah when reworked reinforces, or one might even say "seconds," the mystery of existence in that this use of the Decalogue emphasizes the created order and replaces "Torah" with the mystery of existence in the Shema-Decalogue combination.[133]

---

be explained by interference from Mal 1:6 where the honor of אב ("father") and אדונים ("masters") are mentioned; in Mal the two terms are not synonymous.

131   The combination of the Decalogue's command to honor parents because they are co-creators is also known from Philo (*Spec. Laws* 2.224–227) and Clement of Alexandria (*Strom.* 6.146.1–2).

132   Directly after the use of the Decalogue in 4Q416 2 iii 15–18, the speaker moves to the topic of marriage (4Q416 2 iii 20–iv 13) and does so with several allusions to Gen 2. However, 4Q416 2 iv 3–7 are concerned to instruct, *contra* Gen 2:24 (where man leaves his parents and joins with his wife's family), that when a daughter is given in marriage she moves from her own household to her husband's, and that he is the one who then has rightful authority over her. 4QInstruction alludes to the separation of woman from man (Gen 2:22) and refers explicitly to them joining as "one flesh" (4Q416 2 iii 21, iv 4; cf. Gen 2:23–24). In 4QInstruction, although the authority of parents over children is established, questions arise as to how parental authority functions, changes, and transfers when daughters are married. Parents, as co-creators, have authority over their children; yet, woman's derivation from man justifies a shift in authority from parents to husband at marriage. In 1Q26 4 is the statement "watch out for yourself in case she honors you more than him" (השמר לכה למה תכבדכה ממנו); this line likely relates to how women are to show respect for father and husband in their role as both daughter and wife. Moreover, in 4Q416 2 iii 14–17 gendered terms are used to introduce the commandment (גבר, איש ×2), mothers are compared with אדונים while fathers to אל (terms that may be in synonymous parallel, but this would imply equality not otherwise present, and raises the question why the rare term אדונים is used), and the father is also included in the gestational process, "*they* are the womb." The hierarchy of the family in 4QInstruction places women under the authority of men; moreover, men usurp the female's womb, women are emphasized as "helpers," and dominance over women is justified based upon creation of male before female (Gen 2:22). Cf. Wold "Genesis 2–3."

133   Najman, *Seconding Sinai*.

Nickelsburg observes that "[f]or the Enochic authors, law is tied to cosmic order" and that these "laws" do not have formal parallels to those found in the Mosaic Torah, such as honoring parents, observing Sabbaths and feasts, circumcision, and cultic laws. Instead, the focus is on imminent eschatological judgment, which "implies a corpus or collection of laws and commandments that form the criteria for this judgment."[134] 4QInstruction in contrast ties "laws" to cosmic order only when Torah and its laws evoke or reinforce issues related to cosmology. One possible explanation of this use of Torah is as the speaker-sage interpreting the Torah's hidden or deeper meaning, thereby transforming it in a way so as to demonstrate the mystery of existence and its preeminence.[135] In this respect, the *maśkîl* in 4QInstruction would be similar to the Teacher of Righteousness to whom "all the mysteries of his servants the prophets" have been made known (1QpHab II 8–9; VII 4–5). Indeed, in 4Q418 221 2 where the sage likely uses first person speech, "prophets" are also mentioned. Although the speaker of 4QInstruction is certainly not a scribe who writes down his visionary experiences, one title given to Enoch in the Book of Giants is illuminating: ספר פרשא (4Q203 8 4; 4Q206 2 2), perhaps best translated as "scribe of discernment."[136] Revelation as the source of authority when interpreting scripture is well known, so too exegesis vis-à-vis angelic mediation.[137]

4.2   *4Q423 1*

The garden metaphor of 4Q423 1 has been interpreted as an Edenic Garden in which pursuing wisdom is likened to tending the garden. The knowledge of good and evil is closely related to wisdom in 4QInstruction and those who seek knowledge are likened to those who dwell in a garden. There is some disagreement about whether 4Q423 1 should be joined to 4Q423 2. The consequence of not joining fragments 1 and 2 is that there may be no explicit mention of "good

---

134   Nickelsburg, "Enochic Wisdom," 84.

135   Cf. Brooke's work on Qumran wisdom as *pesher*, in "Biblical Interpretation," 149–156.

136   The title given Enoch is "scribe," e.g., "scribe of the righteous" (12:4); "scribe of truth" (15:1); these are translated in Ethiopic as "scribe of righteousness" and may derive from an Aramaic original ספר קושטא; Knibb, "The Book of Enoch," 196.

137   Alfred R.C. Leaney, *The Rule of Qumran and Its Meaning: Introduction, Translation and Commentary* (Philadelphia, PA: Westminster Press, 1966), 63–75; Michael Mach, "The Social Implication of Scripture-Interpretation in Second Temple Judaism," in *The Sociology of Sacred Texts*, ed. Jon Davies & Isabel Wollaston (Sheffield: Sheffield Academic, 1993), 166–179; Hindy Najman, "Angels At Sinai: Exegesis, Theology, and Interpretive Authority," *DSD* 7 (2000): 313–333.

and evil" in this passage. However, even if fragment 2 is not joined to fragment 1, a metaphor based upon the creation narrative of Genesis 2–3 is clearly present.

4Q423 1, Transcription and Translation:[138]

]וֹכֹל פרי תנובהֹ וכל עץ נעים נחמד להשכיל הלוא גן נ]עים [ ]	1
נחמד]לֹ[ה]שֹׁכֹיל מ[ואֹ]דֹה ובו המשילכה לעבדו ולשמרו גֹ]ן vac תֹ[ ]	2
האדמה] קֹוץ ודֹרֹדר תצמיח לכה וכוחה לא תתן לכה ○[ ] [ ]	3
במועלכה vacat [ ]	4
ילדה וכל רחמי הורֹ]ת לֹ[] ○○○[ ] vac [ ]	5
בכל חפציכה כי כל תצמיחֹ] לכה [ ]	6
ובמטע [] בם הֹ○] מואס ה] [ ]	7

1 [   ] and every fruit of produce,
and every pleasant tree desirable to make wise;
is it not a pl[easant] garden,
2 [desireable]to[ma]ke one exceedingly wise?
And He has given you authority to tend it and to keep it.
vacat g[arden   ]t
3 [the earth] will sprout forth thorns and thistles to you,
and its strength it will not yield to you [   ]
4 [   ] in your being unfaithful
vacat
5 Her child and all the mercy of her that is pregna[nt
[   ] 6[   ]
] in all your pleasure,
for everything it sprouts forth [for you
[   ] 7 [   ]
]and in a planting [] them *h*[

In the description of the garden in 4Q423 1 every tree yields wisdom and the *mēvîn* is to cultivate them and partake of their fruit. The observation of the woman in Gen 3:6 (וַתֵּרֶא הָאִשָּׁה כִּי טוֹב הָעֵץ לְמַאֲכָל וְכִי תַאֲוָה־הוּא לָעֵינַיִם וְנֶחְמָד הָעֵץ לְהַשְׂכִּיל) is that the tree of the knowledge of good and evil is pleasant to make

---

138   DJD 34:507–508 Elgvin joins 4Q423 1, 2 i; Tigchelaar, *To Increase Learning*, does not join 4Q423 1 and 2, 141, "I am not completely convinced"; Rey, *4QInstruction*, does not transcribe or discuss 4Q423 1; Goff, *4QInstruction*, 289 does not join; Qimron, *Dead Sea Scrolls*,

one wise.[139] This is the same tree that God commands Adam not to eat from in Gen 2:17 (וּמֵעֵץ הַדַּעַת טוֹב וָרָע לֹא תֹאכַל מִמֶּנּוּ), 3:1, and 3:11. The description of the entire garden in 4Q423 1 1–2 is indebted to the description of the tree of the knowledge of good and evil in Gen 3:6.

Similar to Sir 17:7, which is not preserved in Hebrew, 4Q423 1 appears to ignore the prohibition of eating from the tree of the knowledge of good and evil found in Genesis. Instead, God endows Adam and Eve with the knowledge of good and evil from the beginning (ἐπιστήμην συνέσεως ἐνέπλησεν αὐτοὺς καὶ ἀγαθὰ καὶ κακὰ ὑπέδειξεν αὐτοῖς).[140] The meaning of the Garden of Eden, as found in Ben Sira 15:14–17, is that before each person are life and death and whichever one chooses will be given (15:17, לִפְנֵי אָדָם חַיִּים וּמָוֶת וּמָה אֲשֶׁר יַחְפֹּץ יִנָּתֶן לוֹ). There is neither a primordial sin of Adam, nor "fall" of humanity, nor original sin, but rather God leaves humanity in the garden in the power of their own free will and exhorts them to stretch forth their hand to choose.[141] After Sir 17:7 underscores that wisdom is given to humankind from the beginning, in the verses to follow (17:11–12) it describes the allotment of the "law of life" (νόμον ζωῆς), establishment of an "eternal covenant" (διαθήκην αἰῶνος), and the revealing of "decrees/judgments" (κρίματα). Collins observes that the "law of life" in 17:11 identifies it with revelation at Sinai because in Sir 45:5 God made Moses equal in glory to the angels by giving him "the law of life and knowledge" (καὶ ἔδωκεν αὐτῷ … νόμον ζωῆς καὶ ἐπιστήμης). This is derived from Deut 30:11–20 where Moses tells Israel that he has set "life and death" before them. Therefore, the "eternal covenant" in Sir 17:12 is convincingly read as a reference to Sinai. Collins explains further that in Ben Sira "the law set before Adam and Eve was no different from the law given to Moses on Mount Sinai" and "the law of creation and the law of Sinai are one and the same."[142] As we have seen,

---

2:179 does not join. Qimron is alone in rejecting the reconstruction לֹ[ה]שְׂכִּיל מַ[וּא]דָּה in l. 2 commenting that the traces are not suitable and the place narrow ("השרידים אינם מתאימים והמקום צר"), and reconstructs the beginning of l. 2 instead as לֹ[ו] וֹבֹכֹ(ו)לֹ מֹ[עַ]שֹׂה ("[…]to [him], and in e(ve)ry d[ee]d, and over it He has placed you in authority"). Qimron may be correct; however, his reconstruction adds an additional letter space. Whether there are remains of a *beit* or *shin* is ambiguous; however, regardless of whether l. 2 begins by re-emphasizing the nature of the garden as making one wise or not, l. 1 is unambiguous on this point.

139   The serpent claims (Gen 3:5) that eating from the tree of the knowledge of good and evil results in becoming like אֱלֹהִים. It is purely speculative, but the metaphor here could, conceivably, feed into the angelology of 4QInstruction.

140   Collins, *Jewish Wisdom*, 125.

141   Cf. Sir 25:24 and the attribution of sin and the beginning of death to Eve.

142   Collins, *Jewish Wisdom*, 59–60.

however, "Torah" is absent from the discourse of 4QInstruction and there is, therefore, no reason to suppose that 4Q423 1 similarly collapses the interval between creation and Sinai. Instead, 4QInstruction portrays that access to wisdom is given in Eden (i.e., in this metaphor trees make wise) and wisdom is equated with the mystery of existence rather than Torah.

The addressee of 4Q423 1 has been placed in authority over a wisdom producing garden, he is to guard and keep it.[143] In Genesis, once Adam has partaken of the fruit of the tree a series of well-known curses follows (3:14–19), shortly thereafter God confirms, by way of direct speech, that because Adam knows good and evil he is "like one of us" (3:22); in conclusion (3:23) Adam is expelled from the garden to tend the earth (לַעֲבֹד אֶת־הָאֲדָמָה). The description in 4Q423 1 2 is that the *mēvîn* is tending the Edenic garden and not laboring in post-Edenic fields. Why then the reference to "thorns and thistles" in line 3? In Gen 3:18 this is the language of God's cursing of the earth (קוֹץ וְדַרְדַּר תַּצְמִיחַ לָךְ); however, it is hard to conceive how in 4QInstruction those laboring in the garden are under a curse, as this would imply that the prohibition not to eat of the tree was in effect, when it clearly is not. Therefore, when the description of "thorns and thistles" is used it is more likely part of a metaphor: wisdom trees, thorns, and thistles grow together in the same garden. Caution should be shown when cultivating wisdom because it is an arduous task. Indeed, there is concern for vigilance in pursuing wisdom on several occasions in 4QInstruction in the form of exhortations not to weary in pursuing it (e.g., 4Q418 69 ii 10–11). Within this metaphor a serious challenge is present when tending the garden: the earth does not necessarily yield its "strength" (ll. 3–4; cf. Gen 4:12). Lack of vigilance when cultivating wisdom trees could result in a complete failure acquiring wisdom. The failure to cultivate the garden results in this privilege being taken away, the very description we read in the Vision of Hagu that the fleshly spirit is "no longer" given "Hagu" because he did not know the difference between good and evil.

In the Thanksgiving Hymns (XVI 5–28) the psalmist uses the metaphor of an Edenic garden (1QHᵃ XVI 21 "But the plantation of fruit trees ○[...] eternal [fo]unt becomes a glorious Eden and [an everlasting] splen[dor]") to describe

---

143 In the Apocryphon of John, or Secret Book of John, from Nag Hammadi the tree of the knowledge of good and evil from Gen 2:15–17 is a tree of *gnosis*, a vehicle of esoteric knowledge, and its fruit should be eaten. While there is no doubt that early Christian "Gnostic" teaching is deeply indebted to Neo-Platonism, three commonalities—negative associations with "flesh," a positive view of eating from the tree of knowledge in Eden, and pursuit of esoteric knowledge—suggest some continuity in religious patterns between 4QInstruction and Apocryphon of John.

his own pursuit of knowledge and mysteries. When the speaker withdraws his hand from tending the garden it becomes like junipers in the wilderness, nettles and salt, and "thorns and thistles" (קוץ ודרדר, l. 26). When the psalmist works the garden in the heat of the day, the earth retains its strength (ובעת חום יעצור מעוז, ll. 24–25). The metaphor in the hymns uses the word עולם frequently (ll. 6, 8, 12, 14, 20), and among these are the expressions מטעת עולם ("eternal planting" l. 6) and מקור עולם ("eternal spring" l. 8), both of which are found in 4Q418 81 + 81a (ll. 1, 14) with regard to the role of the elevated sage figure. Similarity in language found here and in Gen 2–3 suggest that other fragments from 4QInstruction may also belong to a garden metaphor. 4Q415 2 i + 1 ii is highly fragmentary, but preserved are the broken phrases בהתהלכו תמים ("in your walking perfectly" 2 i 3), עולם וזרע קדושכה ("eternity and seed of your holiness" 2 i + 1 ii 4–5), לוא ימוש זרעכה מנחלת ("your seed will not depart from the inheritance of" 2 i 5), תשיש בפרי ("rejoice in your fruit" 2 i 6), and לכו[ל קצים יפרח ("at a]ll times it will blossom" 2 i 8). 1QH[a] XVI 11–13 describe that the "planting of truth" (i.e., Eden) conceals itself, that the mysteries of the garden are sealed up, and that God protects these mysteries with "strong warriors" (גבורי כוח) and "spirits of holiness" (רוחות קודש). As discussed previously, concealment of wisdom is not emphasized in 4QInstruction and if the Edenic garden is sealed off in 4QInstruction, it is from those who have left the garden.[144] The similarities between the hymns and 4QInstruction should be interpreted in light of their comparatively different anthropologies (cf. Ch. 2). For the hymns, the issue is "getting in" (i.e., acquiring access to knowledge) while in 4QInstruction it is "staying in" (i.e., remaining faithful to one's created purpose). Indeed, according to 1QH[a] XVI 15 the psalmist is "as a thing [wa]shed up by rivers" upon the garden's shores.

The association of the Garden of Eden with the temple in Ezek 40–48 is taken up by several early Jewish authors and beyond (e.g., Book of the Watchers, Ben Sira, John's Apocalypse). Moreover, temple imagery also evokes traditions associated with Sinai.[145] However, an identification of Eden with Sinai in 4QInstruction is not to be found; just as the re-writing of Ps 1:2b indicates that the mystery substitutes Torah as an explicit theme, so too 4Q423 1 seems to substitute Sinai with Eden, a place where the faithful (metaphorically) dwell. While one might speculate that the *maśkîl*, when he is appointed as firstborn son, is

---

144   One small fragment from 4Q418 76 has a broken reference to "spirits of holiness" (רוחי קודש), which is likely a reference to angelic beings, but there is no connection to the garden. Both רוחי קודש and רוחות קודש are angelic epithets known also from Songs of the Sabbath Sacrifice.

145   Himmelfarb, *Between Temple and Torah*, 12.

(metaphorically) placed in the garden, this would conflict with 4Q417 1 i where humanity is created with the ability to meditate and understand. If the garden were interpreted in an exclusive way, as a place only for the exalted sage, then it would evoke an identification of Eden with (the heavenly) temple. However, if this were the case, then the garden's description as full of thorns and thistles and not yielding its strength simply does not align with the positive description of the *maśkîl's* situation in 4Q418 81 + 81a.

The garden metaphor of 4Q423 1 and Ben Sira's references to Eden share an important commonality, that is they both ignore the prohibition of eating from the tree, but here the similarities cease. Indeed, as we have seen, the place of Torah in Ben Sira and 4QInstruction is starkly different. Wisdom in 4QInstruction is identified with the רז נהיה, the mystery itself relates to the cosmic order, and pursuing it is frequently depicted by reworking Gen 2–3. Eden in 4Q423 1 is a place where one pursues the mystery of existence, the garden is where humanity began and where some still remain. The *maśkîl*, it seems, has become more like God and the angels, by knowing good and evil (Gen 3:22).

5   Conclusions

If any reference to Mosaic Torah were present in 4QInstruction it would be found in the expression "hand of Moses." An examination of the two instances where Harrington, Strugnell, and Elgvin transcribe the "hand of Moses" leads to the conclusion that there is in fact only one occurrence (4Q418 184); however, *contra* the editors it is not preceded either with the statement "he spoke" or "he commanded." The occurrence of "Moses hand" alone, without the activity of God speaking or commanding by it, opens up another plausible association with Moses' hand other than giving Torah at Sinai, namely turning away wrath or delivering judgment, both of which are motifs in 4QInstruction. In addition to the assessment of Moses' hand two passages were examined that take traditions in which Torah is typically in focus and supplant "Torah" with the "mystery of existence," these are: (1) Ps 1:2b in 4Q417 1 i 6 and (2) the Shema-Decalogue combination in 4Q416 2 iii 14–19. A third passage, 4Q418 55 3, appears to substitute "Torah" with "truth," a term used to describe the foundations of the cosmos (4Q417 1 i). Negative evidence regarding the presence of "Torah" in 4QInstruction, vis-à-vis Moses' hand, begins to clarify the author(s') attitude toward Sinai, but taken alone would leave ambiguities. The supporting evidence from the three passages that omit Torah in order to give supremacy to the mystery of existence, or truth, clarify the author(s') attitude and provide persuasive evidence that "Torah" is intentionally absent.

Instead of placing emphasis on Sinai, 4QInstruction turns repeatedly to creation in reference to Gen 1–3. When scripture is interpreted, whether vis-à-vis
literary allusion or re-writing, a pesher-like style has been observed where concealed, often cosmological, meaning is found. In this assessment of Torah, it has
become evident that 4QInstruction maintains the preeminence of (revealed)
wisdom, which is identified with the רז נהיה, and only incorporates Torah by
way of these non-explicit uses. The absence of "Torah" from 4QInstruction's
discourse sets it in contrast with, especially, Ben Sira who equates Torah with
wisdom. The combination of a non-explicit use of scripture and absence of
thematized Torah is also found in Enochic literature, which suggests that 4QIn-
struction's provenance may be more closely associated with these circles than
with Ben Sira's. In Stuckenbruck's study of 4QInstruction and Enochic literature he observes common terms found in both; however, he does not posit a
direct literary relationship between the two.[146] Michael Knibb likewise offers
a study on Enochic literature and 4QInstruction and concludes that parallels
between them evidence a shared thought-world. Indeed, on the basis of this
assessment of Torah, which takes a different point of departure than either
Stuckenbruck or Knibb, we may likewise conclude that 4QInstruction presents
us with a theological perspective on wisdom and Torah much more closely
aligned with Enochic literature than Sirach.[147] This conclusion is not so much
about genetic relationships, but milieu and common theological patterns.

4QInstruction is not simply neutral toward Torah nor ignorant about it.
Indeed, the author is clearly aware of Torah from Genesis to Deuteronomy.
For the speaker to appeal to the mystery of existence is to invoke an authoritative source outside and beyond himself and humanity. It is possible that
this reaction to Torah as a source of authority may relate to the association of
Torah with Jerusalem priests, their abuse of power, and exclusionary practices;
4QInstruction appeals to a universal and inclusive authority outside of history,
society, and politics. Human beings are created with spirit, they are aware of
and are given meditation on right and wrong from the beginning. Moreover,
the addressees of 4QInstruction are taught that they too may become a sage
and, as a *maśkîl*, they have authority not just over the children of Israel, but
over the sons of mankind (4Q418 81 + 81a 3).

---

146   Stuckenbruck, "4QInstruction and the Possible Influence," 245–261; cf. Elgvin, "The Mys-
      tery to Come," 150, suggests that 4QInstruction may be dependent on the Epistle of Enoch
      and concludes that "4QInstruction represents a bridge between the apocalyptic Enoch
      literature and the clearly-defined sectarian community."
147   Knibb, "The Book of Enoch," 210.

The multiple copies of 4QInstruction discovered at Qumran indicate that the Torah-centered Yaḥad copied and apparently used this composition in the late first century BCE and early first century CE. Similar to many other Scrolls found in the Qumran caves, 4QInstruction does not always align with their theological views. However, the use of a non-Torah text by a Torah loving community may be explained in several ways. 4QInstruction likely interested the Yaḥad because of its pedagogical function as a *maśkîl*-text. Moreover, it is so replete with allusions to Torah, especially Gen 1–3, that it may not have concerned them that Torah was not thematized.

Does 4QInstruction include gentiles into this universal outlook? Whether fellow Jews or non-Jews 4QInstruction provides an explanation for how someone comes to be on the outside of the faithful community; this is based on merit rather than an appeal to election. 4QInstruction's sapiential discourse offers a distinctive way of thinking about being "inside" and "outside" of a faithful community. That even elect Israel can go astray, as seen in CD I 13–14 ("like a wayward heifer so Israel has strayed"), is indicative of a struggle with the very notion of "election" and in some documents the solution is the formulation of "true Israel" or "the elect of the elect." 4QInstruction never mentions Israel and yet the community is called the "eternal planting," which designates them as the remnant community who has faithfully pursued the mystery of existence. This righteous community remains, metaphorically, in Eden where they tend wisdom producing trees that grow among thorns and thistles.[148] In the beginning, all of humanity was metaphorically within the Garden of Eden and anyone who did not tend wisdom producing trees was expelled.

The rationale that someone is "outside" of the community because they did not distinguish between good and evil according to their own creation applies to both Jews and gentiles. In terms of inclusion, however, does this mean that not only Jews but also gentiles may be included within the faithful community? The framework that 4QInstruction sets for itself, particularly its anthropology and view of revelation, leads to an affirmative answer; however, this document is not composed to function universally. Written in Hebrew and reliant upon scriptural traditions to express a universal framework, 4QInstruction's outlook reflects a distinctively Israelite/Jewish identity and its speech is directed only to insiders. Those within the community, the ones addressed,

---

148   There is no indication that there is an expectation for future restoration of the elect like Enochic literature, *pace* Elgvin, "The Mystery to Come," 121: "Similar to the Enochic books, 4QInstruction does not ascribe to the remnant community a clearly-defined role in history as do later sectarian writings, although the designation 'eternal planting' indicates that the community is the nucleus of the future-restored Israel."

range from simpletons verging on outright foolishness to sages and, while they have financial interactions with people outside of their community, the ideal is to keep separate from all that God hates. The *maśkîl* is a figure who by dint of discipline is separated from the fleshly spirit.

Finally, "general" revelation in Rom 1:18–19 (cf. Ch. 2 §1.1.5.) serves to establish the guilt of humanity and justify judgment upon them ("for the wrath of God is revealed from heaven against all ungodliness and wickedness of men who by their wickedness suppress the truth. For what can be known about God is plain to them, because God has shown it to them"). Creation in 4QInstruction serves a similar purpose to that found in Rom 1, and yet there is more than general revelation, there are mysteries to be taught too. The same beginning point sets humanity on an even plane and from there one may go up or down, suppress the truth and become fleshly spirit or pursue the mystery of existence, guard one's spirit, and grow in actualized wisdom. In 4QInstruction the way of the wise leads to honor in one's community and a life hereafter, but to the unfaithful fool exclusion and judgment awaits.

Concluding Remarks

The three chapters of this book are interested in distinct but intersecting notions of divisions and hierarchies. Chapter 1 addresses hierarchies within the community and what separates different members from one another. While there are clear divisions between the activities and attributes of the speaker-sage and his varied students, one's place within the community's hierarchy is not immutable. In Chapter 2, the focus of questioning turns from the community to the whole of humanity. What is the nature and character of human beings and how is one group of humanity distinguished from another? The conclusion reached is that all humankind is created with the ability to distinguish right from wrong and that individual behavior separates the righteous from the wicked. Chapter 2 challenges a *status quo*, one which concludes that 4QInsruction conceives of a particular hierarchy, namely the bestowing of special revelation (i.e., רז נהיה) only to the elect "spiritual people" while those who are "fleshly" are created without this privilege. The conclusion that 4QInstruction conceives of a universal creation, as well as a view that act-consequence are rooted in personal ethics and human merit, stands in sharp contrast with the *status quo*. Finally, in Chapter 3, the relationship of Mosaic Torah to the mystery of existence is addressed. These two types of revelation are each authority constructs and one may, therefore, ask: if these two are not identified with one another (Torah = Mystery), then what is their relationship within a hierarchy of authorities? This chapter addresses the place of Torah within 4QInstruction and finds that it is never thematized nor mentioned (not even by way of "Moses' hand"). Moreover, on three different occasions traditions that typically refer to "Torah" supplant "Torah" with the mystery of existence (or "truth"). This mystery, as argued in Chapters 2 and 3, is closely associated with creation. By placing emphasis on the mystery rather than Torah, 4QInstruction gives creation precedent over Sinai. These three chapters taken together contribute to a view of 4QInstruction as a composition distinct from the outlook and theological viewpoints of Yaḥad literature, one that is concerned with universal revelation and creation and hierarchies within which movement is possible.

1   Function and Reception

Disparate teachings are found in 4QInstruction, ranging from warnings to the foolish (4Q418 69 ii+60) to an address to one who is placed as a most holy one over the earth (4Q418 81+81a). A variety of solutions have been

© KONINKLIJKE BRILL NV, LEIDEN, 2018 | DOI: 10.1163/9789004364240_006

offered to explain the stark contrast between the character of these different addressees. For instance, it has been suggested that some sections have a
different provenance or that at times non-community members are directly
addressed. From this study, we see that 4QInstruction is addressed to pupils in
various standings—the sage speaks to students across a spectrum—some who
are more advanced and others less so. This insight into the pedagogical function and purpose of 4QInstruction assists in fundamentally resolving many
problems reading this fragmentary composition. Moreover, the assessment of
4QInstruction as an address by a *maśkîl* to understanding ones provides at least
a partial explanation for why it may have been copied and used at least a generation or more after it was first composed. Understanding this composition
as speech by a *maśkîl* influences how we understand its function. The figure of
maśkîl in literature found at Qumran is often seen to embody a community's
ideals and in the specific example of 4QInstruction this sage is the pinnacle
of the community's desire to actualize wisdom (cf. Ch. 1 § 2.3. "*ḥokma* of the
hands"). As we have seen, the role of *maśkîl* is not exclusive, which fits with the
broader inclusive theological outlook of 4QInstruction.

Another important avenue for exploring function is the way that poverty
themes in 4QInstruction have been used to suggest a *Sitz im Leben* and original audience. Even before analyzing poverty within the context of a *maśkîl's*
speech, we asked why recipients of this composition, ones we infer are literally lacking and living at subsistence level, would need to be reminded that
they are "poor." Furthermore, why would a community living at a later time, an
estimated one hundred and fifty years later, be interested to transmit and copy
this teaching if it were so unambiguously grounded in the specific realities of
an impoverished community? In Chapter 1 we see that "poverty" in 4QInstruc-
tion may relate to material and economic impoverishment, but is also used as
a metaphor that is associated with humility. 4QInstruction holds to a type of
Armenfrömmigkeit and, as such, meaning could have been found within this
text in multiple generations that experienced more than one social condition.
Issues related to poverty are taught to an aspiring sage and the values imparted
are not simply about finances, debt, and hardship, but also viewpoints on what
it means to live humbly, human nature, and how a leader should care for others
within his community.

When members of the Yaḥad copied this document, they would likely have
been interested in it because they shared similar, or at least partially overlap-
ping, ideas about the pursuit and acquisition of revealed wisdom. They may
have found in 4QInstruction's *maśkîl* a figure that they too found worthy of
emulation and who encapsulated their values. Readers of 4QInstruction in
later generations would likely have accepted instruction about poverty, with

all of its nuances, as a topic related to a sage's pursuit of revealed wisdom and not so much as isolated sapiential advice about how members of a specific, and financially monolithic, audience should negotiate their financial circumstances. 4QInstruction is not straightforwardly and consistently addressing the socio-economic status of his addressees, but rather establishes ethical categories that have a particular rhetorical function.

Priestly prerogatives are associated with the *maśkîl* in 4QInstruction; however, this is neither an exclusive privilege nor one that is confined to the Jerusalem temple. The ones addressed are not identified as being of priestly progeny, and yet they have it within their remit to become a sage and, when they become one, they are placed in authority over the whole earth. The description of being a unique, firstborn son carries priestly connotations and yet this position is by appointment in response to faithful pursuit of, and lived out, wisdom. This perspective on priestly privileges begs the question: to what is the author of 4QInstruction reacting? Entirely plausible is that 4QInstruction is responding to corruption at the Jerusalem temple and presents an alternative model of selection (versus "election") to priestly duties. If this is the case, then it also offers an explanation for the reception of this composition by the Yaḥad community at a later stage. These same characteristics likewise offer insights about why 4QInstruction may not have become popular among other communities; not only is priesthood disassociated with temple and Levitical progeny, but also the authority of Mosaic Torah is subordinate to the revelation of the mystery of existence. Creation has precedence over Sinai. While this is different from Yaḥad literature, even there the interpretation of Mosaic Torah and its mysteries is dependent upon revelation and the character of its interpreter. In contrast to the writings of the Yaḥad, 4QInstruction does not evoke Torah as a theme and yet to some degree viewpoints on revelation and interpretation of Torah are shared; one reason that this composition was valued by a later community may be related to these common beliefs.

2   Provenance and Relationship to Other Compositions

The study of divisions and hierarchies results in a portrait of 4QInstruction that is neither dualistic nor deterministic and, as such, its relationship to other literature requires reassessment. This comes into view especially in Chapter 3 (§ 3.). The understanding ones are exhorted to conduct themselves properly, they are consoled, warned, and even reproved; however, these instructions do not operate within a highly deterministic worldview in which those addressed are reminded about their predetermined paths. Instead, at the center of 4QInstruction is the notion that faithful pursuit of wisdom is what ultimately locates people either within or outside of the community, and for those within it the hierarchy of the group is determined not only by the internal "wisdom of the heart," but also the outward actualization of the mystery of existence by the "wisdom of the hands" (4Q418 81 + 81a 15–20). One's adherence to wisdom ultimately results in either life or death.

Although literary dependency is not a major focal point in this study, how 4QInstruction relates to other compositions comes into view. This is especially the case of Enochic literature; it was seen in Chapter 3 (§ 3.) that 4QInstruction shares similar ideas about how revelation and Mosaic Torah operate. In other studies, significant attention has been given to the relationship of 4QInstruction to the Treatise on the Two Spirits. Indeed, the dating of 4QInstruction to the *circa* mid-second century BCE has been partly derived in other studies from comparisons with the Treatise, hypothesized interdependence and evolutionary trajectories. Shared terminology alone is insufficient to postulate that the two works originate from, or belong to, the same group. The frequency of key terms in 4QInstruction and Yaḥad literature have been carefully studied and yet the majority of scholars are not convinced that this alone is persuasive evidence that 4QInstruction is a "sectarian" product. When relating 4QInstruction to the Treatise, the division of humanity into two groups is crucial to understanding the possible relationship of these two compositions. In Chapter 2 the creation and division of humanity is addressed and I challenge the translation and interpretation of the Vision of Hagu passage which finds in it the creation of two types of humanity. Not only is the Hagu passage more convincingly taken as depicting the singular creation of all humanity, but also in the remainder of 4QInstruction there is no other expression of two opposing groups of human beings. This fundamental difference with the Treatise, as well as the lack of interest in opposing good and evil spirits in 4QInstruction, or their respective actors, distance these two compositions.[1] That the Vision of Hagu similarly conceives of two types of humanity within the particular dualistic framework of the Treatise has been a lens through which 4QInstruction as a whole has been interpreted. I suggest an alternative reading, a less deterministic one that is absent of dualities, which results not only in a different understanding of the Hagu pericope, but the entirety of 4QInstruction. The reassessment of determinism and dualism affects how one postulates the rela

---

1 The Treatise on the Two Spirits is an imported source to 1QS with an earlier provenance. If the author(s) of 4QInstruction is aware of the Treatise, then 4QInstruction is not modeling itself on the Treatise, but rather distancing itself from an overt dualism.

tionship of 4QInstruction to the Treatise; a greater distance is seen between them, which consequently challenges one means used to date 4QInstruction.

In Chapter 2, 4QInstruction is compared with the Thanksgiving Hymns and although common terms are found their views on human nature and access to wisdom differ. Nonetheless, the parallel phrase דעתם יכבדו איש מרעהו found in 1QHᵃ XVIII 29–30 and 4Q418 55 10 may suggest a direct dependence of the hymns on 4QInstruction. Therefore, in regard to the provenance of 4QInstruction, the Thanksgiving Hymns may, if this is correct, offer a *terminus ad quem* but how do we arrive at a *terminus post quem*? 4QInstruction may be aware of some Enochic writings, suggested by similar vocabulary and theological patterns, here as related to Torah, and this general milieu would seem to offer a *terminus a quo*. Would the date of 4QInstruction then fall between the time that Enochic authors began to exert influence (e.g., the Book of Watchers is dated fairly early, perhaps to the third century BCE) and the beginning of the Yaḥad? Dating 4QInstruction's provenance in relationship to Ben Sira seems highly problematic, although this is not to deny that 4QInstruction and Ben Sira share common characteristics and interest in similar themes. The identi-fication of 4QInstruction with *maśkîl* literature calls into question its straightforward designation as "wisdom literature" and, therefore, its classification in terms of genre and form. Identifying 4QInstruction's "cross-talk" as a means of dating this composition should include other *maśkîl* literature as well as Enochic tradition. By calling into question how 4QInstruction shares, or does not share, ideologies and theologies the provenance of 4QInstruction is much less certain. A date to the mid second-century BCE remains a possibility, indeed nothing in this study definitively speaks against this possible date, but it is also not inconceivable that it was composed earlier.

Commonalities between 4QInstruction, the Thanksgiving Hymns, and the Songs of the Sabbath Sacrifice have been observed and studied. The identification of 4QInstruction with the speech of a *maśkîl* denotes a liturgical aspect and, as such, provides a way to triangulate these three compositions. When one is instructed in the ways of a sage in 4Q418 81+81a this figure serves as an intermediary and, I have argued, participates with angelic beings similarly to *maśkilîm* in other literature as well as the Songs of the Sabbath Sacrifice. While 4QInstruction remains one of our most important witnesses to sapiential trajectories in Jewish antiquity, its exhortations about how to live in this world should not only be seen in light of its cosmological framework and temporal axis (i.e., eschatology), but also the speech of a sage and an audience that aspires to the ideals presented in the figure of its *maśkîl*. 4QInstruction is ultimately interested in ethical distinctions between those who have pursued and acted upon the revealed knowledge of good and evil and those who have not. Among those who continue seeking after the mysteries of revealed wisdom, 4QInstruction presents social distinctions and hierarchies among different divisions of humanity.

Bibliography

Abegg, Martin, "Who Ascended to Heaven? 4Q491, 4Q427, and the Teacher of Righteousness," in *Eschatology, Messianism, and the Dead Sea Scrolls*, ed. C. Evans & P. Flint (Grand Rapids, MI: Eerdmans, 1997), 61–73.

Adam, Douglas, *The Hitchhiker's Guide to the Galaxy* (New York, NY: Random House/Del Rey, 1979).

Adams, Samuel L., *Wisdom in Transition: Act and Consequence in Second Temple Instructions*, SJSJ 125 (Leiden: Brill, 2008).

Anderson, Arnold A., "The Use of Ruaḥ in 1QS, 1QH and 1QM," *JSS* 7 (1962): 293–303.

Angel, Joseph, *Otherworldly and Eschatological Priesthood in the Dead Sea Scrolls* STDJ 86 (Leiden: Brill, 2010)

Angel, Joseph, "Maskil, Community, and Religious Experience in the *Songs of the Sage* (4Q510–511)," *DSD* 19/1 (2012): 1–27.

Angel, Joseph, "The Liturgical-Eschatological Priest of the Self-Glorification Hymn," *RevQ* 96/1 (2010): 585–605.

Argall, Randal A., *1 Enoch and Sirach: A Comparative Literary and Conceptual Analysis of the Themes of Revelation, Creation and Judgment* (Atlanta, GA: Scholars Press, 1995).

Arnal, William E., *Jesus and the Village Scribes: Galilean Conflicts and the Setting of Q* (Minneapolis, MN: Fortress Press, 2001).

Arnold, Russell C.D., *The Social Role of Liturgy in the Religion of the Qumran Community*, STDJ 60 (Leiden: Brill, 2006).

Austin, John L., *How to Do Things with Words* (New York, NY: Oxford Paperbacks, 1965).

Baillet, Maurice, *Qumran grotte 4.III (4Q482–4Q520)*, DJD 7 (Oxford: Clarendon Press, 1982).

Barclay, John M.G., *Paul and the Gift* (Grand Rapids, MI: Eerdmans, 2015).

Baumgarten, Joseph M., "Some Astrological and Qumranic Terms in 4QInstruction," *Tarbiz* 72 (2003): 321–328. [Hebrew]

Baumgarten, Joseph M., "Corrigenda to the 4Q MSS of the Damascus Document," *RevQ* 19 (1999): 217–225

Baumgarten, Joseph M., *The Damascus Document (4Q266–273), Qumran Cave 4, XIII*, DJD 18 (Oxford: Clarendon Press, 1996).

Baumgarten, Joseph M., "On the Nature of the Seductress in 4Q184," *RevQ* 15 (1991–1992): 133–143.

Beavin, Edward Lee, *Ruaḥ Hakodesh in Some Early Jewish Literature* (Ph.D. diss., Vanderbilt University, 1961).

Beentjes, Pancratius C., *The Book of Ben Sira in Hebrew: A Text Edition of All Extant Hebrew Manuscripts and a Synopsis of All Parallel Hebrew Ben Sira Texts*, VTSup 68 (Leiden: Brill, 1997).

Bedenbender, Andreas, "The Place of the Torah in the Early Enoch Literature," in *The Early Enoch Literature*, ed. G. Boccaccini & J.J. Collins, JSJSup 121 (Leiden: Brill, 2007), 65–80.

Berg, Shane A., *Religious Epistemologies in the Dead Sea Scrolls: The Heritage and Transformation of the Wisdom Tradition* (Ph.D. dissertation, Yale 2008).

Berg, Shane A., "An Elite Group within the Yaḥad," in *Qumran Studies: New Approaches, New Questions*, ed. M.T. Davis & B.A. Strawn (Grand Rapids, MI: Eerdmans, 2007), 161–177.

Birnbaum, Ellen, *The Place of Judaism in Philo's Thought: Israel, Jews, and Proselytes*, BJS 290 (Atlanta, GA: Scholars Press, 1996), 1–14.

Blenkinsopp, Joseph, *Wisdom and Law in the Old Testament: The Ordering of Life in Israel and Early Judaism, second edition*, OBS (Oxford: OUP, 2003).

Boccaccini, Gabriele, *Middle Judaism: Jewish Thought, 300 B.C.E. to 200 C.E.* (Minneapolis, MN: Fortress Press, 1991).

Borg, Marcus M., *Conflict, Holiness and Politics in the Teaching of Jesus* (New York, NY/London: Continuum, 1984).

Boring, Eugene M., *Sayings of the Risen Jesus: Christian Prophecy in the Synoptic Tradition*, SNTSMS 46 (Cambridge: CUP, 1982).

Brand, Miryam T., "Belial, Free Will, and Identity-Building in the Community Rule," in *Evil, the Devil, and Demons: Dualistic Characteristics in the Religion of Israel, Ancient Judaism, and Christianity*, ed. J. Dochhorn, S. Rudnig-Zelt & B. Wold, WUNT 2.412 (Tübingen: Mohr Siebeck, 2015), 77–92.

Brand, Miryam T., *Evil Within and Without: The Source of Sin and Its Nature as Portrayed in Second Temple Literature*, JAJSup 9 (Göttingen: Vandenhoeck & Ruprecht, 2013).

Brin, Gershom, "Wisdom Issues in Qumran: The Types and Status of the Figures in 4Q424 and the Phrases of Rationale in the Document," *DSD* 4/3 (1997): 297–311.

Brin, Gershom, "Studies in 4Q424, Fragment 3," *VT* 46/3 (1996): 271–295.

Brooke, George J., "Deuteronomy 5–6 in the Phylacteries from Qumran Cave 4," in *Emanuel: Studies in Hebrew Bible, Septuagint, and Dead Sea Scrolls in Honor of Emanuel Tov*, ed. S. Paul, R. Kraft, L. Schiffman & W. Fields, VTSup 94 (Leiden: Brill, 2003), 57–70.

Brooke, George J., "Biblical Interpretation in the Wisdom Texts from Qumran," in *The Wisdom Texts from Qumran and the Development of Sapiential Thought*, ed. C. Hempel, A. Lange & H. Lichtenberger, BETL 159 (Leuven: Peeters, 2002), 201–222.

Brown, Francis, Driver, S.R., and Briggs, Charles A., *The Enhanced Brown-Driver-Briggs Hebrew and English Lexicon* (Peabody, MA: Hendrickson, 1994).

Brownlee, William H., *Midrash Pesher of Habakkuk* (Missoula, MT: Scholars Press, 1979).

Bruce, Frederick F., "Holy Spirit in the Qumran Texts," *ALUOS* 6 (1966/68): 49–55.

Carmignac, Jean, "Les horoscopes de Qumran," *RevQ* 5/18 (1965): 199–207.

Carmignac, Jean, "Conjecture sur la première ligne de la Règle de la Communauté," *RevQ* 2 (1959): 85–87.

Caquot, André, "4QMess ar 1 i 8–11," *RevQ* 15/57–58 (1991): 145–155.

Cavin, Robert L., *New Existence and Righteous Living: Colossians and 1 Peter in Conversation with 4QInstruction and the Hodayot*, BZNW 197 (Berlin: de Gruyter, 2014).

Charlesworth, James H. (ed.), *The Old Testament Pseudepigrapha*, 2 vols. (New York, NY: Doubleday, 1983).

Chester, Andrew, *Messiah and Exaltation*, WUNT 207 (Tübingen: Mohr Siebeck, 2007).

Christensen, Duane L., *Deuteronomy 1:1–21:9*, WBC 6a (Nashville, TN: Thomas Nelson Publishers, 2001).

Cohen, Naomi G., "Philo's Tefillin," *WCJS* 9/A (1985): 199–206.

Cohen, Shaye J.D., *From the Maccabees to the Mishnah*, 2nd ed. (Louisville, KY: Westminster John Knox Press, 2006).

Collins, John J., "The Transformation of the Torah in Second Temple Judaism," *JSJ* 43 (2012): 455–474.

Collins, John J., *Beyond the Qumran Community: The Sectarian Movement of the Dead Sea Scrolls* (Grand Rapids, MI: Eerdmans, 2009).

Collins, John J., "The Eschatologizing of Wisdom in the Dead Sea Scrolls," in *Sapiential Perspectives: Wisdom Literature in Light of the Dead Sea Scrolls*, ed. J.J. Collins, G.E. Sterling & R.A. Clemens, STDJ 51 (Leiden: Brill, 2004), 49–65.

Collins, John J., "The Mysteries of God: Creation and Eschatology in 4QInstruction and the Wisdom of Solomon," in *Wisdom and Apocalypticism in the Dead Sea Scrolls and in the Biblical Tradition*, ed. F. García Martínez, BETL 168 (Leuven: Peeters, 2003), 287–305.

Collins, John J., "In the Likeness of the Holy Ones: The Creation of Humankind in a Wisdom Text from Qumran," in *The Provo International Conference on the Dead Sea Scrolls: Technological Innovations, New Texts, and Reformulated Issues*, ed. D.W. Parry & E. Ulrich, STDJ 30 (Leiden: Brill, 1999), 609–618.

Collins, John J., "Wisdom Reconsidered, in Light of the Scrolls," *DSD* 4/3 (1997): 265–281.

Collins, John J., *Jewish Wisdom in the Hellenistic Age*, OTL (Louisville, KY: Westminster, 1997).

Collins, John J., *The Scepter and the Star: The Messiahs of the Dead Sea Scrolls and Other Ancient Literature*, ABRL (New York, NY: Doubleday, 1995).

Coulot, Claude, "L'image de Dieu dans les écrits de sagesse 1Q26, 4Q415–418, 4Q423," in *Wisdom and Apocalypticism in the Dead Sea Scrolls and in the Biblical Tradition*, ed. F. García Martínez, BETL 168 (Leuven: Peeters, 2003), 171–181.

Crawford, Sidnie White, *The Temple Scroll and Related Texts* (Sheffield: Sheffield Academic Press, 2000).

Crawford, Sidnie White, "Lady Wisdom and Dame Folly at Qumran," *DSD* 5 (1993): 255–266.

Cross, Frank M., "The Development of the Jewish Scripts," in *The Bible and the Ancient Near East: Essays in Honor of W.F. Albright*, ed. G.E. Wright (New York, NY: Anchor Book Edition, 1965), 133–202.

Davies, Philip R., "Dualism in the Qumran War Texts," in *Dualism in Qumran*, ed. G.G. Xeravits (London: T & T Clark, 2010), 8–19.

Davies, Philip R., *The Damascus Covenant: An Interpretation of the Damascus Document* (Sheffield: JSOT Press, 1982).

Davila, James R., "4QMess ar (4Q534) and Merkavah Mysticism," *DSD* 5/3 (1998): 367–381.

Delcor, Mathias, *Les Hymnes de Qumrân (Hodayot): texte hébreu, introduction, traduction, commentaire* (Paris: Letouzey et Ané, 1962).

Desmond, William D., *The Greek Praise of Poverty: Origins of Ancient Cynicism* (Notre Dame, IN: University of Notre Dame, 2006).

Dimant, Devorah, "The Library of Qumran: Its Content and Character," in *The Dead Sea Scrolls Fifty Years after Their Discovery: Proceedings of the Jerusalem Congress, July 20–25, 1997*, ed. L.H. Schiffman, E. Tov & J.C. VanderKam (Jerusalem: IES, 2000), 170–176.

Dimant, Devorah, "The Qumran Manuscripts: Contents and Significance," in *A Time to Prepare the Way in the Wilderness. Papers on the Qumran Scrolls by Fellows of the Institute for Advanced Studies of the Hebrew University, Jerusalem, 1989–1990*, ed. D. Dimant & L.H. Schiffman, STDJ 16 (Leiden: Brill, 1995), 23–58.

Dimant, Devorah, "A Synoptic Comparison of Parallel Sections in 4Q427 7, 4Q491 11 and 4Q471B," *JQR* 85 (1994): 157–161.

Dombrowski-Hopkins, Denise, "The Qumran Community and 1Q Hodayot: a Reassessment," *RevQ* 10 (1981): 323–364.

Duhaime, Jean, "Cohérence structurelle et tensions internes dans l'Instruction des deux esprits (1QS III 13–IV 26)," in *Wisdom and Apocalypticism in the Dead Sea Scrolls and in the Biblical Tradition*, ed. F. García Martínez, BETL 168 (Leuven: Peeters, 2003), 103–131.

Elgvin, Torleif, "Priestly Sages? The Milieus of Origin of 4QMysteries an 4QInstruction," in *Sapiential Perspectives: Wisdom Literature in Light of the Dead Sea Scrolls: Proceedings of the Sixth International Symposium of the Orion Center for the Study of the Dead Sea Scrolls and Associated Literature, 20–22 May, 2001*, ed. J.J. Collins, G.E. Sterling & R.A. Clements, STDJ 51 (Leiden: Brill, 2004), 13–47.

Elgvin, Torleif, "Wisdom With and Without Apocalyptic," in *Sapiential, Liturgical and Poetical Texts from Qumran: Proceedings of the Third Meeting of the International Organization for Qumran Studies, Oslo 1998, Published in Memory of Maurice Baillet*, ed. D.K. Falk, F. García Martínez & E.M. Schuller, STDJ 35 (Leiden: Brill, 2000), 15–38.

Elgvin, Torleif, "Wisdom and Apocalypticism in the Early Second Century BCE: The Evidence of 4QInstruction," in *The Dead Sea Scrolls Fifty Years After Their Discovery: Proceedings of the Jerusalem Congress, July 20–25, 1997*, ed. L.H. Schiffman, E. Tov & J.C. VanderKam (Jerusalem: IES, 2000), 226–247.

Elgvin, Torleif, "The Mystery to Come: Early Essene Theology of Revelation," in *Qumran Between the Old and New Testaments*, ed. F.H. Cryer & T.L. Thompson, JSOTS 290 (Sheffield: Sheffield Academic Press, 1998), 113–150.

Elgvin, Torleif, *An Analysis of 4QInstruction* (Ph.D. Dissertation, Hebrew University of Jerusalem, 1997).

Elgvin, Torleif, "'To Master His Own Vessel' 1 Thess 4.4 in Light of New Qumran Evidence," *NTS* 43/4 (1997): 604–619.

Elgvin, Torleif, "Early Essene Eschatology: Judgment and Salvation according to Sapiential Work A," in *Current Research and Technological Developments on the Dead See Scrolls: Conference on the Texts from the Judean Desert, Jerusalem, 30 April 1995*, ed. D.W. Parry & S.D. Ricks, STDJ 20 (Leiden: Brill, 1996), 126–165.

Elgvin, Torleif, "Wisdom, Revelation and Eschatology in an Early Essene Writing," *SBL Seminar Papers, 1995*, SBLSP 34 (Atlanta, GA: Scholars Press, 1995), 440–463.

Elgvin, Torleif, "The Reconstruction of Sapiential Work A," *RevQ* 16/4 (1995): 559–580.

Elgvin, Torleif, "Admonition Texts from Qumran Cave 4," in *Methods of Investigation of the Dead Sea Scrolls and the Khirbet Qumran Site*, ed. M.O. Wise, N. Golb, J.J. Collins & D.G. Pardee, Annual of the New York Academy of Sciences 722 (New York, NY: The New York Academy of Sciences, 1994) 179–196.

Elgvin, Torlcif, Kister, Menaham, Lim, Timothy, Nitzan, Bilhah, Pfann, Stephen, Qimron, Elisha, Schiffman, Lawrence H., *Qumran Cave 4 XV: Sapiential Texts, Part 1*, DJD 20 (Oxford: Clarendon Press, 1997).

Eshel, Esther, "The Identification of the 'Speaker' of the Self-Glorification Hymn," in *The Provo International Conference on the Dead Sea Scrolls: Technological Innovations, New Texts, and Reformulated Issues*, ed. D.W. Parry & E. Ulrich, STDJ 30 (Leiden: Brill, 1999), 619–635.

Eshel, Esther, "Self-Glorification Hymn," in *Qumran Cave 4.XX, Poetical and Liturgical Texts, Part 2*, E. Chazon, et al., DJD 19 (Oxford: Clarendon Press, 1999), 421–436.

Evans, Craig A., "A Note on the 'First-Born Son' of 4Q369," *DSD* 2/2 (1995): 185–201.

Fabry, Heinz-Josef, "Die Armenfrömmigkeit in den qumranischen Weisheitstexten," in *Weisheit in Israel: Beiträge des Symposiums "Das Alte Testament und die Kultur der Moderne" anlässlich des 100. Geburtstags Gerhard von Rads (1901–1971), Heidelberg, 18.–21. Oktober 2001*, ed. D.J.A. Clines, H. Lichtenberger & H.-P. Müller, ATM 12 (Münster: Lit-Verlag, 2003), 163–209.

Falk, Daniel K., *Daily, Sabbath, and Festival Prayers in the Dead Sea Scrolls*, STDJ 27 (Leiden: Brill, 1998).

Fitzmyer, Joseph, *Romans: A New Translation with Introduction and Commentary*, AB (New York, NY: Doubleday, 1993).

Fitzmyer, Joseph, "The Aramaic 'Elect of God' Text from Qumran Cave 4," *CBQ* 27 (1965): 348–372.

Flusser, David, *Judaism of the Second Temple Period, vol. 1 Qumran and Apocalypticism* (Grand Rapids, MI: Eerdmans, 2007).

Frey, Jörg, "Flesh and Spirit in the Palestinian Jewish Sapiential Tradition and in the Qumran Texts. An inquiry into the Background of Pauline Usage," in *The Wisdom Texts from Qumran and the Development of Sapiential Thought*, ed. C. Hempel, A. Lange & H. Lichtenberger; BETL 159 (Leuven: Peeters, 2002), 367–404.

Frey, Jörg, "The Notion of Flesh in 4QInstruction and the Background of Pauline Usage," in *Sapiential, Liturgical and Poetical texts from Qumran: Proceedings of the Third Meeting of the International Organization for Qumran Studies, Oslo 1998, Published in Memory of Maurice Baillet*, ed. D.K. Falk, F. García Martínez & E.M. Schuller, STDJ 35 (Leiden: Brill, 2000), 197–226.

Frey, Jörg, "Die paulinische Antithese von 'Fleisch' und 'Geist' und die palästinisch-jüdische Weisheitstradtion," *ZNW* 90/1 (1999): 45–77.

García Martínez, Florentino, "Old Texts and Modern Mirages: The 'I' of Two Qumran Hymns," in *Qumranica Minora I: Qumran Origins and Apocalypticism*, ed. E.J.C. Tigchelaar, STDJ 63 (Leiden: Brill, 2007), 105–128

García Martínez, Florentino, "Wisdom at Qumran: Worldly or Heavenly?" in *Wisdom and Apocalypticism in the Dead Sea Scrolls and in the Biblical Tradition*, ed. F. García Martínez (BEThL 168; Leuven, Peeters, 2003), 1–16. Reprinted in *Qumranica Minora II: Thematic Studies on the Dead Sea Scrolls*, ed. E.J.C. Tigchelaar, STDJ 64 (Leiden: Brills, 2007), 171–186.

García Martínez, Florentino, "Marginalia on 4QInstruction," *DSD* 13/1 (2006): 24–37.

García Martínez, Florentino, "The Heavenly Tablets in the Book of Jubilees," in *Studies in the Book of Jubilees*, ed. M. Albani, J. Frey & A. Lange, TSAJ 65 (Tübingen: Mohr Siebeck, 1997), 243–260.

García Martínez, Florentino, *Qumran and Apocalyptic: Studies on the Aramaic Texts from Qumran*, STDJ 9 (Leiden: Brill, 1992).

Garnsey, Peter, *Cities, Peasants and Food in Classical Antiquity: Essays in Social and Economic History* (Cambridge: CUP, 1998).

Goering, Greg Schmidt, "Creation, Torah, and Revealed Wisdom in Some Second Temple Sapiential Texts (Sirach, *4QInstruction*, 4Q185, and 4Q525): A Response to John Kampen," in *Canonicity, Setting, Wisdom in Deuterocanonicals: Papers of the Jubilee Meeting of the International Conference on the Deuterocanonical Books*, ed. G.G. Xeravits, J. Zsengellér & X. Szabó (Berlin: de Gruyter, 2014), 121–124.

Goering, Greg Schmidt, *Wisdom's Roots Revealed: Ben Sira and the Election of Israel*, JSJSup 139 (Leiden: Brill, 2009).

Goff, Matthew J., "A Seductive Demoness at Qumran? Lilith, Female Demons and 4Q184," in *Evil, the Devil, and Demons: Dualistic Characteristics in the Religion of*

Israel, Ancient Judaism, and Early Christianity, ed. J. Dochhorn, S. Rudnig-Zelt & B. Wold, WUNT 2.412 (Tübingen: Mohr Siebeck, 2016), 59–76

Goff, Matthew J., *4QInstruction*, WLAW 2 (Atlanta, GA: SBL, 2013).

Goff, Matthew J., "Being Fleshly or Spiritual: Anthropological Reflection and Exegesis of Genesis 1–3 in 4QInstruction and First Corinthians," in *Christian Body, Christian Self: Concepts of Early Christian Personhood*, ed. C.K. Rothschild, T.W. Thompson, WUNT 284 (Tübingen: Mohr Siebeck, 2011), 41–59.

Goff, Matthew J., "Adam, the Angels and Eternal Life: Genesis 1–3 in the Wisdom of Solomon and 4QInstruction," in *Studies in the Book of Wisdom*, ed. G. Xeravits & J. Zsengellér, JSJSup 142 (Leiden: Brill, 2010), 1–22

Goff, Matthew J., "Recent Trends in the Study of Early Jewish Wisdom Literature: The Contribution of 4QInstruction and Other Qumran Texts," CBR 7/3 (2009): 376–416.

Goff, Matthew J., *Discerning Wisdom: The Sapiential Literature of the Dead Sea Scrolls*, VTSup 116 (Leiden: Brill, 2007).

Goff, Matthew J., "Wisdom, Apocalypticism, and the Pedagogical Ethos of 4QInstruction," in *Conflicted Boundaries in Wisdom and Apocalypticism*, ed. B.G. Wright III & L.M. Wills, SBLSP 35 (Atlanta, GA: Scholars Press, 2005), 57–67.

Goff, Matthew J., "Discerning Trajectories: 4QInstruction and the Sapiential Background of the Sayings Source Q," JBL 124/4 (2005): 657–673.

Goff, Matthew J., "Reading Wisdom at Qumran: 4QInstruction and the Hodayot," DSD 11/3 (2004): 263–288.

Goff, Matthew J., "The Mystery of Creation in 4QInstruction," DSD 10/2 (2003): 163–186.

Goff, Matthew J., *The Worldly and Heavenly Wisdom of 4QInstruction*, STDJ 50 (Leiden: Brill, 2003).

Greenfield, Jonas C., "Prolegomenon," in *3 Enoch or the Hebrew Book of Enoch*, ed. H. Odeberg (New York, NY: Ktav, 1973).

Grossman, Maxine L., "Cultivating Identity: Textual Virtuosity and 'Insider' Status," in *Defining Identities: We, You, and the Other in the Dead Sea Scrolls* (*Proceedings of the Fifth Meeting of the IOQS in Groningen*), ed. F. García Martínez & M. Popović, STDJ 70 (Leiden: Brill, 2007), 1–3.

Grossman, Maxine L., *Reading for History in the Damascus Document: A Methodological Study*, STDJ 45 (Leiden: Brill, 2002).

Hadas, Moses, *Aristeas to Philocrates* (Philadelphia, PA: Dropsie College, 1951).

Hammer, Reuven, "What did they Bless? A Study of Mishnah Tamid 5.1," JQR 81/3–4 (1991): 305–324.

Harrington, Daniel J., "Wisdom and Apocalyptic in 4QInstruction and 4 Ezra," in *Wisdom and Apocalypticism in the Dead Sea Scrolls and in the Biblical Tradition*, ed. F. García Martínez, BETL 168 (Leuven: Peeters, 2002), 343–355.

Harrington, Daniel J., "The Qumran Sapiential Texts in the Context of Biblical and Second Temple Literature," in *The Dead Sea Scrolls: Fifty Years after Their Discovery:*

Proceedings of the Jerusalem Congress, July 20–25, 1997, ed. L.H. Schiffman, E. Tov & J.C. VanderKam (Jerusalem: IES, 2000), 256–262.

Harrington, Daniel J., "Two Early Jewish Approaches to Wisdom: Sirach and Qumran Sapiential Work A," *JSP* 8/16 (1997): 25–38.

Harrington, Daniel J., *Wisdom Texts from Qumran* (London: Routledge, 1996).

Harrington, Daniel J., "The *Raz Nihyeh* in a Qumran Wisdom Text (1Q26, 4Q415–418, 423)," *RevQ* 17 (1996): 549–553.

Harrington, Daniel J., "Wisdom at Qumran," in *The Community of the Renewed Covenant, The Notre Dame Symposium on the Dead Sea Scrolls*, ed. E. Ulrich & J.C. Vanderkam (Notre Dame, IN: University of Notre Dame Press, 1994), 137–152.

Harrington, Daniel J., "The Apocalypse of Hannah: Targum Jonathan of 1 Samuel 2:1–10," in *Working with no Data: Semitic and Egyptian Studies Presented to Thomas O. Lambdin*, ed. D.M. Golomb & S.T. Hollis (Winona Lake, IN: Eisenbrauns, 1987), 147–152.

Harrington, Daniel J. and Saldarini, Anthony J., *Targum Jonathan of the Former Prophets*, AB (Edinburgh: T & T Clark, 1987).

Hartin, Patrick J., *James and the Q Sayings of Jesus*, JSNTS 47 (Sheffield: JSOT Press, 1991).

Hempel, Charlotte, "The Qumran Sapiential Texts and the Rule Books," in *The Wisdom Texts from Qumran and the Development of Sapiential Thought*, ed. C. Hempel, A. Lange & H. Lichtenberger, BETL 159 (Leuven: Peeters, 2002), 277–296.

Himmelfarb, Martha, *Between Temple and Torah: Essays on Priests, Scribes, and Visionaries in the Second Temple Period and Beyond*, TSAJ 151 (Tübingen: Mohr Siebeck, 2013).

Hoffmann, Heinrich, *Das Gesetz in der frühjüdischen Apokalyptik* (Göttingen: Vandenhoeck & Ruprecht, 1999).

Hogan, Karina M., *Theologies in Conflict in 4 Ezra: Wisdom Debate and Apocalyptic Solution*, JSJSup 130 (Leiden: Brill, 2008).

Hollander, H.W. and de Jonge, M., *The Testament of the Twelve Patriarchs: A Commentary*, SVTP 8 (Leiden: Brill, 1985).

Holm-Nielsen, Svend, *Hodayot: Psalms from Qumran* (Aarhus: Universitetsforlaget, 1960).

Hooker, Morna D., *From Adam to Christ: Essays on Paul* (Cambridge: CUP, 1990), 73–84.

Horbury, William, "Ezekiel Tragicus 106: δωρήματα," *VT* 36/1 (1986): 37–51.

Horsley, Richard A., *Revolt of the Scribes: Resistance and Apocalyptic Origins* (Minneapolis, MN: Fortress Press, 2009).

Horsley, Richard A., "Logoi Prophētōn: Reflections on the Genre of Q," in *The Future of Early Christianity: Essays in Honor of Helmut Koester*, ed. B. Pearson (Minneapolis, MN: Fortress Press, 1991), 195–209.

Hyatt, Philip J., "The View of Man in the Qumran 'Hodayot,'" *NTS* 2 (1955–1956): 276–284.

Jackson-McCabe, Matt A., *Logos and Law in the Letter of James: The Law of Nature, the Law of Moses, and the Law of Freedom*, SNT 100 (Leiden: Brill, 2001).

Jacobson, Arland D., "Apocalyptic and the Synoptic Sayings Source Q," in *The Four Gospels: Festschrift Frans Neirynck*, ed. F. Van Segbroeck, et al., BETL 100 (Leuven: Peeters, 1992), 403–419.

Jassen, Alex P., *Mediating the Divine: Prophecy and Revelation in the Dead Sea Scrolls and Second Temple Judaism*, STDJ 68 (Leiden: Brill, 2007).

Jeremias, Gert, *Der Lehrer der Gerechtigkeit*, SUNT (Gottingen: Vandenhoeck & Ruprecht, 1963).

Jutta Jokiranta, *Social Identity and Sectarianism in the Qumran Movement*, STDJ 105 (Leiden: Brill, 2014).

Jutta Jokiranta, "Learning from Sectarian Responses: Windows on Qumran Sects and Emerging Christian Sects," in *Echoes from the Caves: Qumran and the New Testament*, ed. F. García Martínez, STDJ 85 (Leiden: Brill, 2009), 177–210.

Kampen, John, "Wisdom in Deuterocanonical and Cognate Literature," in *Canonicity, Setting, Wisdom in Deuterocanonicals: Papers of the Jubilee Meeting of the International Conference on the Deuterocanonical Books*, ed. G.G. Xeravits, J. Zsengellér & X. Szabó (Berlin: de Gruyter, 2014), 89–120.

Kampen, John, " 'Torah' and Authority in the Major Sectarian Rule Texts from Qumran," in *The Scrolls and Biblical Tradition: Proceedings of the Seventh Meeting of the IOQS in Helsinki*, ed. G.J. Brooke et al., STDJ 103 (Leiden: Brill, 2012), 231–254.

Kampen, John, *Wisdom Literature*, ECDSS (Grand Rapids, MI/Cambridge: Eerdmans, 2011).

Kimelman, Reuven, "Polemics and Rabbinic Liturgy," in *Discussing Cultural Influences: Text, Context, and Non-Text in Rabbinic Judaism*, ed. R. Ulmer (Lanham, MD: University Press of America, 2007), 59–97.

"The Šěma and its Blessing: The Realization of God's Kingship," in *The Synagogue in Late Antiquity*, ed. L.I. Levine (Philadelpia, PA: Eisenbrauns, 1987), 73–86.

Kirk, Alan, *The Composition of the Saying Source: Genre, Synchrony, and Wisdom Redaction in Q*, NovTSup 91 (Leiden: Brill, 1998).

Kister, Menahem, " 'Inclination of the Heart of Man,' the Body and Purification from Evil," in *Meghillot: Studies in the Dead Sea Scrolls VIII*, ed. M. Bar-Asher & D. Dimant (Jerusalem: Bialik Institute & Haifa University Press, 2010), 243–286 [Hebrew].

Kister, Menahem, "ספרות החכמה בקומראן," in מבואות ומחקרים—מגילות קומראן / *The Qumran Scrolls and Their World*, 2 vols., ed. M. Kister (Jerusalem: Yad ben-Zvi, 2009), 299–320 [Hebrew].

Kister, Menahem, "Divorce, Reproof, and Other Sayings in the Synoptic Gospels: Jesus Traditions in the Context of 'Qumranic' and Other Texts," in *Text, Thought, and Practice in Qumran and Early Christianity: Proceedings of the Ninth International Symposium of the Orion Center for the Study of the Dead Sea Scrolls and Associated Literature, Jointly Sponsored by the Hebrew University Center for the Study of Christianity*, ed. R.A. Clements & D.R. Schwartz, STDJ 84 (Leiden: Brill, 2009), 195–229.

Kister, Menahem, "Physical and Metaphysical Measurements Ordained by God in the Literature of the Second Temple Period," in *Reworking the Bible: Apocryphal and Related Texts at Qumran. Proceedings of a Joint Symposium by the Orion Center for the Study of the Dead Sea Scrolls and Associated Literature and the Hebrew University Institute for Advanced Studies Research Group on Qumran, 15–17 January, 2002*, ed. E.G. Chazon, D. Dimant & R.A. Clements, STDJ 58 (Leiden: Brill, 2005), 153–176.

Kister, Menahem, "Wisdom Literature and Its Relation to Other Genres: From Ben Sira to Mysteries," in *Sapiential Perspectives: Wisdom Literature in Light of the Dead Sea Scrolls: Proceedings of the Sixth International Symposium of the Orion Center for the Study of the Dead Sea Scrolls and Associated Literature, 20–22 May, 2001*, ed. J.J. Collins, G.E. Sterling & R.A. Clements, STDJ 51 (Leiden: Brill, 2004), 13–47.

Kister, Menahem, "A Qumranic Parallel to 1Thess 4,4? Reading and Interpretation of 4Q416 2 ii 21," *DSD* 10/3 (2003): 365–370.

Kister, Menahem, "Some Aspects of Qumranic Halakhah," in *The Madrid Qumran Congress: Proceedings of the International Congress on the Dead Sea Scrolls, Madrid 18–21 March 1991*, 2 vols., ed. J. Trebolle Barrera & L. Vegas Montaner, STDJ 11 (Leiden: Brill, 1992), 2.575–576.

Klawans, Jonathan, "Josephus on Fate, Free Will, and Ancient Jewish Types of Compatibilism," *Numen* 56 (2009): 44–90.

Kloppenborg, John, *Excavating Q: The History and Setting of the Sayings Gospel* (Philadelphia, PA: Fortress Press, 2000).

Kloppenborg, John, *Trajectories in Ancient Wisdom Collections* (Harrisburg, PA: Trinity Press International, 1981, reprint 1999).

Kloppenborg, John, *The Formation of Q: Trajectories in Ancient Wisdom Collections* (Minneapolis, MN: Fortress Press, 1987).

Kloppenborg, John, "Symbolic Eschatology and Apocalypticism in Q," *HTR* 80/3 (1987): 287–306.

Knibb, Michael A., "The Book of Enoch in the Light of the Qumran Wisdom Literature," in *Wisdom and Apocalypticism in the Dead Sea Scrolls and in the Biblical Tradition*, ed. F. García Martínez, BETL 168 (Leuven: Peeters, 2003), 193–210.

Knohl, Israel, *The Messiah Before Jesus: The Suffering Servant of the Dead Sea Scrolls*, trans. D. Maisel (Berkeley, CA: University of California Press, 2000), 15–21.

Koester, Helmut, "One Jesus and Four Primitive Gospels," in *Trajectories through Early Christianity*, ed. J.M. Robinson & H. Koester (Philadelphia, PA: Fortress Press, 1971), 158–204.

Kosmala, Hans, "Maskil," *JANESCU* 5 (1973): 235–241.

Kugel, James L., "Some Instances of Biblical Interpretation in the Hymns and Wisdom Writings of Qumran," in *Studies in Ancient Midrash*, ed. J.L. Kugel (Cambridge, MA: Harvard University Press, 2001), 155–169.

Kugel, James L., "4Q369 'Prayer of Enosh' and Ancient Biblical Interpretation," *DSD* 5/2 (1998): 119–148.

Kugel, James L., *Traditions of the Bible: A Guide to the Bible as It was at the Start of the Common Era* (Cambridge, MA: Harvard Univeristy Press, 1998).

Kugel, James L., "Levi's Elevation to the Priesthood in Second Temple Writings," *HTR* 86/1 (1993): 1–64.

Kvanvig, Helge S., "Enochic Judaism—a Judaism without the Torah and the Temple?" in *Enoch and the Mosaic Torah: The Evidence of Jubilees*, ed. G. Boccaccinni & G. Ibba (Grand Rapids, MI/Cambridge: Eerdmans, 2009), 163–177.

Langdon, Stephan, *Die neubabylonischen Königsinschriften* (Leipzig: Hinrichs, 1912).

Lange, Armin, "Die Weisheitstexte aus Qumran: Eine Einleitung," in *The Wisdom Texts from Qumran and the Development of Sapiential Thought*, ed. C. Hempel, A. Lange & H. Lichtenberger, BETL 158 (Leuven: Peeters, 2002), 3–30.

Lange, Armin, "The Determination of Fate by the Oracle of the Lot in the Dead Sea Scrolls, the Hebrew Bible and Ancient Mesopotamian Literature," in *Sapiential, Liturgical and Poetical texts from Qumran: Proceedings of the Third Meeting of the International Organization for Qumran Studies, Oslo 1998, Published in Memory of Maurice Baillet*, ed. D.K. Falk, F. García Martínez & E.M. Schuller, STDJ 35 (Leiden: Brill, 2000), 39–48.

Lange, Armin, "In Diskussion mit dem Tempel: Zur Auseinandersetzung zwischen Kohelet und weisheitlichen Kreisen am Jerusalemer Tempel," in *Qohelet in the Context of Wisdom*, ed. A. Schoors, BETL 136 (Leuven: Peeters, 1998), 113–159.

Lange, Armin, "Wisdom and Predestination in the Dead Sea Scrolls," *DSD* 2/3 (1995): 340–354.

Lange, Armin, *Weisheit und Prädestination, Weisheitliche Urordnung und Prädestination in den Textfunden von Qumran*, STDJ 18 (Leiden: Brill, 1995).

Leaney, A. Robert C., *The Rule of Qumran and Its Meaning: Introduction, Translation and Commentary* (Philadelphia, PA: Westminster Press, 1966).

Lesley, Michael J., "Exegetical Wiles: 4Q184 as Scriptural Interpretation," in *The Scrolls and Biblical Traditions: Proceedings of the Seventh Meeting of the IOQS in Helsinki*, ed. G.J. Brooke et al., STDJ 103 (Leiden: Brill, 2012), 107–142.

Levinson, Bernard M., *A More Perfect Torah: At the Intersection of Philology and Hermeneutics in Deuteronomy and the Temple Scroll*, Corpus Scriptorum Historiae Byzantinae 1 (Winona Lake, IN: Eisenbrauns, 2013).

Liddell, Henry G., Scott, Robert & Jones, Henry S., *Greek English Lexicon, Ninth Edition with a Revised Supplement* (Oxford: Clarendon Press, 1996)

Lockett, Darian, "The Spectrum of Wisdom and Eschatology in the Epistle of James and 4QInstruction," *Tyndale Bulletin* 56/1 (2005): 131–148.

Mach, Michael, "The Social Implication of Scripture-Interpretation in Second Temple Judaism," in *The Sociology of Sacred Texts*, ed. J. Davies & I. Wollaston (Sheffield: Sheffield Academic Press, 1993), 166–179.

Mack, Burton, *The Lost Gospel: The Book of Q and Christian Origins* (San Francisco, CA: HarperSanFrancisco, 1993).

Magness, Jodi, *The Archaeology of Qumran and the Dead Sea Scrolls* (Grand Rapids, MI: Eerdmans, 2002).

Maier, Gerhard, *Mensch und freier Wille: Nach den jüdischen Religionsparteien zwischen Ben Sira und Paulus*, WUNT 12 (Tübingen: Mohr Siebeck, 1971).

Maier, Johann, *Die Qumran-Essener: Die Texte vom Toten Meer*, 3 vols. (München/Basel: E. Reinhardt, 1995–1996).

Mays, James Luther, "The Place of the Torah-Psalms in the Psalter," *JBL* 106 (1987): 3–12.

Meyer, Nicholas A., *Adam's Dust and Adam's Glory in the Hodayot and the Letters of Paul: Rethinking Anthropogony and Theology*, SNT 169 (Leiden: Brill, 2016).

Merrill, Eugene H., *Qumran and Predestination: A Theological Study of the Thanksgiving Hymns*, STDJ 8 (Leiden: Brill, 1975).

Metso, Sarianna, *The Textual Development of the Qumran Community Rule*, STDJ 21 (Leiden: Brill, 1997).

Milik, Józef T., *Qumran Grotte 4.II. Tefillin, Mezuzot et Targums (4Q128–4Q157)*, DJD 6 (Oxford: Clarendon Press, 1977).

Montgomery, Eric, *A Stream from Eden: The Nature and Development of a Revelatory Tradition in the Dead Sea Scrolls* (Ph.D. dissertation, McMaster University, 2013).

Moody, Dale, "God's Only Son: The Translation of John 3:16 in the Revised Standard Version," *JBL* 72/4 (1953): 213–219.

Murphy, Catherine M., *Wealth in the Dead Sea Scrolls and in the Qumran Community*, STDJ 40 (Leiden: Brill, 2001).

Murphy, Roland E., "Yēṣer in the Qumran Literature," *Bib* 39 (1958): 334–344.

Najman, Hindy, *Past Renewals: Interpretive Authority, Renewed Revealtion and the Quest for Perfection in Jewish Antiquity*, JSJS 53 (Leiden: Brill, 2010).

Najman, Hindy, *Seconding Sinai: The Development of Mosaic Discourse in Second Temple Judaism*, JSJSup 77 (Leiden: Brill, 2003).

Najman, Hindy, "Angels At Sinai: Exegesis, Theology, and Interpretive Authority," *DSD* 7 (2000): 313–333.

Naudé, Jacobus A., "The Wiles of the Wicked Woman (4Q184), the Netherworld and the Body," *JSem* 15 (2006): 372–384.

Nelson, Richard D., *Deuteronomy: A Commentary* (Louisville, KY: Westminster John Knox Press, 2002).

Newsom, Carol A., "Deriving Negative Anthropology through Exegetical Activity: The Hodayot as Case Study," in *Is There a Text in This Cave? Studies in the Textuality of the Dead Sea Scrolls in Honour of George J. Brooke*, ed. A. Feldman, M. Cioată & C. Hempel, STDJ 119 (Leiden: Brill, 2017), 258–276.

Newsom, Carol A., "Spirit, Flesh, and the Indigenous Psychology of the Hodayot," in *Prayer and Poetry in the Dead Sea Scrolls and Related Literature: Essays in Honor of*

Eileen Schuller on the Occasion of Her 65ᵗʰ Birthday, ed. J. Penner, K.M. Penner & C. Wassen, STDJ 98 (Leiden: Brill, 2012), 339–354.

Newsom, Carol A., *The Self as Symbolic Space: Constructing Identity and Community at Qumran*, STDJ 52 (Leiden: Brill, 2004).

Newsom, Carol A., *Poetical and Liturgical Texts, Part 1*, DJD 11 (Oxford: Clarendon Press, 1998).

Newsom, Carol A., "The Sage in the Literature of Qumran: The Functions of the Maskil," in *The Sage in Israel and the Ancient Near East*, ed. J.G. Gammie & L.G. Perdue (Winona Lake, IN: Eisenbrauns, 1990), 373–382.

Newsom, Carol A., *Songs of the Sabbath Sacrifice: A Critical Edition*, HSS 27 (Atlanta, GA: Scholars Press, 1985).

Newsom, Carol, Stegemann, Hartmut and Schuller, Eileen, *Qumran Cave 1.III: 1QHodayot a, with Incorporation of 4QHodayot a-f and 1QHodayot b*, DJD 40 (Oxford: Clarendon Press, 2009).

Nickelsburg, George W.E., "Enochic Wisdom and its Relationship to the Mosaic Torah," in *The Early Enoch Literature*, ed. G. Boccaccini & J.J. Collins, JSJSup 121 (Leiden: Brill, 2007), 81–94.

Nickelsburg, George W.E., *1 Enoch 1: A Commentary on the Book of 1 Enoch. Chapters 1–36; 81–108*, Hermeneia (Minneapolis, MN: Fortress Press, 2001).

Nickelsburg, George W.E., "Enochic Wisdom: An Alternative to the Mosaic Torah?" in *HESED VE-EMET: Studies in Honor of Ernest S. Frerichs*, ed. J. Magness & S. Gittin, BJS 320 (Atlanta, GA: Scholars Press, 1998), 123–132.

Nickelsburg, George W.E., "Revealed Wisdom as a Criterion for Inclusion and Exclusion: From Jewish Sectarianism to Early Christianity," in *To See Ourselves as Others See Us: Christians, Jews, Others in Late Antiquity*, ed. J. Neusner & E. Frerichs (Chico, CA: Scholars, 1985), 73–91.

Nitzan, Bilhah, "The Ideological and Literary Unity of *4QInstruction* and Authorship," *DSD* 12/3 (2005): 257–279.

Nitzan, Bilhah, *Qumran Prayer and Religious Poetry*, STDJ 12 (Leiden: Brill, 1994).

Nitzan, Bilhah, "Key Terms in *4QInstruction*: Implications for Its Ideological Unity," in *Meghillot: Studies in the Dead Sea Scrolls, III*, ed. M. Bar-Asher & D. Dimant (Jerusalem: Bialik Institute, 2005), 101–124. [Hebrew]

O'Neill, John C., "'Who Is Comparable to Me in My Glory?': 4Q491 Fragment 11 (4Q491C) and the New Testament," *NovT* 42 (2000): 24–38.

Owen, H.P., "The Scope of Natural Revelation in Rom. i and Acts xvii," *NTS* 5 (1959): 133–143.

Patterson, Stephen J., *The Gospel of Thomas and Christian Origins: Essays on the Fifth Gospel*, NHS 84 (Leiden: Brill, 2013).

Pelletier, André, *Lettre d'Aristée a Philocrate* (SC 89; Paris: Les Éditions du Cerf, 1962).

Penner, Jeremy, *Patterns of Daily Prayer in Second Temple Period Judaism*, STDJ 104 (Leiden: Brill, 2012).

Penner, Todd, *The Epistle of James and Eschatology: Re-reading an Ancient Christian Letter*, JSNTSup 121 (Sheffield: Sheffield Academic Press, 1996).

Pennington, Jonathan T., *The Sermon on the Mount and Human Flourishing: A Theological Commentary* (Grand Rapids, MI: Baker Academic, 2017).

Perdue, Leo G., "Mantic Sages in the Ancient Near East, Israel, Judaism, and the Dead Sea Scrolls," in *Prophecy after the Prophets? The Contribution of the Dead Sea Scrolls to the Understanding of Biblical and Extra-biblical Prophecy*, ed. K. de Troyer & A. Lange, CBET 52 (Leuven: Peeters, 2009), 166–174.

Philonenko, Marc, "De la 'Prière de Jesus' au 'Notre Père': (Abba; targoum du Psaume 89,27; 4Q369, 1,2, 1–12; Luc 11,2)," *RHPR* 77/1 (1997): 133–140.

Piper, Ronald A., *Wisdom in the Q-Tradition: The Aphoristic Teaching of Jesus*, SNTSMS 61 (Cambridge: CUP, 1989).

Pryke, John, "'Spirit' and 'Flesh' in the Qumran Documents and Some New Testament Texts," *RevQ* 5 (1965): 345–360.

Puech, Émile, "L' hymne de la glorification du Maître de 4Q431," in *Prayer and Poetry in the Dead Sea Scrolls and Related Literature*, ed. J. Penner, K.M. Penner, & C. Wassen, STDJ 98 (Leiden: Brill, 2012), 377–408.

Puech, Émile, *Qumrân Grotte 4. XXVII: Textes araméens, deuxième partie, 4Q550–4Q575a, 4Q580–4Q587 et appendices*, DJD 37 (Oxford: Clarendon Press, 2009).

Puech, Émile, "Apport des manuscrits de Qoumrân à la croyance à la resurrection dans le judaïsme ancien," in *Qoumrân et le judaïsme de tournant de notre ère: actes de la Table ronde, Collège de France, 16 novembre 2004*, ed. A. Lemaire & S.C. Mimouni (Paris-Louvain: Peeters, 2006), 81–110.

Puech, Émile, "Les fragments eschatologiques de 4QInstruction (4Q416 i et 4Q418 69 ii, 81–81a, 127)," *RevQ* 22 (2005): 89–119.

Puech, Émile, "La croyance à la résurrection des justes dans un texte qumrânien de sagesse: 4Q418 69 ii," in *Sefer Moshe: The Moshe Weinfeld Jubilee Volume. Studies in the Bible and the Ancient Near East, Qumran, and Post-Biblical Judaism*, ed. C. Cohen, A. Hurvitz & S.M. Paul (Winona Lake, IN: Eisenbrauns, 2004), 427–444.

Puech, Émile, "Apports des textes apocalyptiques et sapientiels de Qumrân à l' eschatologie du judaïsme ancien," in *Wisdom and Apocalypticism in the Dead Sea Scrolls and in the Biblical Tradition*, ed. F. García Martínez, BETL 168 (Leuven: Peeters, 2003), 133–170.

Puech, Émile, "La conception de la vie future dans le livre de la Sagesse et les manuscrits de la mer Morte: un aperçu," *RevQ* 21 (2003): 209–232.

Puech, Émile, *Qumrân Grotte 4. XXII: Textes araméens partie, 4Q529–549*, DJD 31 (Oxford: Clarendon Press, 2001).

Puech, Émile, *La croyance des esséniens en la vie future: immortalité, résurrection, vie éternelle? Histoire d'une croyance dans le judaïsme ancien. Vol. II: les données qumraniennes et classiques* (Paris: J. Gabalda, 1993).

Puech, Émile & Steudel, Annette, "Un nouveau fragment du manuscrit 4QInst (XQ7 = 4Q417 ou 4Q418)," *RevQ* 19 (2000): 623–627.

Qimron, Elisha, ‏מגילות מדבר יהודה. החיבורים העבריים‎ /*The Dead Sea Scrolls: The Hebrew Writings*, 3 vols. (Jerusalem: Yad Ben-Zvi Press, 2010–2014). [Hebrew]

Reif, Stefan C., *Judaism and Hebrew Prayer: New Perspectives on Jewish Liturgical History* (Cambridge: CUP, 1995).

Reinhartz, Adele, "The Meaning of *nomos* in Philo's Exposition of the Law," *SR* 15 (1986): 337–345.

Rey, Jean-Sébastien, *4QInstruction: sagesse et eschatologie*, STDJ 81 (Leiden: Brill, 2009).

Rollens, Sarah E., *Framing Social Criticism in the Jesus Movement: The Ideological Project in the Sayings Gospel Q*, WUNT 2.374 (Tübingen: Mohr Siebeck, 2014).

Rosen-Zvi, Ishay, *Demonic Desire: Yetzer HaRa and the Problem of Evil in Late Antiquity* (Philadelphia, PA: University of Pennsylvania Press, 2011).

Rowland, Christopher, "Apocalyptic, the Poor, and the Gospel of Matthew," *JTS* 45 (1994): 504–518.

Sanders, Jack T., "When Sacred Canopies Collide: The Reception of the Torah of Moses in the Wisdom Literature of the Second-Temple Period," *JSJ* 32/2 (2001): 121–136.

Schiffman, Lawrence H., "Non-Jews in the Dead Sea Scrolls," in *The Quest for Context & Meaning. Studies in Biblical Intertextuality in Honor of James A. Sanders*, ed. C.A. Evans & S. Talmon, Biblical Interpretation Series 28 (Leiden: Brill, 1997), 153–172.

Schuller, Eileen M. and Newsom, Carol A., *The Hodayot (Thanksgiving Psalms): A Study Edition of 1QHᵃ* (Atlanta, GA: Society of Biblical Literature, 2012).

Schultz, Brian, *Conquering the World: The War Scroll (1QM) Reconsidered*, STDJ 76 (Leiden: Brill, 2009).

Searle, John R., "A Taxonom of Illocutionary Acts," in *Expression and Meaning: Studies in the Theory of Speech Acts* (Cambridge: CUP, 1979).

Segal, Alan F., "Torah and Nomos in Recent Scholarly Discussion," *SR* 13 (1984): 19–27.

Sekki, Arthur E., *The Meaning of Ruaḥ at Qumran*, SBLDS 110 (Atlanta, GA: Scholars Press, 1989).

Shutt, R.J.H., "Letter of Aristeas," in *Old Testament Pseudepigrapha*, 2 vols., ed. J.H. Charlesworth (Garden City, NY: Doubleday, 1985), 2:7–34.

Smith, Jay E., "Another look at 4Q416 2 ii 21, a critical parallel to first Thessalonians 4:4," *CBQ* 63/3 (2001): 499–506.

Smith, Morton, "Ascent to the Heavens and Deification in 4QMᵃ," in *Archaeology and History in the Dead Sea Scrolls*, ed. L.H. Schiffman, JSPSup 8 (Sheffield: JSOT Press, 1990), 181–188.

Starcky, Jean, "Le Maître de Justice et Jésus," *Le Monde de la Bible* 4 (1978): 53–55

Starcky, Jean, "Un texte messianique araméen de la Grotte 4 de Qumrân," in *Mémorial du cinqantenaire de l'Ecole des langues orientales de l'Institut Catholique de Paris* (Paris: Bloud et Gay, 1964), 51–66.

Steudel, Annette, "The Eternal Reign of the People of God—Collective Expectations in Qumran Texts (4Q246 and 1QM)," *RevQ* 17 (1996): 507–525.

Steudel, Annette and Lucassen, B., "Aspekte einer vorläufigen materiellen Rekonstruktion von 4Q416–4Q418," unpublished handout at *Forschungsseminar: Die Wiesheitstexte aus Qumran, Tübingen, 22–24 Mai; 20–21 Juni 1998*.

Stökel ben Ezra, Daniel, "Old Caves and Young Caves—A Statistical Reevaluation of a Qumran Consensus," *DSD* 14/3 (2007): 313–333.

Strugnell, John, "More on Wives and Marriage in the Dead Sea Scrolls: (4Q416 2 ii 21, cf. 1 Thess 4:4 and 4QMMT § B)," *RevQ* 17 (1996): 537–547.

Strugnell, John, "The Sapiential Work 4Q415ff. and Pre-Qumranic Works from Qumran: Lexical Considerations," in *The Provo International Conference on the Dead Sea Scrolls: Technological Innovations, New Texts, and Reformulated Issues*, ed. D.W. Parry & E.C. Ulrich, STDJ 30 (Leiden: Brill, 1999), 595–608.

Strugnell, John, Harrington, Daniel J., and Elgvin, Torleif, *Qumran Cave 4 XXIV. Sapiential Texts, Part 2: 4QInstruction (Mûsār lĕ Mēvîn): 4Q415ff. with a Re-edition of 1Q26*, DJD 34 (Oxford: Clarendon Press, 1999).

Strugnell, John and Attridge, Harold, "4Q369 '4QPrayer of Enosh,'" in *Qumran Cave 4, VIII: Parabiblical Texts, Part 1*, ed. J.C. VanderKam, DJD 13 (Oxford: Clarendon Press, 1994), 353–362.

Stuckenbruck, Loren T., "Pseudepigraphy and First Person Discourse in the Dead Sea Documents: From the Aramaic Texts to the Writings of the Yaḥad," in *The Dead Sea Scrolls and Contemporary Culture*, ed. A.D. Roitman, L.H. Schiffman & S. Tzoref, STDJ 93 (Leiden: Brill, 2011), 295–328.

Stuckenbruck, Loren T., "The Dead Sea Scrolls and the New Testament," in *Qumran and the Bible: Studying the Jewish and Christian Scriptures in Light of the Dead Sea Scrolls*, ed. N. Dávid & A. Lange, CBET 57 (Leuven: Peeters, 2010), 131–170.

Stuckenbruck, Loren T., *1 Enoch 91–108*, CEJL (Berlin/New York, NY: de Gruyter, 2007).

Stuckenbruck, Loren T., "'Angels' and 'God': Exploring the Limits of Early Jewish Monotheism," in *Early Jewish and Christian Monotheism*, ed. L.T. Stuckenbruck & W.E.S. North, JSNTS 263 (London/New York, NY: T & T Clark, 2004), 45–70.

Stuckenbruck, Loren T., "4QInstruction and the Possible Influence of Early Enochic Traditions an Evaluation," in *The Wisdom Texts from Qumran and the Development of Sapiential Thought*, ed. C. Hempel, A. Lange & H. Lichtenberger, BETL 159 (Leuven: Peeters, 2002), 245–261.

Teeter, D. Andrew, "Torah, Wisdom, and the Composition of Rewritten Scripture: Jubilees and 11QPsª in Comparative Perspective," in *Wisdom and Torah: The Reception of 'Torah' in the Wisdom Literature of the Second Temple Period*, ed. B.U. Schipper & D.A. Teeter, JSJSup 163 (Leiden: Brill, 2013), 233–272.

Thomas, Samuel I., *The "Mysteries" of Qumran: Mystery, Secrecy and Esotericism in the Dead Sea Scrolls*, EJL 25 (Atlanta, GA: SBL Press, 2009).

Tigchelaar, Eibert J.C., "Dittography and Copying Lines in the Dead Sea Scrolls: Considering George Brooke's Proposal about 1QpHab 7:1–2," in *Is There a Text in This Cave? Studies in the Textuality of the Dead Sea Scrolls in Honour of George J. Brooke*, ed. A. Feldman, M. Cioată & C. Hempel, STDJ 119 (Leiden: Brill, 2017), 293–307.

Tigchelaar, Eibert J.C., "Historical Origins of the Early Christian Concept of the Holy Spirit: Perspectives from the Dead Sea Scrolls," in *The Holy Spirit, Inspiration, and the Cultures of Antiquity* (Berlin/Boston, MA: de Gruyter, 2014), 167–240.

Tigchelaar, Eibert J.C., "'Spiritual People,' 'Fleshly Spirit,' and 'Vision of Meditation': Reflections on 4QInstruction and 1 Corinthians," in *Echoes from the Caves: Qumran and the New Testament*, ed. F. García Martínez, STDJ 85 (Leiden: Brill, 2009), 103–118.

Tigchelaar, Eibert J.C., "Wisdom and Counter-Wisdom in 4QInstruction, Mysteries and 1 Enoch," in *The Early Enoch Literature*, ed. G. Boccaccini & J.J. Collins, JSJSup 121 (Leiden: Brill, 2007), 177–194.

Tigchelaar, Eibert J.C., "Towards a Reconstruction of the Beginning of 4QInstruction (4Q416 Fragment 1 and Parallels)," in *The Wisdom Texts from Qumran and the Development of Sapiential Thought*, ed. C. Hempel, A. Lange & H. Lichtenberger, BETL 159 (Leuven: Peeters, 2002), 99–126.

Tigchelaar, Eibert J.C., *To Increase Learning for the Understanding Ones: Reading and Reconstructing the Fragmentary Early Jewish Sapiential Text 4QInstruction*, STDJ 44 (Leiden: Brill, 2001).

Tigchelaar, Eibert J.C., "The Addressees of 4QInstruction," in *Sapiential, Liturgical, and Poetical Texts from Qumran: Proceedings of the Third Meeting of the International Organization for Qumran Studies, Oslo 1998, Published in Memory of Maurice Baillet*, ed. D.K. Falk, F. García Martínez & E.M. Schuller, STDJ 35 (Leiden: Brill, 2000), 62–75.

Tigchelaar, Eibert J.C., "הבא ביחד in 4QInstruction (4Q418 64 + 199 + 66 par. 4Q417 1 i 17–19) and the Height of the Columns of 4Q418," *RevQ* 18 (1998): 589–593.

Tiller, Patrick, "The 'Eternal Planting' in the Dead Sea Scrolls," *DSD* 4/3 (1997): 312–335.

Tiwald, Markus (ed.), *Q in Context I: The Separation between the Just and Unjust in Early Judaism and in the Saying Source* (Göttingen: Vandenhoeck & Ruprecht, 2015).

Tooman, William A., "Wisdom and Torah at Qumran: Evidence from the Sapiential Texts," in *Wisdom and Torah: The Reception of 'Torah' in the Wisdom Literature of the Second Temple Period*, ed. B.U. Schipper & D.A. Teeter, JSJSup 163 (Leiden: Brill, 2013), 203–232.

Tov, Emmanuel, "The *Tefillin* from the Judean Desert and the Textual Criticism of the Hebrew Bible," in *Is There a Text in This Cave? Studies in the Textuality of the Dead Sea Scrolls in Honour of George J. Brooke*, ed. A. Feldman, M. Cioată & C. Hempel, STDJ 119 (Leiden: Brill, 2017), 277–292.

Tov, Emmanuel, "Excerpted and Abbreviated Biblical Texts from Qumran," *RevQ* 16 (1995): 581–600.

Tromp, Johannes, "On Human Disobedience to the Order of Creation (4Q521, fr. 2 and Latin Life of Adam and Eve 29c)," *RevQ* 21 (2003): 109–115.

Ulrich, Eugene, "Pluriformity in the Biblical Text, Text Groups, and Questions of Canon," in *Madrid Qumran Congress: Proceedings of the International Congress on the Dead Sea Scrolls*, 2 vols., STDJ 11 (Leiden: Brill, 1992), 1.23–41.

Ulrich, Eugene, "The Canonical Process, Textual Criticism, and Latter Stages in the Composition of the Bible," in *Sha'arei Talmon: Studies in the Bible, Qumran, and the Ancient Near East Presented to Shemaryahu Talmon*, ed. M. Fishbane & E. Tov (Winona Lake, IN: Eisenbrauns, 1992), 267–294.

Uro, Risto, "Apocalyptic Symbolism and Social Identity in Q," in *Symbols and Strata: Essays on the Sayings Gospel Q*, ed. R. Uro (Göttingen: Vandenhoeck & Ruprecht, 1991), 67–118.

Uusimäki, Elisa, *Turning Proverbs Towards Torah: An Analysis of 4Q525*, STDJ 117 (Leiden: Brill, 2016).

VanderKam, James C., "Jubilees and the Priestly Messiah of Qumran," *RevQ* 13 (1988): 353–365.

van der Woude, Adam S., "Wisdom at Qumran," in *Wisdom in Ancient Israel: Essays in Honour of J.A. Emerton*, ed. J. Day, R.P. Gordon & H.G.M. Williamson (Cambridge: CUP, 1995), 244–256.

Vermes, Geza, "Pre-Mishnaic Jewish Worship and the Phylacteries from the Dead Sea," *VT* 9 (1959): 65–72.

Wachob, Wesley H. and Johnson, Luke Timothy, "The Sayings of Jesus in the Letter of James," in *Authenticating the Words of Jesus*, ed. B. Chilton & C.A. Evans, NTTS 28 (Leiden: Brill, 2002), 431–450.

Wacholder, Ben Zion, "Jubilees as the Super Canon: Torah-Admonition versus Torah-Commandment," in *Legal Texts and Legal Issues: Proceedings of the Second Meeting of the International Organization for Qumran Studies, Cambridge 1995, Published in Honor of Joseph M. Baumgarten*, ed. M. Bernstein, F. García Martínez & J. Kampen, STDJ 23 (Leiden: Brill, 1997), 195–211.

Weinfeld, Moshe, "Grace after Meals at Qumran," *JBL* 111/3 (1992): 427–440.

Werman, Cana, "What Is the Book of Hagu?" in *Sapiential Perspectives: Wisdom Literature in Light of the Dead Sea Scrolls: Proceedings of the Sixth International Symposium of the Orion Center for the Study of the Dead Sea Scrolls and Associated Literature, 20–22 May, 2001*, ed. J.J. Collins, G.E. Sterling & R.A. Clements, STDJ 51 (Leiden: Brill, 2004), 125–140.

Werman, Cana, "The 'תורה' and the 'תעודה' Engraved on the Tablets," *DSD* 9/1 (2002): 75–103.

Wise, Michael O., "מי כמוני באלים: A Study of 4Q491ᶜ, 4Q471ᵇ, 4Q427 7 and 1QHᵃ 25:35–26:10," *DSD* 7/2 (2000): 173–219.

Wise, Michael O., Abegg, Martin and Cook, Edward, *The Dead Sea Scrolls: A New Translation* (San Francisco, CA/London: HarperCollins, 1996).

Wold, Benjamin, "Is the 'Firstborn Son' in 4Q369 a Messiah? The Evidence from 4QInstruction," *RevQ* (2017): 3–20.

Wold, Benjamin, "Genesis 2–3 in Early Christianity and 4QInstruction," *DSD* 23/3 (2016): 329–346.

Wold, Benjamin, "'Flesh' and 'Spirit' in Qumran Sapiential Literature as the Background to the Use in Pauline Epistles," *ZNW* 106/2 (2015): 262–279.

Wold, Benjamin, "The Universality of Creation in 4QInstruction," *RevQ* 102/1 (2013): 211–226.

Wold, Benjamin, "Metaphorical Poverty in Musar leMevin," *JJS* 58/1 (2007): 140–153.

Wold, Benjamin, *Women, Men and Angels: The Qumran Wisdom Document Musar leMevin and its Allusions to Genesis Creation Traditions*, WUNT 2.201 (Tübingen: Mohr Siebeck, 2005).

Wolfson, Elliot R., "Seven Mysteries of Knowledge: Qumran E/Sotericism Recovered," in *The Idea of Biblical Interpretation: Essays in Honor of James L. Kugel*, ed. H. Najman & J.H. Newman, JSJSup 83 (Leiden: Brill, 2004), 177–213.

Wright III, Benjamin G., "Three Ritual Practices in Aristeas §158–160," in *Heavenly Tablets: Interpretation, Identity and Tradition in Ancient Judaism*, ed. L. LiDonnici & A. Lieber, JSJS 119 (Leiden: Brill, 2007), 13–21.

Wright III, Benjamin G., "The Categories of Rich and Poor in the Qumran Sapiential Literature," in *Sapiential Perspectives: Wisdom Literature in Light of the Dead Sea Scrolls: Proceedings of the Sixth International Symposium of the Orion Center for the Study of the Dead Sea Scrolls and Associated Literature, 20–22 May, 2001*, ed. J.J. Collins, G.E. Sterling & R.A. Clements, STDJ 51 (Leiden: Brill, 2004), 125–140.

Wright III, Benjamin G., "Wisdom and Women at Qumran," *DSD* 11/2 (2004): 240–261.

Wright III, Benjamin G., "'Fear the Lord and Honor the Priest': Ben Sira as Defender of the Jerusalem Priesthood," in *The Book of Ben Sira in Modern Research*, ed. P.C. Beentjes, BZAW 255 (Berlin/New York, NY: de Gruyter, 1997), 189–222.

Xeravits, Géza G., *King, Priest, Prophet: Positive Eschatological Protagonists of the Qumran Library*, STDJ 47 (Leiden: Brill, 2003).

Yadin, Yigal, "Tefillin (Phylacteries) from Qumran (XQPhyl 1–4)," *Eretz Israel* 9 (1969): 60–83. [Hebrew]

Zur, Yiphtah, "Parallels between Acts of Thomas 6–7 and 4Q184," *RevQ* 16 (1993): 103–107.

Index of Authors

Index of Ancient Sources

Plate Section

∴

FIGURE 1   *4Q423 11 (B-284563)*
             COURTESY ISRAEL ANTIQUITIES
             AUTHORITY; PHOTOGRAPHER:
             NAJIB ANTON ALBINA

FIGURE 2   *4Q423 11 (B-359355)*   FIGURE 3   *4Q423 11 (B-359356)*
             COURTESY ISRAEL   COURTESY ISRAEL
             ANTIQUITIES AUTHORITY;   ANTIQUITIES AUTHORITY;
             PHOTOGRAPHER: SHAI HALEVI   PHOTOGRAPHER: SHAI HALEVI

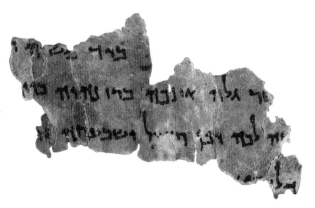

FIGURE 4   *4Q418 184 (B-363727)*
             COURTESY ISRAEL ANTIQUITIES AUTHORITY;
             PHOTOGRAPHER: SHAI HALEVI

FIGURE 5
4Q418 222 (B-364192)
COURTESY ISRAEL
ANTIQUITIES AUTHORITY;
PHOTOGRAPHER: SHAI HALEVI

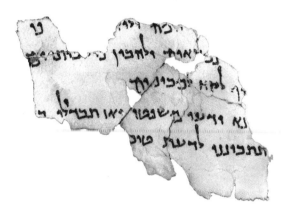

FIGURE 6
4Q418 221 (B-364198)
COURTESY ISRAEL
ANTIQUITIES AUTHORITY;
PHOTOGRAPHER: SHAI HALEVI

FIGURE 7
4Q418 238 (B-480974)
COURTESY ISRAEL ANTIQUITIES AUTHORITY; PHOTOGRAPHER:
SHAI HALEVI

l. 22

FIGURE 8   4Q417 2 i (B-370825)
COURTESY ISRAEL ANTIQUITIES AUTHORITY; PHOTOGRAPHER: SHAI
HALEVI

FIGURE 9   *4Q417 1 i lines 14–18,* Vision of Hagu (*B-370822*)
COURTESY ISRAEL ANTIQUITIES AUTHORITY; PHOTOGRAPHER: SHAI HALEVI

FIGURE 10   *4Q417 1 i lines 14–18,* Vision of Hagu (*B-370823*)
COURTESY ISRAEL ANTIQUITIES AUTHORITY; PHOTOGRAPHER: SHAI HALEVI

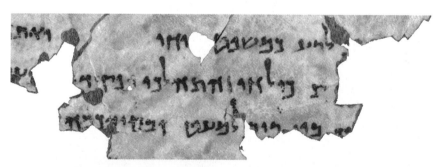

FIGURE 11   *4Q417 1 i lines 18–20* (*B-370823*)
COURTESY ISRAEL ANTIQUITIES AUTHORITY; PHOTOGRAPHER: SHAI HALEVI

FIGURE 12 *4Q417 1 i lines 18–20 (B-370822)*
COURTESY ISRAEL ANTIQUITIES AUTHORITY; PHOTOGRAPHER: SHAI HALEVI

FIGURE 13 *4Q417 1 i (B-370823)*
COURTESY ISRAEL ANTIQUITIES AUTHORITY; PHOTOGRAPHER: SHAI HALEVI